MW01590893

THE BIRTH OF
THE ISLAMIC REFORM MOVEMENT
IN SAUDI ARABIA

THE BIRTH OF
THE ISLAMIC REFORM MOVEMENT
IN SAUDI ARABIA

Muḥammad Ibn ʻAbd al-Wahhāb (1703/4–1792) and the Beginnings of Unitarian Empire in Arabia

George S. Rentz

Edited with an Introduction by
William Facey

AP
Arabian Publishing

The Birth of the Islamic Reform Movement in Saudi Arabia
Muḥammad Ibn ʻAbd al-Wahhāb (1703/4 – 1792) and the Beginnings of Unitarian Empire in Arabia
by George S. Rentz

© The Estate of George S. Rentz Jr.
Introduction © William Facey

Produced and published in 2004 by Arabian Publishing Ltd
3 Devonshire Street, London W1W 5BA
Fax 020 7580 0567

In association with
The King Abdulaziz Public Library,
PO Box 86486, Riyadh 11622, Kingdom of Saudi Arabia

All rights are reserved. No part of this publication may be reproduced, stored in a retrieval system, or transmitted in any form or by any means, electronic, mechanical, photographic or otherwise, without prior permission in writing of the publisher and copyright holder.

A catalogue record for this book is available from the British Library

ISBN 0 9544792 2 X

Typesetting and digital artwork by Falcon Imaging, Cambridge, UK
Printed and bound in the UK by Creative Print and Design (Wales), Ebbw Vale

Contents

Part III
Consolidation in Najd, 1187–1199 AH/AD 1773–1785

Part IV
The Last Years of the Shaikh and the Beginnings of the Expansion of Unitarianism beyond Najd, 1200–1206 AH/AD 1786–1792

Part V
Bibliographical Essay and Bibliography

Maps and Tables

Maps

Genealogical Tables

Introduction

Introduction

Much time has passed and much has changed since 1947, when George S. Rentz (1912–87) submitted his doctoral thesis to the University of California at Berkeley. Entitled *Muḥammad b. 'Abd al-Wahhāb (1703/4–1792) and the Beginnings of Unitarian Empire in Arabia*, it is now, after the lapse of more than half a century, published for the first time.

Though it has been consulted and admired by scholars of Saudi Arabian history ever since its completion, recent developments in the Middle East have generated a wider interest in the history of Saudi Arabia and the background to its culture. Some of this interest is focused most particularly, and with good reason, on the origins of the Islamic Reform Movement that grew with remarkable vigour in settlements of the central region, Najd, in the 18th century. The movement took root at a time before a Saudi Arabian state existed even as an idea. In providing the sense of mission and the force for cohesion in the process of state formation, it played a vital part both in forming the concept of the Saudi state, and in enabling it to be realised as a political entity. The origins of this movement and the life of its founder form the subject of George Rentz's thesis. Hence what its publication lacks in punctuality it makes up for by its topicality and relevance to the Middle East today.

The First Saudi State (AD 1744–1818) had its capital at al-Dir'īyah. Situated in Wadi Ḥanīfah, the populated district of Lower Najd in which Riyadh also lies, al-Dir'īyah was in 1744 the stronghold of a minor ruling house named Āl Su'ūd, more commonly known as Al Saud or the House of Saud. The new state arose with astonishing rapidity during the lifetime of Shaikh Muḥammad b. ʻAbd al-Wahhāb and under his guidance. The Shaikh, who died in AD 1792, did not live to witness the apogee of this politico-religious phenomenon, which propelled the House of Saud to prominence for the first time in Arabian affairs. Between 1803 and 1806 it succeeded in taking control of the holy cities of Makkah and al-Madinah, so challenging the authority of the Ottoman Sultan, who had more or less held sway over the Hijaz since AD 1517. Ottoman retaliation was slow but, in the end, thorough, and the Shaikh was spared the experience of the Saudi State's downfall at the hands of the Ottoman–Egyptian invasion and occupation of Najd in 1816–24. The Second Saudi State rose on the ruins of the First in 1824 and proved to be somewhat less ambitious in scope. Undaunted by a short-lived Egyptian occupation at the end of the 1830s, it maintained itself well in central and eastern Arabia until 1865. Then came a slow dissolution into dynastic strife and loss of allegiance, leading to its final demise in 1891. What might be called (though it is not usual to do so) the Third Saudi State, is with us to this day. It came into being as a result of the series of campaigns waged by ʻAbd al-ʻAzīz Āl Saud (also known as Ibn Saud, and after 1932 as HM King ʻAbd al-ʻAziz) between 1902 and 1930. The united entity was formally proclaimed the Kingdom of Saudi Arabia in 1932. Thereafter the only serious threats to its territorial integrity came from the south: from the flaring of a frontier dispute with the Yemen over Najran in 1932–4, and from uncertainties over the south-eastern border that culminated in the Buraimi Dispute in the 1950s.

George Rentz himself provided a useful summary of the Reform Movement and its role in the emergence of Saudi Arabia in a short article published in 1972 (Rentz 1972). As he played a major part in publicising through his writings, the Reform Movement has reverberated through Saudi Arabian history right up to the present day. Lying very much at the heart of Saudi Arabia's culture and its concept of leadership, it exerts a power in religious, moral, social and political affairs that works at every level in both public and private life to determine judgements of propriety and legitimacy.

The Reform Movement of Shaikh Muḥammad b. ʻAbd al-Wahhāb is known these days in the Arab world as the Salafiyah or

Salafī Reform Movement. The sense of *salaf* (pl. *aslāf*) is here that of "forefather", with the added connotation of worthiness – the "worthy ancestors", that is, the first Muslims, seen as those who abided by the purest belief and practice unsullied by the accretions of time. Western orientalists in the old days not unnaturally named the movement after its founder, using the term *Wahhābī*, as often as not without any derogatory intent. But its disciples right up to the present day have objected to that designation, arguing with cogency that the Shaikh, so far from having contributed any original doctrines which might justify identifying him as the founder of a movement, was doing no more than calling upon people to return to and uphold Islam in its original and purest form – a position with which the Shaikh himself would undoubtedly have agreed. The Shaikh and his followers traced their intellectual descent from Aḥmad Ibn Ḥanbal, the 9th-century AD jurist and founder of the most conservative of the four orthodox schools of Islamic law, and they approached his teachings through the work of the Syrian Ḥanbalī Ibn Taimiyyah (AD 1262–1328). Hence they considered themselves far from sectarian in any respect, but as strictly orthodox, and referred to themselves either simply as Muslims, or else as *muwaḥḥidūn*, "Unitarians". These days the term "Wahhabi" is shunned in print. Rentz himself, as he explains in his Preface, prefers to use "Unitarian". This, as a direct translation of the Arabic *muwaḥḥid*, usefully conveys the central tenet of *tauḥīd* or the Oneness of God, but has not caught on among scholars as it is also the name of a Christian denomination.

Unfortunately "Salafi" is itself an unsatisfactory term, because it does not apply exclusively to the teachings of Shaikh Muḥammad b. ʻAbd al-Wahhāb and his followers. Rather it is a general label open to anyone who may claim, legitimately or otherwise, that his ideology constitutes a return to the original message of the 7th century AD and the practices of the first Muslims. Cloaking one's prescriptions for the ills of the world in the garb of legitimacy, by invoking the noble founders, has been a common enough ploy throughout the history of religious movements, and is by no means confined to the Islamic world. The popularity of the term Salafi among militant Muslims has thus led to a certain amount of confusion in the current climate. It has led many commentators to lay the misdeeds and heterodoxies of every so-called *salafī* or "fundamentalist" group at the door of the teachings of the Reform Movement of Shaikh Muḥammad b. ʻAbd al-ʻWahhāb, and by extension of the Saudi Arabian government, simply because all Salafi groups share with the Shaikh an appeal to a golden age of pristine doctrine and practice (*cf.* Oliveti 2001). In many cases the appeal to the past is the only feature they share with it, and so not all groups claiming to be "Salafi" should be confused with each other. The conclusions they draw from the Qur'ān and Traditions may be and often are as widely disparate as those that Christian fundamentalists draw from their own scriptures. (Azzam 2003: 2)

★

Today, interest in the Najdi Reform Movement extends well beyond the small coterie of specialists who have hitherto studied this area. Anything that provides illumination is thereby all the more welcome. Rentz's doctoral thesis sheds such a bright light on the events of the early Reform Movement and the creation of the First Saudi State that the wonder is that it has never been published before. Rentz himself, as a distinguished scholar of the Arabian Peninsula, was well-used to seeing his work in print. Indeed, with Harry St John Bridger Philby (known to Saudis as Ḥajjī ʻAbd Allāh Philby), he was foremost among the Arabian Peninsula specialists of his day. Yet it is not clear whether Rentz ever seriously tried to get the work presented here into print.

Some scholars, however, have long been aware of its value, even though it has up till now been available only as a photocopy from Rentz's literary executors or on microfilm from the University of California. Both Philby and R. Bayly Winder drew upon it in writing their Saudi Arabian histories, and it is frequently referred to in bibliographies. Philby, greatest of all foreign explorers of Saudi Arabia and one of the most prolific writers on the country, wrote in 1954 (Philby 1955: 5):

> To those who would have more information about the old romantic days of the Saʻudi dynasty, I can indeed hold out the hope that some

> day in the near future, perhaps, they will be able to satisfy their curiosity. I have had the privilege and pleasure of seeing in typescript two admirable works by American scholars of a younger generation, covering the whole story of Wahhabi Arabia from its earliest days to the eclipse of the Sa'udi dynasty in 1891. The first [*Muḥammad ibn 'Abd al-Wahhab (1703/4–1792) and the Beginnings of Unitarian Empire in Arabia* (Berkeley, California, 3/12/1947)] is an account of the rise and fall of the first Wahhabi empire, based on all available original sources, by Mr George Rentz. The second [*A History of the Sa'udi State from 1233/1818 to 1308/1891*] by Mr Bailey [*sic*] Winder of Princeton University, carries on the tale from the fall of Dar'iya in 1818 to the fatal battle of Mulaida in 1891.

Philby's hope that these two Ph.D. theses would soon see the light of day as full-blown publications was to be realised only in the case of Winder, who went on to develop his research into the excellent *Saudi Arabia in the Nineteenth Century* (Macmillan, London, 1965). It is still the standard work on the subject, and in it he paid tribute to Rentz's thesis, calling it "the best study of the first phase of Saudi history" (Winder 1965: 6 n. 2). His preface expressed his warm thanks to both Rentz and Philby and acknowledged their paramount status as scholars of Arabia (Winder 1965: viii):

> Two [individuals] are of transcendent importance. The first is Dr George Rentz of the Hoover Institution, Stanford University, who has always given freely of his kindness and of his own vast knowledge of Arabia and who, in particular, referred me to many choice bibliographical items used in this work and who, by an advance reading of the text, saved me from many howlers, without thereby incurring the slightest responsibility for anything. The other is the late Hajj 'Abd Allah Philby. He was a great man whose work speaks more for him than anyone else could. I can only record that his willingness to share himself with a neophyte was a generosity that I shall always cherish. No two men better exemplify the true community of scholars and scholarship than these.

Philby died in 1960, but if he had still been alive in 1965 he would certainly have appreciated Winder's book as significant publishing milestone. One likes to think he would have hailed it, with justification, as lifting the study of Saudi Arabian history in the West onto a new level of scholarship. And he would doubtless have taken it as another opportunity to promote the publication of Rentz's thesis. It would have come as a great surprise to him, had he had the gift of foresight, that those seeking knowledge of the origins of the Reform Movement and the First Saudi State were going to be kept waiting until the following century for it to be made available in published form.

Rentz's seminal work represents the first thoroughgoing attempt by a foreign historian to come to grips in a systematic way with the local Najdi sources on the Saudi State's beginnings. It is at once a biography of the Shaikh and a chronicle of the expansion of Saudi influence up until his death in 1792. It proceeds principally by comparing the two chief Najdi annals of the period: the *Rauḍat al-afkār*, the major contemporary source on the First Saudi State by the Najdi *'ālīm* Ḥusain b. Ghannām; and the *'Unwān al-majd fī-ta'rīkh Najd* of 'Uthmān b. Bishr.

That this project had been such a long time coming is surprising, especially given that the outside world of the 18th and early 19th centuries had been far from unaware of events unfolding in remote central Arabia. From the 1760s on, travellers and officials such as Carsten Niebuhr, J. L. Reinaud, Harford Jones Brydges, 'Ali Bey al-'Abbasi, Louis de Corancez and Jean Louis Burckhardt had reported what they had heard (Kelly 1968: 48–9; Facey 1992: 104–8; 1997: 45–6). For the most part such observers reached the conclusion – a highly discerning one for the time – that the movement represented no more than a return to the first principles of Islam. But it was not until the armies of Muḥammad 'Alī Pasha of Egypt invaded Najd in 1816–18, attended by various European medics and soldiers of fortune, that first-hand information on the history and conditions of life in the First Saudi State (1744–1818) began to filter out and find its way into the works of Western scholars such as Jomard, Mengin and Crichton. It was that time too that saw the first crossing of the Arabian Peninsula by a European, the British officer George Forster Sadleir, who in 1819 saw for himself the devastation at al-Dir'īyah.

(Jomard 1823 and 1839; Mengin 1823 and 1839; Crichton 1833; Sadleir 1823, 1866.)

For almost a century that period represented the high-water mark in Europe's knowledge of central Arabia. The Second Saudi State of 1824–91 attracted little outside attention and foreign visitors to Riyadh and southern Najd were few: until the European states became concerned to know more about the southern fringes of the Ottoman Empire's influence just before the First World War, only Palgrave (1862) and Lewis Pelly (1865) ventured there (Facey 1992: 120–91).

The idea that there might be local, Najdi documentary sources to draw upon in constructing the history of central Arabia came relatively late. True, there had been one or two glimpses of the existence of such material. For example, as Rentz notes in his Bibliographical Essay, Mengin seems to have had access to a manuscript of the *Rauḍat al-afkār* of Ḥusain b. Ghannām. A manuscript eye-witness account of the entry into Makkah by the reformist warriors, in April 1803, was known to British scholars in India and was published in translation in the *Journal of the Bengal Asiatic Society* in 1874 (O'Kinealy 1874; Facey 1997: 43–4). British officials in the Gulf, notably E. C. Ross, occasionally came by useful local material offered to them by emissaries from Riyadh and included it in their reports (Kelly 1968: 50 n. 1; Ross 1880: 638). J. G. Lorimer's magisterial *Gazetteer of the Persian Gulf, 'Oman and Central Arabia* drew on all sources available at the time, including local ones (Lorimer 1908–15). And one of the only two original manuscripts known to exist of the 19th-century Najdi chronicler 'Uthman b. Bishr's *'Unwān al-majd fī-ta'rīkh Najd*, which brings the history of the First and Second Saudi States up to 1853, was sold to the British Library in 1912 (Ibn Bishr AH 1270; the other is in the King Abdulaziz Public Library in Riyadh). But the first Westerner to rely upon such material to construct a continuous history was Philby.

In the late 1920s Philby, now a businessman resident in Jiddah, was approached by the publisher Benn for a book on Arabia for its series "The Modern World: A Survey of Historical Forces" (Monroe 1973: 157). The book, entitled simply *Arabia*, was published in 1930.

It is in some ways an unsatisfactory work, not least because of its title: "Central Arabia" would have been less misleading, as it is a book not by any means about Arabia as a whole, but about the history of Najd and the rise and fall of the successive Saudi States up to Philby's time. It is a book whose viewpoint from Riyadh reflects Philby's admiration for the figure of 'Abd al-'Azīz Ibn Sa'ud, by whom he had been captivated ever since his first visit to the capital in 1917, and to whose court he was in the process of forming a lifetime attachment. Indeed, it was precisely at the time of writing *Arabia* that Philby was in the process of converting to Islam, and his history very much reflects the standpoint of his sources: the *Rauḍat al-afkār* of Ḥusain b. Ghannām and the *'Unwān al-majd* of 'Uthmān b. Bishr. Both chroniclers had been in their time fervent champions of the Reform Movement. They found a sympathetic interpreter in Philby to whom, for all his shortcomings as a historian, must go the credit for his pioneering approach as the first non-Saudi to make use of the works of these two foremost Najdi chroniclers. (Philby 1930, pp. viii–x; Goldberg 1985: 223–4; Rentz 1979).

In writing his thesis in the late 1930s and 1940s, George Rentz was also a sympathetic interpreter of these native sources. He made good use of Philby's *Arabia*, as is evident from the frequent references to it in his footnotes. Such references mostly set out to correct details in Philby's account, although Rentz graciously conceded in his Bibliographical Essay that the frequency of his criticisms of Philby's *Arabia* might tend to give a false impression of the actual value of that book; the real gauge of his respect for it overall being that it had been his constant companion.

Philby's *Arabia* and Rentz's thesis are, however, works of very different character. Later in life Rentz wrote a short article entitled "Philby as a Historian of Saudi Arabia", in which he set out to assess Philby's strengths and weaknesses (Rentz 1979). His criticisms of Philby reveal the differences between them. Rentz was a much more careful scholar; Philby, although he had a legendary memory for facts and was tenacious in pursuit of details, could be careless in drawing conclusions from evidence. Not only did he not see himself as a professional historian, he was also a romantic who revelled in the big picture and the broad sweep. He enjoyed illuminating his account with historical parallels, as for example in his comparisons of settled rule in Najd with the feudal baronies of mediaeval Europe. There certainly are some resemblances between feudalism and society in Lower Najd in the old days, but Philby perhaps goes too far in conjuring up an image of what one writer has mockingly called a "sun-baked Plantagenet England" in Wadi Ḥanīfah (Kelly 1980: 259). And in his historical works such as *Arabia* and *Sa'udi Arabia* he eschewed notes, so that the reader seeking the evidence for a Philby statement is usually frustrated.

Rentz's approach is more narrow in focus than Philby's and more critical. After all, his work was a doctoral thesis and therefore was not by definition aimed at the general reader. It is a sustained piece of historical detection in which he takes great care to compare the evidence, not to stray beyond his sources, and not to place more weight of interpretation on the evidence than it will stand. In this, his work is at once more limited and far more valuable as historical scholarship than are Philby's two books.

The essential value of Rentz's effort is that it is the first to try to reconcile the accounts of Ibn Ghannam and Ibn Bishr – basic, laborious groundwork that Philby, despite his familiarity with those two chroniclers, did not set out to perform. Inevitably historiography has moved on in the last fifty years, and more local Najdi material for the period is now known (Al-Juhany 2002: 4–17). Nonetheless, as sources Ibn Ghannām and Ibn Bishr still reign supreme, and any study of Najdi history in the 18th and 19th centuries has to start from a comparison and reconciliation of their two accounts. This is where the real strength of Rentz's contribution lies, despite the fact that he was able to consult only published editions and not the original manuscripts. (Readers wishing to know which editions Rentz used should first consult his Bibliographical Essay and Bibliography at the end of this work.)

Rentz himself in his Preface acknowledges that his thesis sticks to the ascertainable facts and risks being a dull recitation of events, no more than the groundwork of history. He proclaims his intention to produce, at a later time, a larger study, "broader in scope and primarily analytical rather than narrative in treatment". He sees the details of his narrative as the raw materials for a "contemplated analysis of Arabian life in this period and the structure and functioning of the Unitarian state". And it is true that one looks in vain for any account of, for example, the processes by which chieftaincy was extended and a centralised state was formed. There is no analysis of the roots of legitimacy of the ruling house; or of the deeper relations between the nomadic and settled people; or of relations between ruler, *'ulamā'*, merchants, farmers and tribesmen, and how those relations might have changed through time; or of economic life, taxation and the evolving administration of the state. Winder's work is far more instructive and insightful in those respects. That Rentz seems never to have found time, during the course of a busy life, to raise a more interpretative edifice upon the foundations of the research presented here, should be a cause for regret among all students of Arabian history.

Philby and Rentz share in common an empathy with the source material that at times can appear over-partial. Both writers seem to have felt a strong personal attachment to the success of the Reform Movement and fully entered into the spirit of the chronicles they used as sources. In Philby's case the reasons, though complex, are not far to seek and have been written about elsewhere (Monroe 1973). With Rentz it may have had something to do with his religious background as the son of a pastor. The Old-Testament style of the Najdi chroniclers no doubt appealed to him. This is reflected in his own rather biblical, old-fashioned prose, a style that is certainly suited to his story, but which also perhaps led to a certain lack of critical detachment where the protagonists are concerned. He never sits in judgement on the Unitarians nor questions their actions, even at unarguably discreditable moments such as the massacres of helpless villagers in Hasa Oasis. There is no general discussion of whether, for example, warfare is an appropriate means of spreading a message of universal brotherhood. It was not in the spirit of 18th-century Najd to pose such questions, and so Rentz does not debate them. In their defence, it is clear that Philby and Rentz, like the British government in the early 19th century, both felt that the Reform Movement was an essentially civilising force (Facey 1992: 125). It was, after all, an improvement, in terms of law and order, social cohesion and the conditions of life, on the constant upheaval and

THE ARABIAN PENINSULA IN THE EARLY 13TH/19TH CENTURY, AT THE GREATEST EXTENT OF THE FIRST SAUDI STATE

Approximate area of influence of the First Saudi State, 1223 AH/AD 1808

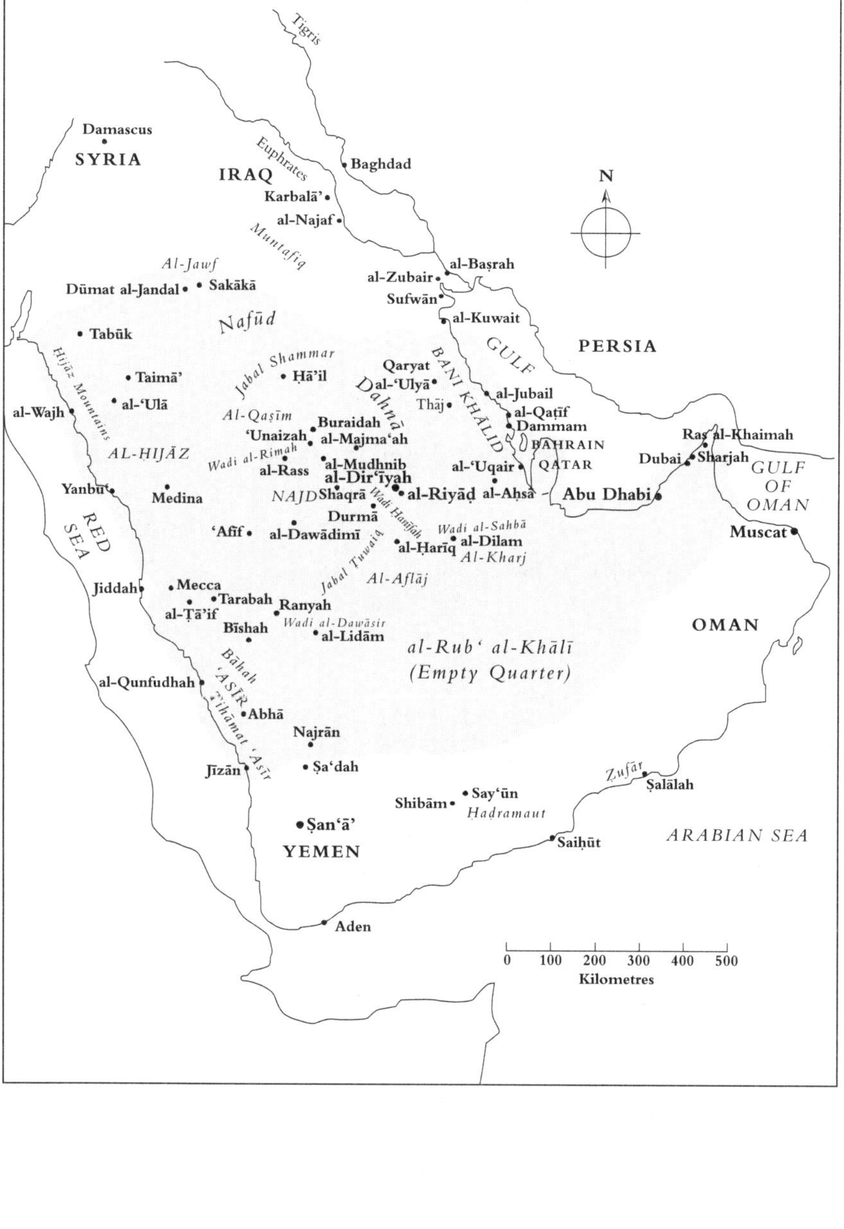

insecurity that had gone before when a chaotic patchwork of petty local amirates and tribes had prevailed. That is the comparison that should be made, rather than with our relatively stable, secure and prosperous societies today.

Taking Rentz's thesis together with Winder's *Saudi Arabia in the Nineteenth Century*, and despite the differences in their approach, students of Saudi Arabian history can now avail themselves of authoritative, scholarly accounts in English of much of the period of the Saudi state's evolution from its origins to 1891. However, Winder does not begin where Rentz leaves off; they do not provide a continuous story, as Philby implied in *Sa'udi Arabia* (Philby 1955: 5, quoted above). Rentz's story ends with the death of the Shaikh in 1792 just as the Unitarian state was beginning to impinge upon the Ottoman Empire; Winder picks up the threads at 1818 and the destruction of al-Dir'īyah at Ottoman–Egyptian hands. Hence the most dramatic period of all in Saudi history, the one that witnessed the greatest highs and lows in Saudi fortunes, still needs a definitive, scholarly history in English, covering the zenith and collapse of the First Saudi State between 1792 and 1818: the Unitarian occupation of Makkah and the Hijaz, Saudi control of the two holy cities, the first-ever foreign invasion of Najd, and the fall of al-Dir'īyah. These can indeed be read about in various publications (e.g. Sabini 1981; Facey 1997), but the period still awaits the scholarly and systematic treatment that it so conspicuously deserves.

★

George Rentz first visited Saudi Arabia in 1944. By that time he was living in Cairo, working for the US Office of War Information (OWI) – he founded the OWI's Department of Research and Translation in Cairo and was to serve as its head until December 1945 (Rentz *c.* 1966). While there he accepted an invitation to the Kingdom from Karl Twitchell, the American mining engineer who had played a role in the negotiations leading to the award of the Eastern Province oil concession to Standard Oil of California in 1933, so contributing to the birth of Aramco and the Saudi oil industry. Twitchell wanted Rentz to accompany him to the Saudi

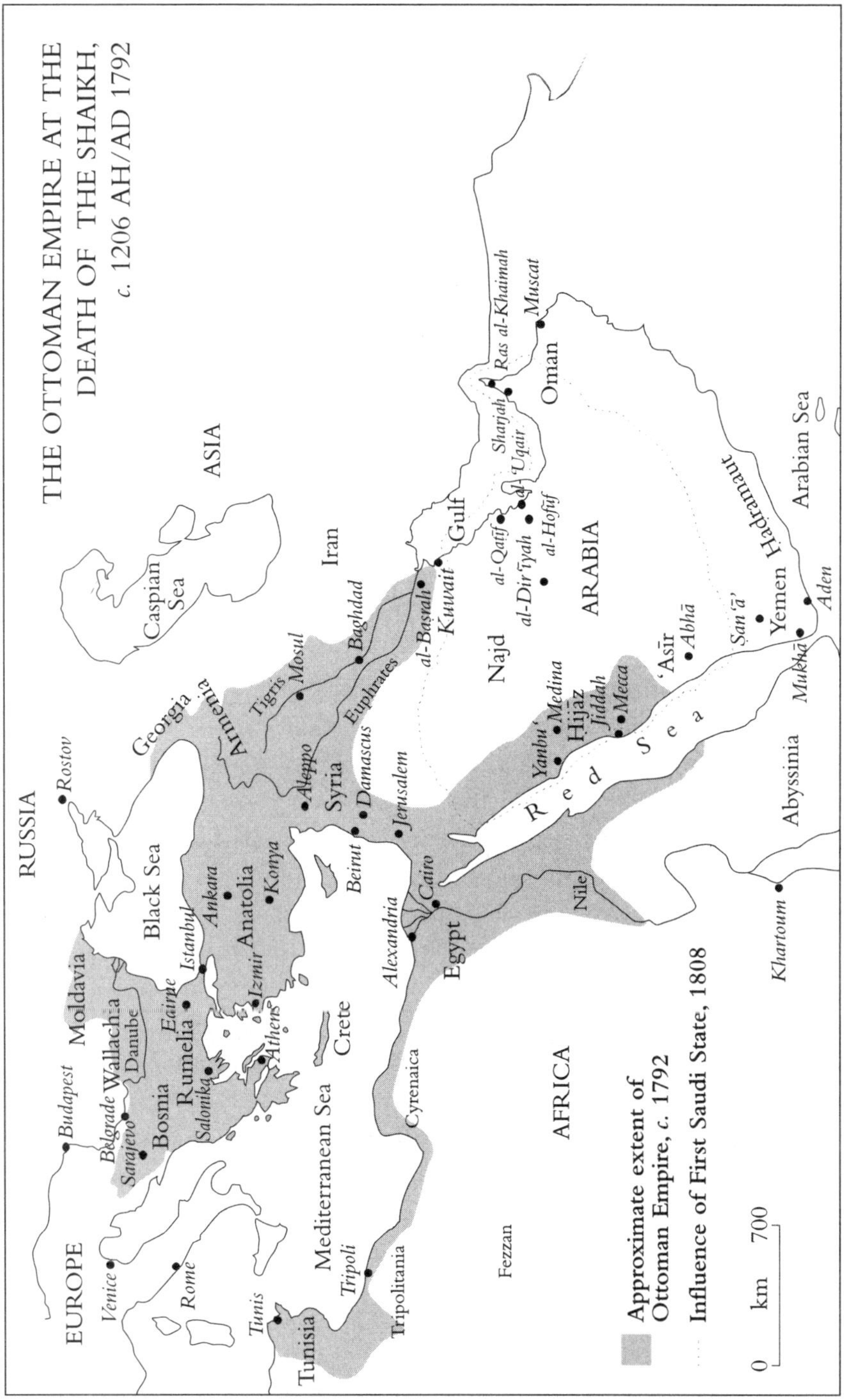
THE OTTOMAN EMPIRE AT THE
DEATH OF THE SHAIKH,
c. 1206 AH/AD 1792
Approximate extent of
Ottoman Empire, c. 1792
Influence of First Saudi State, 1808
0 km 700
EUROPE
RUSSIA
ASIA
AFRICA
ARABIA
Black Sea
Caspian Sea
Mediterranean Sea
Red Sea
Gulf
Arabian Sea
Venice
Rome
Tunis
Tunisia
Tripoli
Tripolitania
Fezzan
Cyrenaica
Budapest
Belgrade
Sarajevo
Bosnia
Wallachia
Danube
Moldavia
Rumelia
Salonika
Edirne
Istanbul
Athens
Crete
Izmir
Ankara
Anatolia
Konya
Rostov
Georgia
Armenia
Tigris
Mosul
Baghdad
Euphrates
Aleppo
Syria
Damascus
Beirut
Jerusalem
Alexandria
Cairo
Egypt
Nile
Khartoum
Abyssinia
Iran
al-Basrah
Kuwait
Najd
al-Dir'iyah
al-Qatif
al-Hofuf
al-'Uqair
Sharjah
Ras al-Khaimah
Muscat
Oman
Hadramaut
Yanbu'
Medina
Hijaz
Jiddah
Mecca
'Asir
Abha
San'a'
Yemen
Mukha
Aden

Arabian Mining Syndicate works at Mahd al-Dhahab, the fabled "Cradle of Gold" south of al-Madinah. Once in Jiddah, however, Rentz found himself unable to join Twitchell. Instead, he was introduced to another type of treasure, in the house of the famous scholar and bibliophile Muḥammad Naṣīf: Arabic books and manuscripts that he had not seen before, and that were not available in the United States.

Most unusually for his time, Rentz was no stranger to Saudi Arabian history, having in 1937 already started work on the Ph.D. thesis published here. The Second World War had interrupted his studies, and he was keen to finish them. The visit to Jiddah merely confirmed his deep interest in the Kingdom and, in January 1946, Rentz accepted the offer of a job at Aramco. As he had received a Rockefeller Fellowship to continue work on his doctorate, he was keen not to let it slide, and so the job he took at Aramco was a temporary one as a translator for a period of nine months, allowing him to plan his return to Berkeley afterwards to complete his Ph.D. requirements.

Those nine months were to turn into 17 years. His command of Arabic and English was so superior that James MacPherson, Aramco's Resident Manager, determined not to lose him, whatever the price. Rentz stipulated that he was ready to stay only if three conditions were met: first, that he was appointed supervisor of a research and translation organisation of considerable size (he was unwilling to be limited to translation); second, that he was granted sufficient time in the near future to complete his Ph.D. requirements; and, third, that he was provided immediately with housing for the wife and baby daughter he had left behind in Cairo. MacPherson had no trouble agreeing to the first two conditions, and true to his promise he saw to it that Rentz was given time to complete his doctoral thesis. But he could concede the third condition only with difficulty. Employees of higher rank and longer service than Rentz were waiting two and a half years for housing that was still scarce, none having been built during the War. Rentz, once his conditions were met, decided to stay with Aramco. His thesis, on completion, was submitted to the University of California at Berkeley in 1947, and he was awarded his Ph.D. in 1948. (Mulligan 1987)

Two qualities combined to prolong his stay in the Kingdom: his command of Arabic, and his abiding interest in Saudi Arabian history and geography. His flair for languages and research made him indispensable to Aramco's fledgling Government Relations Department. Not only was his Arabic, both classical and colloquial, excellent, but he also had a good knowledge of classical Greek and a working knowledge of Latin, and was familiar with literary Turkish and Persian. He could also read and to some extent speak French, German, Spanish and Italian, and was able to use Russian, Serbo-Croat, Polish, Portuguese, Catalan, Dutch and more than one Scandinavian language for research purposes. (Rentz *c.* 1966)

*

George Snavely Rentz Jr was born on 10 April 1912, the eldest of four children of Rebecca Klepper Rentz and George Snavely Rentz Sr, at Welsh Run, Pennsylvania. The family was of Pennsylvania Dutch stock, and George Rentz Sr worked as a Presbyterian minister. It was thus said that George Jr, a boy of literary sensibility, learned his biblical prose style early. His childhood was a rural one, in the farm country around Carlisle, Hershey and Mount Holly Springs, and it was there he conceived the love of natural history that would continue into his travels in Saudi Arabia.

When Rentz Sr joined the US Navy as a chaplain, the family faced a future of continual relocation typical of life in the armed forces. George Jr attended elementary schools in Norfolk, Virginia, Washington DC and at other Navy bases, and completed high school in Pensacola, Florida. He began college at Georgia Institute of Technology, and then made the move with his family to Manila, where he continued his further education at the University of the Philippines.

In 1932, at the age of twenty, on his way home by ship through the Suez Canal, Rentz was invited by a fellow-traveller to teach English to boys in an Arabic school in Aleppo, Syria. He grasped the opportunity, and the three years in Aleppo that followed kindled his lifelong interest in the Middle East (Aramco 1963: 1, 8; Rentz *c.* 1966).

Looking back late in life, Rentz recalled his time in Syria. While he was there a book on King 'Abd al-'Aziz came his way, and he "picked up in the *suq* a large poster with all the pictures of all the rulers in the Arab World, including the first picture of King 'Abd al-'Aziz I ever saw". "Native Arab nationalism", as he put it, especially as expressed in Saudi Arabia, became his abiding interest, and he resolved to pursue it on his return to the United States. He was to start work on his subject just before oil was discovered in 1938, and his fellow students could not understand why he chose to specialise in so obscure a country as the new Kingdom then was. "Little did they know or did I know then," he remarked, "what the future would hold for Saudi Arabia." (Clark 1983)

Returning in 1935 from Aleppo to his family, which was by then stationed at Long Beach, California, Rentz entered the University of California at Berkeley along with his younger siblings William and Mary. There in 1937 he completed his Bachelor's degree, focusing on Middle Eastern history, gaining highest honours. He then spent 1937–8 working on his MA thesis entitled "The Mameluke Empire in the XIV Century".

In 1938, by now the recipient of a university fellowship in history for one year – the first of several such awards – he began work on his doctoral thesis on 18th-century Saudi Arabian history. He studied under Prof. Robert J. Kerner in the Department of History, opting for a minor in Semitics and Arabic with Dr William Popper. He often used to recall his seven years spent as Dr Popper's only Arabic student at UC Berkeley; though he had learnt a smattering of Arabic in Aleppo, it was at Berkeley that his real love for the language blossomed. During this time, he also spent one year at Princeton in the Department of Oriental Languages and Literatures, doing research with the renowned Arab historian Dr Philip K. Hitti (into whose family, incidentally, R. Bayly Winder was to marry).

Rentz's doctoral studies were interrupted by the Second World War. In 1941 his father died a death at sea of heroic self-sacrifice, giving up his life-jacket to save another man – heroism that was to be recognised in 1983–4 when a US Navy guided-missile frigate was named after him. Rentz Jr tried to enlist in the armed services, but was rejected because of his poor hearing. Instead he applied to the

Department of State's Division of Near Eastern Affairs. It was then, in 1942, that he was posted to Cairo. First he acted as representative of the Coordinator of Information (1942), and then of the Office of Strategic Services (1942–3). 1943–5 saw him at the Office of War Information in Cairo, and it was while there that he visited Jiddah, as described above.

While living in Egypt, George Rentz met Sophie Bassili Tadros Badir Ghobrial El-Asfar, an Egyptian Copt who spoke, read and wrote Arabic, French and English, and who had graduated in journalism from the American University in Cairo (AUC). At the time she was working as secretary to Rentz's associate Elmer Lower (who was later to become President of ABC News). They were married on 10 February 1944, after George had appeased Sophie's mother, Lulu Tadros Badir, by eating the traditional Egyptian soup *mulukhīyah* – a seemingly small gesture, perhaps, but it was said to be the one and only time that he was able to bring himself to eat it. Their first daughter, Maureen Sheri, was born in Cairo in late 1944. After Rentz had taken up his post in the Government Relations Department at Aramco, the family moved to Dhahran, Saudi Arabia, and it was there that their second daughter, Tanya Doreen, was born in 1948. Sophie and the two girls stayed in Dhahran for two years but moved back to Cairo in 1950. From then on, for the next 13 years, Rentz would commute between Dhahran and Cairo, where their third daughter, Rebecca Janine, was born in 1955.

His rapid appointment as head of Aramco's Research and Translation Division soon led to higher things. In 1950 he became Senior Arabist and in 1952 he was appointed supervisor of Arabian Research. From 1955 to 1958 he acted as company adviser on Arab affairs, before dual assignment as acting assistant director of Local Government Relations and acting senior representative of the Eastern Province. In October 1958 he joined the Policy and Planning Staff of Aramco's Government Relations Organisation, the post from which he retired in June 1963 (Aramco 1963: 1). His sojourn at Aramco, 1946–63, transformed him into the Company's resident authority on Arabic and Arabian matters and established him as a scholar of international repute.

Rentz's career at Aramco was distinguished by the high quality of research carried out by himself and his colleagues in the Arabian Research and Translation Division that he built up. He became involved at the highest level in Aramco affairs, meeting King 'Abd al-'Aziz, on the King's last visit to Dhahran in 1947 and later (van der Meulen 1957: 226), as well as many other members of the Royal family, and forming a friendship with Philby. Rentz's decision to stay on meant relinquishing his Rockefeller Fellowship, but he never expressed regret. On one occasion, when asked why he had stayed, he replied: "Geography, people and opportunities. Saudi Arabia was not completely *terra incognita* in those days but there were large areas Westerners didn't know about. There were opportunities for constructive research here." (Clark 1983)

Among his achievements at Aramco was the publication of a series of Aramco handbooks in January 1950. Writing the original chapters for these on history, geography, religion and people had been Rentz's first assignment from his boss, Tom Barger and, when the time came for his first vacation in 1947, he had taken them with him for printing in the United States – when he also presented his thesis. These first handbooks were revised and published in 1952 as *The Arabia of Ibn Saud* (Lebkicher, Rentz and Steineke 1952). From this was developed the successive editions, updated every decade or so, of the handsome Aramco Handbook that was made available for general distribution. In successive re-editions this has become a chief source of information on the Kingdom for a wider public. Rentz's concept, albeit much extended and reworked, left its stamp on the series and is identifiable even in the latest edition, *Saudi Aramco and Its World* (Nawwab, Speers and Hoye 1995).

At Aramco Rentz developed and refined the interviewing techniques which he used very effectively to elicit tribal and geographical information from the bedouin (Mulligan 1987), enabling him to fill gaps where no written information existed, and to check and correct written sources that were often sparse. As Mulligan recalls, his office at times seemed swarming with colourful "relators", representing tribes and villages from the far corners of the Kingdom (Mulligan 1987). This process, though inevitably lacking rigour and reliability, was designed to be used with discrimination to produce an enormous amount of new information on the

Kingdom. Rentz used the data to produce, as editor and joint author, *The Eastern Reaches of al-Hasa Province* (Rentz 1950) and *Oman and The Southern Shore of the Persian Gulf* (Rentz 1952), and he and his staff later turned some of the information into articles for the second edition of the *Encyclopaedia of Islam*, the first volume of which appeared in 1954. Among many important new entries, Rentz's *tour de force* must be that on the Arabian Peninsula, which treats the entire region in extraordinary detail (Rentz 1960). Colleagues such as William Mulligan and F. S. Vidal produced other entries, some of them jointly with Rentz.

In 1952 Rentz received a visit from the distinguished Dutch diplomat and scholar Daan van der Meulen, who in giving a graphic account of the Aramco research effort also manages to suggest the potential conflicts inherent in its multiple objectives (van der Meulen 1957: 192–3):

> Aramco had three departments working to smooth the company's way and as a guest of Dr George Rentz, the Head of the Research Department, I was able to see what his department was doing. He and his men were the scholars, the Arabists in the broad sense of studying the people, their language, history and social conditions. And what golden opportunities they had! From the far backsands of the desert they had visitors with whom they could talk the whole day long if they wished. Their guests from the interior were treated with the respect due to men who are in possession of invaluable knowledge. In Aramco's hospitality these men had better fare than they had ever met with before and each, in addition, received a monetary gift. Here the systematic study of Arabia was, for the first time in the long history of the country, being done at home, and in an air-conditioned home at that. Here I met men from the remote wadis of the Hadhramaut … In their daily talks with these men Rentz's able assistants pieced together the information they required of the as yet unexplored regions into which Aramco wished to penetrate. Draughtsmen were busy drawing maps and adding those local features which give a map of the unknown parts of Arabia its real value. Here too were compiled facts never before studied about important parts of Sa'udi Arabia like Al Hasa province, and

> territories such as the inner regions of ʻOman bordering on the southern Saʻudi frontier, hitherto beyond Western exploration. All these publications were produced bilingually in the Latin and the Arabic script, thus fulfilling a triple purpose: first of preparing the ground for Aramco's operations, second of providing the Saʻudi administration with invaluable information and third of furthering the pursuit of learning. Besides collecting its own information on the spot this department kept in close contact with orientalists and scholars the world over and had assembled an admirable specialist library.

Conflict of interest could arise because much of this effort in the early years had a more than academic purpose, and this resulted in accusations of bias (e.g. Kelly 1980: 260–1; Henderson 1993: 110–11). The revival of the oil industry at the end of the Second World War brought a renewed urgency to the demarcation of frontiers between the young states emerging in south-east Arabia. Defined lines in the sand were required in remote desert regions of the eastern Rubʻ al-Khali to establish ownership of oil reserves that might lie beneath. Britain was the protecting power in Abu Dhabi and Oman at that time before independence, and a tussle ensued between the Saudi Arabian government and Aramco on the one hand, and, on the other, the British government with the oil company Petroleum Development (Trucial Coast), the ruler of Abu Dhabi, and the Sultan of Muscat and Oman. Claim and counter-claim hinged on the alleged historic allegiances of the tribes in the area of the Buraimi Oasis, some of whom had acknowledged Saudi overlordship from time to time in the past when Saudi influence had been at its zenith. Much ink has been spilt over the Buraimi Dispute and this is not the place to rehearse the arguments on both sides (e.g. Kelly 1964; Kelly 1980: 60–76, 113–14; Heard-Bey 1982: 302–5; Henderson 1993: *passim* and 110–11 on Rentz; Wilkinson 1987: 286–95; Al-Rasheed 2002: 115–16; McLoughlin 2002: 142–4). Eventually in 1955 it went to international arbitration at Geneva for which extensive legal memorials had been prepared by both sides, citing local oral sources to support their conflicting claims. Rentz had not only been largely responsible for the Saudi *Memorial*, but was attached to the Saudi Arabian delegation at Geneva as a technical expert (Rentz 1955; *c.* 1966). The Dispute bedevilled relations between Britain and Saudi Arabia throughout the 1950s, and inevitably much of the local data supporting the Saudi case was produced by Rentz and the staff of the Aramco Research and Translation Division from 1948 on. The Dispute was not resolved by the Arbitration and Britain eventually enforced the claims of Abu Dhabi and Oman by armed intervention.

That some of this allegedly biased research used to support the Saudi claim was produced by American scholars working for Aramco, and might have subsequently found its way into articles in the august *Encyclopaedia of Islam* has provoked unease in some quarters (e.g. Kelly 1980: 260). But even such critics admit that Rentz himself could be a dispassionate scholar when academic rigour demanded it (e.g. Kelly 1964: 212, 216, 231). Edward Henderson, a British oil company official, once recalled how, in 1951, he went over to Dhahran from the Trucial Coast to meet with Rentz in connection with the Buraimi issue. At the time Rentz was preparing his entry on Abu Dhabi for the *Encyclopaedia of Islam*, and handed Henderson the draft, inviting his comments. Henderson, who himself had compiled much information in support of the British case in the Buraimi Dispute, among other things added a note to the effect that "several villages of al-Buraymī belong to Āl Bū Falāh". Despite this tending to undermine the Saudi–Aramco case, Rentz was first and foremost an objective scholar; he recognised the validity of the information, and retained it in his *Encyclopaedia of Islam* entry. (Henderson 1988: 110–11; Armitage: personal communication; Kelly 1964: 212, 231).

In 1963, due to the political situation in Egypt, and tiring of continual commuting to Cairo, Rentz applied for and received the position of Curator of the Middle Eastern Collection at the Hoover Institution for War, Revolution and Peace at Stanford University in California. His old friend, Wayne Vucinich, was Professor of Slavic Studies at Stanford and facilitated the application. Rentz spent the next 15 years as Curator, but also took up a post as assistant professor in the history department at Stanford, where he worked closely with Michel Nabti, his assistant. There he offered an introductory course on Islamic history and civilisation, and served on doctoral student committees in Islamic and Ottoman studies. He spent the year 1976–7 as a fellow at the prestigious Woodrow Wilson Center at the Smithsonian Institution in Washington DC, and then stayed on as a visiting professor at the School for Advanced International Studies (SAIS) at Johns Hopkins University, Baltimore, before returning west with Sophie to their home on the Stanford campus. In 1977 he returned to Saudi Arabia to participate in the historical conference organised by Riyadh (now King Saud) University, and was able to revisit Dhahran.

In view of his enormous scholarly attainments, one might have expected Rentz to have published more: his full-length publications were limited to the ones listed under his name in the References below. His chief interests covered a vast field: the Arabic language; the contemporary Arab world; Islam and Islamic history; modern movements in Islam; Islam in central Asia and sub-Saharan Africa; the Muslim pilgrimage; Arabian frontiers and exploration; the bedouin tribes of Arabia and their genealogies; the history, geography and culture of Arabia; Arabian flora, fauna and climate; and, of course, the oil industry. He had amassed huge amounts of material on all these subjects. James Mandaville, in the Dhahran days a relatively junior colleague of Rentz at Aramco, vividly recalls his meticulous approach to research and the recording of data and sources (James Mandaville, personal communication):

> One aspect of George's scholarly apparatus that particularly impressed all of us was his huge inventory of 3 x 5 cards recording facts from his readings in several languages. As I remember, at least part of the time he substituted paper slips for cards, thus doubling or tripling the capacity of his rows and rows, stacks and stacks, of trays. We all assumed that they would be used someday in some masterwork in which the footnotes and citations would far outnumber the lines of text. Sometimes, when someone was working on a particular research subject, George would pull out a handful of these slips and loan them as pointers to certain sources. We would go over these cards, marveling at the beautifully inked calligraphy in both Arabic and English. He always used a thick-

> nibbed fountain pen. Every one of these cards was a small piece of art in itself. Some of us, even if semi-consciously, attempted to emulate this note style, only to resign ourselves, finally, to our usual scribble.

Michel Nabti remembers him as a careful and diligent scholar of Arabic and Islam, and as a walking compendium of Arabian erudition. Only a fraction of it was reflected in the large number of pieces he wrote as chapters for books and as articles for periodicals and encyclopaedias (Rentz *c.* 1966).

In retirement he continued to take a keen interest in Arabian affairs. He said that he had embarked upon writing a book about HM King 'Abd al-'Aziz; however, this does not seem to have attained publishable form (Clark 1983). His participation in the "Bahrain Through the Ages" conference in Manamah in December 1983, when he delivered a paper on the Abu Sa'fah oil-field, gave him the opportunity to visit a much-changed Dhahran for the last time. He died at home in Stanford on 22 December 1987, aged 75.

George Rentz left an enduring mark both as an Arabist scholar and as an inspiring teacher. Few would disagree with Prof. Jon E. Mandaville's judgement that he was "the true ground-breaker for modern Saudi Arabian studies, and not just in the USA" (J. E. Mandaville, personal communication). He always had time for students and colleagues and delighted in imparting his knowledge to others. William Mulligan, an old colleague of Rentz's, recalled him with affection shortly before his death in 1987 (Mulligan 1987):

> To compensate for his defective hearing, Rentz developed a deep and agreeably resonant voice. He is gregarious, cheerful and dapper. He has a slightly courtly manner, but he is also among the most truly democratic of men. He treats servants like aristocrats, employees as equals, and earthy bedouins like members of an Academy of Arts and Sciences. His circle of friends and admirers is large indeed. In his scholarly work Rentz combines the methodical and logical processes of his Germanic heritage with a romanticism and exuberance that are typically American and Arabian.
>
> Rentz is a perfectionist and hardest in this regard on himself. This

> helps to explain his relatively meagre literary output, but what he has written is correct and to the point. Much of his finest scholarship appears in the second edition of *The Encyclopaedia of Islam* ...
>
> Rentz is a magnificent teacher, able to correct without hurting and inspire and encourage in the most congenial manner. He writes with ease, but is far more concerned with precision than with style.

At the time of his death Majed Elass, then Vice President of Aramco's Washington Office who had known Rentz well through a long association (Clark 1988), recalled him as

> a dominant contributor to the unique personality of Aramco for nearly 20 of its most formative years ... a part of that remarkable blend of explorers, rig hands, Arabists, anthropologists and historians that made the Aramco experience a model for international enterprises.
>
> He established the high standards of Arabic translation and Arabian research which have given international repute to the company's work in these fields. He was a distinguished scholar whose knowledge of the Arabian Peninsula was unsurpassed. Arab and American employees alike benefited from his brilliance and dedication as a teacher, and he was held in the most affectionate regard by all who knew him.

★

As well as scholar and teacher, George Rentz was a notable bibliophile. At Aramco he started and put his stamp on the company's Middle East collection in Dhahran, which forms the heart of the Headquarters Library. He also built up a truly remarkable personal library in several languages, chiefly in English and Arabic. During the course of a long life it came to include one of the finest private collections in the world of books and papers on the Arabian Peninsula in general and on Saudi Arabia in particular. Rentz himself estimated that his entire personal library, including items not concerned with the Arabian Peninsula, amounted to some 8,000 volumes. It included "a small but respectable collection of Arabic manuscripts", as well as texts in a variety of Semitic languages and scripts, and many works on comparative Semitic philology, the majority in German. (Rentz *c.* 1966; Lunde: personal communication)

Much of this remarkable collection, containing many rare and now unobtainable items, was acquired in the 1990s by the King Abdulaziz Public Library in Riyadh, where it is available to researchers. The books alone total some 3,272 in English and 1,284 in Arabic.

In addition to the books there is a multitude of papers in manuscript and typescript form, arranged in personal and subject files and covering a range of topics of Arabian and international interest: in all there are 1150 files of papers in English, and 1050 of papers in Arabic. The personal files contain miscellaneous correspondence in English, Arabic and German between Rentz and his friends and colleagues, members of the Saudi Royal family, and students and researchers studying various aspects of the history and geography of Saudi Arabia, local conditions, Arab affairs and the life of King 'Abd al-'Aziz Ibn Saud. Among them are to be found, for example, correspondence containing data relating to OPEC and oil companies; drafts of treaties, agreements and disputes, corrected by hand; an analysis, dated 22 March 1958, of the transfer of power from HM King Saud to HM King Faisal; reports of visits to Wadi al-Dawāsir, 'Asīr and al-Dir'īyah; and a brief history of al-Kharj. The document files are classified in the King Abdulaziz Public Library as follows:

- Aramco Affairs
- Saudi Arabia: Internal and External Affairs
- George Rentz's Private Correspondence
- Memoranda, Reports and Articles by George Rentz
- Buraimi: Internal Affairs, Disputes and Arbitration
- Egypt: Internal and External Affairs
- Trucial States and Oman
- The Second World War
- Tribes of Arabia

★

In preparing this work for publication, the editor's task has been unusually simple, for a number of reasons. One may remark, first of all, that most doctoral theses are unsuited to publication in their original form, for reasons of stylistic opacity, pedestrian presentation, repetition, inconsistencies, scholarly apparatus that suffers from too much or too little detail, lack of apparent relevance to a wider context, and so forth. They often need a great deal of rewriting and some reorganisation and abridgement. Rentz's thesis is free of such shortcomings. Not only is his text clearly structured, but it is vividly expressed and perfectly readable as it stands. As observed above, it has a literary quality, being written in a style that befits its subject. Some expressions may seem slightly archaic to the modern reader, but these are part of the character of Rentz's writing and no attempt has been made to render them in a more contemporary style.

Second, it has been a condition of publication set by the author's estate that the text of the thesis should be published unchanged and in full – a stance that is only fair to an author whose work is being published posthumously. Even if extensive editorial interventions had been desirable, therefore, that stipulation would have absolved this editor of the irksome task of carrying them out. As it is, it will relieve scholarly readers of the niggling suspicion that the editor may have changed or deleted something of interest or importance, and that what is published will have to be compared with the original text. Readers can rest assured that no such changes or excisions have been made.

Third, Rentz's system of transliteration from Arabic into English is a simple and adequate one. It has not been tampered with by the editor, because it satisfies that basic criterion of any such system, that it should enable any reader who may wish to do so to put a word or name back into Arabic script with perfect accuracy.

The text of Rentz's original thesis is, hence, published exactly as he presented it in 1947, and editorial intervention has been confined to the following adjustments, structural and otherwise:

- Rentz entitled his work *Muḥammad b. ʻAbd al-Wahhāb (1703/4–1792) and the Beginnings of Unitarian Empire in Arabia.* This has been retained as the subtitle of this publication. The new main title, *The Birth of the Islamic Reform Movement in Saudi Arabia*, has been added to highlight the relevance of the book to the world today.

- The author organised the thesis into the four Parts that appear here. However, he subdivided the Parts not into chapters, but into the short subtitled sections that pepper the book. These subtitles have all been retained, but a chapter structure has now been imposed upon them to signpost the story for the modern reader. Hence none of the 16 chapter headings appeared in Rentz's original. The footnotes have been renumbered accordingly, 1–n, within each chapter, whereas Rentz numbered them 1–n on each page of the thesis.
- An editorial comment has been inserted only when deemed absolutely necessary, for example to draw attention to later research that may correct a statement by Rentz. They are very few and appear only in the footnotes, clearly identified between square brackets and attributed to "Ed.". See, for example, Chapter 1 note 13 on the dating of the Ottoman takeover of al-Aḥsā' in the 10th/16th century (Mandaville 1970; Anscombe 1997).
- Five comments on the text were included on the recommendation of the Scientific Committee of King Abdulaziz Public Library, which has made possible the publication of this work. These comments have been included in the footnotes, where they are clearly indicated between square brackets and attributed to "KAPL". See pp. 101 n. 96, 108 nn. 9 and 11, p. 121 n. 18, and p. 217 n. 4.
- Rentz referred to centuries by the somewhat cumbersome use of Latin numerals, e.g. "XVII century". For the convenience of the reader who may find this an impediment, however slight, all these have been rendered as "17th century" etc.
- The single chart in the text, comparing the genealogies of Shaikh Muḥammad b. 'Abd al-Wahhāb, originally formed a note in Rentz's thesis, but has been presented as a chart in its own right (see Chapter 2 note 11). The two tables forming the Appendix have been added.
- Finally, the seven maps in the text have been added; Rentz submitted no maps with his thesis.

★

King Abdulaziz Public Library and the editor would like to thank the literary estate of George S. Rentz Jr, and in particular Rentz's daughters Maureen Sheri Wernicke, Tanya Doreen Rentz and Rebecca Janine El-Tal, for permission to publish this thesis. The editor would also like to thank them for their patience during the prolonged process of seeing the work into print, for information about their father's life, and for their ready help and advice throughout.

The editor would like to express his gratitude to Mr Faisal Al-Mu'ammar, Supervisor-General of King Abdulaziz Public Library, Riyadh, for his staunch support of this long-overdue publication.

Warm thanks are also due to Arthur P. Clark of *Aramco World* magazine, who has been free with his research and newspaper articles on George Rentz, and for making available William E. Mulligan's unpublished appreciation of him. As it can hardly be improved upon, Arthur Clark's obituary of Rentz has been shamelessly plundered for this Introduction. Dr Michel Nabti kindly supplied an appreciation of Rentz's years at Stanford. St John Armitage has been generous with his time, advice and personal memories, and with contacts such as James and Jon Mandaville whose recollections are much appreciated. Dr Colin Baker, Head of the Near and Middle Eastern Collections and Curator for Arabic, introduced me to the Ibn Bishr manuscript in the British Library. I am especially grateful to Jamie Crocker for drawing the maps and tables. Greg Dowling, Paul Lunde, Russell McGuirk, James Parry, Carl Phillips and Paul Robertson provided valuable insights and encouragement along the way. Thanks go to all.

In conclusion, it is hoped that this publication would have satisfied George Rentz's own exacting scholarly and editorial standards.

William Facey
2004

References

Anscombe, F., (1997), *The Ottoman Gulf*, Columbia University Press.

Aramco, (1963), *Sun and Flare* newspaper, Vol. XIX, No. 21, Dhahran, 29 May 1963.

Azzam, Maha, (2003), "Al-Qaeda: the misunderstood Wahhabi connection and the ideology of violence", The Royal Institute of International Affairs, Middle East Programme, Briefing Paper No. 1, London, February 2003.

Crichton, Andrew, (1833), *History of Arabia, Ancient and Modern*, 2 vols., Edinburgh.

Clark, Arthur P., (1983), "Rentz Brings Back Memories of Earlier Aramco", *The Arabian Sun*, Aramco Services Department, 21 December 1983.

— (1988), "George Rentz, Noted Arabist, Dies; Lauded as a Pioneering Aramco Figure", *The Arabian Sun*, Aramco Services Department, 6 January 1988.

Facey, William, (1992), *Riyadh – The Old City*, London, Immel Publishing. Arabic edition: *Al-Riyāḍ – al-madīnah al-qadīmah*, published by the King Abdulaziz Public Library, Riyadh, 1419/1999.

— (1997), *Dir'iyyah and the First Saudi State*, London, Stacey International. Arabic edition: *Al-Dir'iyyah wa-'l-Daulah al-Su'udiyyah al-Awalī*, published by Al-Turath, Riyadh, 1419/1999.

Goldberg, J., (1985), "Philby as a Source for Early 20th-century Saudi History: A Critical Examination", *Middle Eastern Studies* 21, pp. 223–43.

Heard-Bey, Frauke, (1982), *From Trucial States to United Arab Emirates*, London, Longman.

Henderson, Edward, (1993), *This Strange Eventful History: Memoirs of Earlier Days in the UAE and Sultanate of Oman*, Abu Dhabi, Dubai and London, Motivate Publishing.

Ibn Bishr, (AH 1270): 'Uthmān b. 'Abd Allāh Ibn Bishr al-Ḥanbalī, *'Unwān al-Majd fī-ta'rīkh Najd*, unpublished MS (Or. 7718) in the British Library, Oriental and India Office Collections, dated AH 1270 (AD 1873–4), 258 folios.

Jomard, E. F. (1823), *Notice géographique sur le pays de Nedjd en Arabie centrale*, Paris.

— (1839), *Etudes géographiques et historiques sur l'Arabie avec des observations sur l'état des affaires en Arabie*, Paris.

Al-Juhany, Uwaidah M., (2002), *Najd before the Salafi Reform Movement: Social, Political and Religious Conditions during the Three Centuries Preceding the Rise of the Saudi State*, Reading, UK, Ithaca Press.

Kaplan, Robert D., (1993), *The Arabists: The Romance of an American Elite*, New York, The Free Press, Macmillan Inc.

Kelly, J. B., (1964), *Eastern Arabian Frontiers*, London, Faber and Faber.

— (1968), *Britain and the Persian Gulf*, Oxford University Press.

— (1980), *Arabia, the Gulf and the West*, London, Weidenfeld and Nicolson.

Lebkicher, R., Rentz, G., and Steineke, M., (1952), *The Arabia of Ibn Saud*, New York, Russell F. Moore.

Lorimer, J. G., (1908–15), *Gazetteer of the Persian Gulf, 'Oman and Central Arabia*, 2 vols., Calcutta.

McLoughlin, Leslie, (2002), *In a Sea of Knowledge: British Arabists in the Twentieth Century*, Reading, UK, Ithaca Press.

Mandaville, J. E., (1970), "The Ottoman Province of al-Ḥasā' in the Sixteenth and Seventeenth Centuries", *Journal of the American Oriental Society*, 90.

Mengin, F., (1823), *Histoire sommaire de l'Egypte sous le gouvernement de Mohammed-Aly*, 2 vols., Paris.

— (1839), *Histoire sommaire de l'Egypte sous le gouvernement de Mohammed-Aly ou récit des principaux événements qui ont eu lieu de l'an 1823 à l'an 1838. Précédé d'une introduction et service d'études géographiques et historiques sur l'Arabie par M. Jomard …* [= Jomard 1839], Paris.

van der Meulen, D., (1957), *The Wells of Ibn Sa'ud*, London, John Murray.

Monroe, Elizabeth, (1973), *Philby of Arabia*, London, Faber and Faber.

Mulligan, W. E., (1987), Untitled and unpublished short biographical appreciation of George Rentz.

Nawwab, I., Speers, P., and Hoye, P., eds., (1995), *Saudi Aramco and Its World*, Dhahran, The Saudi Arabian Oil Company (Saudi Aramco).

O'Kinealy, J., (1874), "Translation of an Arabic Pamphlet on the History and Doctrines of the Wahhabis, written by 'Abdullah, grandson of 'Abdul Wahhab, the Founder of Wahhabism", *Journal of the Bengal Asiatic Society*, no. 43, part 1, pp. 68–82.

Oliveti, V., (2001), *Terror's Source: the Ideology of Wahhabi-Salafism and its Consequences*, Amadeus Books, Birmingham.

Philby, H. St J. B., (1930), *Arabia*, New York, Scribner's.

— (1955), *Sa'udi Arabia*, London, Ernest Benn Ltd.

Al-Rasheed, M., (2002), *A History of Saudi Arabia*, Cambridge University Press.

Rentz, George S., (1950), editor and joint author, *The Eastern Reaches of al-Hasa Province*, Dhahran, (English edition xiii + 213 pp.; Arabic edition viii + 167 pp.)

— (1952), editor and joint author, *Oman and The Southern Shore of the Persian Gulf*, Cairo, Imprimerie Misr, (English edition xii + 326 pp.; Arabic edition xii + 318 pp.)

— (1955), joint editor and author, *Memorial of the Government of Saudi Arabia* [Buraimi Arbitration], Cairo, Dar al-Ma'arif, 3 vols. English and 3 vols. Arabic. [The editing was shared with Richard Young, Counsel to the Saudi Arabian Government in the Buraimi Arbitration. Rentz and Young worked under the supervision of 'Abd al-Raḥmān 'Azzam, Agent of the Saudi Arabian Government in the Arbitration. Rentz's principal contribution as author was Chapter IV of Vol. I (pp. 97–382 in the English text and pp. 97–362 in the Arabic), dealing with the history of the disputed areas. (Rentz *c.* 1966)]

— (1956), *A Sketch of the Geography, People and History of the Arabian Peninsula*, Dhahran, (i + 67 pp.). [A somewhat modified version, privately printed, of Rentz's article on the Arabian Peninsula for *The Encyclopaedia of Islam* (Rentz 1960a; Rentz *c.* 1966).]

— (1960a), "Djazirat al-'arab", *Encyclopaedia of Islam*, 2nd edition, Vol. 1, Leiden, pp. 533–56.

— (1960b), joint author, *Aramco Handbook*, Harlem, The Netherlands. [In part a revised edition of *The Arabia of Ibn Saud*, New York, 1952, (Lebkicher, Rentz and Steineke, 1952).]

— (*c.* 1966), typescript *curriculum vitae* of and by George S. Rentz, 8 pp., unpublished (appears to have been compiled no later than 1966).

— (1972), "Wahhabism and Saudi Arabia", in *The Arabian Peninsula: Society and Politics*, ed. Derek Hopwood, London, George Allen and Unwin, pp. 54–66.

— (1979), "Philby as a Historian of Saudi Arabia", *Sources for the History of Arabia*, Part 2, University of Riyadh, pp. 25–35.

Ross, E. C., (1880), "Memoir on Nejd", Persian Gulf Administration Report, Government of India, reprinted in *Records of Saudi Arabia: Primary Documents, 1902–1960*, Vol. 1 Historical Background, ed. Penelope Tuson and Anita Burdett, Archive Editions, 1992.

Sabini, John, (1981), *Armies in the Sand: The Struggle for Mecca and Medina*, London, Thames and Hudson.

Sadleir, G. F., (1823), "Account of a Journey from Katif on the Persian Gulf to Yambo on the Red Sea …", *Transactions of the Literary Society of Bombay*, III, pp. 449–93.

— (1866), *Diary of a Journey across Arabia*, Bombay. (Reprinted Cambridge 1977.)

Wilkinson, J. C., (1987), *Arabian Frontiers*, London, I.B. Tauris.

Winder, R. Bayly, (1965), *Saudi Arabia in the Nineteenth Century*, London, Macmillan.

Muḥammad Ibn ʻAbd al-Wahhāb (1703/4–1792) and the Beginnings of Unitarian Empire in Arabia

Author's Preface

The present study is the outgrowth of an interest in the Near East and its people that began fifteen years ago when I was a teacher of English in Aleppo, Syria. The completion of the study was delayed five years by the war against Hitlerism, but there was a measure of consolation in the delay, the five years having been spent in the Near East, in Egypt and in Arabia itself.

Ten years ago, when I selected the modern history of the Near East as a field of specialization, I had the conviction that any work done in this field would be superficial and of slight account unless based upon familiarity with the Arabic language, the character of the Arab people, the story of their past, and the nature of their dominant religion, Islam, a conviction which, it may be added, has grown stronger with the passage of time and the acquiring of experience. A Westerner might find somewhat strange this emphasis on religion in the modern world, but a brief visit to the Near East would persuade him that it is not misplaced, for he would find that religion there is politics, that it is law, that it is education, that is is in a sense the whole of life. For one holding the conviction referred to, the choice of Arabia as the subject of his inaugural dissertation was easy and natural. As far back as the memory of man runs, Arabia has been the fountainhead of the Arabic language, the purest forms of which are still to be heard on the tongues of the inhabitants of the Peninsula. The Arabs of the Near East are a diverse folk, but there is a bit of the old Arabian of the desert in every one of them, and if one wishes to find the common denominator in their traditions and manners and habits of thought, he can do no better than to go to the home, as they will say, of Abraham and of Ishmael. There is likewise an intimate association between Arabia and the past of the Arabs, particularly in the days of their great glory and power. But above all else, the significance of Arabia lies in its being the birthplace and eternal center of Islam, the religion that an Arab transmitted to his fellow Arabs and that few of them have rejected for other faiths.

Since few aspects of the history of Arabia in the centuries after the time of the Prophet have been examined by Arabists and students of the Near East, a number of specific matters were available for investigation. The choice fell upon the career of the Shaikh Muḥammad b. ʻAbd al-Wahhāb and the early history of the theocratic movement he set in motion because this subject, more than any other, seemed fundamental to an understanding of Arabia and the Near East in the modern age. Islam as preached by the Shaikh was essentially Islam as promulgated by the Prophet; it was a bringing of the 7th century back to life in the 18th, an act of resurrection that has been prolonged through the 19th century and into the 20th, for Unitarianism, as the Shaikh and his followers called their religion, is the official form of Islam in the Kingdom of Saudi Arabia today. The maintenance of puritan Unitarianism in the most conservative of the Arab lands has an important bearing on the position and fate of Islam in the present and the future. Again, the Shaikh Muḥammad b. ʻAbd al-Wahhāb, like the Prophet before him, had the vision to see that political unity was indispensable to the securing of religious triumphs. Arabia disunified would count for little in the world of today or of any other time; the same holds true for the Near East as a whole. The modern unity of Arabia and the trend toward the unity of the larger area are in history inextricably intertwined with the Unitarianism that originated in Najd.

When the study of the Shaikh's career and the rise of the Unitarian state in Arabia was undertaken, it at once became apparent that the first problem was the elucidation of what had happened and the establishing of the proper sequence of events. Gibbon, writing *The Decline and Fall* about forty years after the founding of the Unitarian state, referred to the motive power of that state as "the visions and arms of a modern prophet, whose tenets are imperfectly known". Had Gibbon had access to better sources of information than what the astute Niebuhr had learned by hearsay during his visit to Arabia in the early 1760s, he would have known that the tenets of the Shaikh Muḥammad b. ʻAbd al-Wahhāb were basically those of the Seal of the Prophets, the propounder of Islam in the 7th century. The tracing of the progress of Unitarian arms, the instruments used in erecting the state, is a different matter, an involved and complicated story that no one, writing either in Arabic or the Western languages, has set down with sufficient clarity and authority. The present work is an attempt so to set it down. The Bibliographical Essay appended will show that the sources of value for this purpose have all been consulted; it is hoped that the results of this labor bring us as close as we may come to the true narrative of what went on in central Arabia in the 18th century.

The biography of the Shaikh Muḥammad b. ʻAbd al-Wahhāb has been taken as the framework of the story, but the substance is rather the spread of Unitarianism and how it was fixed in its expanding environment. The presentation is largely chronological, but an effort is made to avoid a dull recitation by frequent comments on the underlying meaning of the events. There may seem to be an excess of inconsequential details, but the details are there to be used in a contemplated analysis of Arabian life in this period and the structure and functioning of the Unitarian state. In conclusion, it may be remarked that this whole study is preliminary to a larger one, broader in scope and primarily analytical rather that narrative in treatment, that is to be carried out as soon as time permits.

★

The movement here dealt with is commonly called Wahhabism by Westerners and by many Near Easterners, particularly those who oppose it, Wahhābi being an adjective derived from the name of the founder, the Shaikh Muḥammad b. ʻAbd al-Wahhāb. In the title of this dissertation and throughout the body of the work, the term Unitarian has been preferred to Wahhabi, since Unitarian represents exactly the Arabic used by the Shaikh and his disciples for one of their own number, *Muwaḥḥid*. The character of the Shaikh's Unitarianism is explained in Part I, which contains a brief discussion of Unitarianian beliefs. It is felt that no harmful confusion will result from the likelihood that the term Unitarian will suggest first of all to Western readers the sect in Christendom, for the Unitarians of the West and the Unitarians of Islam share their absolutely fundamental tenet: God is One.

The main sources for the story date events according to the Moslem calendar, the years of the Hegira. Since the use of only Christian dates would cause considerable awkwardness, the device has been adopted of giving in most instances the Moslem date with the corresponding Christian date following, separated from the first by a diagonal stroke. The tables of Wüstenfeld and Mahler have been used for working out the correspondence of dates.

There is no novelty in the system of transliteration, which agrees in all particulars with one or another of the systems having currency among Arabists. Care has been taken to indicate the presence or absence of the definite article with proper names; where there is disagreement among the Arabs themselves, as there sometimes is, the prevalent form in Arabia itself is given weight in determining preference. The definite article *al* of the Arabic is omitted only when the English *the* is used in its place: for example, the 'Ajmān and the Dahnā'. The definite article in English is not used before a proper name if it is lacking in Arabic: reference is always made to "the Hijaz" (in Arabic al-Ḥijāz), but never to "the Najd" (in Arabic simply Najd). Notice should be taken of the distinction between the definite article *al* and the word *āl*, meaning "family, house". To emphasize the distinction, the definite article is always, excepting at the outset of a sentence, written with a small "a" and is connected with the following name by a hyphen, as in al-Ḥasan and al-Ḥusain, the names of the Prophet's grandsons; whereas the other word is always written with a capital "A" and is separated from the following name, no hyphen being used, as in Āl Zāmil, the Family or House of Zāmil. Where only the English "House" is used, it may be taken to stand for the Arabic "Āl". This matter is further complicated by the modern usage in Arabia, where Āl is usually pronounced and written as if it were identical with the definite article.

In Arabia the word ibn/"son" has two uses: it may be placed before the name of a man's father or before the name of the eponymous ancestor of his family or house. An effort, not always successful, has been made to distinguish between the two by employing the abbreviation "b." in place of *ibn* when it precedes the father's name, excepting in cases where the man's own first name is not cited: for example, Muḥammad b. 'Abd al-Wahhāb, but Ibn 'Abd al-Wahhāb when Muḥammad is omitted. When the term precedes the name of an eponymous ancestor, it is written out in full with a capital "I": for example, Zaid Ibn Zāmil, since his father's name was Mishārī and Zāmil was the founder of his house. In the case where Ibn precedes the name of the founder of the house, modern Arabian usage sanctions the interchangeability of Ibn and Āl: for example, the reigning King of Saudi Arabia may be called 'Abd al-'Azīz Ibn Su'ūd or 'Abd al-'Azīz Āl Su'ūd. The form with Ibn is more colloquial, the form with Āl more formal and proper.

The name Su'ūd deserves a word of comment, particularly since it occurs in the names of the present monarch and his kingdom. The correct form in Arabic is unquestionably Su'ūd, which for the sake of accuracy in transliteration has been used throughout this study, excepting where reference is made to Ibn Saud or Saudi Arabia of the 20th century.

A departure from the classical norms usually adhered to will be observed in the use of Banī/"sons" instead of Banū in the names of Bedouin tribes.

★

I am profoundly in debt to Dr Robert J. Kerner, Sather Professor of History at the University of California, for his guidance and scholarly example and for the faith he has had in me over the years. The interest he has shown in this work, which one might suppose to be somewhat removed from his own field, is a measure of the breadth of his vision in surveying the history of mankind. Dr William Popper of the University of California has been my master in the study of Arabic; I am persuaded that he has no peer. Dr Philip K. Hitti of Princeton University, where part of my research was done, has been generous with knowledge and advice. I am grateful to three friends who provided me with materials of fundamental importance for this work: Rushdī Bey Malḥas, Director of the Diplomatic Branch of the Royal Cabinet in al-Riyāḍ, who presented me with a copy of Ibn Ghannām's rare chronicle; Shaikh Ḥusain Muḥammad Naṣīf, formerly Director of the Office of Waqfs in Jiddah, who presented me with a copy of Ibn Bishr's chronicle and a number of other books on Unitarianism; and Dr Edwin E. Calverley of the Hartford Theological Seminary, who made available to me his very valuable collection of books on this subject. Many others have helped, some more than they know or I could tell; to all I offer thanks.

George S. Rentz
1947

PART I

The Early Career of the Shaikh and the Founding of the State

1115–1159 AH/AD 1703/04–1746

1

Arabia at the Beginning of the 18th Century

The land and the people

The land and the people of Arabia provide a remarkable study in unity and diversity. Ever since the Arabs set foot on the stage of history there have been forces exerting influence in the direction of Arabian unity, and at the same time there have been other forces operating to prevent the attainment of that unity.

The Arabian Peninsula is cut off on the north by desert wastes, lava tracts, and badlands, on the west by a sea, on the east by two gulfs, and on the south by an ocean. The dwellers in the Peninsula recognize, perhaps unconsciously, its isolation in the name they have given it, the Island of the Arabs.[1] Within this vast and lonely landmass there are distinct divisions. The grazing grounds subtending the Fertile Crescent are set off by the sand dunes of the Great Nafūd on their southern skirt. The Tihāmah or Coast-land along the Red Sea is walled off by heights and peaks often rising a mile or even two above sea-level. The coast of the Persian Gulf on the other side of the Peninsula is separated from the interior by the desert strip known as the Dahnā'. In the rear of Hadramaut and the coast on the Indian Ocean there sprawls the widest and most forbidding of Arabia's deserts, the Empty Quarter.[2] In this fashion is Najd, the highland heart of Arabia, separated from all the regions that encircle it. But these barriers are not impassable; nomads and pilgrims and merchants and fighting men traverse them, and, indeed, much of the desert land at certain times of the year provides succulent herbage upon which the herds and flocks grow fat.[3] Since the barriers can be crossed, Najd

[1] Jazīrat al-'Arab
[2] Al-Rub' al-Khālī

occupies the best strategic position for unifying and controlling the Peninsula.

In Najd itself there is unity and diversity. The chief feature of unity is Jabal Ṭuwaiq, running in a slight curve from north to south for a distance of perhaps five hundred miles. This range or escarpment[4] presents a series of more or less sheer bluffs on the western side, facing Mecca and Medina, but towards the Dahnā' and the Persian Gulf in the east it descends in a gentle slope, a fact that tends to link Najd more closely with the east than with the west.[5]

The backbone of Ṭuwaiq is pierced by numerous wadis or arroyos, running roughly from west to east and to a certain extent isolated from each other. The most important of them is Wadi Ḥanīfah, which cleaves through mid-Ṭuwaiq just above 24° north latitude; in it lie al-'Uyainah, the birthplace of the Shaikh Muḥammad b. 'Abd al-Wahhāb, and al-Dir'īyah, the seat of his alliance with the House of Su'ūd that conquered Arabia.

The inhabitants of Arabia exhibit characteristics of both homogeneity and heterogeneity. Among the strongest of their common bonds is the Arabic language, a language notable for its cohesion and resistance to change.[6] There are in addition the concepts of a single race and a single religion. While there have been infusions of foreign elements, particularly of black Africans brought over by the institution of slavery, these elements have on the whole been successfully absorbed into the community and have come to regard themselves as Arabs, though they fail to attain the status of

[3] A poet of the time of the Umayyads, Taubah b. Ḥumayyir al-'Uqailī, vividly expresses the danger of death in the desert: "I have crossed with her [his Mahri camel] the very heart of every desert, in which there is fear of perishing whenever its dust whirls about … You will see weak men there as if they were water-tadpoles whose pool has dried up" – Theodor Noeldeke, *Delectus Veterum Carminum Arabicorum*, p. 6. It should be emphasized, however, that it is easy to exaggerate the fearsomeness of the desert, as, for example, Palgrave has done in his description of the crossing of the Dahnā', which is extremely unrealistic – Palgrave, *Narrative of a Year's Journey*, II, 130–4.

[4] "Not a mountain range but merely the western escarpment of a plateau … formed by denudation" – Musil, *Northern Neǧd*, p. 256.

[5] Jabal Ṭuwaiq does not run the full length of Najd, for beyond it in the north is al-Qaṣīm and then Jabal Shammar just below the Great Nafūd.

[6] The Arabic of today is far closer to the Arabic of the 6th-century poems than modern French or German is to the phrasing of the Strassburg oaths of 842 AD.

purebreds.[7] In the sphere of religion Arabia has followed Islam since the days of its inception, but the devotion of the people has flagged more often than it has held firm.

Despite these unifying forces, the Arabs in Arabia at the beginning of the 18th century stood at the opposite extreme from brotherly comradeship. Throughout the ages hostility had smoldered and blazed between town Arab and nomad, between the desert and the sown. At the same time town had been at strife with town, and tribe with tribe. The Prophet and his first successors had united Arabia, mainly through the prowess of the Sword of God, Khālid b. al-Walīd, but when the Caliphate moved to Damascus the structure fell apart. True and lasting political unity vanished from the Peninsula until the Unitarians of Najd came as restorers in the 18th century.

The political situation

The Ottoman Empire claimed sovereignty over Arabia, the home of Islam, but its claim had little basis in reality. When Salīm the Grim conquered Egypt in 1517, the Sharif of Mecca tendered his allegiance as a diplomatic means of forestalling an invasion.[8] There is no contemporary evidence that al-Mutawakkil, the last of the Abbasid Caliphs, who had been living in Cairo under the shadow of the Mameluke Sultans, designated Salīm as his successor.[9] As a matter of fact, since the institution of the Caliphate had sunk low in popular esteem after the destruction of Baghdad by the Mongols in 1258 AD,

[7] The Bedouins attach much more importance to purity of descent than do the townspeople. A non-Arab origin is no bar to the winning of a high position in society.

[8] Quṭb al-Dīn al-Nahrawālī, ed. Ferdinand Wüstenfeld, *Die Chroniken der Stadt Mekka*, III, 247–8; C. Snouck Hurgronje, *Mekka*, I, 102–3, from al-Sinjārī, *Manā'iḥ al-karam*, pp. 158–9. The Sharif Barakāt b. Muḥammad b. Barakāt sent his twelve-year-old son Muḥammad Abū Numayy to salute the Turkish conqueror, "to tread on the Sultan's carpet in Cairo," as Quṭb al-Dīn expresses it.

[9] The only contemporary historian who gives the career of al-Mutawakkil in detail is Ibn Iyās (d. 1524 AD), *Badā'i' al-zuhūr* (History of Egypt to 928/1522), eds. Moritz Sobernheim, Paul Kahle, Muhammed Mustafa, vol. V, *Bibliotheca Islamica*, Bd 5 e (Istanbul 1932) xii, 493 pp. The chapter on "Sultan Salīm in Egypt" in Sir Thomas W. Arnold, *The Caliphate*, pp. 139–58, reviews the evidence available in both Arabic and Turkish and reaches the firm conclusion that no transfer took place. Arnold has apparently used the Bulaq edition of Ibn Iyās (1894–5), 3 vols.

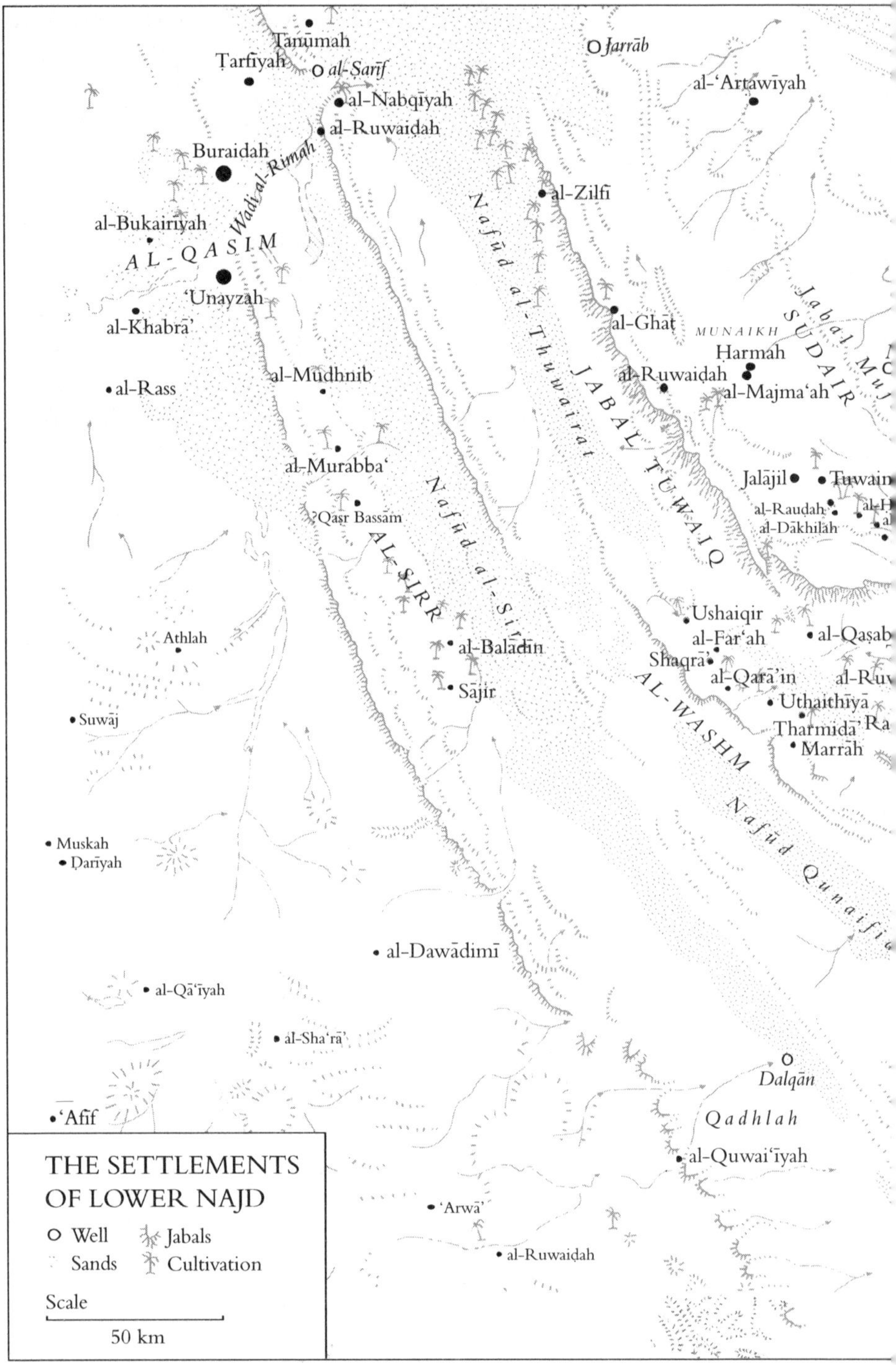
Tanūmah
Ṭarfiyah
al-Sarīf
Jarrāb
al-'Artawīyah
al-Nabqīyah
al-Ruwaiḍah
Buraidah
Wadi al-Rimah
al-Zilfī
al-Bukairiyah
AL-QASIM
'Unayzah
al-Khabrā'
Nafūd al-Thuwairat
al-Ghāṭ
MUNAIKH
SUDAIR
Jabal Mu
Ḥarmah
al-Ruwaiḍah
al-Majma'ah
al-Mudhnib
al-Rass
JABAL TUWAIQ
al-Murabba'
Jalājil
Tuwain
al-Rauḍah
al-Dākhilah
?Qaṣr Bassām
AL-SIRR
Nafūd al-Sirr
Ushaiqir
al-Far'ah
al-Qaṣab
Athlah
al-Baladin
Shaqrā'
al-Qarā'in
Sājir
AL-WASHM
Uthaithīyā
Suwāj
Tharmidā'
Marrāh
Nafūd Qunaifi
Muskah
Ḍarīyah
al-Dawādimī
al-Qā'īyah
al-Sha'rā'
Dalqān
'Afīf
Qadhlah
al-Quwai'īyah
THE SETTLEMENTS OF LOWER NAJD
Well
Jabals
Sands
Cultivation
Scale
50 km
'Arwā'
al-Ruwaiḍah

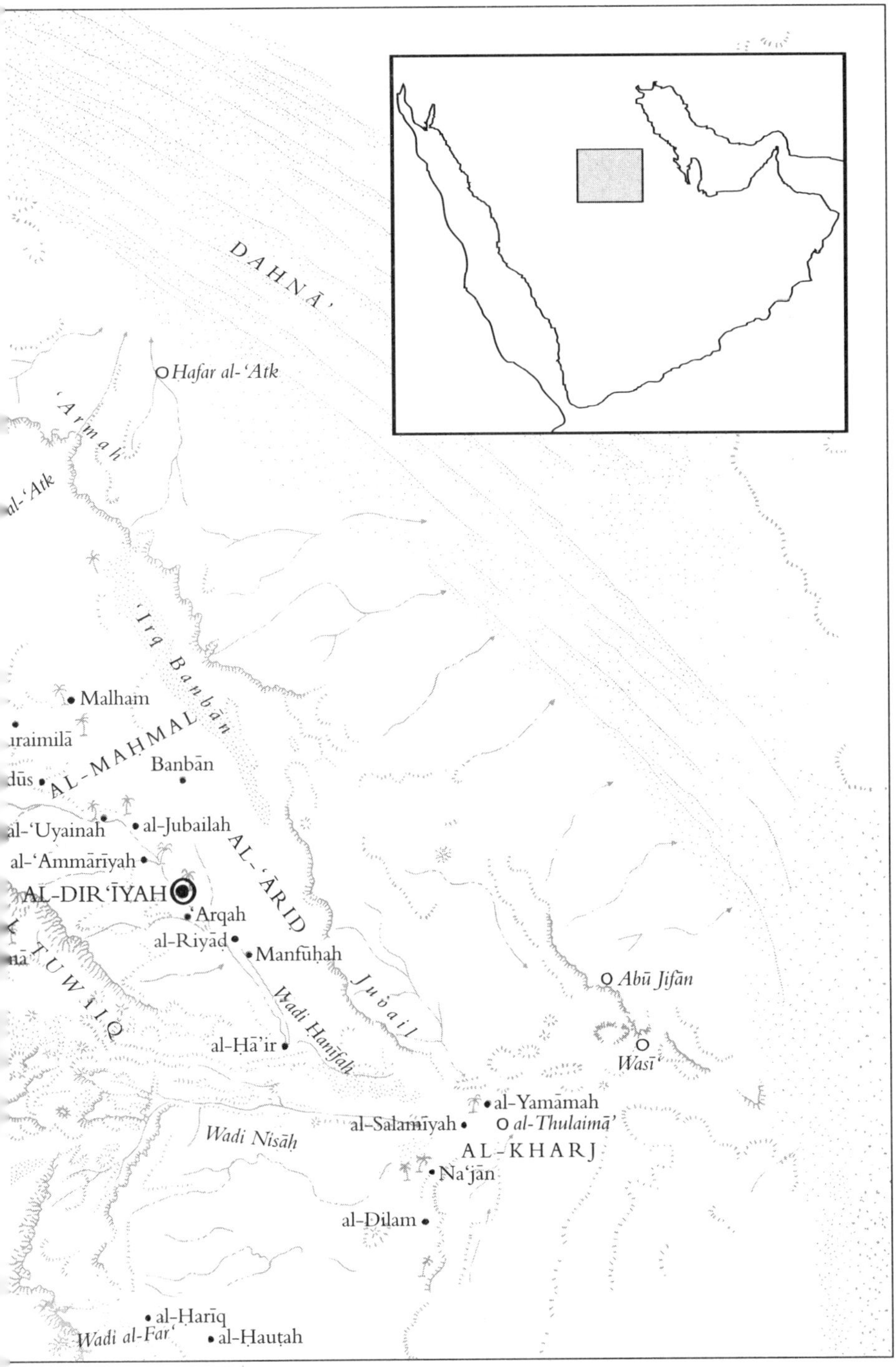
DAHNĀ'
Hafar al-'Atk
'Armah
al-'Atk
'Irq Banbān
Malham
AL-MAHMAL
Banbān
al-'Uyainah
al-Jubailah
al-'Ammārīyah
AL-DIR'ĪYAH
'Arqah
al-Riyāḍ
Manfūḥah
AL-'ĀRID
Jubail
Wadi Hanīfah
al-Ḥā'ir
TUWAIQ
Abū Jifān
Wasī'
al-Yamāmah
al-Salamīyah
al-Thulaimā'
AL-KHARJ
Wadi Nisāḥ
Na'jān
al-Dilam
al-Ḥarīq
Wadi al-Far'
al-Ḥauṭah

the Ottoman conqueror prized more highly another title that in his day gave him greater prestige, the title of Servant of the Holy Cities.[10] The chief concern of the Sultans in Arabia was to keep the Holy Cities inviolate so that they might be ornaments to their rule as the grandest lords in Islam. Particularly in the 16th century they lavished much care and heavy expenditures on the shrines of Mecca and Medina. To guard the flank of the Holy Land of the Hijaz, especially against the threat of the Portuguese, who had sailed up the Red Sea as far as Jiddah, the port of Mecca,[11] the Turks advanced into the Yemen and set up a governor there about twenty years after the establishment of their authority in Mecca.

Meanwhile the Turks had also drawn close to Arabia in the east, where Baghdad fell to Sulaimān the Magnificent in 1534 and al-Baṣrah immediately afterwards offered submission. The Arab ruler of al-Qaṭīf[12] on the Persian Gulf coast of Arabia sent an embassy to the Ottomans as a result of which they proclaimed al-Aḥsā', the eastern region of the Peninsula, a part of their empire, though the embassy had probably done no more than present congratulations.[13] The subjection of al-Aḥsā' to effective Ottoman rule did not take place until in or about the year 1000 AH/about 1592 AD.[14]

[10] At the Friday service in Aleppo following Salīm's decisive victory over the Mamelukes on the way to Egypt, "when Sultan Salīm heard the words of the preacher acknowledging him as Servant of the Holy Cities [*Khādim al-Ḥaramain al-Sharīfain*], he bowed down to God in gratitude and said, 'Praise be to God, who reveals to me that I have become the Servant of the Holy Cities', and he resolved to bestow handsome largess on the people of the two cities. He showed great joy at his investiture as Servant of the Holy Cities, and he gave robes of honor to the preacher while he was in the pulpit and afterwards rewarded him liberally" – Quṭb al-Dīn, pp. 278–9. On the last day of 922/late January 1517 Salīm's name was mentioned in the Friday sermon in the pulpits of Cairo with the same title – Ibn Iyās, V, 145.

[11] Snouck Hurgronje, *Mekka*, I, 102.

[12] Perhaps a member of the House of Ajwad b. Zāmil al-'Āmirī al-Jabarī al-Qaisī, on whom see Ibn Bishr, I, 18, 22, 25, 65. Ajwad himself, who is called Shaikh of al-Aḥsā' by Ibn Bishr, flourished in the early part of the 16th century.

[13] Longrigg, *Four Centuries of Modern Iraq*, pp. 25 and 38, n. 1. [The dating of the Ottoman takeover of al-Aḥsā' to the late 16th century AD has been demonstrated to be too late: J. E. Mandaville in his article "The Ottoman Province of al-Ḥasā' in the Sixteenth and Seventeenth Centuries", in *Journal of the American Oriental Society* 90, 1970, shows it to have taken place in 956 AH/1549 AD. See also Anscombe, *The Ottoman Gulf*, 1997. Ed.]

[14] Ibn Bishr, I, 25.

In this manner the Turks came to exercise a degree of control over segments of the circumference of the Peninsula, but such control as it was gradually weakened with the decline of the Ottoman state. The Sultans after Sulaimān, beginning with Salīm II the Sot (1566–74), were mostly men of meager stature; Murād IV (1623–40) was the only real fighter among them, and he was followed by Ibrāhīm (1640–8), whose bid for fame was the extraordinary fatness

THE TRIBES OF ARABIA

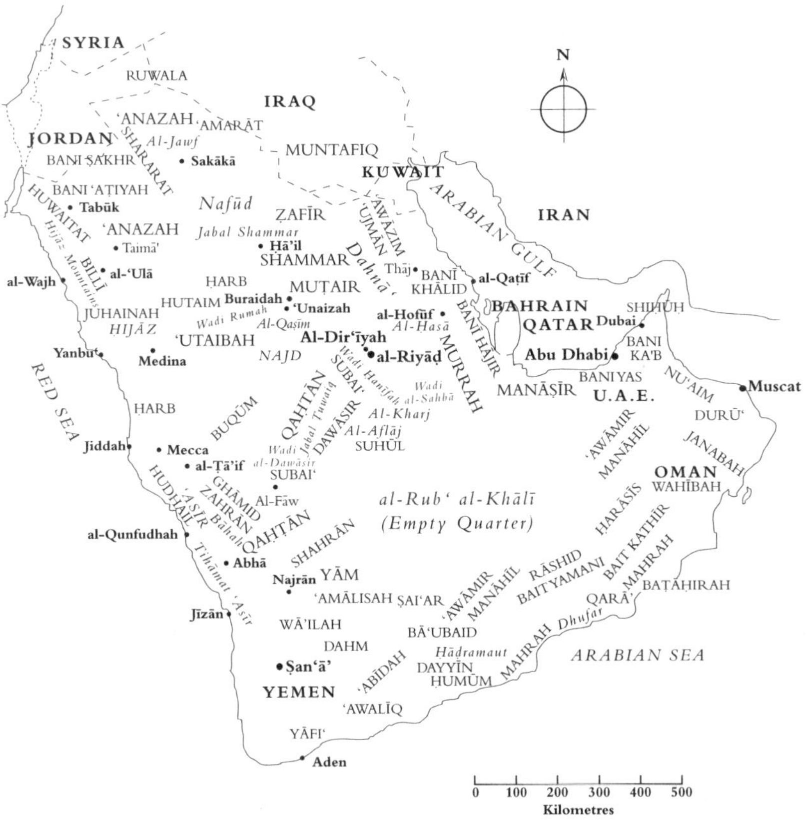

of his wives. In the second half of the 17th century the Koprülü Grand Viziers managed a revival only to be checked abruptly by Sobieski at Vienna in 1683. Half the powers of Europe then joined in the assault on the Turk that did not subside until the Peace of Carlowitz in 1699. The 18th century began with Russia looming on the northern shores of the Black Sea and Austria eager to press forward in the Balkans, and the century was not old before the Persians on the other side found a master of the arts of war in Nādir Qulī Khān, afterwards Shah (1736–47). Seemingly oblivious to these dangers, officials and members of society at the Ottoman capital in the days of Aḥmad III (1703–30) amused themselves with the cultivation of carnations and tulips.[15]

Turkish sovereignty became little more than a hollow shell in Egypt, Syria, and Iraq, and likewise in Arabia. The Imams of the Zaidi sect at Ṣaʻdah[16] after years of warfare drove the Turks from the Yemen in 1636[17] and set up an independent Arab state with its capital at Ṣanʻā'. In al-Aḥsā' the main Turkish garrison was stationed in the Kūt, the great castle at al-Hufūf in the central oases.[18] In 1080/1669–70 Barrāk b. Ghurair of the House of Ḥumaid, the chief of the ancient and powerful Bedouin tribe of Banī Khālid, fell upon the Turks and expelled them from the Kūt and the whole province, thus making himself ruler of the towns as well as the nomads.[19] After this the Hijaz remained the one place in Arabia where the Sultan's word carried at least an ounce of weight; the Sharifs of Mecca continued to recognize the Ottoman as their overlord and to look to

[15] This is the period of Turkish history known as *Lāle devri*/the Time of Tulips, which were imported from the Netherlands and became the rage in Constantinople. Hammer mentions the carnation or pink (*Nelke*) as another favorite of Aḥmad's, which fact would of course have recommended it to the court – Joseph von Hammer, *Geschichte des Osmanischen Reiches,* VII, 390.

[16] The Zaidi Imams, who claimed descent from the Prophet, had been established at Ṣaʻdah in the northern mountains of the Yemen since the 3rd century of the Hegira/since about 900 AD – 'Abd al-Wāsiʻ b. Yaḥyā al-Wāsiʻī, *Ta'rīkh al-Yaman* (Cairo 1346/1927–8), p. 21; A. S. Tritton, *The Rise of the Imams of Sanaa* (Madras 1925), p. 5. The present ruler of the Yemen is a descendant of this line.

[17] Al-Wāsiʻi, p. 53; Tritton, p. 110

[18] The Kūt is to the present day the residence of the Governor of the province.

[19] Ibn Bishr, I, 65. Among those with Barrāk in the attack on the Kūt was Muhannā al-Jabarī, who may have been a descendant of the House of Ajwad – see above, p. 16, n. 12.

Istanbul for protection and support, though even they joined to some extent in the trend towards independence.

While along the coasts there existed governments of some importance in full or in partial measure, political power in the region of Najd in the interior had for centuries been broken up into minute particles. The Turks had not ventured very far inland, so that Najd had not even known a unity imposed by aliens. Bedouin tribes roamed the wider spaces, subject to the often tenuous authority of their great or petty chiefs. The settled territory was parceled out among the lords of little towns and oases, "petty barons", Philby has called them, comparing them to their contemporary Rob Roy in the Highlands of Scotland.[20] To show to what lengths particularism could then go, an Arab chronicler in the 19th century cites the case of the tiny settlement of al-Tuwaim in Sudair, where, in 1120/1708–09, there were four contestants for the right to rule. None of the four being strong enough to overcome his rivals, they divided the place up into four sections so that each could at least be lord of a quarter of a town.[21]

The religious situation

Islam, which had once penetrated into every corner of the Peninsula, is a powerful force for unity among a people who profess it sincerely, binding them together into a single body with its fundamental tenets that God is One and universal and that all Moslems are brothers. But Islam had decayed among the Arabians. The Unitarians later borrowed an old term, al-Jāhilīyah, which is used classically for the state of affairs in Arabia preceding the revelation of Islam, and applied it to the situation that prevailed in the early 18th century. The Jāhilīyah is the Age of Moral Ignorance, ignorance of or disregard for the Right Way laid down by God for the followers of Islam. In this new Jāhilīyah before the coming of Ibn 'Abd al-Wahhāb the Arabs had forsaken the worship of God for their ancient idolatry, the worship of stones and sacred trees and the graves of saints. The reputed tomb of Zaid b. al-Khaṭṭāb, brother of the noble Caliph 'Umar and a

[20] Philby, *The Heart of Arabia*, I, xvi.

[21] Ibn Bishr, I, 157–8.

martyr of the early days of Islam,[22] at al-Jubailah in Wadi Ḥanīfah was a famous shrine; many came there to offer prayers to Zaid that should have been directed to his Maker. Farther down the valley at al-Dir'īyah there were other tombs attributed by popular fancy to companions of the Prophet who had been slain under the banner of the faith in Najd; these were the objects of visitation in the same manner as the tomb of Zaid.[23] A male date palm[24] at the little town of al-Fidā[25] was sought by women who had waited in vain to be wedded; they would embrace the trunk and cry out, "O male palm of the male palms, I desire a husband before I become barren."[26] Men and women used to come to the same tree in the mornings and evenings and perform reprehensible rites, seeking the blessing of the tree. The tamarisk tree[27] was a favorite place on which to hang bits of cloth[28] when a boy was born in the belief that this would protect him from the hand of death. Below al-Dir'īyah there was a great cleft in the mountain known as the Cave of the Daughter of the Amir,[29] which according to the story then current had been opened by God in the mountainside in response to a cry for help uttered by a girl of noble birth when a certain one sought to do her wrong in that

[22] Zaid had fallen fighting in the army of Khālid b. al-Walīd against the false prophet Musailimah in the battle of al-Yamāmah in 11 AH/633 AD – al-Balādhurī, *Futūḥ al-buldān,* ed. M. J. de Goeje, p. 91. When the Moslems were blinded by sand in the south wind, Zaid cried, "Close your eyes and clench your teeth – Forward like men!" He fell in the forefront – Sir William Muir, *The Caliphate*, rev. ed. by T. H. Weir, p. 29. The Unitarians maintained, probably with justice, that the shrine at al-Jubailah was not the true tomb of Zaid.

[23] Ibn Ghannām, I, 7, also mentions the reputed tomb of Darrār b. al-Azwar in Sha'īb Ghubairā' not far from al-Dir'īyah as a similar shrine.

[24] Philby, *Arabia*, p. 5 reads *al-niḥāl* as *al-fiḥāl* and says that the palm tree was "familiarly known as the 'Stallion'". The word should rather be read *al-fuḥḥāl*/"the male date palm".

[25] Bulaidat al-Fidā.

[26] *Yā faḥl al-fuḥūl, urīd zaujan qabl al-ḥaul* – Ibn Ghannām, I, 7. Ibn Ghannām states that women did not come to the tree to be married by it; he may be referring to a custom such as that followed by the Bedouins of Āl Murrah in the south before they adopted Islam: a man and a woman would come to an *'ablah* or *'uballah* tree and walk around it, announcing that they were married, so that the tree took the place of the Qadi or Judge in the ceremony.

[27] *Shajarat al-ṭarafīyah* – Ibn Ghannām, I, 7. The classical form is *ṭarfā'* or *ṭarafah*.

[28] The tying of bits of cloth to shrines, particularly the tombs of saints, is an extremely prevalent practice among the unlearned and superstitious in the world of Islam.

[29] Ghār Bint al-Amīr – Ibn Ghannām, I, 7–8.

spot. People would visit the cave and leave meat and bread there as offerings.

The paying of undue reverence to saints was not restricted to those long dead, for there flourished in Najd in the early 18th century the cult of a blind holy man of al-Kharj in the south, Tāj b. Shamsān by name. The Arabs who had wandered away from Islam believed that Tāj possessed powers that the orthodox would ascribe to none other than God. His devotees, drawn in numbers to al-Kharj to see him, gave him animals for sacrifice and directed their prayers to him. The rulers of the region feared him and went out of their way to propitiate him.[30] Over and over again people repeated the tales of the miraculous feats of Tāj, such as his making his way over the whole distance from al-Kharj to al-Dir'īyah with none to guide him in his blindness.[31]

Beyond the borders of Najd, the residents and pilgrims in the Holy Cities were held guilty by the Unitarians of attaching too great importance to the tombs of mortals. In particular, the orthodox scholars in the interior were incensed at the high respect shown the tomb of the Sharif Abū Ṭālib,[32] who in his day had penetrated into Najd and imposed feudal dues[33] and other demands on the people there, attacking those who failed to pay. If a robber or one who had broken the peace entered the tomb built over the grave of Abū Ṭālib,

[30] See, for example, the offer of Dahhām b. Dawwās, the lord of al-Riyāḍ, in 1159/1746–7, as set forth on p. 60 below.

[31] Ibn Ghannām, I, 8. Here Ibn Ghannām refers to the holy man simply as Tāj; in II, 8, he gives his full name as Tāj b. Shamsān.

[32] Abū Ṭālib b. Ḥasan b. Muḥammad Abū Numayy was Sharif of Mecca from 1008 to 1012 AH/early 17th century of the Christian era – Snouck Hurgronje, *Mekka*, I, Table III. Snouck gives nothing in his text on the reign of this Sharif.

[33] *Kharāj* – Ibn Ghannām, I, 9.

[34] Ibn Ghannām, I, 10, says that the tomb had been constructed by devils (*shayāṭīn*) in the distant past. Rif'at Pasha, who was in the Hijaz in the early years of the 20th century, says that the false tomb of Eve was about 150 meters long, four meters broad, and one meter high. It had three domes, one at the head, one at the navel, and one at the feet – Ibrāhīm Rif'at Pasha, *Mir'āt al-Ḥaramain* (Cairo 1343/1925), I, 22. The tomb is no longer in existence, having been destroyed by the Wahhabis following their conquest of the Hijaz [in 1925–6. Ed.], but the site where it stood, not far from al-Bāb al-Jadīd of Jiddah, is still surrounded by a wall.

[35] Ibn Ghannām, I, 10. The chronicler goes on to describe shrines of the same sort in Egypt, the Yemen, Hadramaut, Syria, and Iraq.

he was granted sanctuary there. At other tombs, such as those of the Prophet's wives, Khadījah and Maimūnah bint al-Ḥārith, men mingled together with women in a fashion considered objectionable by conservative Moslems and raised their voices in prayers to the elect of long ago. In Medina many prostrated themselves before the tomb of the Prophet and rubbed their cheeks in the dust, or they came there to celebrate a festival, thus committing acts that according to tradition the Prophet had forbidden to his followers. The city of Jiddah by the sea had a tomb sixty cubits long in which Eve, the mother of mankind, was said to be buried;[34] the keepers of the tomb amassed large sums by collecting a fee for admission from everyone who wished to enter and greet the wife of his first ancestor.[35]

As a result of the corruption of religion and the spread of superstitious practices, the common people were oppressed by lords unrestrained by the precepts of Islam, which in its pure form goes far in an effort to establish equitable relations between ruler and ruled. Here and there in the Peninsula, though, like tiny oases in the heathen desert, there were men who read the old books and saw the evil of the times. It is with one of these that this study is concerned, the greatest of them, for he was not content to read, but he set out to restore Islam in its old purity, to bring peace and unity to the land, and to lighten the lot of all those, rich and poor, who should become brothers in the faith.

2

Muḥammad b. ʻAbd al-Wahhāb: The Early Years

Birth and upbringing

In the first years of the 18th century the little town of al-ʻUyainah in the upper reaches of Wadi Ḥanīfah was ruled by an able and energetic lord, ʻAbd Allāh b. Muḥammad of the House of Muʻammar,[1] whose family had been masters in the place for more than two centuries.[2] ʻAbd Allāh Ibn Muʻammar was diligent in building up the settlement of his people, and together with various allies he waged war against those who opposed him in central Najd. The Qadi or Judge, that is the chief man of religion, under Abd Allāh Ibn Muʻammar in al-ʻUyainah was Shaikh ʻAbd al-Wahhāb b. Sulaimān, a scholar of the Hanbalite school[3] whose father before him had been a Qadi learned in the sacred lore.[4] The Shaikh ʻAbd

[1] He was ʻAbd Allāh b. Muḥammad b. Aḥmad b. ʻAbd Allāh b. Muʻammar. Ibn Bishr, I, 229, says there was none like him in Najd in his own time or before in leadership and power and possessions, which indicates that he was a remarkable figure. Unfortunately, few details of his career have been preserved.

[2] In the mid-9th century of the Hegira/mid-15th century of the Christian era, Ḥasan b. Ṭauq, the ancestor of the House of Muʻammar, bought al-ʻUyainah from the House of Yazīd, the inhabitants of al-Waṣīl and al-Naʻmīyah in Wadi Ḥanīfah above al-Dirʻīyah, from whom the modern House of Dughaithir is descended. Ḥasan b. Ṭauq, who had been living at Malham in the district of al-Maḥmal, took up permanent residence in al-ʻUyainah and developed the place – Ibn Bishr, I, 16.

Shaikh Muḥammad Ibn Dughaithir of the House of Dughaithir referred to above has been in charge of telegraphic correspondence for King Ibn Saud for a number of years.

[3] There are four main schools of religious law in Islam: the Hanafite, the Malikite, the Shafiite, and the Hanbalite. Of the four, the Hanbalite, founded by Aḥmad Ibn Ḥanbal (d. 855 AD), is in most respects the strictest and most conservative, and as such has always had special appeal to the scholars of Najd.

[4] Ibn Bishr, I, 62, calls ʻAbd al-Wahhāb's father the Shaikh, scholar, *faqīh* (one skilled in *fiqh*/Islamic jurisprudence), and Qadi Sulaimān b. ʻAlī Ibn Mushrif, who was outstanding

al-Wahhāb, like many if not most of the inhabitants of Najd, was a townsman of Bedouin descent, for he traced his lineage back to the ancient tribe of Tamīm.[5] The men of Tamīm, though the greater part of them in Najd had gradually settled down and become mainly villagers and farmers, still retained in their blood something of the fierce simplicity of the Arabian nomad.[6] The bringing forth of a prophet or preacher for the Arabs was no new

among the scholars of Najd in his time. Other scholars used to refer to the Shaikh Sulaimān whenever they encountered difficult problems in *fiqh* or other theological studies. Ibn Bishr himself had seen many questions that had been submitted to the Shaikh Sulaimān in writing and his answers thereto. Shaikh Sulaimān was the author of a book on the rites of the pilgrimage (*al-manāsik*). He also wrote a commentary on *al-Iqnā'*, a standard manual of Hanbalite law by Sharaf al-Dīn Mūsā al-Ḥijāwī of Jerusalem, but when he learned that Manṣūr al-Buhūtī, a famous Egyptian Hanbalite, had completed a commentary on the same work, he destroyed his composition (on al-Ḥijāwī who lived in the 10th/16th century, and his work, see Henri Laoust, *Essai,* p. 486, n. 1; on al-Buhūtī, who was an older contemporary of Shaikh Sulaimān of al-'Uyainah, see Laoust, p. 486, n. 2, and Ibn Bishr, I, 50). Shaikh Sulaimān transmitted his learning to a number of students, among them being the Shaikh Aḥmad b. Muḥammad al-Quṣayyir, a prominent Qadi in the town of Ushaiqir in the district of al-Washm, who died the year before Sulaimān's grandson Muḥammad was born (on al-Quṣayyir see Ibn Bishr, I, 120, 136), and his own sons 'Abd al-Wahhāb and Ibrāhīm.

Shaikh Sulaimān made the pilgrimage to Mecca about thirty years before his death – Ibn Bishr, I, 47. About seven years before his death he accompanied 'Abd Allāh Ibn Mu'ammar and a large number of troops in an attack on the town of al-Bīr in al-Maḥmal, the people of which had plundered a cloth caravan belonging to al-'Uyainah, and was instrumental in making peace after the wall of the town collapsed on the attackers and killed many of them – Ibn Bishr, I, 59. Shaikh Sulaimān died in 1079/1668–9, thirty-five years or so before the birth of his grandson – Ibn Bishr, I, 62.

Euting, *Tagbuch*, I, 157, and Musil, *Northern Neğd*, p. 258, are wrong in saying that Sulaimān was the father of the Shaikh Muḥammad and that Ibn 'Abd al-Wahhāb was the family name. Al-Rīḥānī wrongly gives Sulaimān as Muḥammad's great-grandfather in his Arabic version, *Ta'rīkh Najd al-ḥadīth*, pp. 23, 26, and as his great-great-grandfather in his English version, *Maker of Modern Arabia*, p. 238.

The early travellers, reporting on the spread of Unitarianism at a time when information about the movement was still fragmentary, name the founder himself 'Abd al-Wahhāb – Niebuhr, *Beschreibung von Arabien*, p. 346 and *passim*; Burckhardt, *Notes on the Bedouins and Wahabys*, II, 97 and *passim*.

[5] Al-Rīḥānī, *Ta'rīkh Najd al-ḥadīth*, p. 26; Burckhardt, *Notes*, II, 97. Doughty heard reports that the founder of Unitarianism had sprung from the tribe of 'Anazah, no doubt because of his connection with the House of Su'ūd of that tribe, but even Doughty found the prevailing opinion to be that he was a Tamīmī – *Travels in Arabia Deserta*, II, 425. Neither Ibn Ghannām nor Ibn Bishr refers directly to the descent of Muḥammad b. 'Abd al-Wahhāb from Tamīm.

experience for this tribe: in the time of Abū Bakr, the first Caliph, a prophetess named Sajāḥ had arisen among the members of Tamīm settled in Mesopotamia to challenge the new faith of Islam; she married Musailimah the False Prophet[7] and together they fought the Moslems until the Sword of God, Khālid b. al-Walīd, smote them down. The Shaikh 'Abd al-Wahhāb knew his texts of religion and law, though neither his knowledge nor his influence was as great as his father's,[8] and he was not a man of the boldness to face trouble in the propagation of his beliefs.[9]

This judge in al-'Uyainah had two sons, Muḥammad and Sulaimān.[10] Muḥammad b. 'Abd al-Wahhāb,[11] the future founder and sharer in the upbuilding of Unitarianism in Najd, who was perhaps the older of the two brothers,[12] was born in the year 1115 of the Hegira/mid-May 1703 to early May 1704.[13] The little boy, living among mudbrick houses shaded by date palms in the sun-burnt land, studied at the feet of his father and learned his lessons rapidly. His first great task as a student was memorizing the Koran,

[6] For the old tribe of Tamīm, see Giorgio Levi della Vida in *The Encyclopaedia of Islam*, IV, 644; for the tribe in modern times, see *A Handbook of Arabia* (Admiralty), I, 76, 81, 610–11. On the settlers of Tamīm in al-Qaṣīm, see below, p. 128. The men of Tamīm later accepted the doctrines of Unitarianism in a wholehearted manner: Doughty thought the men of Tamīm in 'Unaizah "somewhat soured by the rheum of the Waháby religion", and Philby called the men of Tamīm in Jabal Ṭuwaiq "devout Wahhabis of the old type" – Doughty, *Travels*, II, 401; Philby, *The Heart of Arabia*, II, 277.

[7] Al-Kadhdhāb. The home of Musailimah was Najd; the opponents of Unitarianism later used the argument that nothing good could come out of Najd, the land that had produced such an enemy of Islam.

[8] Ibn Bishr does not mention any works composed by him, though the chronicler says that he has seen questions submitted to him and his answers – Ibn Bishr, I, 90. In later times 'Abd al-Wahhāb used to consult his son Muḥammad whenever knotty problems in law arose.

[9] See his attitude towards his son's preaching – p. 37 below.

[10] Ibn Bishr, I, 90.

[11] See chart, p. 26

[12] The sources do not specify which of the two was the older. Ibn Bishr, I, 90, names Muḥammad first and Sulaimān second.

[13] Ibn Ghannām, I, 30; Ibn Bishr, I, 138. The authors who have not followed the written Arabic sources have been wide of the mark in giving the date of Muḥammad's birth: Wilfrid Scawen Blunt in Lady Anne Blunt, *A Pilgrimage to Najd*, II, 251, sets it as early as 1691, while Philby in one of his earlier books, *The Heart of Arabia* (1922), I, xvi, has it as late as the 1720s, a mistake that he afterwards corrected in *Arabia* (1930), p. 8.

GENEALOGIES OF THE SHAIKH MUḤAMMAD B. ʻABD AL-WAHHĀB

	Wahīb
	ʻAlawī
	Muḥammad
	Zākhir
	Rīs (or Rais)
Mushrif	Miʻḍād
Buraid	ʻUmar
Muḥammad	Mushrif
Buraid	Buraid
Rāshid	Rāshid
Aḥmad	Aḥmad
Muḥammad	Muḥammad
ʻAlī	ʻAlī
Sulaimān	Sulaimān
ʻAbd al-Wahhāb	ʻAbd al-Wahhāb
Muḥammad	Muḥammad

The two most reliable genealogies for the Shaikh Muḥammad b. ʻAbd al-Wahhāb are in Ibn Ghannām, I, 29–30, and Ibn Bishr, I, 89. They are given in the chart above, the one from Ibn Ghannām, the shorter of the two, being on the left. It will be seen that the genealogies agree only as far back as eight generations; it may be assumed that anything farther back than that is likely to be fanciful (see for example the genealogy covering twenty-two generations and going back through Tamīm to ʻAdnān in al-Rīḥānī, *Ta'rīkh Najd al-ḥadīth*, p. 23, and the genealogy covering thirty-two generations and going back to Tamīm given by al-Atharī, the editor of al-Ālūsī, *Ta'rīkh Najd*, p. 1111, n. 1, on the authority of one of Shaikh Muḥammad's descendants); excepting that Mushrif, who appears in both lists, must have been one of the ancestors, for Sulaimān, the grandfather of the Shaikh Muḥammad, was known as Ibn Mushrif – Ibn Bishr, I, 62 and *passim*. The men of the House of Mushrif were known collectively as the Mashārifah.

It is possible that Ris [or Rais] in Ibn Bishr's list is a mistake for or a corruption of the commoner name Idrīs – see al-Atharī's note in al-Ālūsī cited above.

a feat that he is said to have accomplished before reaching the age of ten.[14] From this task he went on to the receiving of instructions in *fiqh* or Islamic jurisprudence,[15] and the reading of books of *tafsīr* or interpretation of the Koran and *ḥadīth* or traditions of the Prophet. According to the testimony of his brother Sulaimān, his father 'Abd al-Wahhāb was amazed at the understanding and quickness of perception shown by the youth, so that he said in effect: I have benefited from my son Muḥammad in the study of the precepts of our faith.[16] In addition to the father's teaching, the lad may have gained much from association with other relatives, for the whole family kept alive the scholastic tradition. The father's brother, Ibrāhīm b. Sulaimān, was acquainted with *fiqh* and other branches of knowledge, as was Ibrāhīm's son 'Abd al-Raḥmān, Muḥammad's cousin, who also grew up to be an author of religious works.[17] Muḥammad's brother Sulaimān followed much the same course of studies, being trained so that in after years he was fitted to hold the office of Qadi.

In 1121/March 1709 to March 1710, when Muḥammad was a child of about six, 'Abd Allāh Ibn Mu'ammar, the lord of his town, in conjunction with the townspeople of al-'Āriḍ[18] and Bedouins of the tribe of Subai' made an unsuccessful attack on the town of Ḥuraimilā to the northwest.[19] Five years later, in 1126/January 1714 to January 1715, Ibn Mu'ammar and the people of al-'Āriḍ[20] joined forces with Sa'dūn b. Muḥammad Āl Ghurair,[21] the chief of the Bedouins of Banī Khālid in the east, to plunder houses in the oasis of al-Yamāmah in the south.[22] There

[14] Muḥammad 'Abduh, the Egyptian Mufti and reformer (d. 1905 AD), mastered the Koran, a book of nearly eighty thousand words, in two years, between the ages of ten and twelve – Muḥammad Rashīd Riḍā, *Ta'rīkh al-ustādh al-imām*, I, 20.

[15] This seems to have been the main discipline in which his father instructed him – Ibn Bishr, I, 6.

[16] Ibn Ghannām, I, 30.

[17] Ibn Bishr, I, 90. 'Abd al-Raḥmān b. Ibrāhīm died in the same year as Muḥammad b. 'Abd al-Wahhāb, 1206/1791–2, so that the two cousins had not much less than a century of close fellowship in life – Ibn Bishr, I, 97.

[18] Al-'Āriḍ is the district of Najd through which Wadi Ḥanīfah runs.

[19] Ibn Bishr, I, 160.

[20] These brief references suggest that 'Abd Allāh Ibn Mu'ammar may have been to a degree at least the overlord of the whole district of al-'Āriḍ.

may have been other campaigns unrecorded in the meager annals of the time; at any rate it may be said that the future reformer found himself from boyhood on immersed in the martial atmosphere that had prevailed in Najd for centuries, where few were the towns that could reckon their neighbors friends.

The ending of the first period in the life of the young Muḥammad was described by his father in a letter:[23]

> I discovered that he had reached maturity before completing his twelfth year, and I felt that he was ready to take his place in the congregational prayer, so I brought him forward because of his knowledge of Islamic precepts. I found a wife for him in that year after he had reached maturity. He then asked me to allow him to make the pilgrimage to the Sacred House of God [in Mecca]; I granted his request and assisted him to achieve his aim.

Early marriage is very common in Arabia, so that there was nothing particularly unusual about Muḥammad's being given a wife when he was only twelve. More striking was the preference of the stripling for spiritual duties over physical pleasures in expressing the desire to go straightway to Mecca to salute the Kaʻbah, the black-robed House of God. After performing all the rites of the pilgrimage in Mecca, Muḥammad went on to Medina to visit the Prophet's tomb.[24] After lingering in the City of the Prophet for a space of two months, the young devotee returned home to al-ʻUyainah,[25] no doubt profoundly impressed by all he had done

[21] Saʻdūn was the nephew of Barrāk b. Ghurair, who had expelled the Turks from al-Aḥsāʼ – see above, p. 18. Saʻdūn's father Muḥammad had succeeded Barrāk in 1093/*c.* 1681, and Saʻdūn had become chief of the tribe and ruler of al-Aḥsāʼ in 1102/1690–1 – Ibn Bishr, I, 80, 103. [See Table, p. 254.]

[22] Ibn Bishr, I, 183.

[23] Ibn Ghannām, I, 30, says that the letter was addressed to one or some (*baʻḍ*) of ʻAbd al-Wahhāb's brothers, which is perhaps to be taken in the figurative sense of brothers in the faith.

[24] Muḥammad's Unitarians were later accused by some of their enemies of denouncing the practice of visiting the Prophet's tomb, an accusation that was unjust, as shown by Muḥammad's own experiences. What the Unitarians did denounce was the paying of excessive reverence to the Prophet or the worship of him as a being of more than human powers.

[25] Ibn Ghannām, I, 30. Ibn Bishr does not mention Muḥammad's boyhood pilgrimage.

and seen in the far-off land of the Hijaz in the west.

Very soon after Muḥammad arrived from his trip al-'Uyainah was at war with Ḥuraimilā again. In 1128/December 1715 to December 1716 'Abd Allāh Ibn Mu'ammar raided Ḥuraimilā and killed the people known as the Za'ā'īb there.[26] In the following year Ibn Mu'ammar seized sheep and goats belonging to the enemy and killed ten of their men.[27] Young Muḥammad's education was progressing: in the Holy Cities he had seen the brotherhood of Moslems, men from many lands, wearing different costumes and speaking tongues that were strange to each other; at home he saw the fratricidal strife of Moslems, men from the same mountain valleys who all used a familiar dialect.

The conduct of many of the people of Najd also contributed to Muḥammad's informal education. Trees and stones, graves and tombs were dear shrines to them.[28] Instead of taking refuge in God in the manner of true Moslems, they took refuge in the *jinn* or genii, making sacrifices to them and placing food for them in the corners of the houses so that they might be induced to cure the sick ones of the people. When men took solemn oaths, they swore, not by God, but by others. At the time of the date harvest each year Bedouins coming to collect their share of the dates would camp on the outskirts of the towns, bringing with them men and women reputed to have the power of healing. When a townsman approached the nomad healers seeking a remedy, they would say to him: Go to such-and-such a place and sacrifice a black lamb or a small-eared ram[29] without mentioning the name of God;[30] then give the sick one such-and-such a piece of the beast, eat such-and-such yourselves, and leave such-and-such. Although all such acts were violations of the law of Islam, there was no one to forbid them, since the lords of the land, in the words of the chronicler, "knew nothing but oppression of their subjects, wrongdoing, and fighting with each other".[31]

[26] Ibn Bishr, I, 185.

[27] Ibn Bishr, I, 189.

[28] See above, pp. 19–22.

[29] *Tais aṣma'* – Ibn Bishr, I, 7.

[30] A good Moslem should never eat the flesh of an animal if the phrase "In the name of God" has not been uttered at the time of the slitting of its throat.

[31] Ibn Bishr, I. 7.

By putting together what he read and what he observed, Muḥammad b. 'Abd al-Wahhāb acquired the conviction that it was his duty to speak out against the sins of his people. He was in his late teens or very early twenties when he began to point out to others that many current practices were forbidden by Islam.[32] Some of those who heard him found his arguments convincing, but the ignorant mass of the people paid him no heed and continued in their ways. When Muḥammad discerned that his words were having slight effect, he decided to set off once again on the pilgrimage, perhaps with the thought that his inspiration and resolution would be renewed by another sojourn in the Holy Land.

Travels: Medina

Muḥammad's second visit to Mecca passed without incident worthy of note; then the sober young man from Najd traveled on again to Medina. The Prophet in his time had been confronted with problems similar to those that now existed in Arabia; perhaps Ibn 'Abd al-Wahhāb felt that he could secure the answers to his problems in the environment that had surrounded the Prophet as he built up his theocratic state. In any event, when Ibn 'Abd al-Wahhāb reached Medina he did fall in with two scholars who exercised considerable influence on his still formative mind.

The first of these two scholars was an expatriate from Najd, a native of the town of al-Majma'ah in the district of Sudair, the Shaikh 'Abd Allāh b. Ibrāhīm Ibn Saif,[33] who like many others from all parts of the world of Islam had settled in Medina to enjoy proximity to the Prophet. When Muḥammad first appeared as a student at the

[32] No dates are given for this period until 1138–9/1725–7, at which time Muḥammad, still in his early twenties, was away on his travels – see below, pp. 36–7. Ibn Bishr, I, 7, states definitely that Muḥammad began denouncing forbidden practices before starting out on his travels, though there is no direct reference to public preaching by him. Ibn Ghannām has nothing on this activity by Muḥammad, but Ibn Ghannām provides fewer details on this stage of Muḥammad's career than does Ibn Bishr.

[33] The members of the House of Saif were formerly the chief men of al-Majma'ah. Shaikh 'Abd Allāh was the father of Ibrāhīm, author of *al-'Adhb al-fā'iḍ fī 'ilm al-fawā'iḍ* – Ibn Bishr, I, 7.

home of Ibn Saif outside the city, Ibn Saif commenced by repeating the tradition of the Prophet that each of a long line of Hanbalite teachers before him had chosen to inaugurate his course with: "'Amr b. al-'Āṣī[34] said that the Prophet of God, may God grant him blessings and peace, said: 'The Merciful will grant mercy to those who show mercy. If you grant mercy to those who are on the earth, the One Who is in heaven will grant you mercy.'"[35] Another tradition repeated by Ibn Saif that remained with the young student ran: "Anas b. Mālik, may God be pleased with him, said that the Prophet of God, may God grant him blessings and peace, said: 'If God desires good for His servant, He will use him.' They said: 'How will he use him?' He said: 'He will grant him success in a righteous undertaking before his death.'"[36] There can be little doubt that when Muḥammad b. 'Abd al-Wahhāb heard this tradition he thought of the righteous undertaking for which plans were being formed in his own mind, the mission that awaited him in Najd.

On one occasion when the student was with his teacher, Ibn Saif suddenly asked: "Do you want to see weapons that I have prepared for al-Majma'ah?" When Muḥammad indicated his desire to see them, Ibn Saif led him to a house of his that was full of books and said: "This is what I have prepared for my town."[37] When in after times the Unitarians broadcast tracts as a means of combatting their enemies and forwarding their own doctrines, they may well have harked back to that day in the Prophet's city when the founder of their movement learned to think of books as weapons.

Upon Muḥammad's completing the course of study, Ibn Saif awarded him a diploma.[38] Among the things Muḥammad had to

[34] 'Amr was the Moslem conqueror of Egypt.

[35] Ibn Ghannām, I, 31–2, where the whole *sanad* or chain of those who had repeated the tradition is given. Ibn Ghannām admits that the chain is unreliable in the first links, that is in the names of those closest to the Prophet. Ibn Ghannām took the tradition and its *sanad* from Muḥammad b. 'Abd al-Wahhāb's own handwriting.

[36] Ibn Ghannām, I, 32. The full *sanad* contains the names of a number of Hanbalites, including that of Aḥmad Ibn Ḥanbal, founder of the school. Ibn Ghannām's comment on this tradition is that it is first-rate (*ḥadīth 'aẓīm*).

[37] Ibn Bishr, I, 7, where the story is told in Muḥammad b. 'Abd al-Wahhāb's own words.

[38] An *ijāzah* or license to teach others what he had learned in the course.

thank the sage from al-Majmaʻah for was an introduction to the other scholar who left his mark on the student in Medina, the Shaikh Muḥammad Ḥayāh al-Sindī al-Madanī,[39] also an authority on the traditions of the Prophet.[40] The Shaikh Muḥammad Ḥayāh, like Ibn Saif, gave the student from al-ʻUyainah a regular course of instruction. One day when Ibn ʻAbd al-Wahhāb was standing beside the chamber that contains the Prophet's tomb in the great mosque of Medina, a throng of people gathered about, praying to the Prophet and beseeching him to aid them. Muḥammad Ḥayāh chanced along and joined his pupil, who asked him what he had to say about he behavior of the throng. The teacher replied that what the people were doing was futile and vain,[41] an answer in full accord with Unitarian doctrine as understood by the young man of Najd: prayers such as these should be directed to God alone and to no other, not even the Prophet, noble as he had been.

Travels: al-Baṣrah

From Medina the student in search of learning crossed Najd to al-Baṣrah in Iraq, whence he hoped to press on to Syria,[42] where Hanbalite studies were energetically cultivated at Damascus.[43] In al-Baṣrah he settled down for a while to perfect his knowledge of the Arabic language and its grammar and to acquire additional skills in composition.[44] The teacher with whom he did most of his work in al-Baṣrah was the Shaikh Muḥammad al-Majmūʻī,[45] who was renowned for his uprightness and his mastery of *tauḥīd*, the branch

[39] The *nisbahs* al-Sindī al-Madanī indicate that he had come originally from the district of Sind in India and had taken up residence in Medina. Ḥayāh or Ḥayāt is a common name among the Moslems of India.

[40] Ibn Bishr, I, 25–6, gives a brief obituary of him under the year 1165/1751–2.

[41] Ibn Bishr, I, 7.

[42] Ibn Bishr, I, 7.

[43] On Damascus as a center of Hanbalite studies at this time and in former times, see Henri Laoust, *Essai*, p. 508 and *passim*.

[44] Ibn Ghannām, I, 32.

[45] Al-Majmūʻī came from al-Majmūʻah or Majmūʻat al-Baṣrah, a village in the vicinity of al-Baṣrah.

of learning that deals with the aspects of the unity of God.[46]

In al-Baṣrah the Shaikh Muḥammad b. 'Abd al-Wahhāb[47] came into close touch with the Shiite form of Islam. The two greatest shrines of Shiism, the tomb of 'Alī at al-Najaf and the tomb of al-Ḥusain[48] at Karbalā', both lie in lower Iraq not far from al-Baṣrah, and the population of al-Baṣrah contained a strong Shiite element. There is much in Shiism that is an abomination to Sunnite fundamentalists like the Hanbalites of Najd, particularly since the worship of saints is widespread and tenacious among the Shiites. Furthermore, al-Baṣrah as a busy entrepôt of trade[49] was alive with a huckstering spirit and a cosmopolitanism which do not provide a favorable atmosphere for religion to thrive in. The budding reformer from Najd could not hold his peace in the face of what he saw; he began to denounce both privately and publicly[50] the innovations and examples of *shirk* or association of others with God[51] that were corrupting the religion of the people. As the Shaikh prolonged his stay in al-Baṣrah,[52] he acquired a circle of his own made up of men who came

[46] Ibn Bishr's own teacher, the Qadi 'Uthmān b. Manṣūr al-Nāṣirī, had heard from a man from al-Majmū'ah that the sons of the Shaikh Muḥammad al-Majmū'ī were outstanding in their own town for uprightness and mastery of *tauḥīd*, both of which they owed to their father – Ibn Bishr, I, 8.

[47] The young man of Najd had doubtlessly progressed far enough in his studies by this time to merit the title of Shaikh; in fact, he may have borne it before coming to al-Baṣrah. From this point on, whenever reference is made in this study to "the Shaikh", it may be taken to mean the Shaikh Muḥammad b. 'Abd al-Wahhāb.

[48] Al-Ḥusain, the son of 'Alī and Fāṭimah, the Prophet's daughter, is the "arch-saint and martyr" of the Shiites – P. K. Hitti, *History of the Arabs*, p. 183.

[49] See Douglas Carruthers, ed., *The Desert Route to India, being the journals of four travellers by the great desert caravan route between Aleppo and Basra 1745–51*, Publications of the Hakluyt Society, 2nd ser., LXIII (London 1929), xxxvi, 196 pp. These Englishmen were in al-Baṣrah twenty years or so after Muḥammad b. 'Abd al-Wahhāb, but the conditions they depict were probably very similar to those existing at the time of Shaikh Muḥammad's stay there.

In 1751 Carmichael left Aleppo with a caravan carrying merchandise to the value of "near £300,000 sterling" accompanied by an "escort of 240 Arab soldiers" – *op. cit.*, p. 138. Some of the caravans, which went out twice a year, were even bigger than this.

[50] Ibn Ghannām, I, 33, says that he spread the doctrine of the unity of God among certain of the people in al-Baṣrah (*nashara al-tauḥīd fīhā ladā ba'ḍ al-nās*). Ibn Bishr, I, 8, says that after denouncing innovations and examples of *shirk* he made his denunciation public (*a'lana bil-inkār*).

[51] See below, pp. 42–3.

to hear his religious pronouncements or to dispute with him. If anyone in the circle mentioned the symbols of the idols or saints[53] worshipped by the people, the Shaikh would forbid such worship and explain that holy men, deserving of admiration as they might be for the exemplary lives they led, could not share with God the rights of divinity. In the Shaikh's circle one day a man spoke to him about these matters; then as the Shaikh set forth his views a changed expression came over the man's face and he exclaimed: What he says is true; the people are all wrong.[54] The Shaikh himself described what used to take place in his circle:

> Certain men among the Mushrikūn[55] of al-Baṣrah used to bring equivocations and lay them before me. Then I would say while they were sitting in front of me: "The whole of worship belongs to God alone", whereupon they would all be left amazed and speechless.[56]

Although the Shaikh's teacher al-Majmū'ī and others approved of such preaching and exhortation, a number of the people in the town, including some of the chief men, resented the Shaikh as an upstart and a creator of disturbance. At the noontide hour one day these enemies assembled against the Shaikh, laid hold of him, bruised him, and threw him forth from their midst, after which they sought out his teacher al-Majmū'ī and handled him roughly too. Leaving al-Baṣrah, the Shaikh Muḥammad b. 'Abd al-Wahhāb stumbled barefoot along the road towards al-Zubair to the southwest. Overcome by thirst and fatigue and the heat of the sun, he was on the point of collapsing when a donkey-master[57] of the town of al-Zubair, Abū Ḥumaidān by name, happened by. This man was impressed by the dignity and gravity of the Shaikh even though his

[52] Ibn Ghannām, I, 32–3, says that the greatest part of the Shaikh's period of study abroad was spent in al-Baṣrah.

[53] *Shārāt al-ṭawāghīt au al-ṣāliḥīn* – Ibn Ghannām, I, 33.

[54] Ibn Ghannām, I, 33.

[55] The Mushrikūn are those guilty of *shirk*/the association of others with God – see below, pp. 42–3.

[56] Ibn Ghannām, I, 33.

[57] *Ṣāḥib ḥimār mukārī* – Ibn Bishr, I, 8.

knees were giving and he was near to fainting; he gave the weary traveler water and carried him on his donkey into al-Zubair.[58] Thus unwittingly this obscure man with his samaritan kindness saved the new life that was coming to Arabia.

Travels: al-Aḥsā'

After recuperating at al-Zubair from the ordeal of the journey out of al-Baṣrah, the Shaikh bethought himself of his old plan to visit Syria and study with the Hanbalite doctors there,[59] but he lacked the means to make the trip and so in the end he gave it up.[60] The Shaikh may have been responding, consciously or unconsciously, to a call from his homeland, a call to come and battle the forces of iniquity and godlessness entrenched there in every palm grove and Bedouin *dīrah*. From al-Zubair he journeyed southwards to the central oases of al-Aḥsā',[61] the last stop on the way back to Najd. In these oases,

[58] Ibn Bishr (Mecca), I, 8; (Baghdad), pp. 11–12. The Baghdad edition is the only one that describes the Shaikh as being barefoot while on the way. Ibn Ghannām has nothing on this incident.

[59] See above, p. 32.

[60] Philby in *The Heart of Arabia*, I, xvii, and in *Arabia*, p. 8, refers to the possibility that the Shaikh may have studied at Damascus, mentioning in the former work a "University of Damascus". However, the testimony of both Ibn Ghannām and Ibn Bishr, the two authors best acquainted with the career of the Shaikh, to the effect that his travels were restricted to Arabia and Iraq is sufficient to rule out the possibility of his having been in Syria. Strictly speaking there was of course no University of Damascus at that time; there were only mosque-schools and circles of scholars.

According to the biography of the Shaikh entitled *Lam' al-shihāb*, which is abstracted by D. S. Margoliouth in *The Encyclopaedia of Islam*, IV, 1086, and is characterized by him as being "somewhat but not excessively hostile", the Shaikh spent five years in Baghdad, where he married a rich woman who bequeathed him two thousand dinars when she died. From Baghdad he drifted on to Kurdistan for a year, then east to Hamadhān in Persia for two years, and then southeast to Iṣfahān in 1148/1736, the year in which Nādir Qulī Khān usurped the throne to begin his rule as the last great conquering warrior among the Shahs (1736–47). In the atmosphere of Nādir Shah's Sunnite revival and persecution of the Shiites the Shaikh is reported to have studied and taught the Sufi mystic doctrines for a span of five years. From Iṣfahān he wandered on to Qumm, a site revered by the Shiites for the tomb of Fāṭimah, sister of 'Alī al-Riḍā the eighth Imam, after which he forsook Sufism for the legal school of Aḥmad Ibn Ḥanbal. The incongruous dates in this account, which is utterly at variance with what is known of the Shaikh's character, are enough to damn it as excessively romantic, even if not "excessively hostile".

probably in the settlement of al-Hufūf, he alighted as the guest of the Shaikh ʻAbd Allāh b. Muḥammad b. ʻAbd al-Laṭīf, a scholar of the Shafiite school.[62] He remained for a time to take lessons from the Shaikh ʻAbd Allāh, probably concentrating on the points in which the Shafiite school differs from the Hanbalite. Then at last he turned his face towards Najd;[63] his years of study and wandering and preparation were coming to an end, and his great work was soon to begin.

Muḥammad b. ʻAbd al-Wahhāb in Ḥuraimilā

While Muḥammad b. ʻAbd al-Wahhāb was absent from al-ʻUyainah on his travels, disease swept through the town in 1138/September 1725 to August 1726 and carried off many of the inhabitants,[64] including their chief ʻAbd Allāh Ibn Muʻammar, who was succeeded by his grandson Muḥammad b. Aḥmad, nicknamed Khirfāsh.[65] The

[61] It is uncertain, whether al-Aḥsāʼ at this time was under the rule of ʻAlī b. Muḥammad, the successor of his brother Saʻdūn (see above, p. 28), or under the rule of the third brother Sulaimān (see below, p. 46, n. 34), who was later instrumental in driving the Shaikh forth from al-ʻUyainah.

[62] Ibn Ghannām, I, 60–74, gives the full text of a letter written by Ibn ʻAbd al-Wahhāb in after times to Shaikh ʻAbd Allāh, consisting of a discussion of theological matters.

[63] Ibn Bishr, I, 8. Ibn Ghannām, I, 31, refers to the Shaikh's coming to al-Aḥsāʼ but gives no details, even though Ibn Ghannām was himself a native of that region.

[64] Ibn Bishr, I, 229, says that the majority of them died.

[65] Ibn Bishr, I, 8, 229. The meaning of this nickname is not clear; it may be derived from the verb *kharfasha*/"to mix" or *kharfasha fī al-kalām*/"to speak in a confused manner".

[66] Ibn Ghannām, I, 33; Ibn Bishr, I, 8, 235.

[67] There is no indication in the sources as to how long Muḥammad had been away or the date of his return. Hardly an event is mentioned by either Ibn Bishr or Ibn Ghannām in the period between 1139/1726–7, the year of the deposition of ʻAbd al-Wahhāb by Khirfāsh, and 1153/1740–1, the year of the death of ʻAbd al-Wahhāb. The last flashback given by Ibn Bishr (see below, p. 237) is for the year 1139 and his annals proper do not begin before the death of ʻAbd al-Wahhāb and the commencement of his son's preaching in public – see below, p. 41.

[68] Ibn Bishr, I, 8, says simply that "words were exchanged between him and his father". The interpretation given here is based on what is known of the characters of the father and son.

[69] The account given here follows Ibn Bishr, I, 8–9. Ibn Ghannām, I, 33, states that Muḥammad stayed in Ḥuraimilā with his father proclaiming *tauḥīd* or the doctrine of the unity of God. Ibn Ghannām has nothing on the relations between the father and the son and does not even mention the death of ʻAbd al-Wahhāb.

new ruler did not get along with the Qadi of the town, Muḥammad's father ʿAbd al-Wahhāb b. Sulaimān; after a dispute with the Qadi, Khirfāsh deposed him in 1139/August 1726 to August 1727 and gave the post to Aḥmad b. ʿAbd Allāh b. ʿAbd al-Wahhāb b. ʿAbd Allāh. Feeling that there was no hope for a reconciliation, ʿAbd al-Wahhāb, who apparently lacked a combative spirit, decided to emigrate from al-ʿUyainah and settle in Ḥuraimilā off to the northwest.[66] He was established in Ḥuraimilā when his son Muḥammad arrived from al-Aḥsā.[67] The scholar home from the road found that times had not changed since his departure; the majority of the people were still sunk in moral ignorance and they were as actively engaged in superstitious practices as ever. As he had done in al-Baṣrah, the Shaikh Muḥammad began to point out to people the error of their ways and to exhort them to be guided by God's word in the Koran and the example of the Prophet and his companions. The father saw that his son's attempt to reform men who had no desire to be reformed might lead to trouble, and he remonstrated with Muḥammad,[68] though an open break between the two does not seem to have taken place. The father's cautiousness was doubtless an important factor influencing Muḥammad's decision to bide his time and not precipitate matters, a decision that may also have been based in part on the strong opposition shown by the townspeople to the arguments he presented. As long as his father remained alive Muḥammad proceeded with restraint, never concealing his views or trimming his beliefs, yet making no public issue of his conviction that many if not most of his fellow townsmen were sinners destined for hellfire. It appears that his policy during these years was to gain adherents by quiet persuasion. The death of his father ʿAbd al-Wahhāb in 1153/March 1740 to March 1741 was, however, the signal for the adoption of a new policy; the moment had arrived for the open declaration of war on those who by word or act denied the Oneness of God.[69]

3

To al-'Uyainah and al-Dir'īyah

Accession of Muḥammad b. Su'ūd in al-Dir'īyah

Arab tradition held that the towns of al-Dir'īyah[1] and al-'Uyainah in Wadi Ḥanīfah were founded in the same year.[2] The founders of al-Dir'īyah were members of a family descended from the Bedouin tribe of 'Anazah who had been living in the neighborhood of al-Qaṭīf in al-Aḥsā'.[3] According to one version, Māni' al-Muraidī[4] was the leader of the migration from the east into Najd; according to another version, it was his son Rabī'ah. In either event, the newcomers enjoyed cordial relations with their kinsman Ibn Dir',[5] who was then the lord of Ḥajar al-Yamāmah on or near the site of the modern city of al-Riyāḍ. Ibn Dir' gave them land out of his own property to settle on at al-Mulaibīd and Ghaṣībah, and there they built up the new town of al-Dir'īyah.

[1] The form al-Dir'īyah is preferred to the commoner form of al-Dar'īyah because the name seems without question to be derived from the name of the House of Dir'. The *dir'* is the coat-of-mail that the old Arab warriors wore; it was still in use in the 19th century – Burckhardt, *Notes on the Bedouins and Wahábys*, I, 55–6. The plural is *durū'*.

[2] Ibn Bishr, I, 16, gives the year as 850 AH. The probability is that both towns were founded about the middle of the 9th century of the Hegira/mid-15th century AD – see above, p. 23, n. 2.

[3] Ibn Bishr, I, 16, says that their old home al-Dir'īyah was in the neighborhood of or at (*'inda*) al-Qaṭīf; in II, 5, he says their old home was the town of al-Durū' in the district of (*min nawāḥī*) al-Qaṭīf. At the present time there is a spot in the sand dunes to the south-west of al-Qaṭīf called by the Bedouins al-Dir'īyah; no ruins are to be seen there, but the dunes may cover the site where the town once stood.

[4] Māni' is said to have been the ancestor of the well-known House of Māni', the Manāni'ah or Mawāni'ah, of Najd – Sulaimān al-Dakhīl, *Lughat al-'arab*, III, 228; al-Rīḥānī, *Ta'rīkh Najd al-ḥadīth*, p. 51; Martin Hartmann, *Die Welt des Islams,* II, 318.

[5] Ibn Dir' may have invited or even urged them to make the migration – Ibn Bishr, I, 16; II, 6.

The great-grandson of Rabī'ah b. Māni' was Mirkhān, whose two sons, Rabī'ah and Muqrin[6] produced a galaxy of rulers among their descendants. In the late 17th and early 18th century several of the members of the House of Waṭbān b. Rabī'ah ruled al-Dir'īyah; then their star went into decline and that of the House of Muqrin began to rise. In the last years of the reign of 'Abd Allāh Ibn Mu'ammar at al-'Uyainah, Muqrin's grandson Su'ūd b. Muḥammad[7] was lord of al-Dir'īyah. Su'ūd died on the eve of the Feast of the Breaking of the Fast in 1137/mid-June 1725,[8] only a year or so before the sickness in al-'Uyainah claimed 'Abd Allāh Ibn Mu'ammar as one of its victims.[9] Muḥammad b. Su'ūd did not succeed his father immediately; for some unspecified reason the rule reverted to the House of Waṭbān in the person of his grandson Zaid b. Mirkhān.[10]

Upon the spread of the disease in al-Uyainah and the death of 'Abd Allāh Ibn Mu'ammar in 1139/August 1726 to August 1727, Zaid of al-Dir'īyah sought to take advantage of the situation and enrich himself by plundering the stricken place. In company with Bedouin allies of the tribes of Subai' and Āl Kathīr he advanced up the valley, but Khirfāsh, the successor of 'Abd Allāh Ibn Mu'ammar, tricked him and a party of his men into his castle,[11] where his musketmen shot Zaid down. Muḥammad b. Su'ūd and his comrades, who were with Zaid at the time, escaped and fortified themselves in a strong place, which they refused to leave until guaranteed safe-conduct by al-Jauharah, the daughter of 'Abd Allāh Ibn Mu'ammar and the future wife of the Shaikh Muḥammad b. 'Abd al-Wahhāb.[12] The Shaikh in Ḥuraimilā may have reflected at this time upon the ways of the men of Najd who had been lost to Islam: when disease sapped

[6] Hartmann, *Die Welt des Islams*, III, 311 and *passim*, is wrong in reading this name Muqarrin. The common pronunciation of the name in Najd is Mijrin; the letter *qāf* there often has the sound of *jīm*.

[7] Su'ūd's father Muḥammad, who had been lord of al-Dir'īyah for a time, died in 1106/1694–5 – Ibn Bishr, I, 117.

[8] Not in 1140/1727, as incorrectly stated in al-Rīḥānī, *Ta'rīkh Najd al-ḥadīth*, p. 48.

[9] See above, p. 36.

[10] Ibn Bishr, I, 234, depicts Muḥammad b. Su'ūd as a supporter, not as a rival, of Zaid.

[11] Khirfāsh said to Zaid in effect: You will gain nothing if the Bedouins are partners in your plundering; come to see me and I shall give you satisfaction. Zaid went to the castle with forty men – Ibn Bishr, I, 235.

[12] See below, p. 43.

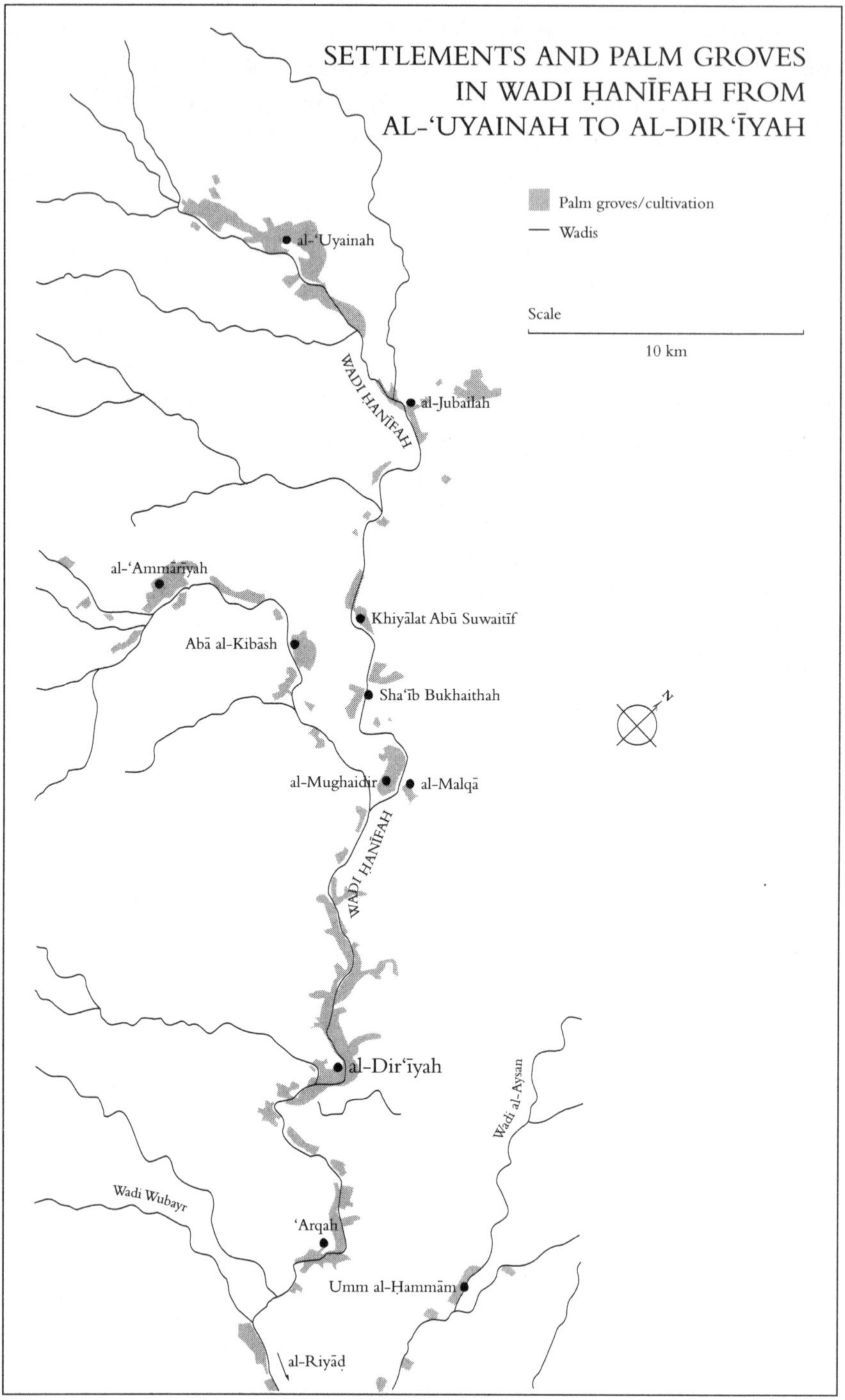
SETTLEMENTS AND PALM GROVES
IN WADI ḤANĪFAH FROM
AL-'UYAINAH TO AL-DIR'ĪYAH
Palm groves/cultivation
Wadis
Scale
10 km
N
al-'Uyainah
WADI ḤANĪFAH
al-Jubailah
al-'Ammārīyah
Khiyālat Abū Suwaitīf
Abā al-Kibāsh
Sha'īb Bukhaithah
al-Mughaidir
al-Malqā
WADI ḤANĪFAH
al-Dir'īyah
Wadi al-Aysan
Wadi Wubayr
'Arqah
Umm al-Ḥammām
al-Riyāḍ

the strength of their neighbors, they came to steal the goods of those in distress. He could hardly divine that before long one of those who had come to plunder would be his ally in propagating the faith, and that he would have the woman who had saved this man to share his bed.

After the return of Muḥammad b. Su'ūd from the unhappy expedition to al-'Uyainah he became the sole and independent ruler of al-Dir'īyah, a position that he and his descendants were to hold, with certain interruptions, to the present day. In recognition of the accomplishments of Muḥammad as ruler, the name of his father Su'ūd was taken as the name of the great house that sprang from his loins, the House of Su'ūd, a branch of the House of Muqrin.[13]

Public preaching of Unitarianism by the Shaikh in Ḥuraimilā, c.1153/1740–1

Soon after the death of the Shaikh 'Abd al-Wahhāb b. Sulaimān in 1153/March 1740 to March 1741, his son the Shaikh Muḥammad began publicly to hurl his doctrines into the teeth of the evildoers in Ḥuraimilā. So vigorous was his challenge that followers flocked to him from among the people of the town and his fame spread.[14] Now the years spent in study and discussion and preparation proved not to have been wasted. To assist him in his enterprise he had a circle of intimates that had been built up during his stay in Ḥuraimilā, men who had sat at his feet and read with him books of traditions of the Prophet and jurisprudence and interpretation of the Koran, men who were faithful to him under any circumstances and for whom his words and actions were guidance.[15] He himself had composed at least one work at Ḥuraimilā, his *Kitāb al-tauḥīd*,[16] in which he set forth the principles of Unitarianism.

[13] Muḥammad was Ibn Su'ūd because his father was named Su'ūd; any of his descendants might also be called Ibn Su'ūd because Su'ūd was the eponymous ancestor of them all – compare above, p. 7.

[14] Ibn Bishr, I, 9.

[15] On the Shaikh's circle see Ibn Ghannām, I, 34–5.

[16] Ibn Ghannām, I, 36. This book was probably written before the Shaikh began his public preaching.

Word of the Shaikh's activity at Ḥuraimilā was carried all over the district of al-'Āriḍ, to al-'Uyainah, al-Dir'īyah, al-Riyāḍ, and Manfūḥah. Men ready and eager to accept the doctrines he preached appeared in every town, but at the same time there also appeared men who denounced him and reviled him, and those who were against him outnumbered those who were for him.[17] The stage was being set for the conflict between Unitarians and anti-Unitarians that was to be waged in Najd for many years.

The basic doctrines of Unitarianism

The Unitarianism of the Shaikh Muḥammad b. 'Abd al-Wahhāb was founded on the concept of the unimpaired and inviolate Oneness of God. There was nothing original in the Shaikh's creed, nor did he intend that there should be. The Prophet Muḥammad in the Arabia of the 7th century had grown up in an environment in which many gods existed; the Almighty had revealed to him the Koran, which affirmed that God was One and that there were no other Gods beside Him. The Prophet had recited the Koran to his people and won their acceptance for its teachings. To Muḥammad b. 'Abd al-Wahhāb, living in an Arabia that greatly resembled the pre-Koranic land, the solution of the problem of how to rid his home of the sinfulness that beset it was crystal clear: Go back to the Word of God in the Koran and the interpretation and putting into effect of that Word by the Prophet and his pious companions. This was in essence the aim of the preaching of the Shaikh; to achieve this he and his followers strove with all their energy.

There were two types of sinful action and thought condemned by the Unitarians with unceasing vehemence: *shirk* and *bida'*. *Shirk* is the association of any being or thing with God, Who in His Oneness can have no associate,[18] or the attribution to any being or thing of powers that rightly belong only to God. In the literature of Unitarianism the denunciations of the *mushrikūn*, those who are guilty of *shirk*, occupy far more space than the denunciations of the

[17] Ibn Ghannām, I, 35.

[18] A favorite Moslem saying with reference to God is *lā sharīk lah*/"He has no associate".

kāfirūn, the unbelievers. *Bida'* or innovations[19] were likewise abhorred. Since the Prophet and his companions had led lives that were model even if not altogether perfect, practices introduced in later times were unworthy of true Moslems, for they were the outgrowth of ignorance or of evil desires. The Shaikh and his Unitarians believed that if they stamped out *shirk* and *bida'*, so that God was acknowledged throughout Islam as the One and Only God and men trod the Right Way He had set for them, all Moslems would indeed become brothers, peace would prevail, and the world would prosper. They were prepared to fight for success.

Departure of the Shaikh from Ḥuraimilā: his alliance with 'Uthmān Ibn Mu'ammar of al-'Uyainah

When the Shaikh began his public preaching of Unitarianism in Ḥuraimilā, the rule over the town was being contested by two branches of a single family, neither of which could gain the upper hand. The members of one branch were supported by their slaves known as the Ḥumayyān, a group notorious for their vile behavior. As one of the first steps towards subjecting the land to the authority of Islam, the Shaikh endeavored to reform this group of slaves. Their reply was a plot to kill him secretly at night. They climbed the wall that protected his dwelling, but some people who were on hand saw them coming and cried out, whereupon they fled.[20]

This incident was enough to make the Shaikh wonder whether it was desirable to remain any longer in Ḥuraimilā. One of the converts who had been won over by his preaching was 'Uthmān b. Aḥmad Ibn Mu'ammar,[21] the new ruler of his native town of al-'Uyainah. The Shaikh decided to move back to al-'Uyainah and work in alliance with 'Uthmān, who received him with respect and honor and gave him as wife al-Jauharah, the daughter of 'Abd Allāh Ibn Mu'ammar.[22] The Shaikh expressed to his new ally the hope he

[19] The singular *bid'ah* means "something new".

[20] Ibn Bishr, I, 9.

[21] No indication is given as to when 'Uthmān had succeeded his brother Khirfāsh (Muḥammad b. Aḥmad).

[22] Al-Jauharah was the paternal aunt of 'Uthmān.

had in mind: If you support the doctrine of the unity of God, through God's help you will possess Najd and its Arabs.[23] For his part 'Uthmān commanded that all the people of his town should obey the precepts of Islam as expounded by the Shaikh.[24]

The Shaikh at al-'Uyainah

Strengthened by the active support of a ruler and at least some of his subjects, the Shaikh selected as the next step the destruction of visible evidences of idolatry in the land. He informed 'Uthmān Ibn Mu'ammar that the sacred trees were to be cut down and the tombs over the graves of saints were to be demolished; 'Uthmān indicated his willingness to comply, and the two assembled their men for the work. The Shaikh himself lent a hand in felling the Tree of the Wolf,[25] being the one to strike the first blow with the axe. When another tree, known as the Tree of Quraiwah, was cut down, the Unitarians were joined by a number of men from the town of al-Dir'īyah who shared their beliefs, among them being Thunayyān and Mishārī, brothers of the ruler Muḥammad b. Su'ūd,[26] and the Shaikh Aḥmad Ibn Suwailim al-'Urainī, one of the most distinguished of the Shaikh Muḥammad's pupils in the early days.[27]

23 Ibn Bishr, I, 9.

24 Ibn Ghannām, I, 36.

25 *Shajarat al-Dhīb* – Ibn Ghannām, I, 37. The colloqual *dhīb* is used instead of the classical *dhi'b*. Like the male palm tree mentioned above, p. 20, the Tree of the Wolf was the resort of women who had not succeeded in getting husbands.

26 Thunayyān b. Su'ūd may have been older than his brother Muḥammad, as Musil, *Northern Neğd*, p. 258, says, but there is no evidence in the chronicles that he was a "born commander, a 'prince of the camel saddle'". He was noted for his piety; it is not clear whether he was blind at this time or became so later on. Compare below, p. 49, n. 47.

Mishārī b. Su'ūd was the father of Ḥasan, one of the captains of Unitarianism in later times – see below, p. 169.

27 Ibn Ghannām, I, 37, names one other tree, *Shajarat Abū Dajjānah*, that was cut down at this time. Ibn Bishr, I, 9, gives two stories that do not sound in keeping with the character of the Shaikh or his position in al-'Uyainah. The first is that the Shaikh hired a man to go out secretly and cut down one of the sacred trees. The second is that the Shaikh himself later went out alone and by stealth and cut down the most sacred of all the trees in the neighborhood.

Ibn Bishr, *loc. cit.*, says that as the cause of the Shaikh prospered a company of about seventy men, among them being some of the chiefs of the House of Mu'ammar (the Ma'āmirah), gathered about him. The word used for company is *'iṣabah*, the same word

The cutting down of trees regarded as sacred by large numbers of people was a daring move on the part of the Shaikh and 'Uthmān Ibn Mu'ammar, but even more daring was their decision to raze the tomb over the reputed grave of Zaid b. al-Khaṭṭāb at al-Jubailah.[28] Ibn Mu'ammar hesitated to do the deed unless the Shaikh accompanied him; he feared armed opposition by the residents of al-Jubailah. As matters turned out, the residents did appear with the intention of protecting their shrine, but Ibn Mu'ammar's force of six hundred men intimidated them and they left without a fight. When the Unitarians reached the tomb, Ibn Mu'ammar held back at the last moment, but the Shaikh asked for the axe and himself leveled the tomb to the ground. The night after the deed the superstitious Bedouins expected disaster to overtake its perpetrator, but the Shaikh arose the next morning in the best of health.[29]

The demolition of the tomb of Zaid, like the cutting down of the trees, served in a dramatic way to make people aware of the new movement with its center at al-'Uyainah, but the impact of these actions was perhaps surpassed by that of another, which Philby, with a certain exaggeration, has called the beginning of the story of modern Arabia.[30] A woman of al-'Uyainah confessed adultery. The Shaikh having learned of her case, she was examined and found sane; then of her own free will she continued to repeat her confession. The Shaikh postponed the rendering of judgment in the case for some days in the hope that she would retract her confession, but this she refused to do. Under the early Caliphs of Islam the punishment for this sin when so confessed was stoning,[31] but with the corruption

used by Ibn Ghannām in referring to the Shaikh's circle at Ḥuraimilā (see above, p. 41), so that Ibn Bishr may be speaking of a select group among the Shaikh's followers.

[28] See above, pp. 19–20.

[29] Ibn Bishr, I, 9–10. Ibn Ghannām gives none of these details, saying simply that the Shaikh instructed Ibn Mu'ammar to destroy the tombs (*qubab*) and places of prayer (*masājid*) built over the graves of the Prophet's companions in al-Jubailah – Ibn Ghannām, I, 36.

[30] Philby, *Arabia*, p. xix.

[31] Although stoning is not given by the Koran in its present form as the punishment for adultery, the Verse of Stoning (*Āyat al-rajm*) is said on the authority of the Caliph 'Umar to have been originally included in the Koran. Stoning is still the prescribed penalty in the Moslem books of law but is rarely carried out in practice. See Theodor Noeldeke, *Geschichte des Qorans*, rev. ed. by Friedrich Schwally, I, 248–51, and Joseph Schacht, art. "Zinā'" (fornication, adultery), *The Encyclopaedia of Islam*, IV, 1227.

of morals in Arabia the sentence of stoning had not been executed for many years. Here was the acid test of the sincerity of the Shaikh's endeavor to restore the ways of the past, and he met it unflinchingly. The woman was stoned to death, 'Uthmān Ibn Mu'ammar himself casting the first stone. The Shaikh had not forgotten the Prophet's injunction to show mercy that he had heard in Medina;[32] he had tried to save the woman by having her retract the confession of sin, and after the application of the law proved unavoidable and the woman had perished, he had her buried properly and prayers said for her.[33]

Intervention of the lord of al-Aḥsā', 1157/1744

The report of the stoning of the adulterous woman convinced the enemies of Unitarianism of the seriousness of the Shaikh's purpose. In casting about for a means of stopping the movement before it could grow to dangerous proportions, they decided to enlist the aid of the power in the east that was held by the chief of Banī Khālid and the lord of al-Aḥsā', Sulaimān b. Muḥammad of the House of Ḥumaid.[34] Coming to Sulaimān, the men who hated and feared the Shaikh informed him that the Shaikh desired to cut off the revenue he derived from taxes and to expel him from his realm.[35] Sulaimān, who seems to have been alarmed by the prospect, wrote to 'Uthmān Ibn Mu'ammar ordering him in no uncertain terms to kill the Shaikh or send him into exile.[36] The lord of al-'Uyainah at this time received

[32] See above, p. 31.

[33] Ibn Ghannām, II, 2; Ibn Bishr, I, 10. Philby has a long and illuminating discussion of the significance of this incident and a translation of the full account given by Ibn Ghannām – *Arabia*, pp. 9–11.

[34] Sa'dūn b. Muḥammad (see above, p. 36) had died in 1135/1722–3. After his death his brothers 'Alī and Sulaimān fought against his sons over the succession; the brothers won and 'Alī became the ruler – Ibn Bishr, I, 218. Ibn Bishr does not say when 'Alī died and Sulaimān, the third of the brothers to rule, took his place. 'Alī was still the ruler in the latter part of 1139/1727, when he foiled an attempt by Dujain b. Sa'dūn and the Muntafiq to unseat him – Ibn Bishr, I, 235.

[35] Ibn Ghannām, II, 3. Ibn Ghannām, who was a native of al-Aḥsā', says that Sulaimān was a notorious adulterer; the story of the stoning may have helped to make him apprehensive.

[36] Ibn Ghannām, II, 3, says that Sulaimān presented these two alternatives; Ibn Bishr, I, 10, says simply that the order was that the Shaikh should be killed.

certain feudal dues each year from the region of al-Aḥsā';[37] Sulaimān threatened to cancel these if Ibn Mu'ammar did not comply with the order. Ibn Mu'ammar was torn between two emotions: he wished to maintain his loyalty to his faith and to the Shaikh, and at the same time he was frightened by the might of Banī Khālid and fearful that he might lose his income. When he told the Shaikh of his dilemma, he was reminded that no earthly power could prevail over those who enjoyed the support of God and he was promised that if he held fast he would in time come to rule over Sulaimān's land and territories beyond it. As Ibn Mu'ammar reflected over the matter, however, the present threat outweighed the promise for the future, and so at last he sorrowfully told the Shaikh he would have to leave.[38]

Departure of the Shaikh from al-'Uyainah and his arrival in al-Dir'īyah, 1157/1744

When 'Uthmān Ibn Mu'ammar told the Shaikh that he would have to leave al-'Uyainah, he appointed a squadron of cavalry under the command of one named al-Furaid al-Ẓafīrī[39] to escort him and instructed them to accompany him to whatever place he chose. The Shaikh said: I choose al-Dir'īyah.[40] He already had influential supporters there in Thunayyān and Mishārī, the brothers of the ruler of the place, and in members of the House of Suwailim,[41] and he may have singled out Muḥammad b. Su'ūd as an ally of excellent poten-

There is no evidence in the chronicles to bear out the statement by Philby, *Arabia*, p. 11, that Sulaimān appeared to be the suzerain of al-'Uyainah; if he issued orders to Ibn Mu'ammar, it was only because he possessed vastly superior power.

Sulaimān's intervention took place shortly before the Shaikh moved from al-'Uyainah to al-Dir'īyah, that is in 1157/1744 – see below, pp. 47–8.

37 Ibn Bishr, I, 10, says that he had heard that the *kharāj* received by Ibn Mu'ammar from al-Aḥsā' amounted to twelve hundred gold pieces along with quantities of food and clothing.

38 These details are taken from Ibn Bishr, I, 10–11. Ibn Ghannām, II, 3, states briefly that Ibn Mu'ammar ordered the Shaikh to go.

39 *Al-Zahrā'*, III, 425; Ibn Bishr, I, 11.

40 Ibn Bishr, I, 11.

41 See above, p. 44.

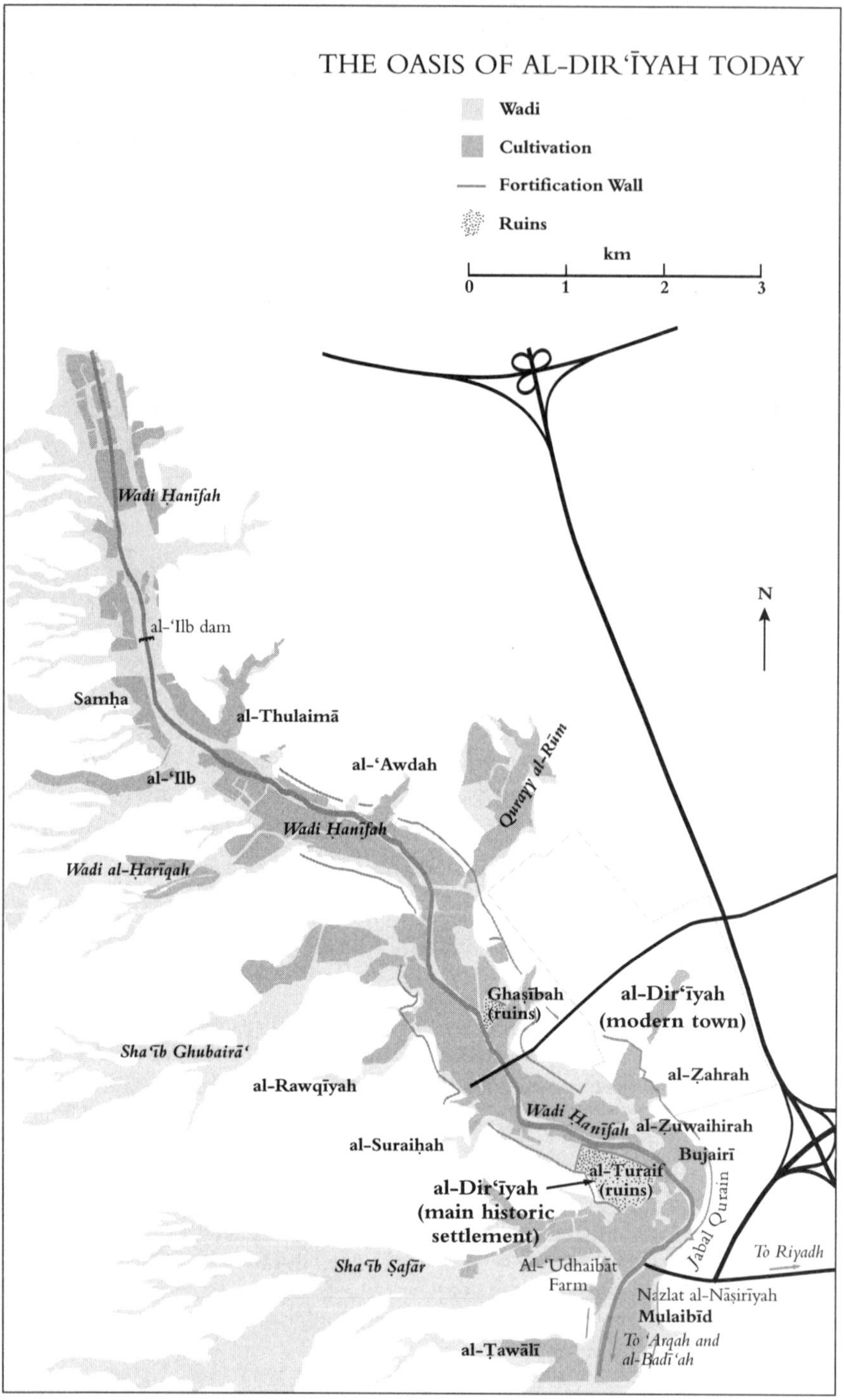
THE OASIS OF AL-DIR'ĪYAH TODAY
Wadi
Cultivation
Fortification Wall
Ruins
km
0
1
2
3
N
Wadi Ḥanīfah
al-'Ilb dam
Samḥa
al-Thulaimā
al-'Awdah
Qurayy al-Rūm
al-'Ilb
Wadi Ḥanīfah
Wadi al-Ḥarīqah
Ghaṣībah (ruins)
al-Dir'īyah (modern town)
Sha'īb Ghubairā'
al-Ẓahrah
al-Rawqīyah
Wadi Ḥanīfah
al-Ẓuwaihirah
al-Suraiḥah
Bujairī
al-Ṭuraif (ruins)
al-Dir'īyah (main historic settlement)
Jabal Qurain
Sha'īb Ṣafār
Al-'Udhaibāt Farm
To Riyadh
Nazlat al-Nāṣirīyah
Mulaibīd
To 'Arqah and al-Badī'ah
al-Ṭawālī

tialities, for Muḥammad, though he had not yet accepted the truths of Islam, was known in Najd as a man of worth and character.[42]

In the summer heat of the year 1157/1744[43] the party set out from al-'Uyainah, the horsemen of the escort mounted and the Shaikh on foot, carrying with him only a fan.[44] On the way the Shaikh kept repeating such phrases as "Praise be to God", "There is no God but God", and "God is greatest".[45] His first venture into the sphere of politics and his first alliance had failed, but he was not disheartened; his faith buoyed him up. In the late afternoon he arrived at al-Dir'īyah and went straight to the house of 'Abd Allāh b. 'Abd al-Raḥmān Ibn Suwailim,[46] where he spent the night. Then he moved to the home of 'Abd Allāh's cousin, the Shaikh Aḥmad Ibn Suwailim, who had studied under the Shaikh in al-'Uyainah or Ḥuraimilā.

Compact between the Shaikh and Muḥammad b. Su'ūd: foundation of the Unitarian State at al-Dir'īyah, 1157/1744

The members of the House of Suwailim who had given the Shaikh shelter were not sure just how their lord, Muḥammad b. Su'ūd, would react to the coming of the preacher of reform. They took counsel with Thunayyān,[47] the brother of the lord, and with Mūḍī

[42] Ibn Ghannām, II, 4.

[43] Ibn Bishr, I, 11, speaks of the extreme summer heat. Ibn Ghannām, II, 4, says that the trip took place in 1257, which is obviously a copyist's slip for 1157/February 1744 to February 1745. Combining the two references gives the date of the trip as the summer of 1744. Ibn Bishr in the Mecca edition, I, 15, and the Baghdad edition, p. 19, says that the Shaikh moved to al-Dir'īyah in 1158, but on p. 16 of the Baghdad edition he agrees with Ibn Ghannām in placing the trip in 1157, which is here taken to be the correct date.

[44] Ibn Bishr, I, 11.

[45] Ibn Bishr (Mecca), I, 11, describes in detail an unsuccessful attempt by 'Uthmān Ibn Mu'ammar to have the Shaikh killed en route, but in the Baghdad edition, p. 15, Ibn Bishr states that he had learned that the story was entirely without foundation.

[46] Ibn Bishr (Mecca), I, 11, gives the name incorrectly as Muḥammad Ibn Suwailim al-'Urainī. The correct name is to be found in Ibn Ghannām, II, 3; Ibn Bishr (Baghdad), p. 15; *al-Zahrā'*, III, 425.

[47] Ibn Bishr (Baghdad), p. 15, here refers to him as the blind Thunayyān.

[48] *Al-Zahrā'*, III, 425, says that she was from the tribe of Āl Kathīr.

bint Abū Waḥṭān, the Bedouin wife[48] of the lord, who was deeply stirred by what they told her of the Shaikh's belief in the unity of God. The Shaikh and his disciples agreed that nothing could be more effective than the persuasiveness of a woman; Mūḍī was delegated to deal with her husband. To him she said: "This man was driven to you by God as booty to be laid hold of, so show him honor." When Muḥammad b. Su'ūd desired to send for the Shaikh, he was told that it would be better to go in person to call on him, since this would elevate the Shaikh in the opinion of the townspeople.[49]

The momentous meeting took place in the home of the Shaikh Aḥmad Ibn Suwailim, the meeting that gave birth to an alliance that still endures in Arabia. According to one account,[50] as soon as Muḥammad b. Su'ūd had greeted the Shaikh he exclaimed: "I bring you tidings of a home that is better than your native home." The Shaikh replied: "And I bring you tidings of glory and power; whoever holds fast to this word of unity[51] will by means of it rule lands and men."[52] The Shaikh then expounded his doctrines at length and dwelt upon the evils in Najd that needed correction. After listening attentively, Muḥammad b. Su'ūd said: "O Shaikh, this is without doubt the religion of God and His Prophet; I shall help you and hold myself ready to take the field against whoever denies the unity of God." Then Muḥammad b. Su'ūd informed the Shaikh that he wished to impose two conditions upon him: first, that he should pledge himself not to forsake al-Dir'īyah for another place, and secondly, that he should not deny the right of the ruler to his income from the harvest. With regard to the first, the Shaikh held forth his hand and offered the oath: Blood with blood and ruin with ruin.[53] With regard to the second condition,

[49] Ibn Bishr, I, 11–12. Ibn Ghannām, I, 4, is briefer, saying no more than that Muḥammad b. Su'ūd went immediately with his brothers Thunayyān and Mishārī to see the Shaikh in the home of Aḥmad Ibn Suwailim.

[50] Ibn Bishr (Mecca), I, 12; (Baghdad), pp. 15–16.

[51] *Lā ilāh illā Allāh*/"There is no God but God".

[52] According to Ibn Bishr (Baghdad), p. 16, the Shaikh went on to say: "I hope that you and your seed after you will be Imams under whom will gather the Moslems of these lands."

[53] Our blood is your blood, and our ruin is your ruin, i.e. if blood is shed for you, it is shed for us, and if you suffer ruin, we suffer it too. This oath was in use among the Arabs

the Shaikh said: "Perhaps God has in store for you conquests and booty better than the share of the harvest." However, Muḥammad b. Su'ūd was allowed to continue the collecting of his local revenue until in after times booty did pour into al-Dir'īyah.

After the Shaikh had set forth his beliefs and outlined his aims, Muḥammad b. Su'ūd stretched out his hand and swore allegiance to the Shaikh in the cause of the religion of God and His Prophet, the struggle in God's path,[54] and the establishment of the rule of Islam in the territory of al-Dir'īyah.[55] He assured the Shaikh that he would defend him as he would defend his own wives and children against any aggressor.[56] Together the two turned and entered the town. The Shaikh Muḥammad b. 'Abd al-Wahhāb had come to al-Dir'īyah, his home for the rest of his life. The minute theocracy thus brought into being by the compact between the Shaikh and Muḥammad b. Su'ūd became in the 20th century, after many vicissitudes, the Kingdom of Saudi Arabia, the name of which commemorates the father of the Amir of al-Dir'īyah.

The Shaikh in al-Dir'īyah, 1157–8/1744–5

When the Shaikh arrived in al-Dir'īyah there were already Unitarians there among the townspeople. With the help of these[57] and the Amir Muḥammad b. Su'ūd the Shaikh spread the faith in his new home during the first two years of his activity there.[58] His powers of persuasion and personal magnetism and the compelling rightness of his cause drew many to him, not only from among the dwellers in his own oasis but from other towns as well. Members of his old circle at al-'Uyainah, including men of the House of Mu'ammar, left their

far back in pre-Islamic times, and it was the oath that the Prophet swore with the Anṣār, his allies at Yathrib or Medina, when he reached the end of the Hegira from Mecca – Abū Isḥāq al-Najīramī, *Aimān al-'arab fī al-jāhilīyah* (Cairo 1343/1924–5), pp. 29–30; al-Ālūsī, *Ta'rīkh Najd*, p. 116, n. 1.

[54] *Al-jihād fī sabīl Allāh.*

[55] Ibn Bishr, I, 12.

[56] Ibn Ghannām, II, 4.

[57] Ibn Ghannām, II, 4, and Philby, *Arabia*, pp. 12–13, give the names of the leading Unitarians among the residents of al-Dir'īyah in these early days.

[58] Ibn Ghannām, II, 4, says that he spent nearly two years giving advice to the people and revealing the truth.

homes and became citizens of al-Dir'īyah. The immigrants often underwent hardships in order to be near the Shaikh; making a living was not always easy for the newcomers, and some of them plied their trades at night so that they could sit with the Shaikh during the day and hear him repeat traditions of the Prophet.[59] The Shaikh felt himself responsible for the keep and welfare of these people of his and did all that he could to help them, but it was not until later, when conquests increased the income of the state, that he was able to care for them in a satisfactory manner.

'Uthmān Ibn Mu'ammar came to regret his action in expelling the Shaikh when he saw members of his own house moving away from al-'Uyainah to join the throng of disciples at al-Dir'īyah. Swallowing his pride, he came with a party of his notables to induce the Shaikh to return to the place of his first alliance. The Shaikh said simply that he had pledged his word to Muḥammad b. Su'ūd that he would not forsake al-Dir'īyah, so that the matter rested in the hands of the Amir. Muḥammad b. Su'ūd when approached by Ibn Mu'ammar was adamant in his refusal to let the Shaikh go.[60]

During the first two years in al-Dir'īyah the Shaikh spent much time composing letters to the rulers of other towns and to judges and scholars in an effort to win them to his views.[61] Sometimes his correspondents evinced a willingness to uphold the doctrines of Unitarianism, but often they proved to be indifferent or hostile.

Always a practical man, the Shaikh realized that words and letters and books alone would not secure the triumph of his beliefs, given the corrupt and chaotic condition of Najd at that time. The weapons of Ibn Saif would have to be supplemented by weapons of another kind. The Prophet had made use of the armies of Islam; the Shaikh could ask for no better or higher precedent. The Amir Muḥammad b. Su'ūd at the time of the making of the compact had indicated his

[59] Ibn Bishr, I, 13.

[60] Ibn Ghannām, II, 5; Ibn Bishr, I, 13.

[61] Ibn Bishr, I, 14. The first volume of Ibn Ghannām contains the texts of a number of such letters, some of which may have been written at this time, though Ibn Ghannām unfortunately does not give dates for them. They consist almost exclusively of discussions of a theological nature.

[62] See above, pp. 51–2.

[63] Ibn Bishr, I, 14–15. Ibn Ghannām does not record this expedition.

readiness to take the field for the struggle in God's path.[62] During this period the Unitarians of al-Dirʿīyah sent out their first military expedition. It started in sorry fashion, but the ending turned out to be more auspicious than the beginning.

A party of riders mounted on seven camels left al-Dirʿīyah. Unaccustomed to the speed of their beasts, the riders were falling out of their saddles before they had gone very far. But they persevered – perseverance was to become a sterling trait of the Unitarians – and before returning home they had found their quarry, a band of roving Bedouins, and had taken from them the booty they were after.[63] It may be assumed that this booty, or at least the major portion of it, was assigned by the Shaikh to the needy Unitarian immigrants.

This trifling affair was the prelude to years of raiding and sieges as the Unitarians fought to extend the realm of their faith. During the first two years at al-Dirʿīyah the Shaikh had fortified himself firmly; now he and the House of Suʿūd were poised to embark on the struggle for Najd.

PART II

The Struggle for Central Najd

1159–1187 AH/AD 1746–1773

4

The First War between al-Dir'īyah and al-Riyāḍ

Beginning of the long war between al-Dir'īyah and al-Riyāḍ, 1159–60/1746–7

A year or two after the Shaikh Muḥammad b. 'Abd al-Wahhāb moved to al-Dir'īyah there began the struggle that was to absorb much of the energy of the reformers for more than twenty-five years to come, the struggle with Dahhām b. Dawwās, the lord of al-Riyāḍ, which lies only ten miles down the valley from al-Dir'īyah.[1] As long as this neighboring oasis was in the hands of a bitter opponent of the new movement the opportunities for expansion and consolidation were bound to be limited. Najd without al-Riyāḍ could not be conquered and made secure.

The rule of Dahhām b. Dawwās[2] in al-Riyāḍ was of recent origin. About 1093/*c.* 1681 his father Dawwās had by force made himself master of the settlement of Manfūḥah next door to al-Riyāḍ.[3] After the death of Dawwās in 1139/1726–7[4] the people of Manfūḥah drove out his sons, including Dahhām, who chose al-Riyāḍ as their new home. Some time subsequent to their arrival the ruler of al-Riyāḍ, Zaid b. Mūsā Abā Zar'ah, was killed by a crazy cousin of his who stabbed him as he lay asleep. A slave of Zaid's, Khumayyis, revenged his master by putting the assassin to death; he then seized the government in the guise of guardian for Zaid's young sons and

[1] Al-Riyāḍ is today the citadel of Wahhabism in the Kingdom of Saudi Arabia and is one of the two capitals of the country, the other being the Holy City of Mecca.

[2] He was Dahhām b. Dawwās b. 'Abd Allāh b. Sha'lān – Ibn Bishr, I, 80. The name Dahhām means Crusher; Dawwās, from the root *dawasa*/"to tread upon", means Courageous or Lion. Dahhām's family or tribe is not given.

[3] Ibn Bishr, I, 80, 82.

[4] Ibn Bishr, I, 235.

held sway for about three years. When the discontent of the populace finally resulted in the flight of Khumayyis, there was none to command in the city. The newcomer Dahhām, who had been a servant of Khumayyis during the period of his rule, saw his chance and took it. Asserting that his sister was the mother of one of Zaid's sons, he named himself regent for the youth, though it was not long before he sent his charge, the lawful heir, into exile. The people of al-Riyāḍ did not take kindly to the acts of the usurper; a mob gathered and shut him up in his castle, but it was a mob without a leader. Dahhām sent his brother Mishlab on horseback to appeal for aid from Muḥammad b. Suʿūd, the Amir of al-Dirʿīyah, who responded by sending an expedition under the command of his brother Mishārī. This help enabled Dahhām to crush the opposition, after which Mishārī stayed with him in al-Riyāḍ for some months until he was firmly seated as sole ruler.[5]

When the Shaikh and Muḥammad b. Suʿūd made their compact and set out to enlarge the realm of their religion, they naturally made overtures to Dahhām, who was indebted to the Amir Muḥammad. The ruthless Dahhām, however, was hardly one to welcome the morality of Islam; one of the historians of Wahhabism declared him guilty of such cruel and unusual punishments as sewing up the lips of a woman, cutting a piece out of a man's thigh and forcing him to eat it raw, and knocking out with an iron bar the teeth of a prisoner who had tried to escape by gnawing at the iron of his prison.[6] When Dahhām found subjects of his accepting the religion preached by the Shaikh, he vented his wrath upon them. In 1159/January 1746 to January 1747 his enmity came out into the open when, in company with Bedouins of the Ẓafīr, he organised an attack on his neighbors in Manfūḥah, who had become adherents of the Shaikh. Dahhām and some of his men concealed themselves in one of the houses of Manfūḥah with the connivance of the owner while the Bedouins and the cavalry were sent in the morning to raid the fields and the palm groves in order to draw out the inhabitants. The ruse worked and not a fighting man was left in the town, whereupon Dahhām and his band rushed in and occupied the castle of the Amir. Nothing

[5] Ibn Ghannām, II, 5–6; Ibn Bishr, I, 80–81

[6] Ibn Ghannām, II, 7.

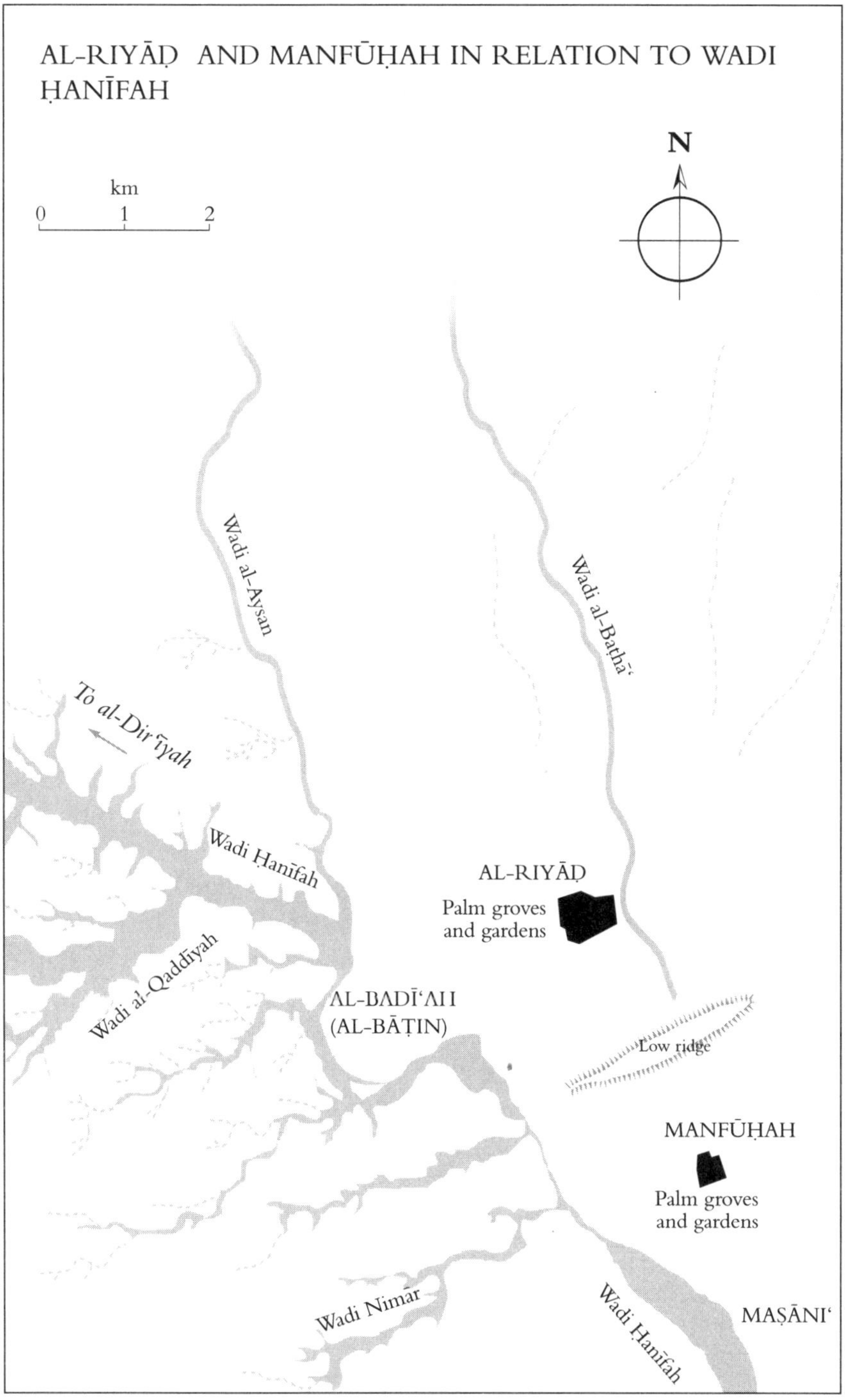
AL-RIYĀḌ AND MANFŪḤAH IN RELATION TO WADI ḤANĪFAH
km
0
1
2
N
Wadi al-Aysan
Wadi al-Baṭḥā'
To al-Dir'iyah
Wadi Ḥanīfah
AL-RIYĀḌ
Palm groves and gardens
Wadi al-Qaddīyah
AL-BADĪ'AH
(AL-BĀṬIN)
Low ridge
MANFŪḤAH
Palm groves and gardens
Wadi Nimār
Wadi Ḥanīfah
MAṢĀNI'

daunted, 'Alī b. Mazrū'[7] and other Unitarians went up into houses overlooking the castle and opened such a hot fire that Dahhām and his followers leaped down from the wall and fled. Dahhām, who was wounded twice, lost the toes of one foot and had his horse killed.[8]

Upon receipt of the news from Manfūḥah, the Shaikh and Muḥammad b. Su'ūd decided that war against Dahhām was necessary, a decision that was reinforced when they heard that Dahhām had offered to devote sacrificial beasts to the cause of the blind holy man of al-Kharj, Tāj b. Shamsān,[9] should the lord of al-Dir'īyah reach al-Fawwārah[10] in an advance on al-Riyāḍ. Carrying out this decision, a party of Unitarians penetrated into al-Riyāḍ and sawed off the door of Dahhām's castle. Entering the houses of Nāṣir b. Mu'ammar and Turkī b. Dawwās, they hamstrung many camels and fired a number of shots, but they failed to hit the man they were seeking.

Dahhām showed his boldness by taking the offensive immediately after his narrow escape. Sweeping around al-Dir'īyah, he fell on the town of al-'Ammārīyah farther on up Wadi Ḥanīfah. Muḥammad b. Su'ūd with men of al-Dir'īyah and 'Arqah laid an ambush at Faiḍat Laban[11] to catch Dahhām on his way home, and Dahhām had to flee until another group of his men came down from al-'Ammārīyah and took the pursuing Unitarians in the rear, completely turning the tables.[12]

Once the adversaries had locked horns, they lunged at each other at every opportunity. Two other battles were fought in 1159/1746–7, one known as the Battle of the Old Men and the other as the Battle of the Slaves; both resulted from Unitarian raids on al-Riyāḍ. On the first occasion Muḥammad b. Su'ūd was supported by 'Uthmān Ibn Mu'ammar and the people of al-'Uyainah; after the battle was joined on al-Wishām,[13] a spacious hill outside al-Riyāḍ, the soldiers

[7] 'Alī b. Mazrū' was of the family of the Mazārī', who had suffered at the hands of Dahhām's father Dawwās – Ibn Bishr, I, 82.

[8] Ibn Ghannām, II, 7–8; Ibn Bishr, I, 17.

[9] See above, p. 21.

[10] The Spring or The Place of Bubbling Water, on the way from al-Dir'īyah to al-Riyāḍ.

[11] *Faiḍah* in the language of the north is the same as *rauḍah*.

[12] Ibn Ghannām, II, 9, is franker than Ibn Bishr, I, 18, in admitting the defeat of the Unitarians.

of this town retired, leaving two old men of the House of Shams among their dead on the field. In the second battle Muḥammad b. Suʿūd, his forces increased by contingents from ʿArqah and other villages near al-Dirʿīyah, set his ambush in a place called Jurf ʿUbayyān.[14] The attackers smashed a sortie led by Dahhām and killed about ten of his followers, the majority of them slaves. This Battle of the Slaves was also known as the Battle of the Unburied,[15] since the corpses of the slain were left lying for a number of days.

Either late in 1159 or early in 1160[16] Dahhām tried to even the score with a raid on al-Dirʿīyah. Fearing an ambush, Muḥammad b. Suʿūd warned his men against recklessness, but the sight of Dahhām giving ground was too tempting and they fell into his trap. Two of Muḥammad's own sons, Faiṣal and Suʿūd,[17] were among those who in the eyes of their fellows won martyrdom by dying in the fight. This grave loss redoubled the determination of the Unitarians to rid themselves of Dahhām, but they were to find this no easy task.

In Rabīʿ I 1160/March to April 1747 the Unitarians mustered their strength from al-Dirʿīyah, al-ʿUyainah, Ḥuraimilā, Manfūḥah, and the subordinate villages, and marched on al-Riyāḍ.[18] A man of Ḥuraimilā, however, slipped on ahead and warned Dahhām of the impending blow, so that he was prepared for it when it fell. In the morning the allies penetrated into Dalqah,[19] the hollow of al-Riyāḍ, where they engaged the defenders in fierce hand-to-hand fighting. At the gate of the castle the Unitarian Aḥmad b. Muḥammad b. Munais[20] slashed at Dahhām's head and body with his sword. Dahhām

[13] Al-Wishām is the plural of al-Washm, the name of one of the districts of Najd; both names apparently refer to plants as they first sprout out of the ground.

[14] A *jurf* or *juruf* is a bank that has been undermined by water; also what lies below such a bank, i.e. a ravine.

[15] Ibn Ghannām, II, 9. The Arabic word, *ghabībah* or *ghubaibah*, refers to meat that is left overnight and acquires a bad smell.

[16] According to Ibn Ghannām, II, 9, near the end of 1159; according to Ibn Bishr, I, 19, early in 1160, so that very likely the time was December 1746 or January 1747.

[17] Muḥammad had at least two other sons, ʿAbd al-ʿAzīz and ʿAbd Allāh, of whom much will be heard later.

[18] Ibn Ghannām, II, 10, says nothing about Muḥammad b. Suʿūd having a share in the expedition; Ibn Bishr, I, 19, states that he went along.

[19] Hence the encounter was known as the Battle of Dalqah. Ibn Bishr, I, 19, says that it was also called the Battle of al-Shirāk, the name of a place, or possibly a road, in al-Riyāḍ.

might have gone down had not one of his men, Mūsā b. 'Īsā Āl Ḥarīṣ, come upon Ibn Munais from behind and killed him. Dahhām's savior received a wretched reward; when Dahhām later discovered that he had been won over by the teachings of the Shaikh Muḥammad b. 'Abd al-Wahhāb, he cut off his hand and foot and exiled him to al-Dir'īyah, where he died three days after his arrival.

Plotting of the Amir of al-'Uyainah against the Shaikh, 1160/1747

Although a contingent from al-'Uyainah was present at the Battle of Dalqah, the expedition had been undertaken with the disapproval of 'Uthmān Ibn Mu'ammar. When the contingent from Ḥuraimilā passed by al-'Uyainah on the way home, Ibn Mu'ammar called in its commander, Muḥammad Ibn Mubārak, the Amir of Ḥuraimilā, and conferred with him regarding the feasibility of a confederation to combat the rising power of al-Dir'īyah. In addition, Ibn Mu'ammar ordered Ibrāhīm b. Sulaimān,[21] the Amir of Tharmidā in al-Washm, to ride to Dahhām and induce him to come to al-'Uyainah. After a while both Dahhām and the Amir of Tharmidā appeared and put their heads together with Ibn Mu'ammar. When those among the people of al-'Uyainah who were loyal to the Unitarian Shaikh got wind of what was going on, they assembled in the presence of Ibn Mu'ammar and demanded to know what he was planning. Ibn Mu'ammar sought to placate them by insisting that his sole purpose was to win Dahhām to acceptance of the religion of the Shaikh. At the same time Ibn Mu'ammar sent a messenger to the Shaikh asking him to come to al-'Uyainah. The Shaikh, however, had been warned of the plot or at least had an inkling of it; he declined the invitation. His action convinced the Unitarians of al-'Uyainah that there was more to the business than their lord had told them; they ran to Ibn Mu'ammar's castle seeking Dahhām. The ruler of al-Riyāḍ escaped under cover of darkness, and Ibn Mu'ammar once

[20] This is the name as given in Ibn Ghannām, II, 10. Although Ibn Bishr does not mention this incident, he lists Abū Munais Aḥmad b. Muḥammad b. Sulaimān b. Ḥasan among those who fell on this day; this seems to be the same man – Ibn Bishr, I, 19.

[21] Ibrāhīm b. Sulaimān b. Nāṣir b. Ibrāhīm b. Khunaifir al-'Anqarī – Ibn Bishr, I, 52.

more exerted himself to persuade his subjects that he was not an enemy of their religion. He sent a friendly message to the Shaikh and Muḥammad b. Su'ūd, asking pardon for his shortcomings and assuring them of his loyalty and sincerity; afterwards he went in person with the notables of al-'Uyainah and Ḥuraimilā to renew the treaty in which he pledged himself to aid the reformers in expeditions to any region whatsoever.[22] His protestations of good faith were accepted, and in the following year he held the rank of commander-in-chief of the Unitarian forces in the field.

Unitarian expeditions against al-Riyāḍ commanded by the Amir of al-'Uyainah, 1161/1748

In 1161/January to December 1748 Ibn Mu'ammar brought out the troops of al-'Uyainah and Ḥuraimilā and was joined by the Unitarians from al-Dir'īyah[23] and Ḍurmā. He proceeded down Wadi al-Watar,[24] approaching al-Riyāḍ from the east, until he made camp between al-'Aud and al-Bunayyah.[25] On the first day there was skirmishing between the two sides until the evening, when the attackers moved past al-Riyāḍ to Manfūḥah, where they stayed for three days taking counsel among themselves regarding the next stage of the campaign. At length they divided their forces into two parties and advanced again on al-Riyāḍ. The first party entered Ṣiyāḥ, one of the settlements of the oasis, and plundered the place, while the other party, made up of the men of Ḥuraimilā and 'Arqah, went through Muqrin, another settlement, as far as al-Ẓuhairah, a part of the town

[22] Ibn Ghannām, II, 11–12. Ibn Bishr has nothing to say about this backsliding of Ibn Mu'ammar beyond the fact that he was not present at the Battle of Dalqah.

[23] Ibn Ghannām, II, 13, gives Muḥammad b. Su'ūd as the leader of the contingent from al-Dir'īyah, while Ibn Bishr, I, 21, gives his son 'Abd al-'Azīz. In either case Ibn Mu'ammar was the commander-in-chief, for Ibn Ghannām, II, 11, states explicitly that Muḥammad b. Su'ūd accepted orders from Ibn Mu'ammar in the field following the renewal of the treaty between them. If 'Abd al-'Azīz, then in his late twenties, accompanied the expedition, it was the first time he went to battle, or, more probably, the first time he played a prominent enough part to be mentioned in the account of the campaign.

[24] The Valley of the Bowstring, the valley in which the town of Sadūs in the district of al-Maḥmal is situated.

[25] The Little Building, the name of a square fort that stood in the environs of al-Riyāḍ.

proper. At al-Ẓuhairah the defenders were waiting for them in the shadow of the castle of Dahhām. Fortune favored Dahhām and his men, who killed about twenty-five of the Unitarians and put the rest to flight. Dahhām then hastened to Ṣiyāḥ, where he found the other Unitarian party scattered about among the houses and palm groves; he killed another twenty here. The discomfited Unitarians had just enough strength left to pull down the walls of the fort of al-Bunayyah as they retreated homewards.[26]

Very shortly thereafter the same allies again set out under the command of 'Uthmān Ibn Mu'ammar, with 'Abd al-'Azīz b. Muḥammad b. Su'ūd as captain of the band from al-Dir'īyah, and returned to Ṣiyāḥ in the oasis of al-Riyāḍ. When the residents made a sortie, the fighting took place at a spot called al-Ḥuzaizah.[27] The attackers suffered the greater losses; their main accomplishment was the cutting down of four palm trees.

Unitarian expeditions against Tharmidā commanded by the Amir of al-'Uyainah, 1161/1748

The allies under Ibn Mu'ammar next turned to the west to attack Tharmidā in the district of al-Washm, probably because of the part played by the Amir of Tharmidā in the plotting against the Shaikh. The issue was joined in the low region known as al-Buṭain not far from the town, where a well executed ambush led to the killing of about seventy of the people of Tharmidā. The survivors took refuge in the nearby fort of al-Ḥurayyiṣ, leaving the town itself virtually unprotected. 'Abd al-'Azīz and his colleagues from al-Dir'īyah urged their commander Ibn Mu'ammar to enter and seize the town, but he demurred, prompted perhaps by his knowledge of the complicity he shared with the Amir of Tharmidā. The young 'Abd al-'Azīz harangued his superior at length, reproaching him for his inaction, but Ibn Mu'ammar, whose mind was set on returning home, started off with the majority of the troops. Left behind with only a small

[26] The Wahhabi historians record this as the campaign of al-Bunayyah – Ibn Ghannām, II, 13–14; Ibn Bishr, I, 21.

[27] Thus in Ibn Ghannām, II, 14; al-Khuraizah in Ibn Bishr (Mecca), I, 21; and al-Jazīrah/The Island in Ibn Bishr (Baghdad), p. 28.

party, 'Abd al-'Azīz debated for a time whether to try to break into the town; in the end he yielded to the advice of his companions and his own better judgment and turned away. Overtaking Ibn Mu'ammar on the road, 'Abd al-'Azīz and his men snatched from him the whole booty of the campaign and took it with them, saying that it was necessary to deliver it to al-Dir'īyah, where the Shaikh and Muḥammad b. Su'ūd would oversee the distribution of it.[28]

Despite the disagreement that had arisen between Ibn Mu'ammar and 'Abd al-'Azīz, Ibn Mu'ammar remained in command of the combined forces, which he led in a second expedition against Tharmidā before the end of the year. This time the people of the town refused to be provoked into coming out from behind their walls, and the attackers had to be content with spoiling some of the fields. A raid carried out farther to the northwest against the town of Thādiq[29] ended in the killing of a few men and the capture of a number of sheep and goats.

Unitarian raid against al-Riyāḍ, 1162/1748–9

In 1162/December 1748 to December 1749 the command of the Unitarian forces reverted to Muḥammad b. Su'ūd, who led a raid against Dahhām in al-Riyāḍ that got no farther than the palm grove of al-Ḥabbūnīyah. The Unitarians stayed in the grove for a day, mounting the towers that had been built for defense and exchanging random shots with their opponents; then they destroyed the defense works and moved on to Manfūḥah, the home of their companions in the faith.

Assassination of the Amir of al-'Uyainah, 1163/1750

With the war against Dahhām b. Dawwās of al-Riyāḍ at a standstill and no other major operations under way, relations with 'Uthmān Ibn Mu'ammar of al-'Uyainah became the most important matter confronting the champions of reform. Indications given by his conduct and complaints registered against him by people from various

[28] Ibn Ghannām, II, 14–15, gives a fuller account of the expedition than Ibn Bishr, I, 21–2.
[29] The chief town of the district of al-Maḥmal.

towns who came to al-Dir'īyah finally persuaded the Shaikh and Muḥammad b. Su'ūd that Ibn Mu'ammar was not a sincere supporter of their cause. The Shaikh told Unitarians arriving from al-'Uyainah to consult him that he asked for allegiance to the religion of God and His Prophet, loyalty to those who were loyal to this religion, and enmity towards those who were inimical to it, even if it proved to be their own Amir 'Uthmān.[30] Perceiving that the political ties with the Unitarians were weakening, Ibn Mu'ammar sought to maintain himself by enlisting the aid of others. He wrote to Ibrāhīm b. Sulaimān al-'Anqarī, the lord of Tharmidā, and to Faiṣal Ibn Suwaiṭ,[31] the head chief of the Bedouin tribe of the Ẓafīr, urging them to meet him in al-'Uyainah. Ibrāhīm of Tharmidā had collaborated with Ibn Mu'ammar in the plotting against the Shaikh three years earlier, and his town had been an object of Unitarian attacks in 1161/1748. The Ẓafīr, a numerous and powerful tribe, had already, in partnership with Dahhām of al-Riyāḍ, fought against the followers of the Shaikh.[32] Before Ibn Mu'ammar's negotiations proceeded any farther, a number of resolute men among the Unitarians of al-'Uyainah determined to kill their Amir. He had unsheathed his sword in defense of their faith and he was the father-in-law of the young Unitarian captain 'Abd al-'Azīz b. Muḥammad b. Su'ūd,[33] but they greatly feared that he would turn against them and become another Dahhām, and so the deed was done. After the congregational prayer on a Friday in Rajab 1163/May 1750 they struck him down in the place where he had been praying. A messenger immediately carried the news to the Shaikh and Muḥammad b. Su'ūd in al-Dir'īyah. Fearful that the assassination might be followed by turmoil in al-'Uyainah, the Shaikh hurried there in person, arriving within two days. His coming served to calm the people, and they indicated their willingness to accept whatever dispositions he might make. There was no great desire on the part of the Unitarians to have another member of the House of Mu'ammar as their Amir, particularly since those who had partici-

[30] Ibn Ghannām, II, 16. On the basis of this, Philby, *Arabia*, p. 16, states that Ibn Mu'ammar was murdered by his fellow citizens at the instigation of the Shaikh.

[31] His family name means Little Whip.

[32] See above, p. 58.

[33] The Shaikh Muḥammad b. 'Abd al-Wahhāb was also related to the House of Mu'ammar by marriage – see above, p. 43.

pated in the assassination were afraid that one of that house might take revenge on them, but the Shaikh disregarded their views and appointed Mishārī b. Ibrāhīm Ibn Mu'ammar as the new ruler.[34]

Unitarian raids against al-Riyāḍ and Tharmidā, 1163–4/1750–1

While the Unitarian cause benefited by the elimination of the threat of dissension by Ibn Mu'ammar on the northern flank, the threat of Dahhām remained on the southern flank. Muḥammad b. Su'ūd took a party of men into the oasis of al-Riyāḍ at night, but after a brisk fight at the gate of al-Marwah he had to withdraw.[35]

Tharmidā in the west likewise remained a stronghold of resistance to the spread of the reform movement. Mishārī Ibn Mu'ammar and 'Abd al-'Azīz, with Mishārī in command, went raiding in that direction, but word of their intent preceded them and the people of Tharmidā called in the people of Uthaithīyā and Marrāh[36] for support. Despite these reinforcements, the ambush prepared by the raiders at al-Waṭīyah outside Tharmidā worked very well; twenty-five of the trapped were slain, including 'Alī b. Zāmil, the Amir of Uthaithīyā.

Another attack on al-Riyāḍ in the following year, 1164/ November 1750 to November 1751, ended in the repulse of the Unitarians and the death of one of their bravest, 'Alī b. 'Īsā Āl Durū', who, contrary to the conventions of Arab warfare, stood his ground against hopeless odds and fought to the last breath. The war of attrition against Dahhām was wearing both sides down, but there was a sustaining religious conviction on one side that was lacking on the other.

[34] Ibn Ghannām, II, 16–17.

[35] According to Ibn Ghannām, II, 17, the affair was known as the Battle of al-Baṭḥā'; according to Ibn Bishr, I, 24, al-Buṭaiḥā'/the Little Baṭḥā'. A *baṭḥā'* is a broad torrent bed.

[36] Ibn Ghannām, II, 18, uses this form of the name; Ibn Bishr, I, 24, uses Marrāt.

[37] The House of 'Abd al-Raḥmān of Ḍurmā and Muḥammad's family had as a common ancestor Ibrāhīm b. Mūsā – Ibn Bishr, II, 6, 10.

[38] The members of this house were known collectively as the Sayāsirah.

[39] The accounts of Ibn Ghannām, II, 18–19, and Ibn Bishr, I, 25, need to be checked carefully against each other.

Elimination of the anti-Unitarian Amir of Ḍurmā, 1164/1750–1

Ibrāhīm b. Muḥammad Ibn 'Abd al-Raḥmān, the Amir of the town of Ḍurmā beyond the western edge of Ṭuwaiq, chose this time to break with the Shaikh and Muḥammad b. Su'ūd,[37] after his town had been one of the first of importance to join the Unitarian movement. His lack of sympathy for Unitarianism or his greed for worldly goods led him to dispossess and put to death three of his subjects, who were staunch Unitarians and at the same time endowed with wealth. One of the murdered men was a relative of the House of Saif,[38] so that the members of this house, for the sake of the bloodwit and their own devotion to the religion of the Shaikh, resolved to secure revenge. Four months after the crime they killed its perpetrator and his two sons as they were sitting in the council chamber; three wives put on mourning just as three wives cast it off. Muḥammad b. Su'ūd appointed 'Abd Allāh b. 'Abd al-Raḥmān al-Raidī as the new Amir of Ḍurmā.[39]

Unitarian raid against al-Zilfī in the north, 1164/1751

The last event recorded for the year 1164/1751 was a raid against al-Zilfī in northern Sudair towards al-Qaṣīm, the furthest point to the north reached by a Unitarian expedition up to this time. 'Abd al-'Azīz, the captain of the raiders, suffered an attack of fever at al-Ḥisā[40] and had to turn over the command to 'Abd Allāh b. 'Abd al-Raḥmān.[41] The raiders came back with a large number of sheep and goats they had taken in the neighborhood of al-Zilfī.

[40] Al-Ḥisā is the singular of al-Aḥsā', the name of the eastern region of Arabia. It refers to sandy ground in which water is found near the surface.

[41] It is not stated whether this was the new Amir of Ḍurmā or another man with the same name.

[42] Munaikh is a subdistrict in Sudair embracing the towns of Ḥarmah and al-Majma'ah.

[43] Ibn Ghannām, II, 19; Ibn Bishr, I, 25.

[44] Al-Ḥarīq and al-Ḥauṭah in Wadi al-Far' to the southwest of al-Kharj are famous centers of fanaticism, having been at times fierce opponents of Wahhabism and at other times

Opposition to Unitarianism in the north and south, 1165/1751–2

Incidents in 1165/November 1751 to November 1752 illustrated how strong the opposition to the Shaikh's doctrines remained in the regions about al-Dir'īyah. The town of Raghbah to the northwest in al-Maḥmal had accepted these doctrines, thereby invoking the enmity of its neighbors. The people of the districts of Sudair and al-Washm, prominent among them being the people of Munaikh[42] and al-Zilfī, united with the anti-Unitarian Bedouins of the Ẓafīr under Faiṣal Ibn Suwaiṭ to plunder the town of all its movable property.[43] These same allies, reinforced by contingents from the south, especially from the town of al-Ḥarīq,[44] and by those who had recently fled from Ḍurmā after the killing of its recalcitrant Amir, next marched south to strike at the revived power of the Unitarians in Ḍurmā. The reception accorded them was stern and unflinching. When they placed ladders against the walls and sent about thirty men scaling up, not a man returned. The defenders of the town killed more than twenty of the allies in the other phases of the fighting,[45] and in the end the aggressors withdrew.

First Unitarian expedition to al-Kharj, 1165/1751–2

Although there were still many enemies close at hand, the men guiding the affairs of the new Unitarian state were now ready to send their raiders out farther from home. They had already reached al-Zilfī and Tharmidā and Thādiq in the north and west; the next direction to turn towards was the south. Men from the south had

fervent supporters of it. The two towns are the only places of consequence in Arabia that have not been visited by Westerners; see Philby, *The Heart of Arabia*, II, 6, for the reasons given in 1918 by the present King of Saudi Arabia for avoiding these towns. The same work, II, 275–88, gives an excellent summary of what is known about the places.

Before the middle of the 11th century of the Hegira/roughly about 1640 AD, the Hazzānī family, known collectively as the Hazāzinah, who claim descent from Bakr b. Wā'il, took possession of al-Ḥarīq – Ibn Bishr, I, 42. They maintained themselves as rulers there until their revolt against Ibn Saud in 1912.

[45] The contingent from al-Ḥarīq suffered the heaviest losses, including one of the members of the Hazāzinah.

appeared among their foes in the assault on Ḍurmā. In the province of al-Kharj, beginning sixty miles or so south of al-Dir'īyah, the center of the ancient and flourishing Kingdom of al-Yamāmah had once stood. The elaborate old irrigation system there had fallen into decay and the great reservoirs of water for which al-Kharj is renowned were no longer being tapped, but the numerous oases of the district still harbored sturdy inhabitants who might be converted to the true religion. In 1165/1751–2 the new Amir of al-'Uyainah, Mishārī Ibn Mu'ammar, rode south as far as al-Dilam,[46] then as now the most important oasis in al-Kharj, where his raiders rounded up and made off with the flocks they found in pasture. As the raiders rode back with their booty the people of al-Kharj came after them in hot pursuit, overtaking them at 'Afjat al-Ḥā'ir.[47] Since the Unitarians did not exceed forty in number, while their pursuers were more than a hundred, Mishārī's men felt that death was at hand for them. Determined to sell their lives dearly, they dismounted and unslung their guns, thinking perhaps of God's word in the Koran, "God is with those who stand fast," or of the Arabic saying, "Standing fast [*ṣabr*] is like *ṣabir* [the extract of a certain tree], bitter to taste but afterwards sweeter than honey."[48] Much to their surprise the people of al-Kharj did not rush upon them; they remained at a distance, firing sporadically. Emboldened by this turn of events, the Unitarians dashed in to close quarters, killed about thirty, put the rest to flight, and captured many of their weapons and mounts.

Apostasy of Ḥuraimilā and war with the Unitarians, 1165–6/1752–3

Ḥuraimilā, the former home of the Shaikh and the place where he had first proclaimed his doctrines in Najd, had given moral and material support to the movement since its infancy, but there were some

[46] Or al-Dalam.

[47] Al-Ḥā'ir is at the point where Wadi al-Ausaṭ and Wadi al-Ḥā' empty into Wadi Ḥanīfah, more than twenty miles south of al-Riyāḍ. It is often called Ḥā'ir Subai', for it is a gathering-place for the Bedouins of the tribe of Subai'. For a good description of the town in 1918, see Philby, *The Heart of Arabia*, II, 10–14.

[48] Ibn Ghannām, II, 20.

among the chief men of the town who desired to break out of the Unitarian circle. Among them was the Shaikh's own brother, Sulaimān b. 'Abd al-Wahhāb. In or about 1165/1751–2 Sulaimān wrote a cordial letter to his brother in which he affirmed his loyalty to the Shaikh's principles and avowed that if there should be backsliding on the part of the people of Ḥuraimilā he would not linger in that town a single day. Nevertheless, rumors began to reach al-Dir'īyah to the effect that Sulaimān and others were casting doubts upon the validity of the Shaikh's teaching. The Shaikh sternly warned his brother in writing of the harsh consequences of such action and assured him that he would fail to attain his ends, but the warning went disregarded. The first overt act was the deposition and expulsion of the Amir, Muḥammad b. 'Abd Allāh b. Mubārak of the House of Aḥmad, who had become a faithful adherent to Unitarianism,[49] who departed with his sons and other leaders of the town who shared his views. Journeying to al-Dir'īyah, they informed the Shaikh and Muḥammad b. Su'ūd of what had happened. A few days later the exiled Amir received letters from the members of his house and party who had remained behind urging him to return and promising that he would regain his position in the town. When he consulted the Shaikh and Muḥammad b. Su'ūd, they told him that if he felt that he ought to go he should take with him a force from al-Dir'īyah. This he refused to do; he went with fewer than ten companions from among his own people. They arrived in Ḥuraimilā at night. Soon after dawn his enemies among the House of Rāshid discovered his presence; they came to the dwelling where he had alighted and killed him and all those with him, excepting Mubārak b. 'Adwān b. Mubārak,[50] who escaped to carry the tale to al-Dir'īyah.

The men who thus came into power in Ḥuraimilā realized that what they had done would mean war with the Unitarians, so they bent their efforts to prepare for the conflict. Among other things, they communicated with Mishārī Ibn Mu'ammar, the lord of al-'Uyainah, in the hope that he would join them, but he declined at this time to be won away from his allegiance to the Shaikh. The war

[49] Compare above, p. 62.

[50] The cousin of the murdered Amir? This event took place in Shawwāl 1165/August to September 1752 – Ibn Ghannām, II, 22.

broke out in 1166/November 1752 to October 1753, during the course of which year the people of Ḥuraimilā launched an attack on al-Dir'īyah which was answered by a series of raids commanded by 'Abd al-'Azīz b. Muḥammad b. Su'ūd, seconded by Mubārak b. 'Adwān of the Ḥuraimilā exiles. No conclusive decision was reached in the fighting, particularly since the attention of the Unitarians was diverted by the appearance of apostasy in another quarter.

Apostasy of Manfūḥah, 1166/1753

The town of Manfūḥah beside al-Riyāḍ had been an active ally of al-Dir'īyah for an even longer time than Ḥuraimilā. With Dahhām b. Dawwās of al-Riyāḍ the bitterest foe of the Unitarian movement, it was especially convenient to possess a stronghold lying hardly more than a stone's throw away from Dahhām's oasis. In the latter part of 1166/1753 the men in Manfūḥah who hated Unitarianism won control and banished the Imam of the worshippers as a sign that Unitarianism was no longer the official religion of the place. Many who held fast to their beliefs found it best to move away from Manfūḥah; seventy of them left in one day.

First submission of Dahhām of al-Riyāḍ, 1167/1753–4

The irony of events was nicely illustrated when the apostasy of Manfūḥah was followed almost immediately by the submission of Dahhām b. Dawwās. This bold baron, the last in whom one might have expected to find repentance, for reasons of his own in 1167/October 1753 to October 1754 requested the Shaikh to reckon him among the upholders of Islam as interpreted in al-Dir'īyah and applied for the appointment of an Imam to instruct the people of al-Riyāḍ in the code of conduct they were to follow. As a token of good faith Dahhām was required to send horses and weapons to al-Dir'īyah. The Imam delegated to reside with him was 'Īsā b. Qāsim,

[51] Ibn Ghannām, II, 23; Ibn Bishr, I, 28. 'Īsā b. Qāsim had been an early disciple of the Shaikh – Ibn Ghannām, II, 4.

one of the most learned and persuasive of the Unitarian doctors of law; during his tenure he succeeded in bringing many of the inhabitants of al-Riyāḍ to see the light.[51]

5

More Local Opposition in Najd

Unitarian convocation at al-Dir'īyah, 1167/1753–4

Notwithstanding the adhesion of Dahhām, the examples of apostasy in Ḥuraimilā and Manfūḥah were so disturbing that the Shaikh in 1167/1753–4 summoned to al-Dir'īyah deputations of his followers from all the towns where they were to be found. To the assemblage he preached and gave counsel; he warned of the dangers of apostasy, made a fresh exposition of the Unitarian doctrine, exhorted his listeners to trust completely in God, and promised them ultimate victory. The delegates went away greatly inspired and impressed.[1]

War of propaganda

During lulls in the fighting between the Unitarians and their opponents the war of propaganda continued. A man from al-'Uyainah named Sulaimān b. Khuwaiṭir went to Ḥuraimilā, which he had to do secretly because of the state of belligerency that existed. The Shaikh's brother Sulaimān b. 'Abd al-Wahhāb gave him a letter and instructed him to read it in the homes of al-'Uyainah and before gatherings of people there; it was contrived so as to cast doubts in the minds of those who had embraced the doctrines of the Shaikh. When the Shaikh learned what Sulaimān b. Khuwaiṭir had done, he ordered that he should be killed, and the order was carried out. Despite this stern measure, the propagandist of Ḥuraimilā found other men coming out of al-'Uyainah and returning there who were willing to bear his messages. To counteract the effect of this activity, the Shaikh composed a long letter addressed to the people of al-

[1] Ibn Ghannām, II, 23. Ibn Bishr does not mention this convocation.

'Uyainah in which he endeavored to dispel the doubts that had been raised by his brother.[2] The Shaikh's letter, which was learned and theological in tone, referred directly to Sulaimān's propaganda in two places:

> They believe that the Unitarians are in error and that the idol-worshipers possess the truth, as their Imam [Sulaimān] declared in the letter which you received prior to this one, written in his own hand. He states that between himself and you are the people of these lands, who are the best nation created for mankind, and so on. If, by describing them as the best nation created for mankind, he wishes them to be the judges, why does he impute to them the association of others with God?[3] …
>
> The people of Ḥuraimilā and those who are behind them proclaim that our religion is cursed and that the truth is what the majority of the people hold. They use the argument of numbers to show that their religion is good, yet what they do and say is the worst of apostasy. If they said that Unitarianism is truth and association of others with God is falsehood and if they did not set up idols in their towns, the unbelievers would oppose them.[4]

The Shaikh presented quotations drawn from the early traditions to show that those who opposed Islam would be many, while those who accepted it would be few. Other quotations justified the branding as unbelievers of those who associate others with God and who are guilty of other theological sins, and the making of war against the enemies of the true religion. Ibn Taimīyah was quoted as saying that the judgment against the apostate is worse than the judgment against the Jews and the Christians.[5] After saying that Ibn Taimīyah had denounced as an unbeliever anyone who recognised as lawful the eating of hashish, the Shaikh closed with the question, "Then

[2] Philby, *Arabia*, p. 17, is wrong in stating that this letter, which he refers to as "a long written sermon", was sent to Ḥuraimilā after its capture by the Wahhabi forces.

[3] Ibn Ghannām, II, 34. The full text of the letter is quoted in Ibn Ghannām, 24–52.

[4] Ibn Ghannām, II, 36.

[5] Ibn Ghannām, II, 51.

how is it with what we have to deal with, which is a thousand times worse than this?"[6]

Capture of Ḥuraimilā by the Unitarians, 1168/1755

In Jumādā I or II 1168/February or March 1755[7] eight hundred of the Unitarians, of whom only a score were horsemen, descended on Ḥuraimilā from the east. 'Abd al-'Azīz varied the usual tactics by posting two parties in ambush during the night instead of one; he himself led the first party into Sha'īb 'Aujā',[8] and Mubārak b. 'Adwān took two hundred men to al-Juzai'.[9] The onslaught began early in the morning as the farmers of the town were coming out to the fields. After the garrison made its sortie, 'Abd al-'Azīz appeared with the men in the first ambush and the struggle grew hot until the men in the second ambush rushed out and turned the tide. The people of Ḥuraimilā fled pellmell, about a hundred of them being killed,[10] with the rest escaping to the surrounding hills and valleys. The victors entered the town[11] and proclaimed an amnesty for all excepting the members of the House of Rāshid and their partners in apostasy and the killing of their ruler. The Shaikh's brother Sulaimān slipped out and made his way on foot to the district of Sudair. 'Abd al-'Azīz designated as the new Amir Mubārak b. 'Adwān, who had fought side by side with the Unitarians ever since he had been driven out of his native town, and showered him with precious articles from among the booty, besides giving him his choice of the confiscated houses and gardens. When the Shaikh in al-Dir'īyah heard of what had been done, he insisted that early Islamic custom required that the booty should become the property of the whole Moslem

[6] Ibn Ghannām, II, 52.

[7] Ibn Ghannām, II, 53, gives the earlier date; Ibn Bishr, I, 30, the later.

[8] Ibn Ghannām, II, 52. Ibn Bishr, I, 29, gives the name of the valley as 'Uwaijā'/Little 'Aujā'. The name means "winding".

[9] The Little Jaz' or Crossing of the Valley.

[10] The attackers were said to have lost only seven or eight men.

[11] Ibn Bishr, I, 29, says that after the battle 'Abd al-'Azīz turned about and headed for home, but Muḥammad b. 'Abd Allāh, the Amir of Ḍurmā, with about thirteen camelmen penetrated to the council chamber known as al-Ḥuwaish/the Little Courtyard in the center of the town and dismounted there. Word of this action was sent to 'Abd al-'Azīz, who hastened back and completed the occupation of the town.

community; 'Abd al-'Azīz had to bring it back to al-Dir'īyah, where the division took place.[12]

Strengthening of Unitarianism in Ḍurmā and the west, 1167–9/1753–6

In the meantime, all had not been peaceful in Ḍurmā, which was still the westernmost outpost of Unitarianism. The men of the House of Saif,[13] after they had killed the apostate Amir of the town, flaunted their importance and made themselves obnoxious both to the new Amir, Muḥammad b. 'Abd Allāh,[14] and to many of his subjects, especially the Unitarians among them. It was rumored that the House of Saif had dealings with the people of al-Ḥarīq who had given assistance in the earlier attempt to wipe out Unitarianism in the town, and a warning reached the Amir that this house was planning his assassination. All this was reported to the Shaikh and Muḥammad b. Su'ūd, along with the suggestion that banishment would not be a wise punishment for the House of Saif, since in exile they could continue to make trouble for the town. The Shaikh and the Amir told the men of Ḍurmā that they were ignorant of the state of affairs in their town; then they advised them to make sure that the House of Saif were enemies of the religion and, if they did make sure, to set

[12] Ibn Ghannām, II, 53; Ibn Bishr, I, 30.

[13] See above, p. 68.

[14] No indication is given as to when he had succeeded 'Abd Allāh b. 'Abd al-Raḥmān al-Raidī.

[15] In 1167/1753–4 at about the time the Shaikh was holding the convocation in al-Dir'īyah.

[16] Ibn Ghannām, II, 23–4, mentions this affair briefly; most of the details are taken from Ibn Bishr, I, 28.

[17] Ibn Ghannām, II, 52; Ibn Bishr, I, 29. The Battle of al-Ghufailī was fought in 1167/1754, according to Ibn Ghannām, or in late Muḥarram 1168/November 1754, according to Ibn Bishr. 'Abd al-Karīm was the second Amir of Uthaithīyā to be killed or captured in the fighting against the Unitarians within the space of about five years – see above, p. 67.

[18] The main road today is the one farther to the north through 'Afīf, al-Dawādimī, and Marrāh – *Masāfāt al-Ṭuruq*, pp. 10–11.

[19] The inhabitants of al-Quwai'īyah are mainly of the section of Banī Zaid of the tribe of Tamīm – Philby, *The Heart of Arabia*, I, 135. Tamīm is the tribe from which the Shaikh Muḥammad b. 'Abd al-Wahhāb was descended.

[20] Apparently of the tribe of Banī Khālid rather than of Tamīm – see Fu'ād Ḥamzah, *Qalb jazīrat al-'arab*, p. 147, and Philby, *The Heart of Arabia*, I, 137. *Jammāz* means "fleet, speedy."

upon them. Not long afterwards[15] Ṣaqr and his brothers of Āl Saif were set upon and killed in cold blood.[16]

Although a relentless fate had overtaken all those who had risen up to oppose the rule of Unitarianism in Ḍurmā, there was a man by the name of al-Ghufailī, the owner of a fort in the oasis, who refused to heed the lessons of the past. With the plan in mind of organising another uprising against the Unitarians, he requested assistance from Ibrāhīm b. Sulaimān al-'Anqarī, the Amir of Tharmidā and the old enemy of al-Dir'īyah. Ibrāhīm sent him horsemen and camelmen from Tharmidā and the neighboring towns of Marrāh and Uthaithīyā with thirty-five mounts that carried extra riders. Muḥammad b. 'Abd Allāh, the loyal Amir of Ḍurmā, discovered what was under way and notified Muḥammad b. Su'ūd, who called the people of his town and of al-'Uyainah to the defense of their faith. With this support the Amir of Ḍurmā hastened home to deal with the threat. When he drew near the town he hid his men in a field of corn, where they waited until they heard the sound of the hoofbeats of horses coming through the night. Rushing out, they broke the forces from the north and made them scatter, killing sixty or seventy of them and capturing others, including 'Abd al-Karīm b. Zāmil, the Amir of Uthaithīyā. Only the horsemen and their extra riders escaped.[17]

In 1169/October 1755 to September 1756 the Unitarian movement spread to the west beyond the oasis of Ḍurmā. Some of the chief men of the settlement of al-Quwai'īyah, a group of palm groves defended by castles in a valley lying athwart one of the pilgrim roads from Najd to Mecca,[18] came as a delegation to offer submission to the Shaikh and Muḥammad b. Su'ūd.[19] Among the leaders of the delegation was Nāṣir b. Jammāz al-'Arīfī.[20]

6

Al-Riyāḍ, Najd and al-Aḥsā'
1168–77/1754–64

Violation of the compact by Dahhām of al-Riyāḍ, 1168–70/1754–57

Only a year or so after Dahhām b. Dawwās of al-Riyāḍ had submitted and accepted the rule of Islam in his domain he violated the compact he had made with the Shaikh by leaguing himself with Muḥammad b. Fāris, the ruler of the apostate town of Manfūḥah, and directing a raid against Abā al-Kibāsh.[1] When the Unitarians in Manfūḥah and al-Riyāḍ, whose numbers had increased through the efforts of the teacher 'Īsā b. Qāsim, saw what Dahhām was now about, many of them decided to seek safety by migrating to al-Dir'īyah. Among them were men of al-Riyāḍ who had originally moved from there to Manfūḥah out of fear of the tyranny of Dahhām in earlier days.[2]

Having begun by allying himself with Ibn Fāris of Manfūḥah, Dahhām set about rallying to his standard all the enemies of the Shaikh's cause in the north and northwest. In Dhū al-Qa'dah 1168/August to September 1755 contingents from al-Riyāḍ and Manfūḥah joined with others from al-Washm, commanded by Ibrāhīm b. Sulaimān al-'Anqarī of Tharmidā, from Sudair, and from Thādiq to attack the town of Ḥuraimilā, newly captured by the Unitarians. Men who had fled from there at the time of its fall joined

[1] The House of Yaḥyā, the ruling family in Abā al-Kibāsh, were related to the ruling families of al-Dir'īyah and Ḍurmā – Ibn Bishr, II, 6, 10. It is not stated whether they had accepted the Unitarianism of the Shaikh at this time or not, but the fact that they were singled out for attack by Dahhām indicates that they had. The raid took place in 1168/1754–5.

[2] Ibn Ghannām, II, 54, gives a long list of names of emigrants from al-Riyāḍ and from Manfūḥah.

the attackers in the hope of regaining their old positions. Dahhām's force alighted at the settlement of al-Ḥisyān in the upper reaches of the oasis while the majority of the guards were asleep and occupied the houses, gardens, and palm groves. Mubārak b. 'Adwān, the new Amir of Ḥuraimilā, came out to pry them loose from their foothold in the morning.[3] The main strength of the attackers was dispersed, but some of their fighting men were trapped in the houses of al-Ḥisyān, where they held out for five days. In the end the people of Ḥuraimilā scaled the walls and there was widespread slaughter. All of the exiles of the town who were caught were cut down on the spot. Dahhām himself had another narrow escape from the Unitarians, getting away in the nick of time. Ten of the men of Ḥarmah[4] surrendered after having been granted a guarantee of safe-conduct by Mubārak, and after their surrender six of them were killed. When the report of this flagrant breach of the rules of Moslem warfare reached the Shaikh and Muḥammad b. Su'ūd, they became very angry with Mubārak.[5]

The failure at Ḥuraimilā did nothing to diminish Dahhām's energy, for the following year, 1169/October 1755 to September 1756, he was off to Sudair and al-Washm in an effort to keep the opposition alive. 'Abd al-'Azīz b. Muḥammad b. Su'ūd chose this opportunity for a raid on Manfūḥah. In the palm grove of al-Ṣubaikhah he and his men rounded up livestock, camels, cattle, and donkeys. After beating off a sortie by the men of Manfūḥah and another by the men of al-Riyāḍ, 'Abd al-'Azīz hurried back to al-Dir'īyah and went on to the neighborhood of Ḍurmā, hoping to waylay Dahhām as he traveled homewards from al-Washm. Adept by this time at eluding the Unitarians just as their fingers were about to close on his neck, Dahhām avoided the ambush and fled at full speed for al-Riyāḍ, casting away all his heavy equipment and leaving

[3] Ibn Bishr, I, 30, says that Mubārak asked for and got reinforcements from al-Dir'īyah.

[4] A town lying just to the north of al-Majma'ah in the district of Sudair.

[5] Ibn Bishr does not mention this incident, which is described in Ibn Ghannām, II, 55. The dead were said to have numbered sixty from among the attackers and eighteen from among the people of Ḥuraimilā. The battle was known as the Battle of the House, for a large number of the besieged were in a house belonging to a certain Ibn Nāṣir. Among those who got away under cover of darkness during the siege was Sārī b. Yaḥyā, the Amir of Thādiq – Ibn Bishr, I, 30.

behind the mounts that could not maintain the pace. 'Abd al-'Azīz and his men had to be satisfied with picking up the equipment and bringing in the beasts. When the booty had all been turned in, 'Abd al-'Azīz requested permission from the raiders, who ordinarily would have received shares of it, to distribute it all among the Unitarian immigrants who had recently settled in al-Dir'īyah, and they acquiesced in this act of charity towards their Moslem brothers.[6]

Pursuing their policy of not relaxing the pressure on Dahhām, the Unitarians went down the next year, 1170/September 1756 to September 1757, to raid Manfūḥah again. In one of the palm groves they set to work tearing down a barrier called al-Rashā[7] built for protection against the flash floods that periodically rush down the valley. While they were engaged in their work of destruction, Dahhām, who had been informed of what was going on, came up with the men of al-Riyāḍ. In the confusion of the fighting Dahhām became engaged with one of his own men; each struck the other so hard that both fell from their horses to the ground. The Unitarians, however, were so intent on getting away that they failed to take advantage of the mishap that had befallen Dahhām.[8]

Attack on the Unitarians in Shaqrā', 1170/1756–7

The town of Shaqrā' in the district of al-Washm had gone over to the Unitarian side[9] and was becoming a power in its region. The people of al-Washm, many of whom had fought for a long time

[6] The events of this year are mentioned cursorily in Ibn Bishr, I, 31; Ibn Ghannām, II, 56, sets them forth in detail.

[7] Or al-Rishā.

[8] Here again Ibn Ghannām, II, 56–7, gives more information than Ibn Bishr, I, 33.

[9] Ibn Ghannām, II, 53, says that the people of Shaqrā' were split up into factions until 1168/1754–5, when they settled their differences and all agreed to support the cause of Unitarianism. Ibn Bishr, I, 33, on the other hand, says that they were early adherents of the faith, being the first to swear allegiance to the Shaikh and Muḥammad b. Su'ūd. The two statements may perhaps be reconciled if Ibn Bishr's is taken to refer to only a part of the people of the town. In any event, Shaqrā' remained a stronghold of Wahhabism from this time on, though the puritan religion did not sour its people, who are reckoned among the most agreeable of the Najdis.

For a description of the town at the time of the Egyptian invasion, see Félix Mengin, *Histoire de l'Égypte*, II, 114.

against the spreading influence of al-Dir'īyah, resented the rise of Shaqrā' and the way in which it served as an asylum for the Unitarian religious men and raiders who could not reach the safety of the Shaikh's own town. In 1170/1756–7 the people of al-Washm summoned the people of Sudair and Munaikh to join them in an attempt to crush the city they feared. The attackers selected the village of al-Qarā'in[10] close by Shaqrā' as the base for their operations. Muḥammad b. Su'ūd in al-Dir'īyah ordered his son 'Abd al-'Azīz to go to the aid of the threatened town. The Unitarians coordinated a sortie from the town with the arrival of the troops from al-Dir'īyah so successfully that they completely shattered the enemy, who might have been annihilated if they had not been able to fall back on their base at al-Qarā'in. The victors blockaded the remnants of the vanquished there for about three weeks until they got away by night and joined Ibn Suwaiṭ of the Ẓafīr, the anti-Unitarian Bedouins.

A Year of Unitarian raids and brushes with the Bedouins, 1170/1756–7

The year 1170 had already seen the Battle of al-Rashā at Manfūḥah and the Battle of al-Qarā'in near Shaqrā'. 'Abd al-'Azīz had been near the Ẓafīr but had not come to grips with them. Not long afterwards he heard that a band of the tribe of Subai' under Ibn Fā'iz al-Mulaiḥī[11] was hunting down Unitarian stragglers; 'Abd al-'Azīz prepared an ambush for them in the region known as al-Ḥisā[12] near Ḥuraimilā, and dispersed the band, killing many of them and taking Ibn Fā'iz prisoner. Ibn Fā'iz purchased his freedom for five hundred *aḥmars*.[13]

[10] Houses are said to be *qarā'in* when they face each other.

[11] The tribe of Subai' in earlier days had lived in the west, where it gave its name to Wadi Subai', in which a section of the tribe is still to be found. Another section was driven eastwards into central Najd; one of its main gathering-places there is the town of al-Ḥā'ir south of al-Riyāḍ. This tribe was destined to play a prominent part in the history of the Wahhabi movement. On Subai' see Fu'ād Ḥamzah, *Qalb jazīrat al-'arab*, p. 155, and Philby, *The Heart of Arabia*, I, 13–14.

One of the predecessors of this Ibn Fā'iz was apparently an ally of Zaid b. Mirkhān, the lord of al-Dir'īyah about thirty years before this time, for Muḥammad Ibn Mu'ammar (Khirfāsh) of al-'Uyainah plotted against and killed the two of them – Ibn Bishr, I, 234.

Although other enemies were about, Dahhām was not neglected. Assembling the full forces of the Unitarians, 'Abd al-'Azīz rode down for the second raid of the year in the region of al-Riyāḍ and Manfūḥah. An ambush was laid at night not far from the Western Gate[14] of al-Riyāḍ, and in the morning the men in ambush confounded the people of the town who had come out to drive the raiders away. Hurling curses at their enemies, the Unitarians drove them back to the gate, where they scrambled over each other and broke their spears in their efforts to get through the passage that was too narrow for them.[15]

'Abd al-'Azīz followed this raid up with another one, during which he alighted at al-Bunayyah[16] and destroyed all the fields of al-Shamsīyah.[17]

Muḥammad b. 'Abd Allāh, the loyal Amir of Ḍurmā, led another Unitarian expedition into the province of al-Washm. On the way he encountered a raiding party of the Ṣumdah,[18] one of the two principal branches of the Ẓafīr, and, finding that he was heavily outnumbered, decided to turn and flee. Some of the Unitarians were captured and then set free upon payment of a ransom.

The first raid into al-Washm having been fruitless, 'Abd al-'Azīz himself led another there, descending upon the town of Ushaiqir.[19]

[12] See above, p. 68.

[13] Ibn Ghannām, II, 58; Ibn Bishr, I, 34. The *aḥmar*, literally "red", was a gold coin in common circulation at that time, the value of which is uncertain. Although both the chroniclers use the term *aḥmar* in this instance, Ibn Ghannām in other places uses instead of it *zar* or *zarr* (Persian for "gold") – see below, pp. 93, 104 n. 110, 105.

[14] *Al-Bāb al-Qiblī*. The term *qiblī*, coming from *qiblah*/"the direction of Mecca", has different meanings depending upon where one is. In Egypt it means "south"; in eastern and central Arabia, "west".

[15] Ibn Ghannām, II, 58.

[16] See above, p. 63

[17] Al-Shamsīyah, the open ground to the north of the walled city, is now the royal quarter of al-Riyāḍ; the King's great palace al-Murabba' and many palaces belonging to the Princes stand there.

[18] Or the Ṣamadah. See Fu'ād Ḥamzah, *Qalb jazīrat al-'arab*, pp. 168–9. The name is pronounced by the Bedouins *aṣmudah*. The root *ṣamada* means "to aim at, to strike"; *ṣamadah* could be the plural of the active participle. *Ṣumdah* means "a high, firm rock"; *ṣamad*, "a man who neither hungers nor thirsts in battle".

[19] Ushaiqir is the diminutive of *ashqar*/"red", of which *shaqrā'* is the feminine form (compare the name of the town Shaqrā').

A skirmish took place at the end of which the defenders retired, having suffered slight losses.

Next 'Abd al-'Azīz went beyond al-Washm to throw the weight of his forces against the important center of Thādiq in the district of al-Maḥmal.[20] The people of this place had long opposed the Unitarians and had taken part in campaigns against them, but outside of a minor raid conducted by Ibn Mu'ammar in 1161/1748[21] they had escaped retaliation in their home territory. This time 'Abd al-'Azīz and his men set about cutting down the palm trees of Thādiq to teach the residents that the lot of those who spurned God's law was a harsh one.[22] Thus the Unitarians constrained the people of Thādiq to accept Islam as preached by the Shaikh and to offer allegiance to its temporal authorities. A delegation accompanied 'Abd al-'Azīz to al-Dir'īyah to inform the Shaikh of their change of heart. He appointed a new Amir to rule their home, Dakhīl b. 'Abd Allāh b. Suwailim,[23] and assigned the Shaikh Aḥmad b. Suwailim[24] to instruct the people in the fundamentals of the faith they were henceforth to follow.

To complete the swing through the northern regions of defiance during the year, 'Abd al-'Azīz, who had already penetrated into the districts of al-Washm and al-Maḥmal, now marched his campaigners into Sudair. His first target was Jalājil,[25] where he defeated the men of the garrison at the place called al-'Umairī north of the town and drove them in disorder back within their gates. The Unitarians plundered the houses that stood outside the walls. Moving on, 'Abd

[20] It is not clear whether 'Abd al-'Azīz went straight on from Ushaiqir or whether he returned home before heading for al-Maḥmal. In view of the number of campaigns carried out during this year, it is likely that he did not return home.

[21] See above, p. 65.

[22] Ibn Ghannām, II, 59.

[23] Son of the man in whose home the Shaikh was received when he first entered al-Dir'īyah – see above, p. 49.

[24] A pupil of the Shaikh before he came to al-Dir'īyah and one of his earliest supporters in that town – see above, pp. 44, 49.

[25] The origin of this peculiar placename, which means "small ornamental bells" such as those worn by women, camels and horses, is unknown. The name is also borne by a family in Najd.

[26] Ibn Ghannām, II, 59, calls them *maṭāwi'ah*; Ibn Bishr, I, 35, *quḍāh*. Ibn Bishr gives their full names.

al-'Azīz summoned to him the religious judges[26] of the towns of al-Rauḍah, al-Dākhilah, and al-Ḥauṭah,[27] in order that they should accompany him back to al-Dir'īyah and study under the Shaikh there. He also took with him two of the chief men of the town of al-'Audah,[28] 'Uthmān b. Sa'dūn and Manṣūr Ibn Ḥammād, for fear that they might incite the people to apostasy if left at home.[29] With all these representatives of Sudair in his train 'Abd al-'Azīz marched south, bringing to a close the military activity in the north for the year.

Shortly after the expedition reached al-Dir'īyah the Amir of al-'Audah, 'Abd Allāh b. Sulṭān, appeared to request the release of his two fellow townsmen,[30] and for his sake they were allowed to go home. But an Arab proverb says, "If you fatten your dog he will eat you", and the two who had been released soon turned on their benefactor and killed him, Ibn Sa'dūn becoming the Amir in his stead. As Amir of al-'Audah Ibn Sa'dūn then did exactly what 'Abd al-'Azīz had been afraid of: he declared that the town had forsaken the cause of the Shaikh, a stand that he was to maintain for ten years to come.

The tireless 'Abd al-'Azīz had one more expedition to make before the year had run its course. His absence in the north had given Dahhām at al-Riyāḍ a certain respite, but 'Abd al-'Azīz knew that it was Dahhām's custom each year to go over to Manfūḥah to offer holiday greetings to its ruler, Ibn Zāmil, at the time of the Feast of Sacrifice,[31] and he planned to surprise his archenemy as he made his way between the two towns. 'Abd al-'Azīz placed his men in position without their being detected, but while they were waiting a traveler discovered them and they had to leave without catching Dahhām.

[27] Not to be confused with the better known town of the same name in Wadi al-Far' below al-Kharj.

[28] Not to be confused with the place of the same name in the oasis of al-Dir'īyah.

[29] This would suggest that al-'Audah was one place in Sudair that had already accepted Unitarianism.

[30] Ibn Ghannām, II, 59–60, says that he made the request of 'Abd al-'Azīz; Ibn Bishr, I, 35, says it was of the Shaikh and Muḥammad b. Su'ūd.

[31] 10 Dhū al-Ḥijjah, which this year, 1170, fell at the end of August 1757.

[32] The Valley of the Camel.

Operations in the north and west, 1171/1757–8

In 1171/September 1757 to September 1758 'Abd al-'Azīz again took the warpath leading to Tharmidā in al-Washm. He and his men alighted at night in Wadi al-Jamal[32] not far from the town. A man of the garrison of Tharmidā observed their movements, so that the would-be surprisers were themselves surprised. The Unitarians entered a walled enclosure in a palm grove outside the town, concealed themselves behind the trees, and cut a breach in the wall to go out through at the proper time. The men of the garrison they were intending to trap now placed themselves in position just outside the breach and cut the Unitarians down as they issued out one by one until at last the pile of corpses outside darkened the breach and those left inside discovered what had happened. In a body they rushed out by another exit and came to blows with the garrison. A son of Ibrāhīm b. Sulaimān, the Amir of Tharmidā, fell on the field, but the Unitarians could not boast of a great victory.[33]

Next it was the turn of Mubārak b. 'Adwān, the Amir of Ḥuraimilā, to go raiding.[34] He brought back as a prisoner a certain 'Abd Allāh b. Sulaimān,[35] whom he later allowed to go free upon payment of a moderate sum. His failure to consult the Shaikh and Muḥammad b. Su'ūd before doing this made them angry with him for the second time.

From al-Washm 'Abd al-'Azīz turned his attention to Sudair. The people of the towns of al-Ḥauṭah and al-Janūbīyah in that district had sent word to Muḥammad b. Su'ūd that they desired to embrace the beliefs of the Unitarians, as a result of which Muḥammad's son journeyed thither with his fighting men, brushed aside the resistance offered by the anti-Unitarians of Sudair after his arrival, and nominated an Amir and an Imam for each of the towns. After this business

[33] Ibn Ghannām, II, 60, says that this battle was called the Battle of the Breach; Ibn Bishr, I, 40, says that it was the Battle of al-Buṭaiḥā'/the Little Baṭḥā'. Ibn Ghannām reports the losses of the Unitarians as about twenty; Ibn Bishr, as about thirty. 'Abd al-Muḥsin was the son of Ibrāhīm who fell.

[34] Ibn Ghannām, II, 61, does not state in what direction he went. It is possible that a portion of the text has been omitted by the copyist. Ibn Bishr is silent regarding this raid.

[35] Possibly a member of the ruling house of Tharmidā.

[36] 'Abd al-'Azīz may or may not have returned home in the meantime.

had been attended to,[36] 'Abd al-'Azīz swooped down on Jalājil and made off with beasts from the flocks belonging to its inhabitants. When men of Jalājil overtook him, he forced them to scurry back to their homes.

Operations against al-Riyāḍ, 1171/1757–8

A minor raid in the early part of 1171/1757–8 during which some of the fields of Manfūḥah were ruined was followed in Ramaḍān/ May to June 1758 by a more vigorous attack under the command of 'Abd al-'Azīz on al-Riyāḍ itself. The Unitarians reached Umm al-'Aṣāfir[37] at night and prepared their ambush in a spot called al-Qubbah.[38] The encounter took place on the morrow. Among those killed on the defending side was Turkī b. Dawwās;[39] the Unitarians lost only one of their number.

'Abd al-'Azīz came down soon again to fight the Second Battle of al-Bunayyah.[40] On this occasion all the shooting was done at long range, so that the casualties were not serious. 'Abd al-'Azīz, realising perhaps that new measures were required if the prolonged resistance put up by Dahhām was ever to be beaten down, now undertook an enterprise that was to become standard practice in Unitarian warfare in the years to follow. Withdrawing to al-Bāṭin, the low-lying channel of Wadi Ḥanīfah to the west of the oasis of al-Riyāḍ, he built a fort in a place called al-Ghazawānah[41] to serve as a permanent threat on the flank of his enemy. The construction was completed in seven days, and then 'Abd al-'Azīz gave permission to all of his footsoldiers who so desired to return to their hearth-sides, while he himself lingered on for a few days with his mounted troops.[42]

[37] The Mother of (i.e. the Place of) the Little Birds.

[38] The Dome.

[39] Apparently a brother of Dahhām.

[40] For the First Battle, see above, pp. 63–4.

[41] The name is given so in Ibn Bishr, I, 40; Ibn Ghannām, II, 62, has it as al-Ghadhawānah.

[42] It is not stated whether 'Abd al-'Azīz established a garrison in the new outpost on this occasion, though such was usually done in later times when the Unitarians erected forts of this kind.

Deposition of the Amir of Ḥuraimilā, 1171/1757–8

As the contingent from Ḥuraimilā passed through al-Dir'īyah on the way home after the Second Battle of al-Bunayyah, the Shaikh and Muḥammad b. Su'ūd summoned Mubārak b. 'Adwān in to their presence. Twice in the recent past he had angered them by his actions, and it was reported that at other times he had failed to execute orders received from them. They informed him that he could have his choice of the palm groves of Ḥuraimilā, but that from this day on he would abide with them in al-Dir'īyah, where he would be treated with respect and would be granted a fixed income.[43] Mubārak[44] pretended to accept the arrangement outlined; then when the Ḥuraimilā contingent under his newly designated successor, Aḥmad b. Nāṣir b. 'Adwān, was ready to resume its course homewards, he asked permission of the Shaikh to go and give greetings to his sister in Umm Ṣawī,[45] a palm grove belonging to his brother-in-law in the channel of the valley above al-'Uyainah. Upon reaching Umm Ṣawī, Mubārak gathered together the horsemen of the place and rode off with them for Ḥuraimilā, hoping to outstrip his successor, though he did not let his companions know what the game was. In Ḥuraimilā the troops stationed in the citadel, who must have had word of the deposition of Mubārak, locked themselves in as soon as they saw him and refused him entrance. Mubārak had a drum sounded in the council chamber of the town known as al-Ḥuwaish to rally his kinsmen and henchmen, but when they saw the citadel shut against him, most of them deserted him out of fear of the vengeance that would come from al-Dir'īyah. There was nothing to do but flee the town; with him went the few whose closeness to him made their remaining unsafe.[46] Mubārak sought refuge in the nearby

[43] *Kharāj.*

[44] Ibn Ghannām, II, 62, after having referred to him on previous pages as Mubārak, here begins to use the diminutive form of his name, Mubairīk. The diminutive in Arabic may express either affection or contempt.

[45] Mother of (i.e. Place of) Dried-up Palm Trees.

[46] Among them was the Qadi, a descendant of the tribe of Tamīm, the tribe of the Shaikh. Ibn Bishr, I, 41, says that he went to Raghbah, where the Amir 'Alī al-Juraisī seized him and put him to death. A footnote by the editor, however, quotes a source that states that he got away to the Yemen, where he told the people he met that he had been forced to

district of Sudair. In the meantime his attempt to seize Ḥuraimilā had greatly disturbed the Unitarians in al-Dir'īyah. The Shaikh and Muḥammad b. Su'ūd sent for 'Abd al-'Azīz immediately.[47] 'Abd al-'Azīz informed his assembled fighting men that Mubārak had become a rebel and asked them all to renew the oath of allegiance in which they swore to follow loyally and to give up their lives if need be for their religion. Passing through al-Dir'īyah, 'Abd al-'Azīz was hurrying on towards al-Na'mīyah in the valley when he received word of Mubārak's flight, whereupon he turned around and carried the good news back to his father and the Shaikh. Later 'Abd al-'Azīz marched to Ḥuraimilā to straighten out its affairs and calm the troubled spirits of the people.

Mubārak at his refuge in al-Majma'ah in Sudair had not yet given way to despair. Knowing that anti-Unitarian feeling still ran high in Sudair and al-Washm, he negotiated with various rulers for the formation of a common front that would seek to recover Ḥuraimilā: with his host Aḥmad b. 'Uthmān, lord of al-Majma'ah; the House of Mudlij in nearby Ḥarmah; Ibrāhīm b. Sulaimān al-'Anqarī of Tharmidā; and others in both Sudair and al-Washm.[48] They sent detachments to aid him in his purpose, but their numbers were not impressive, for when he reached the water of al-Fuqair[49] on the road to Ḥuraimilā he and his men paused for a time, hesitating over whether they should press on. When they heard that 'Abd al-'Azīz was at Ḥuraimilā, they decided to direct their attack against Raghbah instead. There they besieged the Amir, 'Alī al-Juraisī, in his castle and cut down palm trees in the grove called al-Jau. A strong party in the town opposed to the Amir, the 'Uraināt and their supporters, remained in their homes in the settlement of al-Ḥazm,[50] a settlement in the oasis separate from that occupied by al-Juraisī. As 'Abd al-

leave his home because the Shaikh Muḥammad b. 'Abd al-Wahhāb branded as unbelievers those who prayed to saints, as well as anyone who doubted that such were believers, and because the Shaikh waged war against those who opposed him.

[47] He was probably still at the new fort in Wadi Ḥanīfah.

[48] Shaqrā' was one town that held aloof when many others in al-Washm lent a kindly ear to Mubārak's appeal.

[49] Near the town of Raghbah. The name probably comes from *faqara*/"to dig". The hole in which a date palm is planted is called a *faqīr*; *fuqair* would be the diminutive of this.

[50] A *ḥazm* is high ground, a ridge, or a hill.

'Azīz came marching from Ḥuraimilā to give succor to the besieged Amir of Raghbah, the men who had joined Mubārak melted away to their homes and Mubārak himself returned to al-Majma'ah. 'Abd al-'Azīz destroyed the dwelling places of the people of al-Ḥazm, cut down their palm trees, and gave title to the grove to al-Juraisī, all this as punishment for the failure of these people to stand by their lawful ruler when he was in dire straits.[51]

Invasion of Najd from al-Aḥsā', 1172/1758–9

In 1166/1752–3 the Mahāshīr, one of the sections of the tribe of Banī Khālid,[52] rose up against the chief of their tribe, Sulaimān b. Muḥammad of the House of Ḥumaid,[53] the lord of al-Aḥsā' who had tried to rid Najd of the Shaikh Muḥammad b. 'Abd al-Wahhāb a few years earlier. Unable to withstand the rebels, Sulaimān fled to al-Kharj, where he died in the same year. The rule over Banī Khālid and the province of al-Aḥsā' then reverted to the line of Sa'dūn b. Muhammad,[54] Sulaimān's brother, in the person of his grandson 'Urai'ir b. Dujain,[55] who commenced a reign that was to last for over a score of years.

Little is known of 'Urai'ir's career before 1171/1757–8, but it seems that he, unlike his great-uncle, was not greatly concerned at first over the existence of the Unitarian community in neighboring Najd. In 1171 his interest was aroused for reasons not specified by the chroniclers of the time, and word came to al-Dir'īyah that he had declared his intention of marching on Najd to strike a blow at the new and expanding religious brotherhood. The Shaikh and Muḥammad b. Su'ūd set their people to work making ready to ward off the blow, and in the following year, 1172/September 1758 to August 1759, the preparations were intensified. Orders went out to all the Unitarian towns to throw up defense works, and in al-Dir'īyah

[51] The story of Mubārak b. 'Adwān is given by Ibn Ghannām, II, 62–3, and in greater detail by Ibn Bishr, I, 41–2.

[52] The Mahāshīr of Banī Khālid are said to trace their descent back to the tribe of Banī Hājir – Fu'ād Ḥamzah, *Qalb jazīrat al-'arab*, p. 7, n. 2.

[53] See above, p. 46.

[54] See above, pp. 27–8. [See Table, p. 254.]

[55] 'Urai'ir is the diminutive of *'ar'ar*, the name of a desert plant.

'Abd al-'Azīz superintended the building of two walls joined together with towers in order to forestall the scaling of the walls by the enemy.

'Urai'ir mobilized his own forces from the tribe of Banī Khālid and the people of al-Aḥsā' and made common cause with the Najdis of Sudair, Munaikh, al-Washm, al-Maḥmal, al-Riyāḍ, and al-Kharj who were veterans of the warfare against the Unitarians. The size of the array made an impression in Najd, and many whose loyalty to the Shaikh was only lukewarm went over to what they expected would be the winning side.

Among those from Sudair who joined 'Urai'ir was Mubārak b. 'Adwān, who sought to make capital of this opportunity to regain his old position. With the detachments from Sudair, al-Washm and al-Maḥmal Mubārak laid siege to Ḥuraimilā for a period of three days. Discovering that he was not strong enough to break in, Mubārak asked 'Urai'ir to send him reinforcements, and 'Urai'ir responded by supporting him with Āl 'Ubaid Allāh of Banī Khālid and Bedouins from the tribe of 'Anazah under the command of Ibn Hadhdhāl.[56] Mubārak returned to the attack, but he failed to make much progress, and at last a determined sortie of the defenders drove him and his men out of their camp, where they left a large part of their gear behind.

After the defeat of Mubārak at Ḥuraimilā, 'Urai'ir, who had not yet thrown his weight into the fray, brought up his own troops and the men from al-Riyāḍ[57] and al-Kharj and joined forces with Mubārak. The point selected for their descent on Wadi Ḥanīfah was the town of al-Jubailah, which could not have been a place of much importance, since there is no mention of it in the annals of the time after the destruction of the tomb there by the Shaikh Muḥammad b. 'Abd al-Wahhāb.[58] Nevertheless, al-Jubailah was prepared to resist the host that had cast fear into many hearts, and Unitarians came up from al-Dir'īyah to assist in the defense. 'Urai'ir and Mubārak, after a fruitless siege of some days, launched a final charge against the

[56] These Bedouins were probably of the 'Amārāt, a branch of 'Anazah of whom Ibn Hadhdhāl is the chief.

[57] It is not stated whether Dahhām b. Dawwās accompanied this detachment or not.

[58] See above, p. 45.

citadel, but the effort came to naught. While the charge was under way fresh Unitarian troops fell upon the rear of the allies and scattered them irrevocably.

The people of Thādiq and the rest of the district of al-Maḥmal now saw cause to regret their participation in 'Urai'ir's undertaking. They thus sent delegates to the Shaikh and Muḥammad b. Su'ūd to ask forgiveness and proffer allegiance to Unitarian principles. Forgiveness was granted and allegiance was accepted on condition that a tax of half the produce of the fields and a share of the date crop should be paid.[59] The rulers of al-Dir'īyah appointed Sārī b. Yaḥyā b. 'Abd Allāh b. Suwailim[60] as Amir of al-Maḥmal.

With the Unitarians now holding al-Maḥmal and Shaqrā' in al-Washm, 'Abd al-'Azīz set out to wear down the opposition remaining in the northwest. Outside the town of al-Qaṣab in al-Washm he prepared a successful ambush that weakened the will of the defenders to withstand a siege, so that it was not long before they capitulated and embraced Unitarianism. 'Abd al-'Azīz spared their palm groves upon payment of the sum of three hundred *aḥmar*s.

Expeditions to al-Kharj and al-Washm, 1173/1759–60

Preoccupations in the north and in the vicinity of al-Riyāḍ had prevented the Unitarians from directing any attacks against al-Kharj for eight years, though the presence of men from al-Kharj in 'Urai'ir's company was evidence that the Shaikh's teachings were still unpopular in the south. With the situation stabler in the north following the rout of 'Urai'ir, 'Abd al-'Azīz, who had not yet led an expedition to al-Kharj in person, was free for such an undertaking. After a quick raid against al-Majma'ah in Sudair early in 1173/August 1759 to August 1760 in which the main work proved to be the hamstringing of livestock, 'Abd al-'Azīz pressed on south all the way to al-Dilam, where he entered the oasis at night. Eight of the residents fell during the Unitarian onslaught, and some of the shops were plundered of their goods. On the homeward journey, 'Abd al-'Azīz

[59] Ibn Ghannām, II, 65; Ibn Bishr, I, 42.

[60] Probably the same Sārī b. Yaḥyā who is mentioned as having been Amir of Thādiq in 1168/1755 – see above, p. 80, n. 5.

attacked and killed some of the people of Na'jān, just to the north of al-Dilam.

Some days after the return from al-Kharj to al-Dir'īyah 'Abd al-'Azīz was in the saddle again, riding against Tharmidā, one of the prime centers of opposition in al-Washm. The common sequence of an ambush, a sortie, and the sudden appearance of those who had been crouching out of sight went off according to schedule, but the losses on both sides were of no moment. Upon the withdrawal from Tharmidā 'Abd al-'Azīz gave his infantry leave to disperse to their homes while he and the cavalry made a dash down to al-Kharj. Warning of their approach had preceded them to al-Dilam, and they found the defenders on guard against the attack. Nevertheless, the raiders drove the defenders back into their houses and took away many of their camels.

The second raid into al-Washm followed hard after the second raid into al-Kharj. The target was Ushaiqir, another center of opposition, and the springing of the ambush resulted in the killing of about twenty of the enemies of the cause.

The pattern of raids against hostile towns was varied by a morning attack on Āl 'Askar of the Bedouin tribe of the Ẓafīr at the watering place of al-Tharmānīyah[61] in the neighborhood of Raghbah in al-Maḥmal. The Unitarians killed Fauzān Āl Dhabīḥah, the chief of this band of Āl 'Askar, and about ten of his men, and captured many of their camels.

In the third and final raid of the year into al-Washm 'Abd al-'Azīz by chance encountered on the way a party of fifteen men from Tharmidā, who fled for refuge to the town of al-Ḥarīq[62] under the hill near al-Qaṣab. 'Abd al-'Azīz demanded from the rulers of the town, members of the House of Yūsuf, that they hand over the men, but they replied that it would be base conduct for them to do so. When the Unitarians made ready to take the men by force, their protectors offered to ransom them for fifteen hundred *aḥmars*[63] and 'Abd al-'Azīz accepted.

[61] The *tharmān* is a leafless tree containing much sap.

[62] Not to be confused with al-Ḥarīq in Wadi al-Far' to the south.

[63] Ibn Ghannām, II, 67, uses *zar* or *zarr*, another name for the coin called *aḥmar* – see above, p. 83, n. 13.

Deposition of the Amir of al-'Uyainah, 1173/1759–60

While 'Abd al-'Azīz was ranging far afield with the warriors of the faith, his father and the Shaikh were busy mending fences closer at home. Mishārī b. Ibrāhīm Ibn Mu'ammar had been appointed Amir of al-'Uyainah about ten years earlier by the Shaikh against the advice and wishes of many of the people of the town.[64] In the beginning he had been a grateful and active vassal, and he had had the honor of leading the first Unitarian raid into al-Kharj,[65] but as time wore on his martial spirit seems to have flagged and he was guilty of various reprehensible acts[66] that made his overlords in al-Dir'īyah decide that he was unfit to retain his position. Mishārī was deposed and the authority of his office transferred to Sulṭān b. Muḥsin[67] of the House of Mu'ammar.[68] Once again the Shaikh journeyed to his birthplace to regulate affairs there. After his investigation had been completed he ordered the destruction of the castle of the House of Mu'ammar to prevent any member of the house from stirring up trouble for the cause in the future. This oasis in Wadi Ḥanīfah that had fought both for and against the Unitarians of its native son was thus left to sink into insignificance.[69]

Operations against al-Riyāḍ, 1173–4/1759–61

No matter what the demands for action on more distant fronts, the presence of Dahhām b. Dawwās only ten miles away in al-Riyāḍ

[64] See above, p. 67. [65] See above, p. 70.

[66] What they were is not specified in the chronicles.

[67] So in Ibn Bishr, I, 43; Ibn Ghannām, II, 66, uses the diminutive Muḥaisin.

[68] Ibn Bishr calls him al-Mu'ammarī; Ibn Ghannām identifies him as one of the Ma'āmirah.

[69] The scions of the Mu'ammar family, however, continued to play prominent roles in the affairs of Arabia. Aḥmad b. Nāṣir was one of the most learned and persuasive of the Unitarian theologians – see below, p. 229; p. 229, n. 12. Muḥammad b. Mishārī became the Governor of Najd for a brief period following the Egyptian conquest in 1818. Fahd Ibn Mu'ammar was one of the present King's [i.e. HM King 'Abd al-Azīz Al Saud] captains and Governor of al-Qaṣīm and of al-Kharj for him in the early days of his career. Today Ibrāhīm Ibn Mu'ammar is one of the Royal Counselors and his son 'Abd al-'Azīz, perhaps the best educated young Najdi in the Kingdom, is in charge of the monitoring of radio broadcasts in Arabic, English and French for His Majesty.

could not be ignored. During 1173/1759–60 the Unitarians mounted two attacks on Dahhām's territory, in the first of which[70] they burned some of the fields of Manfūḥah, while the second was capped by the Battle of Āl Rīs, so called because four of that family were among the defenders who fell.[71]

Early in the following year 'Abd al-'Azīz went down to al-Riyāḍ and placed his men in ambush before sunrise. In the light of day Fuhaid,[72] one of Dahhām's brothers, led out a sortie to give battle. Fuhaid suffered a broken leg from which he died forty days later. One after another of Dahhām's relatives and his soldiers were meeting their end, but still the lord of al-Riyāḍ fought on.

Right after this affair 'Abd al-'Azīz came back with the intent of doing more damage to the fields of Manfūḥah. He alighted at al-Muraiqibāt[73] and arranged an ambush that worked smoothly, enabling the Unitarians to repulse both the people of Manfūḥah and their allies from al-Riyāḍ.

On another expedition later in the year 'Abd al-'Azīz set out to strengthen the defenses of al-Ghazawānah, the fort he had built in the valley to the west of al-Riyāḍ. His original purpose was to return home without a fight, for the Feast of the Sacrifice[74] was approaching, but in the end he could not resist the temptation to try to surprise his enemies during their festivities on the eve of the feast. By night he introduced his troops into the oasis, but they were seen by a party of Dahhām's followers coming out of a meeting place for men,[75] who hastened off to notify their chief. Dahhām brought up his cavalry and infantry to attack the post established by the Unitarians in the oasis opposite the town, whereupon the horse and camelry of al-Dir'īyah hit him hard and made him give way, leaving a number of his veterans dead on the field.

[70] Ibn Bishr, I, 43, states that 'Abd al-'Azīz led the troops on this occasion; Ibn Ghannām, II, 66, does not mention him.

[71] Ibn Ghannām, II, 66; Ibn Bishr does not record this event.

[72] Ibn Ghannām, II, 68; Ibn Bishr, I, 44 and 80, calls him Fahd, of which Fuhaid is the diminutive.

[73] The Little Lookouts, the name of hills in the vicinity.

[74] 10 Dhū al-Ḥijjah, which in 1174 fell about the middle of July 1761.

[75] *Nādī* or *nadwah* – Ibn Ghannām, II, 68.

Fighting in Sudair, 1174/1760–61

At the beginning of 1174/August 1760 to August 1761 'Abd al-'Azīz with only eighty mounted men made a minor raid on the town of al-Rauḍah in Sudair, during which only one of the Unitarians was lost. Another raid on the same town immediately afterwards resulted in the killing of six of the townspeople as they turned tail upon the appearance of the attackers who had been lying in ambush. Going on beyond al-Rauḍah on the same raid, 'Abd al-'Azīz paid an unannounced visit to al-Zilfī in the farther reaches of Sudair. There he and his men took the flocks that were out to pasture and started home with them, but when overtaken by pursuers they had to let go of their booty in order to defend themselves.[76]

'Abd al-'Azīz's next expedition in this general direction penetrated into the borderland of *rauḍah*s between Sudair and al-Maḥmal, where the Unitarians made a morning attack on the Nabaṭah of Subai',[77] who were camping with their chief Ibn Fayyāḍ[78] at al-'Atk.[79] The nomads stood their ground for a time until the Unitarian shock troops broke in among them and sent them flying away in confusion. The booty for the victors amounted to eighty head of camels, many weapons, and much household furniture.

While 'Abd al-'Azīz was raiding through Sudair the recalcitrant Mubārak b. 'Adwān, deposed Amir of Ḥuraimilā, was dying of paralysis of one side[80] in the town of al-Majma'ah in the same district, and before the year had ended he was dead.

[76] Ibn Ghannām, II, 67; Ibn Bishr, I, 44, speaks of only one raid on al-Rauḍah and has nothing to say of the venturing on to al-Zilfī.

[77] The Nabaṭah are one of the four divisions of al-Khuḍrān, a section of Banī 'Umar, who are among the Subai' dwelling in al-'Ariḍ – Fu'ād Ḥamzah, *Qalb jazīrat al-'arab*, p. 155, n. 1.

[78] Fayyāḍ means "generous and excellent".

[79] Since the letter "k" is often pronounced as "ts" or "ch" in Najd, this name is frequently misspelled in both Arabic and English. Ibn Ghannām, II, 68, writes it al-'Atsh, which would be pronounced as al-'Ach. Perhaps the commonest spelling in English is al-'Ats; al-'Atj is also used. Musil, *Northern Neǧd*, p. 262, writes it al-'Ataḳ, spelling it incorrectly with a *qāf* instead of a *kāf*.

Wadi al-'Atk proper begins at the town of al-Qaṣab in Sudair and runs to the NNE through Ṭuwaiq and al-'Armah to the watering-place of Ḥafar al-'Atk just before one reaches the western side of the Dahnā'. The wadi runs between Sudair on the north and al-Maḥmal on the south – Philby, *The Heart of Arabia*, I, 325.

[80] *'Illat al-fālij*.

Fourth raid into al-Kharj, 1175/1761

On the second and third raids into al-Kharj two years earlier the Unitarians had struck at al-Dilam, the chief place in the province, and on the first of the two occasions they had attacked Na'jān while homeward bound after bidding farewell to al-Dilam. When they went south early in 1175/1761 they limited their objective by preparing their ambush for Na'jān. Through this maneuver they succeeded in killing seven of the defenders and driving the rest back behind their walls, where they besieged them for some days. The besiegers busied themselves in cutting down the tall palms in the groves outside the walls; then 'Abd al-'Azīz raised the siege and rode away.

Advance of Unitarianism in al-Washm, 1175/1761–2

The year 1175/August 1761 to July 1762 was a time for the introduction of variations on the themes of 'Abd al-'Azīz's campaigns. Instead of al-Dilam in al-Kharj the captain of al-Dir'īyah chose as his target the neighboring town of Na'jān; instead of Tharmidā in al-Washm the neighboring town of Marrāh.[81] There the Unitarians coming out of ambush hurled back the sortie from the town, killing about twenty while losing only two of their own number. The same tactics worked for 'Abd al-'Azīz on his next raid into al-Washm, when he knelt his camels by night outside the town of al-Far'ah.

The unceasing series of blows being struck by 'Abd al-'Azīz in al-Washm year after year was undermining the resistance of the enemy and convincing many that they could secure peace only by going over to the side of Unitarianism. While 'Abd al-'Azīz was winning converts by force, the ardent disciples of the Shaikh, who had a base and a refuge in the town of Shaqrā', were winning them by the gospel. A few days after the Unitarian victory at al-Far'ah the people of that town decided to embrace Unitarianism as their official faith.[82] This conversion led to a war between al-Far'ah and anti-

[81] On the way to Marrāh the expedition replenished its supplies at the Unitarian stronghold of Ḍurmā.

[82] Ibn Ghannām, II, 70, says that the people of al-Far'ah requested the people of Shaqrā' to

Unitarian Ushaiqir that continued until the capitulation of Ushaiqir about seven years later.

The Unitarians lost little time in strengthening their new ally. In a raid on Tharmidā 'Abd al-'Azīz lost the element of surprise when the garrison received notice in advance of his coming, so that he and his men were restricted to shooting ineffectively at the enemy from a distance. After the affair at Tharmidā the Unitarians built a fort called al-Ḥulailah[83] between al-Far'ah and Ushaiqir to serve as a support for al-Far'ah in its struggle against the common foe.[84] The garrison established in the fort was maintained until the final conversion of Ushaiqir. The winning of the whole of al-Washm was now in sight, and to accelerate the process 'Abd al-'Azīz also stationed men and horses in Shaqrā'.

In the same year the people of Shaqrā', of Uthaithīyā and of al-Qarā'in joined together in plundering a caravan in the west of al-Washm.[85] This indicates that the towns of Uthaithīyā and al-Qarā'in had adhered to the Unitarian cause, though no mention is made of when they did so.

accept them into the faith, which was done. Ibn Bishr, I, 45, says that the people of al-Far'ah sent a delegation headed by Manṣūr b. Aḥmad b. Ibrāhīm b. Ḥusain to make this request of the Shaikh Muḥammad b. 'Abd al-Wahhāb and Muḥammad b. Su'ūd in al-Dir'īyah, and that the Unitarian rulers appointed Manṣūr chief of the town. Although Ibn Bishr lived at a later date than Ibn Ghannām, he may, as a native of Shaqrā', have had access to better sources in this case than the older writer.

[83] The Little Alighting Place.

[84] Ibn Ghannām, II, 70, says that 'Abd al-'Azīz and his raiders built the fort. Ibn Bishr, I, 45, who alone gives the name of the fort or tower, says that it was built by the House of Manṣūr of al-Far'ah and the people of Shaqrā'. It may have been local patriotism on the part of Ibn Bishr for him to claim the credit for his own townspeople, or again he may have had better sources than Ibn Ghannām.

[85] Ibn Bishr, I, 45. Ibn Ghannām has no reference to this incident. Ibn Bishr also mentions a clash called the Battle of al-'Ulāwah which took place during a raid made by 'Abd al-'Azīz into al-Washm in this year; Ibn Bishr thinks the battle was fought at Ushaiqir, and Ibn Ghannām ignores it completely. On the other hand, Ibn Ghannām, II, 70, records a raid in which a small number of Unitarians were defeated by Ibn Fayyāḍ of Subai', while Ibn Bishr says nothing about it. The discrepancies between the information in the two chronicles for this year suggest that Ibn Bishr leaned heavily on sources independent of Ibn Ghannām.

[86] The *ḍarab*: those who go about the marketplaces at night to guard the town – Ibn Ghannām, II, 70, and Ibn Bishr, I, 45, n. 1.

[87] A brother of Dahhām?

Unitarian attacks against Dahhām of al-Riyāḍ, 1175–6/1761–3

'Abd al-'Azīz began his campaigning in 1175/1761 with a raid on the oasis of Manfūḥah, the home of Dahhām's allies. The Unitarian ambush was so cleverly managed that the enemy sortie was repulsed and not a single soldier on the attacking side was lost in the process. The Unitarians, busy in al-Washm, left Dahhām's quarter of Najd unmolested from that time until late in the year, when they sent a party down to attack the night watch[86] in Muqrin, a settlement in the oasis of al-Riyāḍ. Three of the men of the watch were killed and Sha'lān b. Dawwās[87] was wounded.

In 1176/1762 'Abd al-'Azīz began his campaigning with a raid on al-Riyāḍ. As usual he placed part of his forces in an ambush where they waited for an auspicious moment to issue forth. In the fighting outside the walls Dahhām's followers yielded the field, but they lost only four men. Very shortly thereafter 'Abd al-'Azīz was back again, bringing with him about two hundred men. The foot soldiers hid themselves in the oasis while the camelry remained some distance away. The Unitarians believed that the sentinels of the town were sleeping and had not seen them, but Dahhām had learned that they were there from one of his men and he came with his infantry and horse in an attempt to cut off the men in hiding before their mounted fellows could reinforce them. The Unitarian foot stood firm, the Unitarian camelry rushed in, and Dahhām had to retreat, losing six of his men and three of his horses.

Dahhām's attack on al-Dir'īyah, 1176/1762–3

For some time past, Dahhām himself seems to have been taking little active part in the fighting, for the chronicles do not speak of his appearance in person until the occasion of 'Abd al-'Azīz's latest raid on al-Riyāḍ. This fresh taste of what he had feasted upon in earlier days may have whetted his appetite; at any rate he now resolved to take the offensive after years of waiting at home for the Unitarian raids to strike. Carefully selecting his men and quietly making his plans, he was on his way before al-Dir'īyah suspected what he was about. The surprise, however, did not prove to be complete, for he was sighted during the advance in time for the Unitarians to summon a council of war in al-Dir'īyah. When Muḥammad b. Su'ūd invited his lieutenants to set forth their views on how to meet the danger, the plan proposed by his son 'Abd al-'Azīz, who had risen from the bed where he lay sick with fever to attend the council, was adopted. 'Abd al-'Azīz argued that the best route for the sortie to take was along al-Qarī,[88] since the way there was low-lying and hidden from view. An advance guard was sent on ahead, and when the sound of firing was heard the cavalry sprinted forward and caught Dahhām unawares. After them came the camelry and the foot in rapid succession. Although the men of al-Riyāḍ fought desperately, they could not win. The Unitarians killed twenty-five of them and captured four of their horses, along with many of their camels.[89] Thus was borne out the Word of God in the Koran: "Our soldiers are the victors."[90]

First Unitarian raid into al-Aḥsā', 1176/1762–3

For nearly a score of years the warriors of the Shaikh and the Amir had been fighting for their religion and gradually enlarging the sphere of its authority in the valleys and mountains of the interior of Arabia. They had raided into farther Sudair in the north and al-Kharj in the south, and their converts were established beyond the barrier of Ṭuwaiq on the road towards Mecca in the west. They knew that there was a rival Arab power in the east, on the other side of the sand dunes of the Dahnā': in the early days the Shaikh had continued preaching in the face of the threats of Sulaimān b. Muḥammad of Banī Khālid,[91] and in 1172/1758–9 the Unitarians had driven back Sulaimān's successor, 'Urai'ir b. Dujain, when he penetrated into Najd as far as Wadi Ḥanīfah.[92] As the Unitarian

[88] A *qarī* is a watercourse running from high ground down to a *rauḍah*.

[89] Ibn Ghannām, II, 72, says that all of their camels were captured; Ibn Bishr, I, 46, says some of them.

[90] Ibn Bishr (Baghdad), p. 34.

[91] See above, pp. 46–7.

[92] See above, pp. 90–2.

movement grew in strength, a number of considerations called for a settling of accounts with the Bedouin lords of al-Aḥsā': politically and militarily, the Unitarians could never be safe in Najd as long as their flank was exposed to an enemy who could strike across the sands at will; religiously, the Unitarians regarded the people of al-Aḥsā' with special loathing, for they counted great numbers of them Mushrikūn; economically, the men of Najd realized that they would be far better off in their barren highland home if they could reach the sea by way of which the imports they needed came.

In 1765 Carsten Niebuhr,[93] the first great European explorer of Arabia in modern times, went through the Persian Gulf on his way back to Copenhagen. Although he did not investigate al-Aḥsā'[94] at first hand as he did the Yemen, he inquired diligently of all those having knowledge of the place whom he encountered, and the brief description he set down bears the semblance of accuracy. The inhabitants were predominantly Shiite in the coast towns, and Sunnite in the inland towns and among the Bedouin tribes.[95] Besides the Shiites, whom the Unitarians naturally placed outside the pale as unbelievers, there were said to be many Sabians,[96] as well as a certain number

[93] Father of Barthold G. Niebuhr, the historian.

[94] Niebuhr, *Beschreibung von Arabien*, p. 339, defined the region of "Láchsa oder al Hássa (الحسا), oder Hadsjar (هجر)" as bounded on the east by the Persian Gulf, on the north by the territory of the Arabs in the vicinity of al-Baṣrah, on the west by Najd, and on the south by Oman. With the exception of al-Kuwait, which at that time was reckoned a part of al-Aḥsā' but is now an independent country under British protection, these boundaries correspond to the present boundaries of the Province of al-Aḥsā' in the Kingdom of Saudi Arabia.

In the usage of the people of the region and of the Arabians in general, the name al-Aḥsā', pronounced colloquially al-Ḥasā, is commonly restricted to the great central L-shaped series of oases in which al-Hufūf and al-Mubarraz are the largest towns.

[95] Al-Qaṭīf on the coast is still the most important Shiite center in Saudi Arabia today, although there is also a strong Shiite element among the farmers in al-Hufūf and its surrounding oases.

[96] Not to be confused with the Sabaeans of ancient South Arabia. The Sabians exist today in small numbers in some of the towns of Iraq, where they are known chiefly for their skill as silversmiths. A handful of them live on the island of Bahrain. [Rentz is here repeating Niebuhr's information on al-Aḥsā' and its people, which as he acknowledges was based on hearsay. The concept of al-Aḥsā' was a vague one in those days, as he implies in note 94, stretching up to the vicinity of al-Baṣrah and the borders of southern Iraq. However, as far as the present al-Aḥsā' region is concerned, there is no evidence to support the claim that communities of Sabians and Jews, however small, existed there at any time. KAPL]

of Jews. The region enjoyed a stable administration[97] and trade flourished, the coast dwellers receiving a large income from their pearlfisheries, the farmers from their date palms, the craftsmen from the woolen cloaks that they sold all over Arabia and Persia, and the Bedouins from their camels, of which every year they sent thousands to be marketed in Syria. The donkeys of al-Aḥsā' were also famous and could be sold to foreigners at high prices.[98]

Niebuhr remarks that al-Aḥsā' had once been a province of the Turkish Empire; in his time there were only a few Turkish families left, who could be singled out from the Arabs by the Turkish clothes they wore. Although these Turks owned much land, they had no share whatsoever in the government.

Niebuhr was given to understand that the ruling tribe of Banī Khālid[99] was one of the mightiest of all Arabia, ranging through the deserts as far as the caravan routes between Baghdad and Aleppo. The other Bedouin tribes in al-Aḥsā' recognized their overlordship. The capital of the chief of Banī Khālid in the oases of al-Aḥsā' was a large and well-built town, but this lord was seldom in residence, spending most of the year with his kinsmen under tents.[100]

The Unitarians were not yet strong enough for a full scale invasion of al-Aḥsā', but in 1176/July 1762 to July 1763 they were ready to dart into the land to show the quality of their steel to the Mushrikūn in their homes. 'Abd al-'Azīz's raiding party included about thirty horse. After crossing the Dahnā'[101] they alighted in the neighborhood of the central oases. The scout sent forward by 'Abd al-'Azīz to the village of al-Muṭairifī found the residents all sound asleep and unsuspecting. During the night the raiders completed their preparations, and in the morning they swooped down on the

[97] This is remarkable in view of the fact that the administration had for a century (since 1080/1669–70) been in the hands of nomad chieftains. Also remarkable was the way in which these chieftains of Banī Khālid had kept the rule in one family throughout this century.

[98] The white donkeys of al-Aḥsā' are large and powerful beasts. Many an Egyptian today who has never heard of al-Aḥsā' knows what a *ḥmār ḥasāwī* is.

[99] He correctly identifies the incumbent Shaikh as Arār – 'Urai'ir – *Beschreibung von Arabien*, p. 340.

[100] Niebuhr, *Beschreibung von Arabien*, pp. 340 and 386.

[101] No information is given on the route followed.

village and swept through the houses, slaying everyone they came upon. The toll of the slaughtered was about seventy; only those who hid themselves or took to flight were saved. Along with the killing, the raiders engaged in plunder, making off with animals, weapons, and household goods. 'Abd al-'Azīz planned to strike suddenly and withdraw without delay to Najd, but as he and his men rode away from al-Muṭairifī they found time for a quick blow at some of the people of the larger town of al-Mubarraz and they killed a number of farmers in the palm groves.

On the way back across the plateau of al-'Armah the raiders overtook a caravan made up of people from al-Riyāḍ and from Ḥarmah in Sudair. They killed the men of al-Riyāḍ and confiscated their share of the caravan, but the men of Sudair they allowed to go scot-free, for there was an armistice in the fighting between them at this time.[102] Coming down from the plateau into Wadi Ḥanīfah, the raiders gathered in sheep and goats belonging to their enemies at Manfūḥah and then went home at last to al-Dir'īyah, where the spoils of the campaign were divided among the men.[103]

Apostasy in al-Washm and among the Bedouins, 1176/1762–3

The people of the town of Uthaithīyā[104] in al-Washm, who had accepted the Islam of the Shaikh only a short time previously, now decided that its provisions were too onerous for them. They got in touch with the Amir of Tharmidā, Ibrāhīm b. Sulaimān al-'Anqarī, the old antagonist of Unitarianism, and informed him of their intention of breaking away from their new allegiance. Assured of Ibrāhīm's support, they brought their defiance out into the open and killed

[102] This is the first mention of this armistice, and it is not clear whether it had been made with the town of Ḥarmah alone or with the whole district of Sudair. There had been fighting in Sudair in 1174/1760–1. In 1175/1761–2 a disease known as Abā Damghah had been prevalent in Sudair, where it carried off among others the Qadi of Ḥarmah; the ravages of this disease may have led to the request for an armistice. See Ibn Bishr, I, 45.

[103] Ibn Ghannām, II, 72–3, who was a native of al-Aḥsā', has a fuller account of this raid than Ibn Bishr, I, 46.

[104] The name of this town is probably derived from the root *aththa*, meaning "(of plants) to multiply".

their Amir 'Abd al-Karīm b. Zāmil.[105]

Apostasy also appeared in this year among Bedouins of the tribe of Subai', some of whom at least, it seems, had allied themselves with the Unitarians not long before.[106] 'Abd al-'Azīz went southwards with a combined force of townsmen and Bedouins of Āl Kathīr until his cavalry and camelry caught up with their quarry at the watering place of Saiḥ al-Dubūl.[107] The men of Subai' gave way after losing their champion Mā'iq b. Shalīyah,[108] leaving about two hundred of their camels in the hands of those who had come to discipline them.

Near the close of this year the Unitarians made a raid into Sudair, seeking some of the Bedouins who were wandering in that district, but they returned empty-handed.[109]

Second submission of Dahhām of al-Riyāḍ, 1177/1763–4

In 1167/1763–4 Dahhām b. Dawwās had accepted the rule of Islam in his oasis stronghold, but after a year or so he had reverted to his position as the nearest and one of the most formidable of the foes of Unitarianism. In 1177/July 1763 to June 1764, ten years after his first submission, he deemed it advisable once again to feign conver-

[105] 'Abd al-Karīm had been captured by the Unitarians in the vicinity of Ḍurmā eight years earlier and had apparently joined the Unitarian side following that experience. For his capture see above, p. 78. On the adhesion of Uthaithiyā to the Unitarian cause see above, p. 98.

[106] Earlier references to Subai' in the chronicles deal with raids directed against them by the Unitarians – see above, pp. 82, 96.

[107] A *saiḥ* is a stream of water flowing on the surface; a *dabl* (pl. *dubūl*) is a rivulet such as might feed a *saiḥ*.

[108] Or Shulayyah. Mā'iq means "stupid"; Shalīyah, "bit of meat".

[109] This raid would not have been considered a violation of the armistice, since no attack was made against the towndwellers.

[110] Again Ibn Bishr, I, 47, uses the term *aḥmar* where Ibn Ghannām, II, 73, uses *zar* or *zarr* – see above, p. 83, n. 13.

[111] See above, p. 84.

[112] Ibn Bishr, I, 47, says that Suwaid (b. Muḥammad), the Amir of Jalājil, and all the people of Sudair came to the Unitarians and swore allegiance to the religion of God and His Prophet. This is likely an exaggeration, for Ibn Ghannām has nothing to say on this score, and Ibn Bishr himself under the year 1181/1767–8 indicates that the town of al-'Audah in Sudair was still anti-Unitarian at this time – see below, pp. 118, 120–1.

sion, and he wrote to the Shaikh and Muḥammad b. Su'ūd asking them to accept him as one of the faithful. Although they entertained grave doubts regarding his loyalty, they felt that they could not refuse anyone who proclaimed that he had seen the light of the true way. In order to punish Dahhām for his past sins, the Shaikh and the Amir imposed on him terms more stringent than those at the time of his first submission; they required him to pay two thousand *aḥmars*[110] and to restore to the Unitarians who had emigrated from al-Riyāḍ to al-Dir'īyah all the property they had left behind. Dahhām showed every sign of complete repentance and promptly paid the cash.

Progress of Unitarianism in Sudair, 1177/1764

As a result of the armistice between the Unitarians and some if not all of the people of Sudair, there had been little action in that region for two or three years. About midway through the year 1177/early 1764, the Unitarian leaders came to the conclusion that if their doctrines were to prevail throughout the district of Sudair they would have to crush the resistance of the town of Jalājil, which had been attacked by the Unitarians seven years earlier.[111] 'Abd al-'Azīz approached the town by night and prepared an ambush in the outskirts. When the people of Jalājil issued forth in the morning to give battle, the attackers enveloped them and threw them back to the shelter of their walls. The Unitarians followed up their success by cutting down some of the palms in the oasis before starting for home. This display of Unitarian power resulted in the adherence of many new converts in Sudair.[112]

7

Najran and al-Aḥsā' Invade Najd

Unitarian victory over the 'Ajmān, 1177/1764

On the return journey from Jalājil 'Abd al-'Azīz and his party had reached the town of Raghbah, when a loyal section of Subai' met them and complained that they had been set upon and their belongings seized by raiders from the 'Ajmān[1] who had come up from the south. As soon as 'Abd al-'Azīz heard this he moved off on the trail of the marauders to secure vengeance for the afflicted. Hard traveling brought him in Ramaḍān 1177/March to April 1764 to Qadhlah, the plain to the west of Ṭuwaiq between Nafūd Dalqān and the oasis of al-Quwai'īyah, where he found that the fleeing Bedouins had jettisoned all their heavy gear. Pressing on, he soon overtook the Bedouins themselves with his horse, who numbered about forty, and camels, who numbered something over a hundred. Driving straight in for the fight, the Unitarians killed fifty or more

[1] This is the first appearance in the history of Wahhabism of the warlike tribe of the 'Ajmān, "the Germans of the Arabs". Claiming descent from the great confederation of Yām in Najrān, the 'Ajmān in the second half of the 18th century still had strong ties with the southwestern part of the Peninsula; the Wahhabi chroniclers refer to them as "people of the Yemen". Their main *dīrah* at the present time is in the north and center of the Province of al-Aḥsā', from al-Ṭaff to al-'Uqair, while in the winter they roam westwards to al-Zilfī, al-Qaṣīm, and al-Kharj. Wadi al-Miyāh/the Valley of the Waters in northern al-Aḥsā' is a great gathering-place for the 'Ajmān. One branch of the tribe, Āl Shāmir, now has its home in the almost inaccessible recesses of Jabal 'Ulayyah in south central Najd. See Fu'ād Ḥamzah, *Qalb jazīrat al-'arab*, pp. 182–3.

[2] Ibn Ghannām, II, 74, says that they killed about fifty and took 240 prisoners, as well as capturing the horses and camels the 'Ajmān had with them; according to him the Unitarians suffered no losses in either men or animals. Ibn Bishr, I, 47, says that they killed fifty, including Ibn Ṭuhaimān, who may have been their chief; in addition, twenty of the Majādhimah were killed, while the prisoners taken numbered about a hundred and the horses captured

of the 'Ajmān and took many prisoners.[2] It was a great victory, but its sequel almost brought disaster to the Unitarian cause.[3]

Unitarian victory over the Ẓafīr at Jarrāb, 1178/1764

In Ṣafar 1178/August 1764 'Abd al-'Azīz took a band of about 130 men, among whom were the newly converted Dahhām b. Dawwās and a contingent from al-Riyāḍ, hurrying through Sudair in a search for the section of the Ẓafīr known as Āl Sa'īd[4] under their chief Ḥammād b. Mudaihīm.[5] The Unitarians made a few halts on the way, for they had heard that Ibn Mudaihīm was encamped at Jarrāb, a watering-place between Sudair and the Dahnā',[6] and they wished to meet him there before he departed. Arriving by night at a point near the water, 'Abd al-'Azīz sent a scout to determine the disposition of the enemy. The scout reported that the Bedouins had their tents pitched in two large camps that were separated from each other. Fearing that an attack on one camp with the small Unitarian force might leave the attackers vulnerable before the fighting men from the other camp, 'Abd al-'Azīz took counsel with his soldiers to see what tactics would fit the situation. The decision was made that the Unitarians should advance in a body against one of the camps on foot; as soon as the enemy gave way the Unitarians should hasten back to their mounts and wheel around to attack in the saddle. When the sun rose this plan was put into execution; it resulted in the complete defeat of the Bedouins, of whom about thirty were killed, and in the taking of great quantities of booty.[7]

about forty. The Majādhimah are not listed by Fu'ād Ḥamzah among the sections of the 'Ajmān, but his list is neither complete nor altogether accurate.

[3] See below, pp. 108–11.

[4] Āl Sa'īd of the Ẓafīr claim descent from Qaḥṭān – Fu'ād Ḥamzah, *Qalb jazīrat āl-'arab*, p. 169.

[5] Mudaihīm is the diminutive of *madhūm*, the passive participle of *dahama*, the root from which the name Dahhām is derived.

[6] Jarrāb was later, in 1850, the scene of a Wahhabi victory over the tribe of 'Utaibah, and still later, in 1915, the scene of one of Ibn Saud's most famous battles, the one in which Captain W.H.I. Shakespear lost his life in the war against the House of Rashīd.

[7] Ibn Ghannām, II, 75, sets forth the plan of attack; Ibn Bishr, I, 47 gives fuller information on the identity of the Bedouins who were attacked.

Invasion of Najd from Najrān: crushing defeat of the Unitarians, 1178/1764

The Bedouins of the 'Ajmān who escaped from the field of Qadhlah[8] fled southwards to the land of Najrān, where they hoped to get help in securing revenge for their defeat and in liberating the prisoners they had left behind in the hands of the Unitarians.[9]

The land of Najrān in the southwestern part of Arabia is one of the remote regions of the Peninsula. Separated from the Red Sea by the mountains of 'Asīr and the Yemen, it can be reached only by overland routes that are not easy. The land takes its name from Wadi Najrān, one of the two large and fertile valleys that run through it from west to east.[10] Its isolation has contributed to making it, both in the past and the present, a center for religious beliefs at variance with those of most of the inhabitants of Arabia. Najrān, the seat of a bishop, was the last outpost of Christianity in the Peninsula during the early centuries of Islam. Christianity there gave way to Ismailism, one of the more esoteric sects developed by the followers of the Prophet,[11] which has held its ground in Najrān to the present day.[12] When the Shaikh and his associates began proclaiming the principles of Unitarianism in Najd, Najrān was one of the neigh-

[8] See above, p. 106.

[9] According to Ibn Ghannām, II, 76, the prisoners were in manacles and were being tortured or maltreated daily. [In this story of maltreatment, Ibn Ghannām in fact reports what the prisoners *claimed* to have been done to them, in order to rouse the people of Najran into helping them take revenge on the *muwaḥḥidūn* for the Qadhlah defeat. KAPL]

[10] The other valley is Wadi Ḥabaunah, which runs roughly parallel to Wadi Najrān one day's journey to the north. Wadi Najrān is three days' journey to the NE of Ṣa'dah in the high Yemen.

[11] Ismailism is a form of Shiism that differs from the more usual form in that only seven Imams are recognized instead of twelve. Carmathianism and various other examples of extreme heterodoxy have sprung from or had a relationship with Ismailism. The present head of Ismailism is the Agha Khan in India. [Rentz in this note correctly describes such doctrines as heterodox. He thus appears to contradict his reference to Ismailism in the text to which this note applies, as having been developed by "followers of the Prophet". KAPL]

[12] Najrān has also harbored for many centuries a comparatively large number of Jews, who are said to be better treated and to enjoy a higher standing in the community here than anywhere else in Arabia.

boring regions they denounced because of the prevalence of practices contrary to the laws of Islam. The people of Najrān, according to the Unitarians, showed such reverence for their ruler, a Sayyid,[13] that they came close to placing him on the same plane with God.[14]

The lord of Najrān to whom the 'Ajmān had recourse, the Sayyid Ḥasan b. Hibat Allāh, was a man famous in Arabia for his bravery and his accomplishments as a general as well as for his holiness.[15] The 'Ajmān seem to have been under the protection of the lord of Najrān, who answered their plea for help by assembling the tribesmen of Yām and the other warriors who fought under his command and marching north into Najd.

The army from Najrān reached Wadi Ḥanīfah at al-Ḥā'ir, which was numbered among the towns professing Unitarianism. When the invaders laid siege to the town, 'Abd al-'Azīz came down from al-Dir'īyah in Rabī' II 1178/late September to late October 1764[16] with the full muster of Unitarian soldiery. When the men of Najd advanced to give battle, they found the array from the south too solid and strong; the Unitarians fell back, leaving behind nearly half a thousand killed and many others captured.[17] 'Abd al-'Azīz rode straight to al-Dir'īyah to give a firsthand report on the defeat to his father and the Shaikh, but despite the heavy losses he had suffered he was not despondent; in firm tones he announced to the older men his conviction that if they trusted in God they would ultimately emerge victorious.[18]

[13] A descendant of the Prophet or one who claimed such descent.

[14] Ibn Ghannām, I, 13. Ibn Ghannām, II, 105, calls him Qarīn Iblīs/The Accomplice of Satan.

[15] Ibn Ghannām, II, 76, calls him al-Ḥasan; Ibn Bishr, I, 47, the Sayyid Ḥasan. Niebuhr, who during his travels in Arabia at this time heard much about the ruler of Najrān, calls him Shaikh Mekkrami, i.e. al-Makramī – *Beschreibung von Arabien*, p. 273. Makramī is the name of a family that has long been dominant in Ismaili affairs in Najrān; the Green Book issued by the Saudi Arabian Ministry of Foreign Affairs on relations with the Yemen, *Bayān 'an al-'alāqāt bain al-Mamlakah al-'Arabīyah al-Su'ūdīyah wal-Imām Yaḥyā Ḥamīd al-Dīn* (Mecca 1353/1934–5), p. 174, says: "(The tribes of Yām in Najrān) have three battle standards ... they all follow the guidance of the Dā'i (a common term in Ismailism, which originally meant the Caller or the Missionary but which may also be used as the title of a leader in the movement), who in the majority of cases is one of the Makārimah (i.e. from the Makramī family)." It is strange that neither Ibn Ghannām nor Ibn Bishr mentions the name Makramī in referring to the lord of Najrān.

[16] Ibn Ghannām, II, 75; Ibn Bishr, I, 47.

From al-Ḥā'ir the lord of Najrān moved up Wadi Ḥanīfah to al-Ghazawānah, the fort built by the Unitarians as a threat to Dahhām b. Dawwās of al-Riyāḍ. The men of the garrison sallied forth and seized about twenty camels belonging to the men of the south, after which they re-entered the fort and prepared to withstand a siege.

The resounding victory of the lord of Najrān at al-Ḥā'ir stirred the old enemies of Unitarianism into action. Dahhām of al-Riyāḍ, who had tendered allegiance to Unitarian rule for the second time just the year before,[19] sent presents to the victor and urged him to follow up the advantage he had won with a campaign to obliterate every trace of Unitarianism in the land.[20] At the same time Dahhām wrote to 'Urai'ir b. Dujain in al-Aḥsā' that the moment was auspicious for him to march on Najd, the affairs of the Unitarians having fallen into disorder. 'Urai'ir communicated with the lord of Najrān directly, promising him rich gifts, including thoroughbred horses,[21] if he would wait in Najd until 'Urai'ir could join him. Zaid Ibn Zāmil of al-Kharj and Faiṣal Ibn Suwaiṭ of the tribe of the Ẓafīr made similar offers.[22]

Although the danger daily grew more menacing, the Shaikh and Muḥammad b. Su'ūd kept their wits about them. Their main fighting force having been severely crippled at al-Ḥā'ir, they knew that they had to act with speed and skill to break up the alliance that was forming against them. Using Faiṣal Ibn Suhail, one of the chiefs of

[17] Ibn Ghannām, II, 77, gives the number of killed as about four hundred and the number of prisoners as about three hundred; Ibn Bishr, I, 48 says that about five hundred were killed and 220 captured. The list given by Ibn Bishr of the number of Unitarians killed from each town may be taken as a rough guide to the composition of 'Abd al-'Azīz's forces:

al-Dir'īyah	77	al-'Uyainah	28
Manfūḥah	70	Ḥuraimilā	16
al-Riyāḍ	50	Ḍurmā	4
'Arqah	23	Thādiq	1

'Abd al-'Azīz also had with him Bedouins and others (presumably townsmen) from among the people of al-Ḥā'ir and the tribe of Subai'.

[18] Ibn Bishr, I, 48.

[19] See above, pp. 104–5.

[20] Ibn Ghannām, II, 77, says that Dahhām offered the lordship of all Najd to the Sayyid Ḥasan in return for the final destruction of Unitarianism.

[21] Najrān was an important center for Arab horses – Adolf Grohmann, *Südarabien als Wirtschaftsgebiet* (Vienna etc. 1922 & 1933), I, 194–5.

[22] Ibn Ghannām, II, 77–8.

the Ẓafīr, as an intermediary,[23] they reached an agreement with the lord of Najrān for an exchange of prisoners. After this agreement had been carried out, the lord of Najrān struck his tents in the camp where he had been staying before the fort of al-Ghazawānah and led his army off to the south, abandoning the gifts that had been promised to him and the opportunity he had had of establishing his authority in Najd.[24]

Second invasion of Najd from al-Aḥsā', 1178/1764

The lord of Najrān made his hasty exit from the scene at a time when 'Urai'ir b. Dujain was en route out of the east with the intention of joining him in a thrust at the Unitarians in their citadel. 'Urai'ir, accompanied by the fighting men of Banī Khālid and the region of al-Aḥsā', had not yet crossed the desert of the Dahnā' as the southerners broke camp. 'Urai'ir was no doubt disappointed when he heard that the Sayyid Ḥasan had left, but he was not dismayed; he had a large force of battle-tried soldiers, he had cannon,[25] and he had other allies awaiting his arrival in Najd. Only the region of al-'Āriḍ and the town of Ḍurmā and Shaqrā'[26] remained faithful to Unitarianism; all the rest aligned themselves with Dahhām b. Dawwās of al-Riyāḍ and Zaid Ibn Zāmil of al-Kharj in extending a welcome to the second invader of the year.[27]

[23] Ibn Bishr, I, 48.

[24] The sources give no satisfactory reason for the departure of the lord of Najrān. Philby, *Arabia*, p. 21, states that he and his men went home "rather than face a long and perhaps dangerous sojourn in the enemy's country, which they had no particular desire to conquer." This interpretation does not ring altogether true in view of the very favorable position held by the lord of Najrān at the time of his departure.

Ibn Ghannām, II, 77, says that the lord of Najrān remained at al-Ghazawānah about fifteen days.

[25] Philby's reference in *Arabia*, p. 21, to artillery as "an arm which had apparently never before been used in Central Arabian warfare" is incorrect. The Ottoman armies had been using artillery in Arabia for a matter of two centuries or so, and cannon had occasionally been brought into the interior, though they were not in common use there.

[26] Ibn Bishr, I, 48. Ḍurmā is usually reckoned as lying within al-'Ārid, even though it is beyond the western rim of Ṭuwaiq – see al-Ālūsī, *Ta'rīkh Najd*, p. 28 and n. 1.

[27] The battle of al-Ḥā'ir was in Rabī' II 1178/late September to late October 1764, and after the battle the lord of Najrān stayed at al-Ghazawānah fifteen days – see above, pp. 109–10 and p. 111, n. 24. Dahhām's truce with the Unitarians after the withdrawal of

When 'Urai'ir sought the advice of his allies from Najd regarding the best site for bringing al-Dir'īyah under the fire of his cannon, they recommended a spot between Qarī al-Quṣayyir and Qarī 'Amrān.[28] After a day's rest had been granted the men, 'Urai'ir's cannon started throwing their balls at the towers and ramparts of the town, but their effectiveness was slight.[29] The Unitarians under the command of 'Abd al-'Azīz left the shelter of their defenses to engage in a race with the enemy to secure a certain height in the vicinity,[30] a race which the Unitarians won. A few days went by with the position of the attackers deteriorating due to the shortness of their water supply. Dahhām and Zaid endeavored to keep 'Urai'ir's spirits up, and the men of al-Ḥarīq in the south volunteered to support the allies in a grand assault on the town. 'Abd al-'Azīz, however, discovered the plans for the assault from a man named Sālim b. Jumhūr and disposed his troops accordingly. The anti-Unitarians drew upon every ounce of their energy on the appointed day. The Mahāshīr, a turbulent section of Banī Khālid, rushed on al-Zulāl; the remainder of 'Urai'ir's own tribe and the contingents from al-Aḥsā' attacked the walls of Ṣamhān;[31] Dahhām of al-Riyāḍ, Muḥammad Ibn Fāris of Manfūḥah,[32] and the men of al-Ḥarīq, of Sudair, and of al-Washm headed for Qarī al-Quṣayyir. The Unitarians fighting for their homes and their faith were invincible; they halted the onward surge of the attackers and then forced them back past the useless cannon. 'Urai'ir had by now had his fill of the war, and the alliance against al-Dir'īyah collapsed.[33]

'Urai'ir from Najd was concluded before the end of 1764 – see below, p. 113, n. 34. Therefore, 'Urai'ir arrived in Najd late in 1764.

[28] Ibn Ghannām, II, 79. In II, 81, Ibn Ghannām gives the name of the first *qarī* as Quṣayyir without the definite article. On the meaning of *qarī*, see above, p. 100, n. 88.

[29] Ibn Ghannām, II, 80, says that the cannon did not make a single brick fly out of the walls.

[30] 'Ulū al-Bāṭin – Ibn Ghannām, II, 80. The main channel-bed of Wadi Ḥanīfah is called al-Bāṭin.

[31] Al-Zulāl and Samḥān were two places outside al-Dir'īyah – Ibn Bishr, I, 48.

[32] The men of Manfūḥah were collaborating with Dahhām during the whole period of 'Urai'ir's invasion.

[33] Ibn Ghannām, II, 81–2, says that about fifty of the attackers were killed during the final assault, while the Unitarians lost six men. Ibn Bishr, I, 48, says that the allies remained outside al-Dir'iyah about twenty days; he puts their losses at more than forty men and the losses of the men of al-Dir'īyah at about twelve.

Third submission of Dahhām of al-Riyāḍ: assassination of the anti-Unitarian Amir of Manfūḥah

Dahhām b. Dawwās of al-Riyāḍ found repentance the best course after his hopes had been dashed by the Unitarian survival in 1178/1764. Late in that year[34] he asked the Shaikh and Muḥammad b. Su'ūd for a truce, which they agreed to.[35] The peace that followed the two alien invasions of Najd was not of long duration. In Manfūḥah, the close neighbor of al-Riyāḍ, the nephews of the ruler, Muḥammad Ibn Fāris,[36] were convinced that their uncle, who had sided with Dahhām and the invaders, was still imbued with animosity towards the Unitarians. The nephews informed the Shaikh and Muḥammad b. Su'ūd of the situation and urged that their uncle and his son 'Abd al-Muḥsin be killed before they went any further with their anti-Unitarian schemes. The Shaikh and the Amir refused to consent to such action on the basis that the laws of Islam enjoined strict adherence to a truce once it had been entered upon.[37] Disregarding the attitude of the preceptors of the faith, the nephews in Manfūḥah slew their uncle and their cousin in the council chamber. News of the assassination flew to al-Riyāḍ and al-Dir'īyah; both Dahhām and 'Abd al-'Azīz set out for Manfūḥah with their fighting men, Dahhām to render aid to the party of the assassinated men and 'Abd al-'Azīz to reinforce the assassins. Since 'Abd al-'Azīz had the greater distance to traverse, Dahhām was the first to arrive and had already gone into action against the Unitarians of Manfūḥah when a messenger, speeding on ahead of 'Abd al-'Azīz and his soldiers,

[34] Ibn Ghannām, II, 83, says the truce lasted about ten months, and in II, 84, he says that Dahhām violated the truce in Rabī' I, 1179/mid-August to mid-September 1765, so that the truce must have been concluded before the end of 1764.

[35] No mention is made of terms imposed on Dahhām in punishment for his activity in support of the lord of Najrān and 'Urai'ir. It is possible that the invasions had so weakened the Unitarians that they were content for the time being with nothing more than the cessation of hostilities.

[36] Ibn Bishr, I, 49, calls Muḥammad Ibn Fāris the Shaikh of Manfūḥah. His nephews were the sons of his brother Zāmil – Ibn Ghannām, II, 83.

[37] Although Ibn Ghannām does not say so explicitly, the truce made with Dahhām must have included his associate Muḥammad Ibn Fāris of Manfūḥah.

[38] Ibn Ghannām, II, 84.

[39] Ibn Ghannām, II, 84; Ibn Bishr, I, 49.

came in with a letter from the Shaikh. In the letter the Shaikh informed Dahhām of the efforts made by himself and Muḥammad b. Su'ūd to restrain the hotheads of Manfūḥah; the Shaikh concluded by telling Dahhām that if he wished to maintain the truce he should avoid causing additional dissension.[38] The written words of the Shaikh had the desired effect; by the time 'Abd al-'Azīz reached the outskirts of Manfūḥah Dahhām had withdrawn to his own oasis. 'Abd al-'Azīz tarried for some days in the fort of al-Ghazawānah until the tide of emotion in Manfūḥah subsided.

Dahhām's break with the Unitarians, 1179/1765

Dahhām was not happy with the truce, particularly since the Unitarians were right at hand in both al-Ghazawānah and Manfūḥah. In Rabī' I 1179/mid-August to mid-September 1765, less than a year after the battle of al-Ḥā'ir, Dahhām violated the truce by combining forces with Zaid Ibn Zāmil of al-Dilam for an attack on the place known as al-Ṣubaikhāt in the oasis of Manfūḥah. The attackers seized a large number of the livestock pasturing there; the residents came out for a fight in which a dozen men were killed.[39] In this way Dahhām resumed the war against the Unitarians; from this day on the enemies fought each other with unrelenting bitterness until, years afterward, exhaustion overtook Dahhām.

8

‘Abd al-‘Azīz b. Muḥammad b. Su‘ūd: First Years as Imam 1179–87/1765–73

Death of Muḥammad b. Su‘ūd and accession of ‘Abd al-‘Azīz as Imam, 1179/1765

At the end of Rabī‘ I 1179/mid-September 1765 Muḥammad b. Su‘ūd, Amir of al-Dir‘īyah and Imam of the Unitarian State, died in his capital.[1] Twenty years earlier the preacher of Unitarianism had come to his town and the two had made a compact for the elevation of the word of God throughout the land. The Shaikh had promised the Amir wide dominions; at the time of his death much of Najd acknowledged his sway, his people had maintained their faith in the face of all the power of al-Aḥsā’ and Najrān, and the infidel state of al-Riyāḍ, though not yet conquered, was so weak from repeated blows that it was to fall within a few years. The Amir had asked the Shaikh to submit to two conditions. The first was that the Shaikh should not leave al-Dir‘īyah for another place, and the Shaikh had not left. The second was that the Shaikh should allow the Amir to retain his feudal income from the people of the town; the Shaikh had promised that the Amir's share of the booty of their conquests would far surpass his old income. When in the course of time this promise was fulfilled, the Shaikh told the Amir: "This is more than you get from the people of your town." After hearing these words the Amir cancelled the old feudal dues.[2]

From the time of the compact on, the Shaikh and the Amir shared

[1] Muḥammad must have been at least in his sixties at the time of his death, for his son ‘Abd al-‘Azīz was about forty-five. The Shaikh Muḥammad b. ‘Abd al-Wahhāb was then about sixty-two.

[2] Ibn Bishr, I, 12.

the rule of the new theocracy; decisions were made and edicts were proclaimed by the two together, and when outsiders wished to treat with the government they addressed themselves to both of them, yet there was never any question that the Shaikh was the senior partner in authority. In the words of the chronicler: "No camels were mounted and no opinions were voiced by Muḥammad or his son 'Abd al-'Azīz without his approval."[3] The Shaikh was the supreme judge in matters of religion and religion ruled the state. Even with the encroachment of old age the Shaikh did not withdraw from active participation in the ordering of affairs until eight years or so after the death of Muḥammad b. Su'ūd and the accession of 'Abd al-'Azīz.[4] Muḥammad and his son after him gratefully accepted the position of the Shaikh as God's will for their little realm, and they showed him the utmost loyalty; there is no suggestion or hint that they ever disputed his views on any matter great or small.

Besides his successor 'Abd al-'Azīz, Muḥammad was survived by at least one other son, 'Abd Allāh,[5] who was to be a brave lieutenant of his brother in the wars to come. Little is known of the private life of Muḥammad b. Su'ūd; it is uncertain whether either 'Abd al-'Azīz or 'Abd Allāh was born of his wife Mūḍī, who had helped to persuade him to welcome the Shaikh to al-Dir'īyah – they may have been full brothers or sons of Muḥammad by different wives.[6]

Upon the death of Muḥammad b. Su'ūd, his son and general 'Abd al-'Azīz was designated[7] as the new Amir and Imam. Since

[3] Ibn Bishr, I, 15.

[4] See below, pp. 137–8.

[5] The present King of Saudi Arabia, 'Abd al-'Azīz b. 'Abd al-Raḥmān b. Faiṣal b. Turkī b. 'Abd Allāh, is the great-great grandson of this 'Abd Allāh.

Two older (?) brothers of 'Abd al-'Azīz and 'Abd Allāh, Faiṣal and Su'ūd, were killed in the early fighting against Dahhām of al-Riyāḍ, about 1159–60/1746–7 – see above, p. 61.

[6] Although Ibn Bishr gives very full obituaries to 'Abd al-'Azīz and his son and successor Su'ūd on the occasions of their deaths, he records the passing of Muḥammad in three lines, one of which is taken up with his genealogy – Ibn Bishr, I, 49. The notice in Ibn Ghannām, II, 85, is even briefer, indicating that only forty years or so after his death little was remembered regarding his life other than his public acts in conjunction with the Shaikh.

[7] The chroniclers do not describe the manner of designation. There is no doubt that 'Abd al-'Azīz was the choice of both his father and the Shaikh, though one wonders, in view of the Wahhabi insistence on doing everything as it had been done in the early days of Islam, whether any consideration was given to the formality of election by the general consent

1161/1748 'Abd al-'Azīz had been leading the men of al-Dir'īyah and their Unitarian allies out to war; his capabilities were well known, particularly his skill in dealing with unexpected situations, and there was none like him to command the loyalty of his people. From every town and tribe in the Unitarian domain the people came streaming in to al-Dir'īyah to take the oath of allegiance to their new ruler. As men of high and low degree gathered there, the figure of the Shaikh dominated the assemblies. He preached and expounded the laws of their state; he warned that whoever violated his oath violated it for himself alone, and he promised those who kept their oath a rich reward. Through the eloquence and flaming sincerity of the Shaikh the ties that bound the diverse elements of the community together were made stronger than they had been before.[8]

With the assumption of the new office by 'Abd al-'Azīz it might have been expected that he would have been kept at home by administrative duties and the risks attendant upon raids into distant territories, but such was not the case. It is true that he began to place the responsibility of leading certain of the campaigns on his brother 'Abd Allāh, but he himself continued for years to come to venture forth with his men as he had done in the old days before he became their Imam.

Further operations against al-Riyāḍ, 1179/1765–6

Since Dahhām b. Dawwās had broken his pledge of loyalty for the third time just before the death of Muḥammad b. Su'ūd, the Unitarians were determined to allow him no ease as soon as they could muster their forces following the installation of their new Imam. 'Abd al-'Azīz in person conducted a party that seized the towers known as Jaṣṣān. Dahhām dispatched a rider to summon to his assistance Bedouins of Subai' who were in the neighborhood. As the

of the community. From the time of 'Abd al-'Azīz on it became the practice in the First Wahhabi Empire for the Imam during his lifetime to designate his successor – see below, pp. 209–10. This same practice is followed in the modern Kingdom of Saudi Arabia. The successor so designated is styled Walī al-'Ahd or Heir Apparent (literally, The One to whom the Covenant is Intrusted).

[8] Ibn Ghannām, II, 85.

horse of Subai' drew near, Dahhām came out from behind his walls, intending to keep the Unitarians busy until the Bedouins could join the fray. 'Abd al-'Azīz ordered his men out of the towers in which they had installed themselves and attacked Dahhām immediately. Dahhām's Bedouin allies arrived to find the Unitarians fighting so fiercely that neither side could gain a decision.

The next attack on al-Riyāḍ was made by a band of only sixty men from al-Dir'īyah. A renegade from the Unitarian capital apprised Dahhām of their coming; the lord of al-Riyāḍ gathered his people together and waited for them. When the raiders began their attack on the settlement of Ṣiyāḥ in the oasis, Dahhām took them unawares. The horse of al-Riyāḍ pursued them as they fled; eight of them were killed and five captured.

To avenge this defeat 'Abd al-'Azīz accompanied an expedition to demonstrate that he had lost none of his old subtlety in the art of ambushing the enemy. When his soldiers made their sudden appearance in the light of early morning, the men of al-Riyāḍ had to take to their heels.

Near the end of the year the Unitarians heard that Dahhām had gone over to Manfūḥah to confer with his allies. A flying squadron was sent down to break up the conference, and at its approach Dahhām scurried out of the palm groves of Manfūḥah and made for home.[9]

'Abd Allāh's raid into Sudair and attack on Subai', 1179/1765–6

While operations were being carried on against al-Riyāḍ throughout the year, 'Abd Allāh, the brother of the new Imam, was given command of an expedition for the first time. He headed for the town of al-'Audah in Sudair, a center of disaffection, but turned away without a fight. Swinging over to the plateau of al-'Armah, he came upon a large encampment of Bedouins of Subai', some of them being from Āl Shalīyah[10] and some from other sections, and made a morning

[9] Ibn Ghannām, II, 86; Ibn Bishr does not record this incident.

[10] Or Shulayyah – see above, p. 104, n. 108.

attack on them. The Unitarians acquired as booty camels, horses, sheep, goats and other belongings of the nomads.

Unitarian attack on Tharmidā in al-Washm, 1180/1766–7

In terms of obstinacy and perseverance Ibrāhīm b. Sulaimān al-'Anqarī, the Amir of Tharmidā, easily ranked second to Dahhām of al-Riyāḍ in the list of Unitarianism's enemies in Najd. In 1180/June 1766 to May 1767 'Abd al-'Azīz took command of an expedition designed to strike at Ibrāhīm's sources of supply. The Unitarians waited in their ambush until all the flocks had left the town for the pasture, whereupon some of the raiders came out and began to drive the animals away. The townspeople rushed forth to save their stock, only to be trapped by the rest of those who had been in ambush, after which they were harried by the Unitarian cavalry. About twenty of the men of Tharmidā were killed, including two of the sons of the Amir Ibrāhīm and the Imam of the town.[11]

Operations against al-Riyāḍ, 1180/1766–7

When 'Abd al-'Azīz left Tharmidā he rode with his camelry for Manfūḥah, not raiding as in the old days but seeking a bride. On the way he encountered a detachment of Dahhām's men and made short work of them. Then swords were sheathed and the bridegroom went on to Manfūḥah, where the daughter of Zāmil was waiting for him to come.[12]

'Abd al-'Azīz by thus allying himself with the people of Manfūḥah helped to draw the noose tighter about al-Riyāḍ. In Shawwāl

[11] This battle was known as the Battle of al-Ṣaḥn/The Level Ground, after the name of the place outside Tharmidā where the fighting occurred – Ibn Ghannām, II, 87; Ibn Bishr, I, 50.

[12] It may be conjectured that political considerations entered into the making of this match, which is mentioned only by Ibn Ghannām, II, 87. The chroniclers offer scant information on the matrimonial alliances of the members of the House of Su'ūd, though the career of the present King would suggest that there were many instances in which political advantages were gained by the wise selection of brides.

1180/March 1767 the newlywed was in harness again, alighting with his men at al-Bunayyah, the fort in the environs of al-Riyāḍ that had been the scene of much fighting between the old enemies. The defenders made their sortie without zest, and the battle that followed proved to be only a minor affair.

Unitarian conquest of al-'Audah: Su'ūd's first raid and the submission of Sudair and al-Washm, 1181/1767–8

The last places in the district of Sudair holding out against the rising tide of Unitarianism were the towns of Jalājil and al-'Audah. 'Uthmān b. Sa'dūn had made himself the ruler of al-'Audah about ten years earlier by killing his benefactor Ibn Sulṭān,[13] and as ruler he had been a persistent enemy of the new dispensation. In 1181/May 1767 to May 1768 a powerful Unitarian force under the command of Hadhlūl b. Faiṣal[14] advanced against al-'Audah, accompanied by the leading men of that town who had been driven into exile by Ibn Sa'dūn at the time of his *coup d'état*, among them being members of the House of Sulṭān and Manṣūr b. 'Abd Allāh b. Ḥammād. Ibn Ḥammād had made an agreement with the Imam 'Abd al-'Azīz by the terms of which he was to be appointed Amir of al-'Audah if he enabled the expedition to take the town. Another soldier under Hadhlūl was Su'ūd b. 'Abd al-'Azīz, who was making the first raid of his career. The young son[15] of the new Imam was destined, after a course of rigorous training in the field, to take his father's place as chief general of the Unitarian armies and to become, after his father's death, master of the Unitarian Empire at the zenith of its power.

Hadhlūl placed an ambush to the west of al-'Audah and then sent the rest of his troops around to the east to make a demonstration. The fighting men of the town came out on the eastern side to meet the attackers, leaving only two or three men with their Amir Ibn

[13] See above, p. 85.

[14] This new captain, who suddenly appears on the scene, is not identified by the sources.

[15] Su'ūd was at this time less than twenty, for he had been an unweaned infant when his grandfather on the mother's side, 'Uthmān Ibn Mu'ammar, was assassinated in 1163/1750 – Ibn Bishr, I, 23.

Sa'dūn inside the walls. At this moment Ibn Ḥammād led the men stationed to the west right into the town. Ibn Sa'dūn tried to save himself by taking refuge in the citadel, but the Unitarians made a breach in the rear of that place, entered, and killed their enemy. The townspeople who had gone out with the sortie retired to the citadel to find it shut in their faces. 'Abd al-'Azīz in fulfilment of his agreement appointed Ibn Ḥammād Amir of al-'Audah.[16]

The reduction of al-'Audah left Jalājil almost alone in Sudair.[17] A show of force by 'Abd al-'Azīz was sufficient to make the Amir of Jalājil seek favor by offering five horses to the Imam in payment for his misdeeds. The Imam accepted the horses with pleasure, for they were excellent beasts[18] and the offer was a sign that Jalājil had been

[16] The members of the House of Sulṭān, the old rulers of the town, who had returned with Ibn Ḥammād and the Unitarians, settled down to live in al-'Audah, but after a time Ibn Ḥammād drove them into exile and they went to the district of al-Maḥmal.

Ibn Bishr, I, 51, gives more details on the expedition against al-'Audah than does Ibn Ghannām, II, 87–8.

[17] Ibn Ghannām, II, 88, describes Suwaid, Amir of Jalājil, as being an apostate at this time, which would suggest that Ibn Bishr may have been correct in stating that Suwaid accepted Unitarianism in 1177/1764 – see above, p. 104, n. 112.

[18] Ibn Ghannām, II, 88; Ibn Bishr, I, 51. The fondness of the ruling house of Najd for fine horses is illustrated by an anecdote Burckhardt relates about Su'ūd b. 'Abd al-'Azīz when he was Imam: "The greatest punishment inflicted by order of the Wahaby chief is the shaving of the culprit's beard. ... Saoud had long wished to purchase the mare of a sheikh belonging to the tribe of Beni Shammar, but the owner refused to sell her for any sum of money. At this time, the sheikh of the Kahtān Arabs had been sentenced to lose his beard for some offence. When the barber produced his razor in presence of Saoud, the sheikh exclaimed, 'O Saoud, take the mare of the Shammary as a ransom for my beard!' The punishment was remitted; the sheikh was allowed to go and bargain for the mare, which cost him two thousand five hundred dollars, swearing that no sum of money could have induced him to part with her, had it not been to save the beard of a noble Kahtāny. But this is a rare example; for Saoud frequently refused considerable offers of money, to remit the punishment of shaving." – Burckhardt, *Notes on the Bedouins and Wahábys,* II, 144–5.

Su'ūd had a horsefarm for his stock at al-Aḥwar, a watering-place near Ḍurmā; they were kept there in the spring – Ibn Bishr, I, 215. The present King of Saudi Arabia has a large horsefarm at al-Sulaimīyah in al-Kharj; he also keeps a number of horses at Buraidah in al-Qaṣīm. [Imam Su'ud b. 'Abd al-'Aziz was noted for his piety and thorough knowledge and application of strict Shari'ah law, as Burckhardt himself describes elsewhere in his book. This story of the threatened shaving of the beard thus seems out of character with what is known of the man. KAPL]

won for the Unitarian cause. The people of the town of al-'Aṭṭār in Sudair also paid a fine of three hundred *aḥmars* at this time.[19]

The enemies of Unitarianism in al-Washm capitulated along with their fellows in Sudair. Ibrāhīm b. Sulaimān al-'Anqarī, the Amir of Tharmidā, gave up after years of resistance[20] and swore allegiance to the Shaikh and 'Abd al-'Azīz, only to die shortly afterwards in the same year.[21] Others like him in al-Washm, even the people of Marrāh, wrote to 'Abd al-'Azīz expressing their desire to come and embrace Islam as preached by the Shaikh; then the delegations arrived to accept the laws of the religion as binding upon themselves and the people they represented.

Unitarian expeditions against al-Riyāḍ, 1181/1767–8

'Abd al-'Azīz in an expedition against the oasis of al-Riyāḍ alighted at al-Mushaiqīq,[22] where he successfully beat off a sortie by the townspeople, after which he returned home. In another expedition led by 'Abd al-'Azīz the fighting took place at al-Mujawwaz; in the long-range sniping between the two sides the number of Unitarians killed was about the same as the enemy's losses in both men and horses.[23] 'Abd al-'Azīz withdrew to the Unitarian outpost of al-Ghazawānah in the streambed of the valley, where he stayed for a time, harassing the rebellious city with quick dashes out of the fort.[24]

[19] According to Ibn Bishr, I, 52; Ibn Ghannām has no reference to this.

[20] Two of his sons had been killed in the last Unitarian attack on his town the year before – see above, p. 119. Another had been killed by the Unitarians ten years earlier – see above, p. 86.

[21] Ibn Bishr, I, 52; Ibn Ghannām has nothing on either the conversion or the death of Ibrāhīm.

[22] This name is the diminutive of the passive participle *mashqūq*, meaning "split". The place is probably a small ravine.

[23] The Unitarians lost about ten men, while the people of al-Riyāḍ lost five men and four horses – Ibn Ghannām, II, 88; Ibn Bishr, I, 52.

[24] Ibn Bishr, I, 52, mentions a battle fought at Bāb al-Thumairī during this year in which some men were killed on each side. This battle may have taken place on one of the Unitarian raids out of al-Ghazawānah. Bāb al-Thumairī in the western wall of al-Riyāḍ is today one of the principal gates of the city, "the regular outlet to the main tracks to the north and east and also to the southern road towards Manfuha" – Philby, *The Heart of Arabia*, I, 71–2.

Battles with the Bedouins, 1181/1767–8

'Abd Allāh, the brother of 'Abd al-'Azīz,[25] led the Unitarians in a raid against the Bedouins of Muṭair[26] that did not have a favorable outcome for the raiders. They found the Bedouins[27] expecting them with a host of cavalry,[28] for warning of the raid had gone on ahead. The Unitarians, who had begun rounding up the pasturing camels of the nomads before the cavalry of Muṭair appeared, seem to have suffered the heavier losses, and they withdrew in some haste.[29]

Later in the year, after the Amir of Jalājil had paid the fine of the five horses, 'Abd al-'Azīz made a morning attack on a party of Bedouins from the south[30] at the watering-place of al-Murabba' to

[25] Ibn Bishr, I, 52; Ibn Ghannām, II, 87, does not name the commander.

[26] Muṭair is a confederation some of whose members are descended from Qaḥṭān and some from 'Adnān; their *dīrah* at the present time stretches from the borders of al-Kuwait and the Persian Gulf to the neighborhood of al-Qaṣīm in the west and the *dīrah*s of the 'Ajmān and Banī Khālid in the south – Fu'ād Ḥamzah, *Qalb jazīrat al-'arab*, p. 192.

In the early 1760s Niebuhr heard of Muṭair, whom he calls Omtar (امطار), as an important tribe on the boundaries of Najd – *Beschreibung von Arabien*, p. 399. Originally Arabs of the south, Muṭair had moved northwards to occupy the lava tracts between Mecca and Medina, whence they gradually migrated eastwards to their present home – Doughty, *Travels in Arabia Deserta*, II, 366. According to Burckhardt, in the early 19th century they were chiefly in al-Qaṣīm and in the area between that district and Medina – *Notes on the Bedouins and Wahábys*, II, 30. Guarmani in 1864 found them living on the plains to the east of 'Unaizah – *Northern Najd*, p. 93.

Burckhardt understood that Muṭair were "inveterate enemies" of 'Anazah. They were among the most fanatical and devoted of the Wahhabi Ikhwān in the early stages of Ibn Saud's program for settling the Bedouins in colonies, but in the late 1920s they revolted against Ibn Saud under the leadership of Faiṣal Āl Dawīsh, chief of the colony of al-'Arṭāwīyah.

Ibn Ghannām, II, 87, refers to the men of Muṭair as al-Miṭrān.

[27] Neither the direction of the raid nor the site of the battle is given.

[28] Ibn Ghannām, II, 87, states that they had more than 600 horse assembled for the battle. Burckhardt, writing in the early 19th century, says that it was well known that Muṭair had "reduced the number of their horses, within a few years, from two thousand to twelve hundred" – *Notes on the Bedouins and Wahábys*, II, 55–6. Guarmani, whose figures are usually somewhat high, gives the strength of Muṭair in 1864 as 2500 horsemen – *Northern Najd*, p. 93. Doughty, who wandered through Najd in the late 1870s, reported that Muṭair "are in multitude (among the middle Arabian tribes) next after the great Beduin nation *Ateyba* ['Utaibah], and may be almost 5,000 souls" – *Travels in Arabia Deserta*, II, 367. In the early 20th century they were said to be "some 1,500 tents strong" – *A Handbook of Arabia* (Admiralty), I, 83.

[29] Ibn Ghannam, II, 87; Ibn Bishr, I, 52.

the west of Nafūd al-Sirr.[31] The Unitarians took camels belonging to the Bedouins and then went home.

Migrations from Najd to the northeast and other migrations, 1181–3/1768–70

In 1181/1768 there occurred a great drought in Najd that was the cause of the hard times known as Sūqah,[32] which lasted for nearly three years. Wells grew dry, prices went up, and many people died of hunger and disease. Large numbers of the survivors[33] migrated to al-Baṣrah, al-Zubair, al-Kuwait, and other places away from Najd. Late in 1183/early spring 1770 the rains fell before their time, and in Munaikh and elsewhere the first rains were followed by others, but there was no planting in midsummer, for swarms of locusts appeared that ate everything in the fields.[34]

Although this is the first great migration recorded in the Arabian chronicles of the period, similar movements by both nomad and town Arabs were no novelty. Since prehistoric times the tendency of the Arabs has been to shift from south to north in their Peninsula and eventually to gravitate to Iraq in the northeast, drawn by the fertility of that land of rivers.[35] One of the most famous of the migrations in the modern age was the advance in the mid-17th century of large sections of the powerful tribe of Shammar into Iraq, where after years of struggle they established themselves in the Jazirah, the area between the Tigris and the Euphrates. The town-dwellers of Najd did not go in large and warlike aggregations such as Shammar, but year after year they went, singly, in small families, or in groups, seeking escape from the droughts and barrenness of their homeland,

[30] Both Ibn Ghannām, II, 88; and Ibn Bishr, I, 52, call them Bedouins of the Yemen, which probably means that they were from Najrān or another district to the south rather than from the Yemen proper.

[31] Al-Murabba'/The Square is not far south of the town of al-Mudhnib.

[32] The Najdis had a habit of giving a special name to every period of this sort where hardships were the result of natural phenomena. Sūqah comes from the root *sāqa*/"to drive".

[33] Ibn Bishr, I, 52, says "most of the people", which is doubtless an exaggeration.

[34] Ibn Bishr, I, 52, gives more specific details on Sūqah than does Ibn Ghannām, II, 87 and 89, who dwells on the high prices and scarcity of supplies in 1181 and 1182.

[35] Their own saying is: "Yemen is the cradle of the Arabs and Iraq their tomb."

seeking trade or new professions or learning in the ancient schools. Sometimes they did not stay, sometimes they stayed and kept their ties with the places from which they had come, sometimes they cut themselves loose entirely from the past.[36]

As the Unitarianism preached by the Shaikh Muḥammad b. 'Abd al-Wahhāb grew and spread in Najd, men who had fought it and lost and men who had no desire to live under its puritanical laws journeyed away to regions not yet violated by the avenging Unitarian armies.

In 1765 Niebuhr was told that the town of al-Zubair near al-Baṣrah, which a short time before had contained only a few houses, had been built up into a considerable place by fugitives from al-'Āriḍ, the central district of Najd.[37] Al-Baṣrah itself was growing in commercial importance[38] and consequently attracting settlers.

The port of al-Kuwait[39] farther down the Gulf, though it had been founded only a century or so earlier,[40] had by Niebuhr's time a population estimated to be in the neighborhood of 10,000.[41] Among this number were many Najdi expatriates, including the prominent family of Khalīfah,[42] who had come to al-Kuwait from the district of al-Aflāj in southern Najd in the 12th century of the Hegira.[43] Because

[36] Yūsuf b. 'Alī al-Qinā'ī, the author of a sketch of the history of al-Kuwait, goes to some lengths in an attempt to prove that his family, the Qinā'āt of al-Kuwait, are not of Najdi origin, though they have strong ties with the town of al-Qaṣab in al-Washm – *Ṣafaḥāt min ta'rīkh al-Kuwait,* pp. 92–100.

[37] Niebuhr, *Beschreibung von Arabien*, p. 349.

[38] Evidence of this growth is to be seen in the fact that the East India Company in 1763 raised its Resident there to the rank of Agent, and a year later he was given consular status – Longrigg, *Four Centuries of Modern Iraq*, p. 188.

[39] The Little Kūt or Fort. Also called al-Qurain/The Little Horn, whence the Anglicized form Grain that was once in common use.

[40] The exact date of founding is not known; al-Qinā'ī places it in the latter part of the 11th century of the Hegira/late 17th century AD – *Ṣafaḥāt min ta'rīkh al-Kuwait,* p. 4. According to al-Qinā'ī, Arab tradition is unanimous in naming Banī Khālid, the lords of al-Aḥsā', as founders of al-Kuwait, not 'Anazah, as stated by Philby, *Arabia*, p. 25. Al-Qinā'ī suggests that Barrāk b. Ghurair of Banī Khālid, who died in 1093 AH/about 1681 AD, was the one who first built the town. [For the most recent research on the origins of Kuwait, see Slot, B. J., ed., *Kuwait: The Growth of a Historic Identity*, London, Arabian Publishing, 2003. Ed.]

[41] Niebuhr, *Beschreibung von Arabien*, p. 342.

[42] The House of Khalīfah, like the House of Su'ūd in Najd and the House of Ṣabāḥ in al-Kuwait, claim descent from the Bedouin tribe of 'Anazah.

of repeated acts of aggression committed by the neighboring Arabs of Banī Ka'b, Muḥammad b. Khalīfah, then the head of the house, decided to move to Qaṭar in 1178/1764–5, where he alighted with his folk at the new settlement of al-Zubārah[44] on the coast opposite Bahrain, to which place he had come before as a buyer of pearls. Here the House of Khalīfah remained until some twenty years later, when fear inspired by the progress of Unitarian arms impelled them to transfer their residence to the island of Bahrain, the seat of their authority to the present day.

Su'ūd's first command in the field: raid against al-Zilfī, 1182/1768

A year after Su'ūd b. 'Abd al-'Azīz had accompanied the Unitarian raiders for the first time, he was given command of an expedition. The stripling who in his maturity was to outdo even his father in boldness and the breadth of his ranging led a quick dash against al-Zilfī in farther Sudair, up near the borders of al-Qaṣīm.[45] Su'ūd and his men killed three of the townspeople and returned straightway.

'Abd al-'Azīz's attack on Subai' and al-Ḥā'ir, 1182/1768

The son still had much experience to gain before the father would resign him the command of every expedition. While Su'ūd was away in the north, or shortly after his arrival home, 'Abd al-'Azīz headed south to settle a score with the Bedouins of Subai', who were encamped not far from their main gathering-place, the town of al-

[43] The first Amir chosen by the people of al-Kuwait was one Ṣabāḥ, the ancestor of the present ruling house in the Shaikhdom. This Ṣabāḥ, whose family had come to al-Kuwait from Qaṭar, was of Banī 'Utbah, sometimes called the 'Utūb, the section of 'Anazah to which the House of Khalīfah belonged. Ṣabāḥ was succeeded by his youngest son, 'Abd Allāh, who is said to have ruled for about seventy years until his death in 1229/1813–14 – al-Qinā'ī, p. 9.

[44] Al-Zubārah was founded by a certain Shaikh Aḥmad b. Rizq, who was still alive in 1212/1797–8 – al-Nabhānī, *al-Tuḥfah al-nabhānīyah: al-Baḥrain*, pp. 119 and 128.

[45] Al-Zilfī may not have joined the rest of Sudair in making submission the previous year, or there may have been signs of apostasy in the place.

Ḥā'ir. The Bedouins had notice in advance of the approach of the Unitarians and the fight proved grim, but 'Abd al-'Azīz at last won the day. The defeated Bedouins found safety in the castle of al-Ḥā'ir, the garrison of which was made up of men who had rejected Unitarianism, so that the victors had to be satisfied with their booty of horses and camels and sheep and goats and the personal possessions in the empty tents.

Defeat of Su'ūd and his raiders by Āl Murrah, 1182/1768–9

The stunning victory of the lord of Najrān at al-Ḥā'ir was a sign that the Unitarians were to have other sorrowful encounters with the people of the south, who in general make excellent fighting men. Su'ūd's second raid as a commander was directed against the wild nomads of Āl Murrah[46] in their camp at Qinā and Qinā.[47] When the Unitarians made their charge, the Bedouins broke and ran. Chasing the enemy to their tents, the Unitarian horse were so engaged that they failed to notice another party of Bedouins who came up and slashed them in the rear until they took to flight.[48]

[46] Ibn Ghannām, II, 89, refers to them here simply as people of the Yemen; Ibn Bishr, I, 53, names them Āl Murrah.

Āl Murrah, the greatest tribe of the Empty Quarter, often range far to the north of that desert. Claiming descent from Yām of Najrān, they acknowledge the 'Ajmān as their cousins but in former times were frequently in feud with them. They are famous all over Arabia for their skill in tracking; their feats in this respect are so marvelous that it is often said that their ancestor was one of the Jinn. A saying current in Saudi Arabia today runs: "In the sky Ibn Saud has his telegraph [*barqīyah*], while on earth he has his men of Āl Murrah [Murrīyah]." Abundant information on this tribe may be found in Philby, *The Heart of Arabia* and *The Empty Quarter*, and in Bertram Thomas, *Arabia Felix*. Arabic sources are disappointing, for there is no Arab writer who has observed these tribesmen closely in their native habitat.

[47] Qinā and Qinā, which are distinguished from each other in Arabic by one being written with a final *alif* and the other with a final *yā'*, قنا وقني , are two hills with a watering place in the vicinity. [*Cf.* Ch. 14 n. 62 for Qinā and Qunayy, two hills north of al-Qaṣīm. Ed.]

[48] Ibn Bishr, I, 53, as usual is readier to admit the defeat than Ibn Ghannām, II, 89.

[49] The lower course of the valley, from al-Qaṣīm to the Gulf, is known as al-Bāṭin.

[50] Doughty, *Travels in Arabia Deserta*, I, 374.

[51] Doughty, *ibid.* II, 312.

First Unitarian expedition into al-Qaṣīm, 1182/1768–9

Once Sudair and al-Washm had been won over to Unitarianism the next step to the north led into al-Qaṣīm. The Shaikh and the Imam knew that the adhesion of this district, with its wealth of fighting men and horses and camels, would be a signal success for their cause. In terms of material civilization al-Qaṣīm was the most advanced district in the whole of central Arabia. Lying athwart Wadi al-Rimah, the great riverbed that from its head in the Hijaz runs most of the way across the Peninsula to empty into the Persian Gulf,[49] al-Qaṣīm has its good share of farmland and pasture. Moreover, this riverbed is the highway from Mesopotamia to the Holy Land of Islam, a road for merchants as well as pilgrims. The Quṣmān, the "civil and industious people"[50] of al-Qaṣīm, are in the most part descended from settled Bedouins of the stock of Tamīm, whose "thick blood" makes them "prudent and adventurous",[51] and of Banī Khālid and Subai' and other tribes. Although what they have to export from their own country is meager,[52] the Quṣmān are busy in commercial affairs as brokers and importers and above all as carriers, for they are the masters and operators of many of the big caravans crossing the land. Metalworking, stone masonry and other handicrafts are more practised in al-Qaṣīm than in the rest of Najd.

The twin cities of al-Qaṣīm, Buraidah and 'Unaizah, have long been the principal urban centers of Najd, rivaled or surpassed in

[52] In the days of the Shaikh and for most of the 19th century Buraidah and 'Unaizah in al-Qaṣīm were important centers for the trade in Arabian horses. The Italian horsedealer Guarmani in 1864 found the horse market at Buraidah, which was supplied with its stock by the Bedouins of Muṭair, superior in numbers but inferior in quality to the market at 'Unaizah, supplied by the Bedouins of Qaḥṭān. The Amir Zāmil of 'Unaizah explained this difference by quoting the proverb: "Men from the north; horses from the south" – Guarmani, *Northern Najd*, pp. 42–3. This business is now for all practical purposes non-existent.

Other exports from al-Qaṣīm in the past were *samn* (cooking fat), dates and cereals.

[53] At the time of the first penetration of Unitarianism into al-Qaṣīm, it is likely that al-Dir'īyah, despite the influx of immigrants, was still considerably inferior as a city to both Buraidah and 'Unaizah. It may be conjectured that al-Dir'īyah did not become preeminent until very late in the 18th century.

[54] Ibn Bishr, I, 53; Ibn Ghannām does not mention this request of al-Duraibī's.

importance only by the development of al-Dir'īyah and later al-Riyāḍ as the religious and administrative capitals of Unitarianism.[53] Buraidah, on the left or northern bank of Wadi al-Rimah, is an imposing walled city filled with inhabitants universally accounted surly and inhospitable despite their many contacts with the world outside Arabia. The extensive palm gardens lie outside the walls. About ten miles to the south, a short distance from the right bank of the valley, stands 'Unaizah, whose people are engaging and gracious to strangers in contrast to the boorishness of their neighbors. There has never been any love lost between the two towns; throughout the years they have fought each other perhaps as much as they have maintained an uneasy peace.

It was in the direction of these towns and their province that the rulers of al-Dir'īyah now looked as they laid their plans for further expansion. An opportunity presented itself when Ḥumūd al-Duraibī, the chief of Buraidah, sent a request to the Imam 'Abd al-'Azīz for assistance against 'Unaizah.[54] In response to this request the young Su'ūd was selected to take a party north; all told, he had with him about a hundred mounts. The attack was pressed home at Bāb Shārikh, the southern gate of 'Unaizah, and after a brisk fight the defenders took refuge in their town, where the attackers made no attempt to pursue them. Su'ūd returned home immediately.

Encounter with men of al-Riyāḍ, 1183/1769–70

In 1183/May 1769 to April 1770 the Imam 'Abd al-'Azīz prepared for an expedition against al-Riyāḍ. He had hardly left al-Dir'īyah before he ran into a large squadron of Dahhām's cavalry coming to raid al-Dir'īyah after a successful attack on Bedouins of Subai' during which they had acquired a number of camels. When neither side gained a conclusive victory, both abandoned the idea of advancing, thus postponing the final decision between the Unitarians and their old enemy until another day.

Second Unitarian expedition into al-Qaṣīm, 1183/1770

The Unitarianism of the Shaikh was a demanding religion; many who had paid it lipservice could be found from time to time slipping into disobedience and returning to the easier paths they had once known. The district of Sudair had formally adopted Unitarianism, but not many months went by before examples of backsliding began to occur. About the middle of 1183/late 1769 the Shaikh and 'Abd al-'Azīz found it necessary to dispatch a punitive expedition against the town of al-Majma'ah.[55] Stopping at Ḥuraimilā on the way, 'Abd al-'Azīz called out the manpower of the districts of al-Maḥmal and Sudair. With this force he alighted at al-Maknas,[56] where he clashed with the people of al-Majma'ah but did not win a clear-cut victory.[57]

'Abd al-'Azīz now ordered his foot-soldiers to return to their homes, for it was Ramaḍān, the month of fasting/January 1770, while he and the camelry rode on northwestwards into al-Qaṣīm until they came to the small settlement of al-Hilālīyah.[58] In the darkness some of the Unitarians took up positions where they would be out of sight when day came; the others made ready to draw out the villagers from behind their walls. Everything went according to plan, and the next day the Unitarians celebrated their triumph by

[55] Al-Majma'ah is not mentioned specifically in the accounts of the submission of Sudair two years before this, but there can be little doubt that this place, which lies a journey of two days southward from the northern boundary of the district, did not then hold aloof. The chronicles have nothing to report on the attitude of al-Majma'ah towards Unitarianism between the death there of Mubārak b. 'Adwān, the exiled Amir of Huraimilā (see above, p. 96), and this expedition, a period of ten years.

[56] A *maknas* is a place where gazelles seek refuge from the heat.

[57] According to Ibn Ghannām, II, 90, 'Abd Allāh and Quwaifil, the brothers of Aḥmad b. 'Uthmān, the Amir of al-Majma'ah, were killed in the battle. According to Ibn Bishr, I, 56, the Amir himself was killed, which is incorrect – see below, p. 164. This Aḥmad b. 'Uthmān was the old ally of Mubārak b. 'Adwān and opponent of Unitarianism – see above, p. 89.

[58] Al-Hilālīyah and its neighbour al-Bukairīyah, both of which are ancient colonies of Subai', lie about a score of miles southwest of 'Unaizah. Al-Hilālīyah takes its name from the medieval tribe of Banī Hilāl famous in Arab legend – Doughty, *Travels in Arabia Deserta*, II, 414.

[59] Ibn Ghannām, II, 90, says that all of the people of al-Qaṣīm were struck with fear and desired to adopt Islam, turning away from the idols they worshiped; they came to 'Abd al-'Azīz and made a pact with him. Ibn Bishr, I, 56, says that most of the people in al-Qasīm sent delegations to swear allegiance to the religion of God and the Prophet in the presence of 'Abd al-'Azīz. Neither gives any information about the attitude of 'Unaizah and Buraidah at this moment.

plundering the settlement, after which an amnesty for the inhabitants was proclaimed. The skill with which this raid from the south was executed made a deep impression on the people throughout al-Qaṣīm, many of whom came forward to embrace the beliefs of Unitarianism.[59] 'Abd al-'Azīz remained at al-Hilālīyah for some days, receiving the new converts and appointing men to instruct them in theology and the laws.

As the Unitarians were bound for home laden with booty to be divided according to custom in al-Dir'īyah, they came across the tracks of a raiding party of Banī Khālid led by Buṭayyin b. 'Urai'ir, son of the lord of al-Aḥsā'. When the raiders learned of the proximity of 'Abd al-'Azīz and his men, they made off without giving battle.[60]

In the following year, 1184/April 1770 to April 1771, the members of the House of Ibn 'Ulayyān in Buraidah rose up against the chief of the town, Rāshid al-Duraibī,[61] drove him into exile, and made themselves masters in his place. There is no indication as to whether the spread of Unitarianism in al-Qaṣīm had anything to do with this or not; the act may have been simply the outcome of a local feud.[62]

Reduction of al-Ḥā'ir by the Unitarians, 1184/1770–1

Since the invasion from Najrān the Unitarian strategists had concentrated their efforts in the north, where their soldiers had ridden all the way to al-Qaṣīm, taking the Word of God with them and overcoming resistance wherever it appeared. Now it was time to give attention once more to the south. Close at hand al-Riyāḍ still held

[60] Ibn Ghannām, II, 91, says that the raiders attacked a number of Bedouins of Subai' who were staying in the neighborhood of Ḍurmā; the townspeople, who were loyal Unitarians, came to the aid of the men of Subai' and the raiders were soundly beaten, losing much of their gear and about six fine horses, which were seized by the victors. Ibn Ghannām does not make it clear whether this took place before or after the raiding party nearly had the collison with 'Abd al-'Azīz's force. Ibn Bishr has nothing at all on the raiding party.

[61] Rāshid had apparently succeeded his relative Ḥumūd, who was chief of the town in 1182 – see above, p. 129.

[62] Ibn Bishr, I, 57, records the act without comment; Ibn Ghannām does not even record it.

out under Dahhām, a little farther on al-Ḥā'ir and then al-Kharj harbored enemies, and in the far distance the formidable power of Najrān had not yet ceased to threaten.

The strategists selected al-Ḥa'ir for the first action. 'Abd al-'Azīz encompassed the town with his troops and began to cut down the palm trees in its gardens. Seeing their staff of life about to be shattered, the inhabitants hastened out to offer allegiance to the Imam and the religion he fought for.[63]

Fighting with the Ẓafīr and the 'Ajmān, 1184–6/1770–3

In 1184/April 1770 to April 1771 'Abd al-'Azīz raided the Muḥammarah of the Ẓafīr and took some of their camels after a fight. In 1185/April 1771 to April 1772 the Unitarians set out on an expedition directed against Munaikh,[64] but when they stopped at Ḥuraimilā news came in that a raiding party of the Ẓafīr under some of their chiefs of the House of Ḍuwaiḥī were behind them at Ghiyānah,[65] between Ḥuraimilā and Sadūs. Turning about, the Unitarians caught up with the Bedouin raiders and dealt them a heavy blow, killing some, including Wahaq[66] Ibn Fayyāḍ, capturing others, and putting the rest to flight.

The next year, 1186/April 1772 to March 1773, 'Abd al-'Azīz went out after Āl Ḥubaish of the 'Ajmān, whom he found camping in the land known as Ṣabḥā'.[67] The Unitarians went into ambush and

[63] Ibn Ghannām, II, 91; Ibn Bishr, I, 58.

[64] Ibn Ghannām, II, 91, names Su'ūd as the commander; Ibn Bishr, I, 58, his father the Imam 'Abd al-'Azīz.

[65] Ghiyānah or Ghayānah, from the root *ghanā*/"to be thirsty".

[66] A *wahaq* or *wahq* is a sort of Arabian lasso.

[67] *Ṣabḥā'* is the feminine of *aṣbaḥ*/"reddish black in color".

[68] A *ṣafāh* is a great hard rock; a *fawwārah* is a spring where the water bubbles up – see above, p. 60, n. 10.

[69] Ibn Ghannām, II, 93, says that Dawwās was the first to be killed in the fight while Sa'dūn was the last. The account in Ibn Bishr, I, 58, suggests that Dawwās was captured while fleeing from the field and then executed in cold blood by the Imam.

The custom of having a boy child named after his grandfather, as in the case of this Dawwās b. Dahhām b. Dawwās, is common in Najd.

waited until they had prayed the morning prayer, after which they rushed out to scatter the nomads from their camp and seize their camels.

Final victory over al-Riyāḍ, Rabī' II 1187/July 1773

Once the Unitarians had begun to exert pressure again in the south with the capture of al-Ḥā'ir, 'Abd al-'Azīz gathered his strength to deliver the *coup de grâce* to the incorrigible Dahhām b. Dawwās, whose resistance over the years in al-Riyāḍ had been a notable obstacle to the imposition of the Shaikh's religion on the whole of Najd. Not long after the fight with the Ẓafīr at Ghiyānah in 1185/April 1771 to April 1772, 'Abd al-'Azīz attacked the settlement of Mi'kāl in the oasis of al-Riyāḍ, lured the inhabitants into an ambush, and killed six of them. The Unitarians then headed for home, but on the road they decided to wheel about and swoop down on al-Riyāḍ of a sudden. This maneuver brought them by chance face to face with Dahhām himself, who had come up with cavalry and camelry to harry the Unitarian residents of 'Arqah, a town between al-Riyāḍ and al-Dir'īyah. In the battle that was joined in the vicinity of 'Arqah the Unitarians won a quick and telling victory. At the rock called Ṣafāt al-Ẓahrah between 'Arqah and al-Fawwārah[68] the horse ridden by Dawwās, Dahhām's son, stumbled, allowing its rider to fall into the hands of the Unitarians. The Imam 'Abd al-'Azīz killed Dawwās, while his men killed about twenty of the enemy, including another son of Dahhām's, Sa'dūn.[69] Dahhām grieved greatly over the loss of his two sons, a loss which sapped his will to continue the struggle. Nor was he to have any rest, for 'Abd al-'Azīz raided al-Riyāḍ later in the same year and killed off a few more of his people, and in the following year, 1186/April 1772 to March 1773, the Unitarians repeated this proceeding. In the first of the two raids carried out in 1186[70] the Unitarians designed their ambush to trap the flocks of the town as they came out to pasture in the morning; when the men lying in wait appeared, the camels of al-Riyāḍ eluded the trap,

[70] Ibn Ghannām, II, 94, names Su'ūd as the commander; Ibn Bishr, I, 59, his father the Imam 'Abd al-'Azīz.

making for the safety of their walls, but seven of their masters met their fate in the fight that took place over them. In the second raid, captained by 'Abd al-'Azīz, the morning attack of the Unitarians resulted in the death of Marzūq al-Muṭairī and Muḥammad Ibn Fā'iz.[71] On the Unitarian side 'Alī b. Muḥammad, the Amir of Ḍurmā,[72] was killed.

The hammering against al-Riyāḍ was taken up again in Ṣafar 1187/April to May 1773. Instead of the usual hit-and-run raid, 'Abd al-'Azīz and his fighting men installed themselves in the oasis and remained there for a number of days, trading blows each day with the defenders. The Unitarians seized some of the towers and walls and destroyed them; they also pulled down the high watchtower.[73] Many of the defenders were killed, and the Unitarians lost twelve out of their ranks. With despair entering the hearts of Dahhām and the citizens of al-Riyāḍ, the conquest of the city was almost within the grasp of the Unitarians, but 'Abd al-'Azīz drew off and marched back to al-Dir'īyah for the time being. In the middle of Rabī' II/early July 1773[74] he made ready, despite the summer heat, to resume the attack, enrolling the strongest force possible for the venture, which all felt would mark the climax of the long-drawn-out struggle. In the meantime Dahhām, after much vacillation, had decided that it was futile to resist any longer and had made up his mind to abandon the town he had ruled for many years as a usurper.[75] In the neigh-

[71] These names suggest that there were elements of the tribes of Muṭair and Subai' supporting Dahhām in the defense of his oasis.

[72] Ibn Ghannām, II, 94; Ibn Bishr, I, 59. Apparently this 'Alī was the son and successor of Muḥammad b. 'Abd Allāh, who had upheld the cause of Unitarianism in Ḍurmā twenty years earlier – see above, p. 77. Philby, *Arabia*, pp. 24, 366, is mistaken in identifying him as the son of Muḥammad b. Su'ūd of al-Dir'īyah, i.e. as the brother of 'Abd al-'Azīz.

[73] Al-Marqab. The other towers were called *burūj* – Ibn Ghannām, II, 94; Ibn Bishr, I, 60.

[74] Philby, *Arabia*, p. 25, is incorrect in placing this towards the end of 1773, for Ibn Ghannām, II, 96, and Ibn Bishr, I, 60, agree that it was in mid-Rabī' II.

[75] Ibn Ghannām, II, 95–96, and Ibn Bishr, I, 60, give detailed but conflicting accounts of what went on in al-Riyāḍ at this time, accounts that may or may not be based on information gathered from persons who were present. In substance, Ibn Ghannām states that Dahhām summoned all the notables of the town and informed them of his intention to flee, after which they and the great majority of the townspeople decided to accompany him. Ibn Bishr, after admitting that all the people of al-Riyāḍ were loyal to Dahhām, says that it was reported that Dahhām made the preparations for his departure privily, so that none beyond his intimates had knowledge of his plan until he came out of his castle with

borhood of 'Arqah a messenger met 'Abd al-'Azīz and the Unitarian host with the news that Dahhām b. Dawwās had fled from his stronghold. Hastening on, 'Abd al-'Azīz arrived at the oasis in the late afternoon to find it deserted save for a handful of dwellers.

When Dahhām rode away with his womenfolk and children and henchmen on horseback and camelback, his subjects took to the road in a frenzied rush. Doors of the houses were left hanging open, camels standing at their watering-places, and meat boiling in the pots.[76] The event became famous; for years thereafter in Najd and elsewhere the saying was repeated upon the occasion of a person's foolishly abandoning or selling a house or a palm grove or moving from one town to another: "Like the evacuation of al-Riyāḍ by Dahhām b. Dawwās."[77] The stream of fugitives flowed southwards, for they hoped to find refuge at al-Dilam in al-Kharj, a town known for its unfriendliness towards the Shaikh and his doctrines. Dahhām, who was better prepared than most for the journey, seems to have reached his goal safely,[78] but many of his compatriots, lacking food and water and burned by the midsummer sun, fell by the wayside.[79] 'Abd al-'Azīz put men on their trail, who gave water to the poor and the weak but the sword to every enemy of the faith they overtook.

In the town itself 'Abd al-'Azīz proclaimed an amnesty, which induced those in hiding to show their faces. He also endeavored to persuade those who had fled with Dahhām to return, excluding only those whose notorious misdeeds in the past had placed them beyond the pale.

The booty taken was without doubt the richest acquired in any

his party and declared: "People of al-Riyāḍ, for years I have been here fighting Ibn Su'ūd, but now I have had my fill of warfare and I am leaving the place to him. Whoever wishes to follow me, let him do so; otherwise let him bide in his place in the town." His flight was then followed by the flight of most of the others.

[76] So Ibn Bishr was told – I, 60.

[77] Ibn Bishr, I, 61.

[78] He may have helped to inspire the bitter opposition offered by Zaid b. Zāmil, the lord of al-Dilam, to Unitarianism during the next few years, though there is no direct evidence to this effect, since the Wahhabi chroniclers ignore Dahhām's career following his evacuation of al-Riyāḍ.

[79] According to Ibn Ghannām, II, 97, about four hundred of them perished.

Unitarian campaign up to this point.[80] The whole town with all its weapons and other contents and its palm gardens was reckoned as won for the Unitarian state. It was said that the sum of 40,000 *muḥammadīyahs*[81] was carried off to al-Dir'īyah and placed in charge of the Shaikh, who did not take a single *dirham* for himself.[82] Since there had been no opportunity for the mounted men in the Unitarian forces to perform special services in the winning of the town, all of the booty was turned over to the public treasury.[83]

'Abd al-'Azīz stayed on in al-Riyāḍ for some days, putting the affairs of the new conquest in order and appointing an Amir as representative of the Unitarian government and an Imam to lead the people in prayer. During this time he received a letter from the Shaikh which read in part:

> I desire for you what I desire for myself. In dealing with your enemy God has shown you what you had not even hoped for. What God has shown you is that you should repeat the words of al-Ḥasan al-Baṣrī,[84] who, when he was about to relate a saying of the Prophet, would declare: "O God, praise be to You, since You have created us and provided for us and guided us and comforted us. Praise be to You for Islam and the Koran. Praise be to You for mankind and what they possess and their wellbeing. You have laid low our enemy, You have bestowed bounty upon us, You have placed us in safe-keeping, and you have granted us wellbeing. Everything we have asked of You, O Lord, You have given to us. Praise be to You for that in abundant measure, so that You may be pleased. Then praise be to You when You are pleased."[85]

[80] When the Unitarians entered the town 'Abd al-'Azīz posted men in the houses to prevent looting – Ibn Bishr, I, 61.
[81] The *muḥammadīyah* was a coin then current in Arabia, the value of which is not known.
[82] Ibn Bishr, I, 15.
[83] Ibn Ghannām, II, 97. Ordinarily the riders received an extra share. The treasury was called Bait al-Māl.
[84] Al-Ḥasan al-Baṣrī (d. 728 AD) was a great religious figure noted in particular for transmitting words and traditions of the Prophet.
[85] Ibn Ghannām, II, 98. This is the only part of the letter quoted by Ibn Ghannām.
[86] Ibn Bishr, I, 61. When Ibn Ghannām, II, 98, says the war lasted thirty years, he is speaking in round numbers, for the first action of the conflict took place in 1159, which began in January 1746 – see above, p. 58.

The occupation of al-Riyāḍ in 1187/1773 was the culmination of the war that had gone on for about twenty-seven years[86] between the Unitarians and Dahhām b. Dawwās. It was estimated that during this period about four thousand men had fallen in the fighting, 2300 from al-Riyāḍ and 1700 from among the Unitarians,[87] enough men to populate what would be an unusually large town in the interior of Arabia. All this bloodshed had served to establish the Unitarian faith without a rival in central Najd, the heartland of the Peninsula. With the foothold gained, the Shaikh and the Imam were ready to set new tasks before their missionary soldiers.

Retirement of the Shaikh from public affairs

Following the conquest of al-Ḥā'ir and al-Riyāḍ, the Unitarian writ ran down to the hostile oasis settlements of al-Kharj in the south. In the east the sands of the Dahnā' had been crossed in a single raid; the Bedouin lords of Banī Khālid still ruled the relatively rich land of al-Aḥsā'. In the north the energetic folk of al-Qaṣīm had recently been taken into the fold; Iraq and Syria lay beyond on the routes but were not to fall prey until a number of years and many events had passed. On the fourth side the Najdi movement was edging westwards towards the domains that the Sharif of Mecca, the great power in the Hijaz, counted his own.

Within these boundaries the religion that the Shaikh expounded and the House of Su'ūd fought for had been, as a result of the campaigns of about three decades, firmly implanted. Its districts were al-'Āriḍ, the home country, al Maḥmal, al-Washm, Sudair and al-Qaṣīm, all lying in or close to the rugged hills of Ṭuwaiq. Opposition to the Shaikh or his teachings had not died out altogether and local politics were not completely extinguished, but the grip of Unitarianism on the region had become too strong to be broken by any force other than foreign intervention.

[87] Both Ibn Ghannām, II, 98, and Ibn Bishr, I, 61, cite these figures.

[88] 'Abd al-'Azīz was then about fifty-three.

[89] Ibn Bishr, I, 15. Ibn Ghannām passes over the retirement of the Shaikh without a word, which suggests that it was probably a gradual process without formal announcements or special emphasis on the change.

The capture of al-Riyāḍ took place nearly eight years after the death of Muḥammad b. Su'ūd in Rabī' I 1179/September 1765. During these years 'Abd al-'Azīz had carried on his father's work as Amir and Imam, and he had done it well. The Shaikh Muḥammad b. 'Abd al-Wahhāb, who was now about seventy, felt that the time had come to transfer his temporal responsibilities, including the management of the public treasury, to the shoulders of his younger colleague.[88] From this time on the Imam was the one to whom reference was made in all the affairs of the state, but such was the prestige of the founder of the movement and the regard in which he was held that 'Abd al-'Azīz continued to consult him as a matter of course and to seek his approval for all major decisions. The Shaikh turned from the business of war and politics to a regime of worship and the instruction of his wide circle of students, to which he devoted the remaining twenty years of his life.[89]

9

First Contacts with the Hijaz

Early relations with the Hijaz

Relations with the Holy Land of Arabia and Islam, the mountainous country of the Hijaz in the western part of the Peninsula, eventually grew to be of supreme importance in the history of the Unitarian movement. As these relations developed in intimacy, they resulted in a state of war that existed through the last years of the 18th century and the first years of the 19th until peace came with the subjection of the Hijaz to Unitarian rule, an event that served as no other had to draw the attention of the outside world to the puritanical interpretation of Islam preached by the men of Najd. Had the Unitarians kept hands off the Hijaz, the armies of Muḥammad 'Alī of Egypt might never have marched into Arabia to destroy the temporal power of Unitarianism.

For the first ninety years of the 18th century, however, the relations between Najd and the Hijaz were intermittent and of slight significance. This was not due to any lack of basic hostility between the principles of Najd and the practices of the Hijaz. Many of the people of the Hijaz and many pilgrims who visited Mecca and Medina were guilty of sins and innovations denounced by the Shaikh Muḥammad b. 'Abd al-Wahhāb, as the thorough cleansing of the Holy Cities by the Unitarians was later to show.[1] The inconsequential character of the relations may be traced back rather to the preoccupation of the Unitarians with local affairs in Najd and the preoccupation of the rulers of the Hijaz with dynastic feuds. The clash was not to come until the Unitarians had riveted fast their control at home and one branch of the Sharifial line in Mecca had subdued all its rivals.

[1] See also above, pp. 21–2.

The modern line of the Sharifs of Mecca goes back to Qatādah b. Idrīs (d. 1221 AD), a direct descendant of al-Ḥasan, grandson of the Prophet. In 1525 AD, less than a decade after the attachment of the Hijaz to the Ottoman Empire, the Sharif Muḥammad Abū Numayy began a reign that was long and peaceful.[2] His descendants, however, had much trouble to experience, for they took to fighting among themselves. By the first half of the 17th century the House of Abū Numayy had split into three contesting clans: Dhawī Barakāt,[3] the 'Abādilah,[4] and Dhawī Zaid.[5] In 1688 AD Sa'īd b. Sa'd of Dhawī Zaid[6] became Sharif for the first time, commencing a career that was distinguished by the fact that he held the office on five different occasions and produced six sons each of whom held it after him. Following Sa'īd's death in 1129/1716, Dhawī Barakāt interrupted the ascendancy of Dhawī Zaid for a few years until Sa'īd's sons succeeded in regaining the authority. Two of the six sons enjoyed lengthy reigns, Mas'ūd from 1146 to 1165/1734 to 1752,[7] and Musā'id from 1165 to 1184/1752 to 1770. It was during the reign of Mas'ūd that the first recorded incident in the relations between the Unitarians and the Hijaz took place, and it was shortly after the death of Musā'id that the two parties for the first time organized an official religious disputation.

When the season of the pilgrimage drew near in each of the years immediately following the creation of the Unitarian state through the sealing of the compact between the Shaikh Muḥammad b. 'Abd al-Wahhāb and the Amir Muḥammad b. Su'ūd, it may safely be assumed that at least a few of their followers in al-Dir'īyah and the neighboring towns took the long road overland to Mecca. The Unitarians considered the pilgrimage a religious duty incumbent upon them, and the preaching of Unitarianism had not yet made

[2] Snouck Hurgronje, *Mekka*, I, 104.

[3] Dhawī Barakāt were the descendants of Barakāt, a son of Muḥammad Abū Numayy who had never held the office of Sharif himself.

[4] The 'Abādilah were the descendants of 'Abd Allāh b. Ḥasan b. Muḥammad Abū Numayy. Both 'Abd Allāh and Ḥasan had held the office of Sharif.

[5] Dhawī Zaid were the descendants of Zaid b. Muḥsin b. Ḥusain b. Ḥasan b. Muḥammad Abū Numayy. All in this line had held the office of Sharif.

[6] Sa'īd b. Sa'd b. Zaid, grandson of the eponym of Dhawī Zaid.

[7] Mas'ūd had previously held the office for three or four months in 1145/1732–3.

such a stir in Najd as to arouse strong suspicions in the breast of the Sharif Mas'ūd, the theocratic potentate in the west.

After four or five years, however, the situation changed. Reports were reaching Mas'ūd of developments in the interior, and many of the reports were distorted and exaggerated. Some of the Unitarian pilgrims were no doubt boldly outspoken in condemning the violations of early Islamic practice that they saw in the Holy City. At the time of the pilgrimage in 1161 or 1162/November or December 1748 or November 1749,[8] the Sharif Mas'ūd ordered the arrest of the Unitarian pilgrims then in Mecca. He held them in confinement for so long that a number of them died before securing release.[9]

It may also be assumed that the barring of the Unitarians from the pilgrimage dated from this time. For the next twenty years or so there is no mention of Unitarians making their way to Mecca, though many of them must have yearned to do so, for it is a bitter thing for a Moslem to leave this life without having offered homage to the House of God on earth.

In 1183/May 1769 to April 1770, when Musā'id was Sharif of Mecca and the troops of the Imam 'Abd al-'Azīz were establishing themselves in al-Qaṣīm, a band of Unitarian raiders came upon the Sharif Manṣūr[10] by chance and took him prisoner. The Imam 'Abd al-'Azīz granted Manṣūr his freedom without payment of a ransom; in appreciation of this action Manṣūr came back from the Sharif Musā'id with permission for the Unitarians to make the pilgrimage.

[8] Ibn Bishr, I, 23, places this event under 1162; then he states that it is also said to have taken place in the preceding year.

[9] Ibn Ghannām has nothing on this incident or on any aspect of the relations between the Unitarians and the Hijaz until the raid of the Sharif Manṣūr – see below, this page.

Snouck Hurgronje, *Mekka,* I, 138–9, taking his information from Aḥmad b. Zainī Daḥlān, *Khulāṣat al-kalām*, states that in the time of Mas'ūd thirty learned Wahhabis came to Mecca to preach Unitarianism and to secure recognition of their right to participate in the pilgrimage without hindrance. These Wahhabi emissaries were very badly treated. The pertinent portion of Daḥlān is not at hand at the moment of writing, but from Snouck's summary it would seem that the thirty were some if not all of the Unitarian pilgrims imprisoned by Mas'ūd. When permission to make the pilgrimage was granted to the Unitarians in 1197/1783, after their faith had expanded greatly in Najd, only about three hundred went to Mecca, though that number may not have been representative because of the existence of famine in Najd that year – see below, p. 185.

[10] Ibn Ghannām, II, 91. Manṣūr is not identified; he may have been a fairly close relative of the reigning Sharif.

That year a party of them went in safety and performed all the rites with satisfaction.[11]

Unitarian mission to Mecca, 1184/1770–1

In the early summer of 1184/1770[12] a large comet appeared in the heavens over the Hijaz. Centuries before, a poet, al-Fāsī by name, had fashioned verses predicting that a glittering star with a long tail would be a sign foretelling the advent thirty years later of heretics from the east who would trample over the land.[13] Although there were probably few in Mecca who heeded or even recalled al-Fāsī's prophecy at the time of the comet's appearance, all the inhabitants of the city were to become aware of the danger in the east before the thirty years had passed.

The Sharif Musā'id b. Sa'īd, who had given the Unitarians of Najd permission to make the pilgrimage in 1183/March and April 1770,[14] died in Muḥarram 1184/late April to late May 1770, only about a month after the pilgrimage season had ended, and was succeeded by his brother Aḥmad b. Sa'īd. Dhawī Barakāt, the rivals of Dhawī Zaid[15] for the Sharifate, took advantage of the change in rulers to advance their own claim to supremacy in the Holy City. Needing outside assistance in the attempt to supplant the sons of Sa'īd, the members of Dhawī Barakāt turned to Egypt.

In the land of Egypt, which since the early 16th century had been a domain of the Ottoman Empire, an able Mameluke named 'Alī Bey had gradually acquired administrative power until he was strong enough to throw off the Ottoman overlordship in 1182/May 1768 to May 1769.[16] 'Alī Bey was a man of large views who perceived that

[11] The pilgrimage in 1183 reached its climax in the first week of April 1770. Philby, *Arabia*, p. 23, is wrong in saying that the pilgrims were "welcomed and nobly entertained by the Grand Sharif, Ahmad Ibn Sa'id", for Aḥmad did not become Sharif of Mecca until after the death of Musā'id in Muḥarram 1184/late April to late May 1770.

[12] Snouck Hurgronje, *Mekka*, I, 138, says in May or June.

[13] Snouck Hurgronje, *Mekka*, I, 138, n. 1, gives the Arabic of al-Fāsī's verses as quoted by Aḥmad b. Zainī Daḥlān. The word used in the verses for heretics is Khawārij/Outgoers, which is what the extremist party in early Islam was called.

[14] See above, p. 141.

[15] The sons of Sa'īd were of Dhawī Zaid – see above, p. 140.

his position in Egypt would be more secure if he extended his influence into Syria and Arabia. Before the death of the Sharif Musā'id the new ruler of Egypt had received 'Abd Allāh b. Ḥusain of Dhawī Barakāt[17] and had without doubt learned much about the internal politics of the Hijaz from him.[18] When the moment seemed opportune for Dhawī Barakāt in 1184/1770, 'Abd Allāh b. Ḥusain visited 'Alī Bey again to implore Egyptian intervention. Hoping to undermine the Sultan's authority and to enhance his own prestige, 'Alī Bey rapidly organised an army and sent it with cannon down the Red Sea from Suez under the command of his lieutenant Muḥammad Abū al-Dhahab. Before Aḥmad b. Sa'īd had completed his first month as Sharif the Egyptian forces were in Mecca, Aḥmad's palace had been plundered of its treasures, and Aḥmad himself was in flight. The invaders installed 'Abd Allāh b. Ḥusain as the new Sharif,[19] and 'Abd Allāh in return recognized 'Alī Bey as Sultan of Egypt and Khāqān of the Two Seas, a title that the Ottoman Sultans had borne for centuries.

Had 'Alī Bey remained in power in Egypt and had the Egyptian occupation of Mecca continued for years, the course of Arabian history might well have been changed. The 19th century later showed how disastrous to the spread of Unitarianism Egyptian rule over the Hijaz could be. Egyptian interference at this time, however, turned out to be very brief. 'Alī Bey's interest shifted to developments in Syria; Abū al-Dhahab and his troops were recalled from the Hijaz after a stay of some weeks in order to prepare for an expedition to challenge the Sublime Porte in such centers as Damascus. Before three years had gone by Abū al-Dhahab had revolted against his

[16] 'Alī Bey asserted the independence of Egypt by expelling the Ottoman Pasha or Governor from the country. C.-F. Volney, *Voyage en Syrie et en Egypte* (Paris 1787), I, 110, says that 'Alī Bey struck money in his own name in 1768, which indicates that he had then assumed the attributes of sovereignty.

The author of the present dissertation has written an article entitled "'Alī Bey and Count Orlov", which he hopes to publish soon, dealing with, among other things, the rise of 'Alī Bey to power in Egypt and his relations with the Hijaz at this time.

[17] 'Abd al-Raḥmān b. Ḥasan al-Jabartī, *'Ajā'ib al-āthār* (Cairo 1880), I, 350.

[18] 'Alī Bey also had firsthand knowledge of the Hijaz, having as a young man accompanied his master Ibrāhīm on the pilgrimage in 1750.

[19] Ibn Bishr, I, 57. Ibn Bishr mistakenly calls 'Abd Allāh by his father's name, Ḥusain.

master 'Alī Bey and encompassed his death on the battlefield.[20] Egypt did not emerge again as a power in international affairs until the coming of a greater mercenary, Muḥammad 'Alī.

The Sharif 'Abd Allāh b. Ḥusain of Dhawī Barakāt could not maintain himself without the guns of the Egyptian army. In Jumādā II 1184/late September to late October 1770 he was deposed and Aḥmad b. Sa'īd of Dhawī Zaid returned to rule as Sharif.

The Unitarians may have requested of the Sharif Aḥmad a renewal of the permission to make the pilgrimage, for the season for visiting the House of God in Mecca was approaching, or Aḥmad may have been moved by curiosity regarding the principles then being proclaimed in Najd; at any rate, Aḥmad wrote to the Shaikh Muḥammad b. 'Abd al-Wahhāb and the Amir Muḥammad b. Su'ūd asking them to send a religious scholar to Mecca to expound their beliefs. The rulers of al-Dir'īyah selected for the mission the Qadi of al-Washm, 'Abd al-'Azīz b. 'Abd Allāh Āl Ḥaṣīn al-Nāṣirī, who had studied under the founder of the movement; with him they sent presents for the Sharif[21] and a letter[22] addressed to him, which read as follows:

> In the name of God, the Merciful and Compassionate.
>
> To the Sharif Aḥmad b. Sa'īd, may God grant him lasting bounty and give him glory both here and hereafter, and may He through him make great the religion of his ancestor, the lord of men and genii [the Prophet].
>
> When your letter was received by your servant and he read the kind words it contained, he raised his hands in prayer to God so that He might strengthen the Sharif, since his purpose was to support the laws of the Prophet and those who obey them and to be an enemy of those who have departed them them. This is the duty of men in authority. Since you requested that we send you a student,

[20] 'Alī Bey in the closing years of his life tried to recoup his crumbling fortunes by securing aid from Count A.G. Orlov, the Russian commander-in-chief in the Mediterranean, who had destroyed the Ottoman fleet at Chesme in the summer of 1770. The Russians gave 'Alī much verbal encouragement but little active assistance – see my paper, "'Alī Bey and Count Orlov". [See n. 16 above.]

[21] The sources do not state what the gifts were.

[22] Philby, *Arabia*, p. 23, refers to the letter as "a lengthy epistle", in actuality, it was rather short, as may be seen from the full text given here.

> we have complied and he is coming to you. He will attend the councils of the Sharif, may God give him glory, together with the 'Ulamā' of Mecca. If they reach an agreement, praise be to God, while if they differ, let the Sharif bring their books and the books of the Hanbalites. It is incumbent upon us and upon them to seek the face of God and the victory of His Prophet by means of our learning, as He Himself has said [in the Koran]: "Since God has bound the prophets" and so on to His words: "Believe in him and give him aid." If God has bound the prophets to believe in and give aid to Muḥammad, God bless him and grant him peace, how is it with us, his people? There is no alternative but to believe in him and give him aid, but neither belief nor aid is sufficient one without the other. The people best fitted for this are the members of the Prophet's own family, out of whom God chose him to give them honor among all the people of the earth, and the ones best fitted for this among the members of his family are those of his own seed, may God bless him and grant him peace.
>
> In closing, the Sharif knows that his servant is truly his servant. May God guard you and keep you in His good care.[23]

In Mecca the Unitarian delegate held a disputation with three of the 'Ulamā': Yaḥyā b. Ṣāliḥ al-Ḥanafī, 'Abd al-Wahhāb b. Ḥasan al-Turkī, who was said to be the Mufti of the Ottoman Sultan, and 'Abd al-Ghanī b. Hilāl. The Meccan scholars brought up three questions: first, the reports concerning the general denunciation by the Unitarians of other Moslems as infidels; secondly, the destruction of tombs built over graves; and thirdly, the Unitarian prohibition on praying to holy persons for intercession. The Unitarian delegate asserted that the reports concerning the general denunciation of other Moslems as infidels were entirely false. With regard to the destruction of tombs, the delegate presented the testimony of scholars approving such action. The question dealing with intercession seems to have provoked the most prolonged discussion; in the end the Unitarian scholar called for *al-Iqnā'* by al-Ḥijāwī, one of the basic

[23] Ibn Ghannām, II, 92.
[24] Ibn Ghannām, II, 93.
[25] See below, p. 184.

Hanbalite works, to prove his contention that the Imams of the four major schools of law had all condemned intercession as *shirk*. According to the Unitarian chronicler who alone has recorded the details of this disputation,[24] the Meccan scholars, convinced of the rightness of Unitarian beliefs, exclaimed: This is the religion of God, and this is the school of the Imam, that is of Aḥmad Ibn Ḥanbal. Due honor was shown to the delegate from Najd when he took his leave.

This Unitarian account, if taken at face value, would suggest that there was no reason for the Sharif Aḥmad b. Sa'īd to refuse permission for the men of Najd to make the pilgrimage. However, there is no mention in the sources of any of them coming to Mecca as a result of this mission, and there is no mention of a Unitarian pilgrimage during the following year, 1185/1772. Aḥmad was driven out of office for the second time just before the pilgrimage season in 1186/1773 and was suceeded by his nephew Surūr b. Musā'id. Early in Surūr's reign the Unitarians were once again trying to get leave from the Sharif for formal visits by their people to the Ka'bah.[25]

PART III

Consolidation in Najd

1187–1199 AH/AD 1773–1785

10

Najran and al-Aḥsā' Repelled Again

Opposition of the lord of al-Dilam in al-Kharj to Unitarianism, and his negotiations with the lord of Najrān, 1187–8/1773–5

No sooner had Dahhām's resistance collapsed than Zaid b. Mishārī Ibn Zāmil, the lord of the important oasis of al-Dilam in al-Kharj, accepted the role of chief of the opposition to Unitarianism in the south. About a decade earlier Zaid had co-operated with Dahhām against the Unitarians at the time of the invasions of Najd from Najrān and al-Aḥsā',[1] and when Dahhām decided to give up the fight the place of refuge he chose was Zaid's town. In 1187/March 1773 to March 1774, the year of the fall of al-Riyāḍ, 'Abd al-'Azīz sent a message to Zaid warning him against violation of the compact and the peace and informing him that the only course for him was to be at one with the defenders of Islam.[2] Zaid disregarded the warning and busied himself in gathering together the forces of his district; he also applied for help to the lord of Najrān, in return for which he promised the payment of a subsidy. The lord of Najrān held off for the time being, seeking an increase in the amount offered and definite assurance that payment would be made properly.

[1] See above, pp. 110–12, 114.

[2] Ibn Ghannām, II, 100; Ibn Bishr has nothing on this. Ibn Ghannām's summary of the contents of the message suggests that Zaid may have made some sort of a treaty with the Unitarians following the withdrawal of the invading troops from Najrān and al-Aḥsā'. 'Abd al-'Azīz's message was probably prompted by the knowledge that Zaid had no great love for the principles of Unitarianism; though Ibn Ghannām does not say so, the occasion of the message was no doubt the flight of Dahhām and other confirmed enemies of the Unitarian movement from al-Riyāḍ to al-Dilam.

In the following year, 1188/March 1774 to March 1775, Zaid Ibn Zāmil communicated with the lord of Najrān, urging upon him the importance of an attack upon the Unitarians without delay.[3] The lord of the south send Zaid's messenger back with a request for precise information on what was to be received in return for assistance rendered.[4] As a result of the negotiations an agreement was reached for the payment of about thirty thousand gold pieces[5] by Zaid, who insisted on the delivery of hostages before making payment. When the hostages, who had been selected from among the chief men of Najrān and the lord's own entourage, arrived, Zaid set about collecting the large sum specified; he labored night and day to extract it from his subjects by harsh measures. As soon as the sum was ready Zaid sent it off post-haste to Najrān.[6] Then the great captain of the south, having received his fee, took his time in coming to honor his pledge and redeem his hostages, and it was not until the next year that he appeared with his army for the battle.

Capture of Buraidah by Banī Khālid, 1188/1774

Early in 1188/early 1774 'Urai'ir b. Dujain, the paramount shaikh of Banī Khālid and lord of al-Aḥsā', invaded al-Qaṣīm and pitched his camp outside the city of Buraidah. With him were Rāshid al-Duraibī, the former Amir of the place who had been driven out by the House of Ibn 'Ulayyān,[7] and troops of the tribe of 'Anazah.[8] By dissimulation 'Urai'ir persuaded the people of Buraidah that his visit was a friendly one and induced the Amir, 'Abd Allāh b. Ḥasan Ibn 'Ulayyān, to come outside the walls for a conference, whereupon he

[3] Ibn Ghannām, II, 100. Although Ibn Ghannām's account indicates that this was Zaid's second communication with the lord of Najrān, the first having been in the previous year, it is possible that this was actually the first communication and that the reference under the year 1187 is simply the historian's anticipation of an event to come.

[4] Ibn Ghannām stresses the cupidity of the lord of Najrān.

[5] Ibn Ghannām here uses the term *zarr* with the double "r" clearly marked – compare above, p. 83, n. 13.

[6] Ibn Ghannām, II, 100–1. Ibn Bishr, I, 63, under the following year, 1189, says that Ḥuwail, the lord of Wadi al-Dawāsir, and other chiefs of the south joined Zaid in paying a subsidy to Najrān, but it is not clear whether they were with him at this time or not.

[7] See above, p. 131.

[8] Ibn Ghannām, II, 101.

seized him and made him prisoner. 'Urai'ir's Bedouins slipped into the city and rushed about breaking down doors and plundering houses, while Rāshid al-Duraibī made his way to the Amir's castle and reinstalled himself there. The Unitarians among the inhabitants fled to save their necks, and so did the remaining members of the House of Ibn 'Ulayyān,[9] who wrote to the Imam 'Abd al-'Azīz informing him that they were coming to stay in al-Dir'īyah. Upon their arrival the Imam received them graciously and treated them with honor. After staying at Buraidah for some days, 'Urai'ir moved on with his army to the region of al-Khābiyah in the neighborhood of the town of al-Nabqīyah,[10] which lies in the sandy stretches of Wadi al-Rimah in al-Qaṣīm.

Death of 'Urai'ir, and struggle among his sons over the succession, 1188–9/1774–6

While 'Urai'ir was tarrying at al-Khābiyah he received letters from the enemies of Unitarianism in Najd urging him to strike directly at the fountainhead of the movement. Feeling that his Bedouins were ready to follow him in any enterprise, 'Urai'ir set about making preparations to march on al-Dir'īyah,[11] but before his tents were folded death overtook him.[12] His son, Buṭayyin, who succeeded him, abandoned the projected attack, though he did win a victory near al-Nabqīyah over a raiding party made up of men of al-Washm under the command of Muḥammad b. Jammāz, the Amir of Shaqrā',[13] in which most of the defeated were killed.[14]

[9] It is not stated whether the members of this house had become enthusiastic Unitarians before this event, but they proved to be from this time on. 'Abd Allāh b. Ḥasan was held a captive by Banī Khālid until the death of 'Urai'ir – Ibn Ghannām, II, 101.

[10] Ibn Bishr, I, 61–2, says that 'Urai'ir left Buraidah about a month before his death in Rabī' without specifying whether it was Rabī' I/May to June 1774 or Rabī' II/June to July.

[11] Ibn Bishr, I, 61.

[12] The chroniclers do not give the precise cause of his death, though Ibn Ghannām, II, 101, says that he fell a victim to the "poisonous" land of al-Khābiyah. His death took place in Rabī' I or Rabī' II 1188/May to July 1774 – see n. 10 above.

[13] According to Ibn Bishr, I, 62, he was also Amir of the whole district of al-Washm.

[14] Ibn Ghannām, II, 107, places this affair in 1189/1775–6; Ibn Bishr does not give any date for it. Philby, *Arabia*, p. 32, is mistaken in saying that Buṭayyin was defeated by the men

Buṭayyin did not have long to enjoy the power of his new position. After returning to his homeland of al-Aḥsā', he began spending the treasure amassed by his father in an attempt to strengthen himself, only to be interrupted by his brothers, Dujain and Sa'dūn, who strangled him in his own house.[15] Dujain, apparently the older of the two fratricides, succeeded Buṭayyin, but he in his turn died within a short space of time, poisoned, according to report, by Sa'dūn, who thus acquired the leadership of the anti-Unitarian forces in the east, a leadership he was to hold for a dozen years or so.[16]

Unitarian raids into al-Kharj, 1188–9/1774–5

While the negotiations were going on between Zaid Ibn Zāmil of al-Dilam and the lord of Najrān, the Unitarians were harrying Zaid in his own territory.[17] Su'ūd and his raiders in 1188/March 1774 to March 1775 descended on al-Dilam one night after the men of the guard and those who frequented the clubs [18] had fallen asleep. Su'ūd stationed some of his men in an ambush and held his horsemen ready to ride down on the flocks of sheep and goats as the herders drove them out after sunrise. The attack on the flocks drew the fighting men of al-Dilam straight into the ambush, from which they recoiled in flight to the shelter of their walls, leaving ten of their number dead on the field. The Unitarians, who lost only two men, marched off towards the north.[19]

When Su'ūd reached al-Ḥā'ir, he detached a flying squadron under 'Adāmah b. Suwairī of Banī Ḥusain[20] and sent them raiding off towards al-Zilfī in farther Sudair. Before reaching that town they encountered a party of about twenty of its inhabitants, whom they wiped out to the last man.

of al-Washm, and his assumption that Buṭayyin was coming to the aid of Rāshid al-Duraibī during the siege of Buraidah (see below, p. 156) seems unfounded.

[15] Not before 1189/1775–6 – see below, p. 154.

[16] Ibn Bishr, I, 62. Ibn Ghannām, who was a native of al-Aḥsā', says that Buṭayyin's evil deeds roused his brothers against him – Ibn Ghannām, II, 107.

[17] There is no indication as to whether the Unitarians had learned of these negotiations at this time or not.

[18] *Ahl al-andiyah.*

[19] Ibn Ghannām, II, 102; Ibn Bishr, I, 62.

[20] There are branches of both Tamīm and the Ẓafīr by the name of Banī Ḥusain.

Early in the following year, 1189/1775, the Imam 'Abd al-'Azīz himself returned to the wars for a raid into al-Kharj. His first objective was al-Ḍubai'ah,[21] a small oasis not far to the north of al-Dilam, where tactics similar to those employed by his son in the preceding raid resulted in the rout of the oasis-dwellers and the killing of twelve of them. The Unitarians cut down many of the date palms in the settlement, including all that stood in the grove of al-Shadī. Going farther on, 'Abd al-'Azīz laid siege to the village of Zumaiqah at the southern extremity of the oasis of al-Dilam, in which place his men also felled palms and ruined some of the fields.[22] When the raid was over the Imam secured permission from those who had taken part in it to turn the booty over to the members of the House of Ibn 'Ulayyān who had taken refuge in al-Dir'īyah after their expulsion from Buraidah by Banī Khālid and Rāshid al-Duraibī.[23]

Submission of Munaikh in the north and al-Ḥarīq in the south, 1188/1774–5

During 1188/March 1774 to March 1775 a delegation came to the Shaikh and the Imam from the towns of Ḥarmah and al-Majma'ah, which together form the subdistrict of Munaikh in Sudair, asking to have their people accepted into the Unitarian circle on condition that they should not be required to furnish contingents for the wars of the state during the next two years, a time of grace that would enable them to recuperate from the exhaustions of the recent past. After a careful examination of the case the Shaikh and the Imam consented to this arrangement.[24]

In the same year Muḥammad b. Rashīd al-Hazzānī and the chief

[21] Where the place got this name, which means The Little She-Hyena, has not been ascertained. It is an old name, being found in al-Hamdānī, *Ṣifat jazīrat al-'arab*, p. 139 (al-Hamdānī died in the early 4th century of the Hegira/10th century AD).

[22] There is no mention of the appearance of Zaid Ibn Zāmil, who was then plotting with the lord of Najrān against the Unitarians, to give battle on the occasion of either of these raids.

[23] Ibn Ghannām, II, 103. Compare above, p. 81.

[24] Ibn Ghannām, II, 102, sets forth the condition proposed by the delegation; Ibn Bishr, I, 62, records the submission of Munaikh without referring to the condition.

men of the town of al-Ḥarīq in the south beyond al-Kharj[25] also came to al-Dir'īyah to tender submission. The Shaikh and the Imam welcomed them, had them swear allegiance to the religion of God and His Prophet, and enjoined them to apply the laws of this religion within the territory over which they ruled.

Second invasion of Najd from Najrān, 1189/1775–6

The lord of Najrān, having enrolled his subjects and allies from the tribes of Yām and the people of Wadi al-Dawāsir,[26] at last marched north to join Zaid Ibn Zāmil and the anti-Unitarians of al-Kharj in another assault on the religious core of Najd. His coming served as a spur to the hopes of the other enemies of al-Dir'īyah. Buṭayyin b. 'Urai'ir of al-Aḥsā', who had not yet been sacrificed to the ambitions of his brothers, supported him with a sum said to have been in excess of six thousand gold pieces,[27] besides furnishing three hundred loads of provisions from al-Aḥsā' for the commissary of the invaders.

The lord of Najrān struck first at al-Ḥā'ir to the south of al-Dir'īyah, the scene of his sweeping victory in the days of the first invasion. The people of the town, who had become loyal Unitarians, resisted valiantly, making daily sorties to fight the besiegers. While the men of al-Ḥā'ir held up the progress of the invaders, the Imam

[25] On al-Ḥarīq and the ruling family of the Hazāzinah, see above, p. 68, n. 44. Ibn Bishr, I, 62, here refers to al-Ḥarīq as al-Ḥariq Na'ām; Na'ām is an older settlement near al-Ḥarīq in Wadi al-Far'. Na'ām means Ostriches; this name is one of many that seem to bear testimony to the fact that the ostrich was a common sight in the Peninsula in earlier times.

Na'ām is mentioned by al-Hamdānī, *Ṣifat jazīrat al-'arab*, p. 153, who died in the 4th century of the Hegira/10th century AD; al-Ḥarīq is not.

[26] The lord of the Wadi at this time was Ḥuwail of the Wadā'īn, a branch of the tribe of the Dawāsir – Ibn Bishr, II, 63. Ḥuwail is a colloquial diminutive of Aḥwal/Squint-eyed.

[27] Ibn Ghannām, II, 103, here uses the term *mushkhaṣ*, which is pronounced colloquially *mishkhaṣ*, a gold coin then current in Arabia that may have been the same as the *aḥmar* or *zarr* – see above, p. 83, n. 13. *Mushkhaṣ* is apparently derived from *shakhṣ* in the sense of a die used for minting coins (*shakhṣ* = person > statue or image> die) – see R. Dozy, *Supplément aux dictionnaires arabes*, II, 734–5. Dozy gives *mushkhaṣ* as meaning a kind of dinar, probably a sequin, minted in Venice (from Buṭrus al-Bustānī, *Muḥīt al-muḥīt*). According to Burckhardt, *Notes on the Bedouins and Wahábys*, II, 150, Venetian sequins circulated in the Peninsula in the early 19th century. At the present time *mishkhaṣ* is perhaps commoner than *dhahab* as the name of the metal gold among the Bedouins, at least in the eastern part of the country.

'Abd al-'Azīz and the Unitarians at al-Dir'īyah exerted themselves in preparing to defend their homes and their faith. Detachments were called up from every town and tribe that owed allegiance to the cause. Reinforcements marched down to al-Riyāḍ to block the way should the invaders come straight up the valley, but the Unitarian strategists rightly divined that the lord of Najrān would rely on a flanking maneuver in the west, so that Su'ūd, the chief commander in the field, stationed himself in the environs of Ḍurmā to guard the avenue of approach from that side. From that position Su'ūd dispatched raiding parties to fall upon any of the southerners who might be separated from the main body of their forces at al-Ḥā'ir. Su'ūd in person led one of these parties over to the plateau of al-'Armah, where he routed a company of the Najrān service of supply who were pasturing flocks. Returning to his base at Ḍurmā, Su'ūd continued his policy of waiting and cautiously avoiding an entanglement with the army that had so bruised the Unitarians a little more than a decade before.

Finding the stubbornness of al-Ḥā'ir too much to overcome, the lord of Najrān made a truce with the town. The besiegers had cut down a number of the palms in the oasis and had lost about forty men in the process. Now, as anticipated, they headed towards the western edge of Ṭuwaiq in the direction of Ḍurmā. The Unitarians had in the meantime strengthened the walls and towers of that town; Su'ūd increased the size of the garrison and withdrew to hover in the vicinity as the invaders advanced. The day after arriving the men of the south mounted a frontal attack on the oasis that cost them dear. The defenders, hiding behind palms and trees, met them with a rain of bullets, forcing them to fall back in confusion. The lord of Najrān decided that he had had enough; the Unitarians of today were

[28] Ibn Ghannām, II, 103–5, treats the invasion in greater detail than does Ibn Bishr, I, 63–4.
[29] Ibn Ghannām, II, 106, calls him simply Judhai' without naming his tribe, but he must have been the same man as Judai' Ibn Hadhdhāl mentioned in II, 121, and by Ibn Bishr, I, 75, as one of the chiefs of 'Anazah in 1195/1780–1. The House of Ibn Hadhdhāl have long been the head shaikhs of the 'Amārāt, one of the most powerful branches of 'Anazah – see above, p. 91. Judhai' is the diminutive of *jadha'*/"young", (especially) "a young sheep"; in the Egyptian colloquial the word, pronounced *gada'* has come to mean "a brave lad, a lively young man". Judai' is also a diminutive, probably referring to a mutilated nose.
[30] Ibn Ghannām, II, 107.

not as those of yesterday, for their military power and steadfastness had grown as their beliefs spread abroad. It may also be that the lord had already fallen ill, for he was ill as his followers the 'Ajmān carried him on his bed on the homeward journey, and he was dead before his native land was reached.[28]

Recovery of Buraidah and the whole of al-Qaṣīm by the Unitarians, 1189/1775–6

As soon as the danger from the south was past, the Unitarians were free to deal with the problem of Buraidah in al-Qaṣīm, where their enemy Rashid al-Duraibī had recently been re-established as Amir by the might of the Bedouins of Banī Khālid and 'Anazah. Su'ūd marched on the city in company with the exiled members of the House of Ibn 'Ulayyān, who had cast in their lot with Unitarianism. An ambush was prepared outside Buraidah, but Rāshid and his men refused to be drawn out from behind their fixed defenses. The siege went on for some days with the two sides firing at each other from a distance. Su'ūd, not wishing to prolong his own stay, built a fort opposite the city and placed 'Abd Allāh b. Ḥasan Ibn 'Ulayyān, the former Amir of Buraidah, in command of the garrison; after the completion of the building Su'ūd returned home. The cavalry from the fort harassed the citizens of Buraidah daily. Rāshid al-Duraibī endeavored to extricate himself from this plight by sending to Judhai' Ibn Hadhdhāl[29] of the Bedouins of 'Anazah for help, but the messenger came back with empty hands. To save his own skin Rāshid made a deal with 'Abd Allāh b. Ḥasan that permitted him to escape from the beleaguered city in safety, though it meant exposing his followers to the swords of the Unitarians, who cut down about fifty of them when they entered and took possession of the place. 'Abd Allāh b. Ḥasan Ibn 'Ulayyān set himself up again as Amir in Buraidah. After a time he led a delegation of the notables of al-Qaṣīm to express their loyalty to Unitarianism and to draw up a compact in the presence of the Shaikh and the Imam 'Abd al-'Azīz in al-Dir'īyah. 'Abd al-'Azīz confirmed the Amir of every town in al-Qaṣīm in his position and designated 'Abd Allāh b. Ḥasan as the Amir of the whole province with authority over all the local officials.[30]

11

Southern Najd and Sudair
1189–91/1776–8

Unitarianism in the south, 1189–91/1776–8: Zaid Ibn Zāmil of al-Dilam and Ḥasan al-Bijādī of al-Yamāmah; victory of Āl Murrah over the Unitarians

Before the end of 1189/March 1775 to February 1776 Zaid b. Mishārī Ibn Zāmil of al-Dilam suddenly appeared in the court of 'Abd al-'Azīz at al-Dir'īyah, accompanied by a number of the leading men of his territory. There had been no negotiations between him and the Unitarians and no notice of his coming had preceded him. When he offered allegiance to Unitarianism, 'Abd al-'Azīz indicated his willingness to accept the offer once Zaid had demonstrated his sincerity by handing over a large quantity of weapons and a number of thoroughbred horses. The lord of al-Dilam delivered what was required of him with such alacrity that the Imam kept only a share for the state, returning the rest to the new adherent.[1]

Only a few months went by before Zaid was at odds with the Unitarians again. Early in 1190/February 1776 to February 1777 Fawwāz[2] b. Muḥammad, the Amir of Nutaiqah, one of the settlements in the oasis of al-Dilam, requested that Zaid, since he had embraced Unitarianism and agreed to the application of Islamic law in his domain, should submit an old dispute that existed between them to judgment according to the provisions of the Shar', the Islamic code. This request enraged Zaid, who blustered that as ruler of the region he would never submit his neck to judgment in court;

[1] Ibn Ghannām, II, 107. Ibn Bishr, I, 64, mentions Zaid's submission without giving details.

[2] Ibn Ghannām II, 107, where it is stated that he was a native of al-Ḥauṭah (Ḥauṭat Banī Tamīm in the south?). Ibn Bishr, I, 65, gives his name as Fauzān and says that he was a noted champion of Unitarianism.

he then punished Fawwāz for his temerity by putting him to death, thus violating the compact with the Unitarians. The Imam ʻAbd al-ʻAzīz took the field in person to bring to task the lord who regarded himself as above the law. When the Unitarians arrived for the attack on Zaid's stronghold, Zaid mounted his horse and fled with his son and a few of his entourage. The people who were left in al-Dilam submitted to ʻAbd al-ʻAzīz and opened their gates; the Imam when he entered granted peace to all excepting the relatives and intimate associates of the departed lord, who were ordered into exile. As successor to Zaid, the Imam appointed Sulaimān b. ʻUfaiṣān Amir of al-Dilam.[3]

In the same year Ḥasan b. Rāshid al-Bijādī,[4] the Amir of al-Yamāmah, came with the elders of his town to affirm his devotion to Unitarianism before the Shaikh and the Imam.[5] When they returned home a religious instructor and propagandist, Aḥmad al-ʻUrainī,[6] accompanied them. In a short time this apostle of Unitarianism and another believer by the name of Ibn Dāʻij began to notice tendencies on the part of the people of al-Yamāmah to revert to their old heathen ways; they also became aware of a plot directed against them as men of religion. Fleeing for sanctuary to the nearby oasis of al-Salamīyah,[7] they paused there briefly and then hurried on to al-Dirʻīyah to report to the Imam. The Imam's son and captain Suʻūd took an expedition down to al-Kharj to protect the recent gains of Unitarianism in that district. Halting at al-Salamīyah,

[3] Ibn Ghannām, II, 107–8; Ibn Bishr, I, 65. This was the beginning of a long association of the House of ʻUfaiṣān with the district of al-Kharj.

[4] Rauḍat al-Bijādīyah, the headquarters of the American agricultural experts not far from al-Yamāmah, no doubt derived its name from Ḥasan's family, the House of Bijād.

[5] Ibn Ghannām, II, 109, speaks of their renewing their pact with Islam, though there has been no earlier reference to submission on the part of the people of al-Yamāmah.

[6] Ibn Ghannām, II, 109. Philby, *Arabia*, p. 32, misreads the name as ʻUzaini. In the early 11th century of the Hegira the ʻUraināt lost possession of the town of al-Bīr in al-Maḥmal – Ibn Bishr, I, 27. Later in that century they are referred to as the people of al-ʻAṭṭār in Sudair – Ibn Bishr, I, 61. At the beginning of the 12th century one of the chiefs of Raghbah in al-Maḥmal was an ʻUrainī – Ibn Bishr, I, 107. There is also a section of the tribe of Subaiʻ called the ʻUraināt – Fu'ād Ḥamzah, *Qalb jazīrat al-ʻarab*, p. 155. On the ʻUraināt of Raghbah, see above, p. 89.

[7] The common form of the name today is the diminutive al-Sulaimīyah. Ibn Ghannām, II, 109; Ibn Bishr, I, 66; al-Ālūsī, *Ta'rīkh Najd*, p. 28, all use al-Salamīyah; al-Rīḥānī, *Ta'rīkh Najd al-ḥadīth*, has al-Salamīyah on p. 15 and al-Sulaimīyah on pp. 118 and 427.

Su'ūd strengthened the garrison there and sent heavy reinforcements to al-Dilam, al-Ḍubai'ah and Na'jān.[8] From al-Salamīyah Su'ūd wrote to Ḥasan al-Bijādī urging him to expel from al-Yamāmah all those who had shown enmity towards the faith. Ḥasan agreed that he would take such action when Su'ūd returned to al-Dir'īyah, but this was only a ruse, for no sooner had Su'ūd couched his mounts and unloaded his gear in the Baṭḥā'[9] at the capital than Ḥasan and his fellow conspirators made public their apostasy. They underlined their change of heart by attempting to pry the Unitarian garrison out of the castle in al-Salamīyah, but the resolute men of the garrison stopped the apostates short of their goal. In the meantime a party hostile to Unitarianism in al-Dilam communicated with Zaid Ibn Zāmil,[10] appealing to him to return. Zaid was wary, but he did agree to delegate his son as his representative to investigate the situation in al-Dilam. Upon the arrival of Zaid's son the anti-Unitarians summoned to their side the Bedouins of Āl Murrah,[11] who were then in the neighborhood, and the apostates of al-Yamāmah. All together these partisans fell upon the Unitarians of al-Dilam in the heart of the town[12] and killed about ten of them; most of those who escaped on this occasion fled from the oasis and made their way to various towns held by sharers in their faith.[13] The news of this uprising convinced Zaid Ibn Zāmil that the time was ripe for him to come back to his native hearth, and after a few days he reappeared in al-Dilam. The Imam 'Abd al-'Azīz now sent Su'ūd down with his troops, but the united front of the anti-Unitarians in al-Kharj had grown too formidable for Su'ūd to risk a direct encounter on the field of battle, so that his main mission was to rescue the loyal Unitarian residents

[8] This would indicate that al-Ḍubai'ah and Na'jān, both of which lie a little to the north of al-Dilam, had accepted Unitarianism at the time of the flight of Zaid Ibn Zāmil.

[9] Compare the Baṭḥā' at al-Riyāḍ, above, p. 67, n. 35.

[10] The place where he had taken refuge is not stated. Ibn Ghannām, II, 110, here refers to Zaid as Qarīn Iblīs/The Accomplice of Satan, the same term he had used for the lord of Najrān – see above, p. 109, n. 14.

[11] Āl Murrah had badly beaten the Unitarians in a fight about ten years before this – see above, p. 127.

[12] *Jauf al-bilād* – Ibn Ghannām, II, 111.

[13] It must have been at this time that Sulaiman b. 'Ufaiṣān, the Unitarian Amir, left al-Dilam, as recorded in Ibn Bishr, I, 66. Ibn Ghannām does not speak of the flight of Sulaimān.

of al-Salamīyah, the one oasis in al-Kharj where the roots of the Shaikh's religion had taken firm hold. In addition to the garrison that was evacuated, a large number of the people moved out under the protection of Su'ūd's forces, taking their animals and furniture with them. They left their homes without regret, for they trusted in their Lord and counted His ways the best.[14]

To deal with the aroused opposition in the south, the Unitarians resorted to the strategy of concentrating first on one enemy and then on another. The Imam 'Abd al-'Azīz led a strong band of raiders far to the south to strike at the Bedouins of Āl Murrah who had assisted the anti-Unitarians at al-Dilam. As the Unitarians pressed on farther from their base, the situation grew more dangerous for them, since word of their coming traveled fast and the Bedouins had time to rally their dispersed and roving numbers. Nevertheless, 'Abd al-'Azīz drove on until he came to grazing land on which Āl Murrah had great herds of camels.[15] Drawing near to the beasts and their herdsmen under cover of darkness, 'Abd al-'Azīz divided his raiders into two groups, one for dashing out and one for lying in ambush. Early in the morning the first group played their part: scattering the herdsmen, they began driving away their charges. From this point on the plans of the Imam went awry. Bedouins poured in for the fight in such numbers that it was impossible to trap them in the ambush. The Bedouin horse and camelry swept the Unitarians back into a narrow mountain pass called Mukhairīq al-Ṣafā,[16] where many of them were slaughtered.[17] The Imam extricated the remnants of his force and headed for home. At al-Ḥā'ir he detached eighty riders and sent them off to al-Yamāmah, where they hamstrung camels belonging to the apostates. The Unitarians suffered a serious loss in this campaign in the death of 'Abd Allāh b. Ḥasan Ibn 'Ulayyān, the recently

[14] Ibn Ghannām, II, 111. The account in Ibn Bishr, I, 66, is confused.

[15] The camels of Āl Murrah are highly prized, for these Bedouins are dwellers in the Empty Quarter, which makes them preeminently men of the camel, and they have access to the camel markets of Oman, the source of the choicest stock in Arabia.

[16] Mukhairīq is the diminutive of *makhrūq*/"pierced", a term used for a natural rock arch such as the well known one in the neighborhood of al-Riyāḍ. Ṣafā is the plural of *ṣafāh*/"a large hard rock" – see above, p. 132. The name of the pass is given only in Ibn Bishr, I, 68.

[17] Ibn Ghannām, II, 112, says that about forty of the Unitarians were killed; Ibn Bishr, I, 66, about sixty. Ibn Ghannām admits that Āl Murrah rescued most of their camels.

appointed Amir of al-Qaṣīm.[18]

Although the raid against Āl Murrah was climaxed by defeat, it proved to be strategically sound, for it prevented these Bedouins for the time being from continuing to make common cause with the anti-Unitarians of al-Kharj. The Imam next singled out al-Yamāmah for attack and chose his son Su'ūd as the instrument. Going down Wadi Ḥanīfah, Su'ūd ran into a party from al-Yamāmah in the Sahbā';[19] an inconclusive fight took place, after which the men on both sides returned home.

The turn of al-Dilam was to follow the turns of Āl Murrah and al-Yamāmah. A Unitarian expedition with contingents from Sudair and al-Washm was all set to depart for the south in 1191/1777 when the Amir of Ḥarmah arrived with news of disturbances in the north that caused a quick change in the military plans.[20] After 'Abd Allāh b. Muḥammad b. Su'ūd, the brother of the Imam, had gone up to Sudair and the situation in that quarter appeared quiet, the expedition went south to carry out its original purpose without pausing to rest. 'Abd Allāh made a morning attack on the oasis of al-Dilam, killed six of the defenders, and hamstrung many cattle and camels. Zaid Ibn Zāmil still held the fort, however, and the Unitarians had much hard fighting ahead of them in the south, but for the present their hands were full in Sudair.

Return of Sulaimān b. 'Abd al-Wahhāb to al-Dir'īyah, 1190/1776–7

During 1190/February 1776 to February 1777 a delegation came from Munaikh and al-Zilfī to pay their respects and renew the

[18] 'Abd Allāh was succeeded as Amir of Buraidah, if not of the whole of al-Qaṣīm, at this time or shortly thereafter by Ḥujailān b. Aḥmad, another member of the House of Ibn 'Ulayyān, who was to become one of the great champions of Unitarianism in Najd.

[19] Both Ibn Ghannām, II, 112, and Ibn Bishr, I, 66, here refer to al-Sahbā' as an *arḍ*/"a land", not as a wadi as it is usually called. Al-Sahbā' is the spacious valley on the northern edge of the district of al-Kharj into which Wadi Ḥanīfah empties. The valley now runs as far as the sands of the Dahnā'; at one time it without doubt reached the shores of the Persian Gulf. For the meaning of the name, compare *suhb* or *suhub* from the same root/"broad level land".

This fight took place early in 1191/February 1777 to February 1778.

[20] Ibn Bishr, I, 66. See below, p. 162.

compact for the upholding of Unitarianism.[21] With them came Sulaimān b. ʻAbd al-Wahhāb,[22] the brother of the Shaikh Muḥammad, who had once made propaganda against the doctrines propagated by al-Dirʻīyah and had later fled when Ḥuraimilā fell.[23] The Shaikh Sulaimān had with the passing of the years changed his mind regarding his brother's teachings and was now prepared to settle with his family and children in al-Dirʻīyah to live as a good Unitarian scholar. His brother Muḥammad, the Imam, and the people received him with honor and rejoicing; perhaps the rejoicing of Muḥammad exceeded that of all the rest, for he harbored great affection for his brother, and it must have hurt him deeply in times past when his brother failed to see the light. The state awarded Sulaimān a stipend, and he passed the remainder of his days in the capital of the faith he had once opposed.[24]

Beginning of resistance in Sudair, 1191/1777–8

For about eight years the Unitarians had been confronted with no serious trouble in the district of Sudair, and in 1188/1774–5 and 1190/1776–7 delegations had come from the towns of Ḥarmah and al-Majmaʻah in the subdistrict of Munaikh to affirm their allegiance to Unitarianism.[25] In 1191/February 1777 to February 1778, however, just as a Unitarian expedition under the command of ʻAbd Allāh b. Muḥammad b. Suʻūd was about to take the road for al-Kharj,[26] ʻUthmān b. ʻAbd Allāh al-Mudlijī, the Amir of Ḥarmah, appeared before the Shaikh and the Imam in al-Dirʻīyah with a tale such as might have been told by many another local official in the Unitarian state. "Why are you going to al-Kharj," he said in effect, "when the signs of apostasy are to be seen in our town of Ḥarmah? I cannot command our people to do good or forbid them to do

[21] See above, p. 153.

[22] Ibn Bishr, I, 65, says that the Shaikh Muḥammad and the Imam ʻAbd al-ʻAzīz sent for him and ordered him to come.

[23] See above, pp. 71, 74–6.

[24] Ibn Ghannām, II, 108; Ibn Bishr, I, 65.

[25] See above, pp. 153–4.

[26] See above, p. 161.

evil,[27] and I cannot maintain myself there unless you humble them and take hostages from among them to keep with you here in al-Dir'īyah. If you do that, I can enforce religion in the town; then I can beat and depose and exile without fear of anyone."[28] The Amir of Ḥarmah was so importunate that the Imam dispatched his brother 'Abd Allāh to Munaikh and Sudair instead of al-Kharj. For the sake of concealment 'Abd Allāh traveled along Wadi al-Ḥaisīyah by way of al-Ḥamādah, marching night and day until he reached Ḥarmah in the darkness while its people lay asleep. Seizing the towers and other defense works, he stationed his men in them and ordered them all to fire their guns simultaneously at daybreak. The shock of the firing was so great that some of the pregnant women in the town were said to have immediately given birth.[29] The Unitarian commander 'Abd Allāh then selected four members of the ruling House of Mudlij, among them being the Amir 'Uthmān's brother Aḥmad and 'Alī al-Ḥusainī, to be taken to al-Dir'īyah as hostages; the people of the town swore allegiance to 'Abd Allāh. Leaving Ḥarmah, 'Abd Allāh passed through Sudair and picked up two more hostages on the way: Ṣa'b b. Muḥammad b. Muhaidib, the Amir of al-Ḥauṭah, and Manṣūr b. 'Abd Allāh b. Ḥammād, the Amir of al-'Audah,[30] both of whom were believed to be plotting apostasy with the people of Ḥarmah. There were rumors that Suwaid b. Muḥammad, the Amir of Jalājil,[31] was also a partner in the plotting, but 'Abd Allāh decided not to take him in order to avoid stirring up unrest in Sudair.

'Abd Allāh's precaution in leaving Suwaid behind proved of no avail, and the tour for the collection of hostages served only to bring the anti-Unitarian plot in Sudair to a head. Juwaisir al-Ḥusainī of Ḥarmah now became the ringleader,[32] working with Suwaid of

[27] *Al-amr bil-ma'rūf wal-nahy 'an al-munkar*/commanding good and forbidding evil are actions much stressed in the teachings of Unitarianism. In Saudi Arabia today there is a Commission for Commanding Good and Forbidding Evil in every important town in the Kingdom – see Nallino, *L'Arabia Sa'ūdiana*, pp. 100–2.

[28] Ibn Bishr, I, 67, gives all this as a direct quotation.

[29] So states Ibn Bishr, I, 67.

[30] On Manṣūr, see above, pp. 120–1.

[31] On Suwaid, see above, pp. 104, n. 112; 121, n. 17.

[32] According to Ibn Ghannām, II, 113; Ibn Bishr mentions Juwaisir, whom he calls Jāsir, only at the end of the story – see below, p. 164. Juwaisir was apparently, like 'Alī al-Ḥusainī (see above, this page), a member of the House of Mudlij.

Jalājil, Aḥmad b. ʿUthmān, the Amir of al-Majmaʿah,[33] and the House of Māḍī, the rulers of the town of al-Rauḍah.[34] The Unitarian religious leaders of al-Majmaʿah were in the habit of paying frequent visits to join in the rites of their faith with ʿUthmān b. ʿAbd Allāh, the Amir of Ḥarmah. One day when about ten of them arrived in Ḥarmah, ʿUthmān was in his palm garden outside the town. The plotters, who included ʿUthmān's brother Khuḍair and one of his cousins, notified ʿUthmān that he was expected at al-Majmaʿ, the place in the town where the religious readings were usually held; when ʿUthmān came in that direction the plotters met him in the marketplace and ran him through with their swords. Next they seized the religious men from al-Majmaʿah, fastened wooden shackles on their feet, and shut them up in al-Majmaʿ, intending to hold them in exchange for their fellows who had been carried off to al-Dirʿīyah as hostages. The final step in the plan called for the plotters of Ḥarmah to join Aḥmad b. ʿUthmān, the Amir of al-Majmaʿah, in getting the upper hand over the Unitarians in his town, but here at last the plan miscarried, for the Unitarians of al-Majmaʿah discovered what was afoot, established themselves in force in their Amir's castle, and sent a messenger by camel to bring help from ʿAbd al-ʿAzīz in al-Dirʿīyah.[35] The Imam lost no time in calling out the fighting men of al-ʿĀriḍ, al-Maḥmal, al-Washm and Sudair, who were sent off to Munaikh under the command of Suʿūd. This force encamped at the palm grove of al-Ẓāhirīyah outside Ḥarmah and laid siege to the town until the inhabitants asked for terms, whereupon Suʿūd agreed to exchange the hostages in al-Dirʿīyah for the religious men who had been seized at the time of the time of the murder of the Amir of Ḥarmah. The people of Ḥarmah were also required to make Juwaisir al-Ḥusainī leave town. The terms were lighter than might have been expected, since Suʿūd still wished to deal with the

[33] On Aḥmad, see above, pp. 89; 130, n. 57.

[34] Mazrūʿ, the ancestor of the House of Māḍī, had come from Qifār in Jabal Shammar and purchased the site of al-Rauḍah for a settlement – Ibn Bishr, I, 52. Several members of the House of Māḍī are among the trusted men of the King of Saudi Arabia at the present time; one of them was the local Amir in the zone of operations of California Arabian Standard Oil Company (now Arabian American Oil Company) a few years ago.

[35] The messenger was the son of Aḥmad al-Tuwaijirī, one of the religious men being held by the plotters in al-Majmaʿ.

lords of al-Majma'ah and Jalājil, who had been privy to the plot. Aḥmad b. 'Uthmān of al-Majma'ah was banished to al-Qaṣab in al-Washm along with his women and children and their property; Suwaid b. Muḥammad of Jalājil was banished to Shaqrā' in the same district along with his women and children and their property, later being transferred to al-Dir'īyah.[36]

Before returning home Su'ūd appointed Nāṣir b. Ibrāhīm[37] Amir of Ḥarmah; he also appointed 'Abd Allāh b. Jalājil as Amir of the whole of Munaikh and Sudair with headquarters in the town of Jalājil.[38]

Continuation of the conflict between the Unitarians and al-Dilam, 1191–2/1778

Towards the end of 1191[39]/February 1777 to January 1778 a band of Unitarian horsemen who were riding along to make a raid on al-Dilam happened to meet troops from al-Kharj while still short of their objective. An indecisive fight followed, after which the Unitarians broke off the raid and returned home.

Even later in 1191 or at the beginning of 1192/late 1777 or early 1778,[40] the soldiers of the faith tried again, this time under the leadership of their Imam 'Abd al-'Azīz. Arriving on a day when Zaid Ibn Zāmil was away from home conferring with Ḥasan al-Bijādī in al-Yamāmah, the Unitarians fought their way past the outposts of al-Dilam as far as the principal settlement,[41] which was entered by some

[36] Ibn Bishr, I, 69. Ibn Ghannām, II, 115, says that 'Abd al-'Azīz later ordered both Aḥmad and Suwaid to come to al-Dir'īyah, where they remained until they died.

[37] Nāṣir, a cousin of the murdered Amir, was a member of the House of Mudlij. One of his brothers had been among the four hostages taken to al-Dir'īyah earlier in the year; another had been one of the plotters and a partner in the murder of the Amir.

[38] Ibn Bishr, I, 69. Ibn Ghannām, II, 115, says that Ḍuwaiḥī b. Suwaid was appointed Amir of Jalājil, which position he no doubt held as subordinate to 'Abd Allāh b. Jalājil. 'Uthmān b. 'Uthmān succeeded his brother (?) Aḥmad as Amir of al-Majma'ah. Ibn Bishr, I, 66–9, gives the whole story in considerably greater detail than does Ibn Ghannām, II, 112–15.

[39] It is assumed that this incident took place towards the end of the year, since Ibn Ghannām, II, 115, records it at the end of his account of the events of 1191. Ibn Bishr overlooks the incident.

[40] Ibn Bishr, I, 69, gives the earlier date; Ibn Ghannām, II, 115, the later.

[41] Al-Ḥillah – Ibn Bishr, I, 69.

of their number. The residents were yielding to despair, and a few had even gone so far as to surrender, when Zaid, who had heard the firing, came up with reinforcements from al-Yamāmah and surprised ʻAbd al-ʻAzīz, who was still outside the town guarding the mounts and the gear of the raiders. Zaid and his men killed about twenty of the Unitarians and captured about fifty of their mounts. The Unitarians inside the town got out as best they could and rejoined their commander.

Withdrawing from al-Dilam, ʻAbd al-ʻAzīz shifted his forces to the oasis of Naʻjān to the north and sat down for a siege of some days. Although the Unitarians were cutting down palms, spoiling fields, and killing men, Zaid did not come to the help of his neighbors, a number of whom fled from their dwellings to escape the vengeance of the righteous enemy. The Unitarians lifted the siege and departed after they had crammed their packs with booty.

12

The Lord of al-Aḥsā' in Najd
1191–6/1778–82

Brief truce with the Unitarians, 1191/1778–9

Sa'dun b. 'Urai'ir, after making himself master of al-Aḥsā' by force and guile, found elements in his realm, especially among the more refined settlers in the towns, resentful of being subjected to rule by nomads of the desert. In 1189/March 1775 to February 1776 rebellion broke out among the people of al-Hufūf and adjacent oases,[1] which led to a battle during the next year between these people and Banī Khālid that ended with Sa'dūn and his Bedouins still in the saddle. As punishment for insubordination Sa'dūn put to death a number of the chief men in the oases.

Perhaps as an aftermath of this rebellion, or perhaps for other reasons, Sa'dūn brought many of his tribe to al-Kharj during 1192/January 1778 to January 1779.[2] While encamped there he sent a messenger to 'Abd al-'Azīz proposing a truce, which the Imam agreed to on condition that Sa'dūn should approach no closer to the Unitarian domains.[3] From al-Kharj Sa'dūn moved on to Banbān in

[1] Ibn Bishr, I, 64, calls them both Ahl al-Ḥasā' and Ahl al-Aḥsā'.

[2] Ibn Ghannām, II, 116; Ibn Bishr, I, 70. There may have been an old connection between Banī Khālid and al-Kharj that the chroniclers neglect to mention. Al-Kharj lies outside the *dīrah* of the tribe, and in the fairly long list given in *A Handbook of Arabia* (Admiralty), I, 608, of towns in which members of this tribe have settled, there is none near al-Kharj. When Sulaimān b. Muḥammad of Banī Khālid had to go into exile in 1166/1752–3, he took refuge in al-Kharj – see above, p. 90. Sa'dūn's brother Buṭayyin had been in effect an ally of Zaid Ibn Zāmil of al-Dilam at the time of the second invasion of Najd in 1190/1776–7 – see above, p. 154; in fact, exactions levied on the oasis dwellers of al-Aḥsā' for the support of the lord of Najrān may have made them more inclined than ever towards rebellion.

[3] Philby, *Arabia*, p. 34, refers to "the curious stipulation that Sa'dūn should not loiter about the frontiers of Najd if his intentions were dishonest". The Arabic of Ibn Ghannām, II,

al-'Āriḍ and then to the watering-place of Mubā'iḍ[4] in Majzal near Sudair, by which time the Unitarians had become convinced that his desire for peace was not sincere, so that they regarded the truce as at an end.[5] Some impelling reason, perhaps fear of a Unitarian attack, drove Sa'dūn on to make the crossing of the sands of the Dahnā' in midsummer, a venture in which he and his people suffered greatly and most of their sheep and goats died of thirst.

Crushing of apostasy in Ḥarmah of Munaikh, 1193/1779–80

The measures taken by Su'ūd in Munaikh and Sudair in 1191/1777–8 had not eradicated all opposition to Unitarianism in those regions. The foes of the faith in Ḥarmah continued to scheme against the men of religion in al-Majma'ah, especially since Su'ūd had stationed a garrison in al-Majma'ah to keep a watchful eye on Ḥarmah. The schemers found willing support in the east, where Sa'dūn b. 'Urai'ir had recovered from his grueling summer march across the Dahnā', and in the north, where al-Zilfī remained a strongly anti-Unitarian center.

When Sa'dūn arrived to within a day's march of Ḥarmah, his allies there, sure at last that they could count on him, put their plan into operation. They dressed a number of their men in women's clothes and sent them over to al-Majma'ah where they were to try to get into the towers of the castle. The Unitarians, however, were on the alert, and the trick failed.[6] This unsuccessful effort was followed by the siege of al-Majma'ah by the combined forces of Banī Khālid,

116, reads, "He set the condition for him that he should not approach the country. Truly his (Sa'dūn's) purpose was deceit and a stratagem that would make apostasy attractive to the people of the country."

[4] Mubā'iḍ is mentioned in al-Hamdānī, *Ṣifat jazīrat al-'arab*, pp. 141, 230. [Majzal: probably should read Mujazzal (= Jabal Mujazzal, bounding the eastern edge of Sudair) – Ed.]

[5] Philby, *Arabia*, p. 34, says "the treaty was denounced in consequence of an attack by Sa'dūn on tribesmen encamped at the watering of Mabaidh". Neither Ibn Ghannām nor Ibn Bishr speaks of such an attack; Ibn Ghannām, II, 116, says that 'Abd al-'Azīz canceled the truce because Sa'dūn's purpose became clear; Ibn Bishr gives no reason at all.

[6] Ibn Ghannām, II, 117. Ibn Bishr has no direct reference to the episode of the men disguised as women.

Ḥarmah, and al-Zilfī. The defenders shut themselves into their castle, the gates of which they stopped up with mud bricks; among them none was more energetic than Aḥmad al-Tuwaijirī, who for his beliefs had been held shackled in Ḥarmah only two years or so before.[7] The besiegers cut down palms in the oasis[8] and pastured their camels and flocks in the fields. At length the exhausted defenders were on the point of coming to terms, but as a last resort they asked Sa'dūn for a stay of two days, and during the two days help came. Ḥasan b. Mishārī,[9] who was at Jalājil with a force drawn from al-'Āriḍ, al-Maḥmal, and Sudair, had been hesitating over the dispatch of reinforcements, but now he acted. Leading his men to al-Majma'ah under cover of darkness, he slipped with them through the encircling lines and reached the walls by dawn. The defenders, whose gates were blocked up, let down ropes and drew Ḥasan and his men up. Discovery of this feat and reports of the coming of additional reinforcements from al-Dir'iyah under the command of the Imam's brother 'Abd Allāh convinced Sa'dūn's Bedouins and the men of al-Zilfī that the siege had lasted long enough; they melted away, leaving the men of Ḥarmah to face the Unitarian wrath alone.[10] The men of Ḥarmah hied themselves back to their own town, where they promptly exchanged the role of besiegers for that of besieged. 'Abd Allāh's Unitarians cut down all the palms in the garden called al-Muwais,[11] but 'Abd Allāh did not have strength enough to carry Ḥarmah by assault; he left cavalry and infantry in al-Majma'ah and went back to al-Dir'īyah. Later in the year Su'ūd came up from al-Dir'īyah to renew the siege with a determination that left the defenders no choice but to give in. When they asked for terms, Su'ūd insisted that all their palm gardens should become the property of

[7] See above, p. 164, n. 35. Aḥmad at the time of his death a year later, 1194/1780, was Qadi of al-Majma'ah – Ibn Bishr, I, 73. He may have been appointed Qadi as a reward for the spirit shown during the siege.

[8] Showing that this was by no means a purely Unitarian practice.

[9] Ḥasan b. Mishārī was the cousin of the Imam 'Abd al-'Azīz. His father, Mishārī b. Su'ūd, an early supporter of the Shaikh at al-Dir'īyah (see above, p. 44), had died in 1189/1775–6 – Ibn Ghannām, II, 105.

[10] The Bedouins had already grown restless over staying so long in one spot with their flocks.

[11] Or al-Muwayyis.

the Unitarian treasury;[12] he also appropriated the belongings and foodstuffs in the houses, which he allowed the people to buy back. Su'ūd wrote to his father the Imam, informing him of the peace, and the Imam wrote back instructing his son to destroy the town because of repeated violations of its compacts. Su'ūd tore down the walls and forts and some of the residences and sent into exile the members of the House of Mudlij and others who had persisted in opposing Unitarianism. A large number of the residents migrated away from Ḥarmah, a part of them settling in al-Majma'ah and many moving all the way to al-Zubair beyond Najd on the edge of Iraq.[13]

Unitarian activity in the south, 1193–4/1779–80

In Rajab 1193/July to August 1779 'Abd al-'Azīz started off on a raid against the oasis of al-Salamīyah, from which the apostates of al-Kharj had forced the Unitarians into exile, but he changed his plans after being sighted by men from that place while en route. Attacking a section of the tribe of Muṭair in the region of 'Arwā,[14] the Imam after a stiff fight got even more than he had hoped for in camels and other booty. Among the three Unitarians who fell was 'Adāmah b. Suwairī of Banī Ḥusain, who had once commanded an expedition.[15]

Late in the following year, 1194/January to December 1780,[16] Su'ūd passed through al-Kharj[17] and pressed on to al-Ḥauṭah at the eastern end of Wadi al-Far', the first time the Unitarians had gone so far south for a raid against a town. Voices that had been stilled as

[12] Bait al-Māl.

[13] The accounts in Ibn Ghannām, II, 116–19, and in Ibn Bishr, I, 70–2, need to be collated carefully, for each contains numerous details not to be found in the other.

On the people of Ḥarmah who settled in al-Zubair and eventually became the rulers of that town see al-Nabhānī, *al-Tuḥfah al-nabhānīyah: al-Baṣrah*, pp. 123–8.

[14] Arḍ 'Arwā Najd.

[15] See above, p. 152. Ibn Ghannām, II, 118, is the only source that deals with this raid that started out against al-Salamīyah and ended with the fight against Muṭair.

[16] Ibn Bishr, I, 73, mentions a Unitarian raid against al-Dilam in 1194 that apparently took place immediately after the last expedition of that year against al-Zilfī (see below, p. 171), but he gives no details.

[17] It is possible that he took the much rougher route through the mountains of Ṭuwaiq, but more likely that he rode straight through al-Kharj. The raiders of that time traveled so light and moved so fast that it mattered little if they had enemy forces between them and their base.

the men took their posts at night in the ambush or among the shock troops pierced the air shrilly on the morrow when the battle raged. Fifteen of the people of al-Ḥauṭah died that day and an undisclosed number of the raiders, including Baṭī al-Muṭairī.[18]

Forcing of al-Zilfī into submission, 1194/1780

During the past few years the people of al-Zilfī in northern Sudair had shown animosity towards Unitarianism, climaxing their efforts by joining the townsmen of Ḥarmah and the tribesmen of Banī Khālid in the siege of al-Majma'ah in 1193/1779. The Imam in al-Dir'īyah was not one to forgive or forget such conduct. Three raids launched against al-Zilfī during 1194/January to December 1780 made its leaders and their followers see the error of their ways. Su'ūd captained the first raid early in the year but lost the chance to take his quarry by surprise and failed to achieve a decisive victory. His uncle 'Abd Allāh tried his hand the next time and had no better fortune, for again al-Zilfī received warning in advance of the approach of the raiders. On the homeward journey 'Abd Allāh became entangled with Sa'dūn of al-Aḥsā'.[19]

In the final months of the year the Unitarians on a third raid burned the fields of the town. The people of al-Zilfī, realizing that if they did not submit these attacks would be followed by others, swore allegiance to the religion of God and His Prophet and pledged obedience to the dictates of al-Dir'īyah.[20]

The lord of al-Aḥsā' defeats the Unitarians in Najd, 1194/1780

When 'Abd Allāh b. Muḥammad got to Raghbah in al-Maḥmal, he dismissed the contingents from Sudair and al-Washm, excepting their leaders, who remained with him. Had he known what was in store for him, he would not have let them go. Sa'dūn b. 'Urai'ir of

[18] Ibn Ghannām, II, 120; Ibn Bishr, I, 73.

[19] See below, pp. 171–2.

[20] Ibn Bishr, I, 73. Ibn Ghannām mentions neither the third raid of the year nor the submission of al-Zilfī.

al-Aḥsā' was in the neighborhood with the warriors of Banī Khālid, and at al-'Atk between Sudair and al-Maḥmal the invaders from the east surrounded 'Abd Allāh's depleted ranks and cut them to pieces. About thirty of the Unitarians met their death, foremost among them being Ḥusain b. Sa'īd, the Amir of al-'Audah[21] and commander of the contingent from Sudair, and 'Abd Allāh b. Sadḥān, a notable of Shaqrā' and commander of the contingent from al-Washm.

Sa'dūn went on from this triumph to attack a party of the Nabaṭah of Subai', Unitarian Bedouins who were accompanied by camelry and cavalry from Ḍurmā returning home from 'Abd Allāh's raid against al-Zilfī. The Unitarians held their ground against the charges of the horsemen of Banī Khālid, several of whom they took prisoner. One of those captured was Sa'dūn Ibn Khālid, a shaikh of the 'Amā'ir,[22] who bought his freedom for three thousand *aḥmars*.[23]

The Unitarian Bedouins of Subai' capped this success by carrying out a raid against the Ẓafīr at Safwān, a watering-place near al-Baṣrah, in which they took about four thousand camels.[24]

Bitter struggle in al-Kharj and the south: the lord of al-Aḥsā' at al-Bid', 1195/1781

Su'ūd opened 1195/1781, a year of bitter battles in the south, by taking a large force of Unitarians to attack al-Dilam. A skilful ambush resulted in the defeat of the defenders and their retirement behind their walls, where Su'ūd kept them in a state of siege while his men cut down about two thousand palms in the grove called Khaḍrā' belonging to Ibn 'Ushbān.

From al-Dilam Su'ūd marched back to the neighborhood of al-Salamīyah and set to work building a fort just to the west of that oasis[25] to serve as an advanced base for the Unitarians in the

[21] Ḥusain b. Sa'īd had probably been appointed Amir of al-'Audah when Manṣūr Ibn Ḥammād was taken as a hostage to al-Dir'īyah in 1191/1777–8 because of suspected complicity in the plotting by the apostates of Sudair – see above, p. 163.

[22] The paramount shaikh of the whole tribe of Banī Khālid at the present day comes from the House of Khālid of the 'Amā'ir; this house has given up nomadism to settle on the island of al-Musallamīyah in the Persian Gulf – *A Handbook of Arabia* (Admiralty), I, 85.

[23] Ibn Ghannām, II, 120, uses *zarr*; Ibn Bishr, I, 73, *aḥmar*.

[24] Ibn Bishr, I, 73. Ibn Ghannām does not speak of this raid.

territory of the apostates. His father the Imam had proposed this step, and this site was selected because a fort there could easily be supplied down Wadi Ḥanīfah and the garrison would be in a strategic position commanding the lines of communication between al-Dilam and al-Yamāmah, the two main centers of disaffection in the area. Su'ūd nominated Muḥammad b. Ghushayyān, a fighter of proved mettle, as commander of the new post, which was named al-Bid',[26] and left with him horses and an ample stock of military equipment for his company. In one of the first sallies out of al-Bid' the Unitarians crossed swords with men of al-Yamāmah and killed Farḥān, the brother of the Amir Ḥasan al-Bijādī.[27] Ibn Ghushayyān and his men were a fearless crew who came out time after time, by day and by night, to worry the people of al-Kharj and deprive them of their peace.

The anti-Unitarians of al-Kharj, finding the existence of this fort in their midst a source of vexation, adopted the proposal of a craftsman who volunteered to build a wooden box, reinforced with lead and steel and large enough to hold a number of men. The box was to be pushed up against the fort and the men inside, protected by coats of mail, would leap out and set to work tearing down the mudbrick walls with their tools. It took some days to build the box, but when the men of al-Kharj began pushing it towards the fort, it stuck in the middle of the way. Afraid that the garrison might seize it and use it for their own purposes, the men of al-Kharj burned it up.[28]

When the stratagem of the box turned out to be a dismal failure, the men of al-Kharj with their allies from al-Ḥauṭah and al-Ḥarīq in Wadi al-Far'[29] decided to try scaling the walls of the fort at night. Equipped with ladders and other gear for the undertaking,[30] they

[25] The road from the King's palace in al-Kharj to al-Riyāḍ today runs between the oasis and the site of the fort.

[26] Al-Bid' means The New.

[27] Ibn Ghannām, II, 121; Ibn Bishr, I, 74.

[28] Ibn Ghannām, II, 122–3. Ibn Bishr has nothing on this incident. Philby, *Arabia*, p. 35, no doubt derived his account of "assaults … on the walls under cover of bullet-proof stockades" from Ibn Ghannām's story of the box, though Ibn Ghannām places this incident before the arrival of Sa'dūn, not after, as in Philby.

[29] This would indicate that some if not all of the people of al-Ḥarīq had become apostates after the chief men of the town had accepted the rule of Unitarianism seven years earlier – see above, p. 154.

[30] Ibn Bishr, I, 74.

made the attempt, only to lose twenty-five men as the wide-awake garrison beat them off.

The last resort of the Houses of Zāmil and Bijād was to call upon Sa'dūn b. 'Urai'ir of al-Aḥsā' for assistance, since Sa'dūn had cannon that might be used to batter down the walls. Sa'dūn's cannon, however, proved ineffective, and when Sa'dūn departed in some haste he stored the cannon in the oasis of al-Yamāmah where they eventually became the property of the Unitarians upon the eradication of apostasy in that place.

During this year[31] the Imam's brother 'Abd Allāh and a band of raiders penetrated into the oasis of al-Yamāmah and arranged an ambush that enabled them to kill nearly twenty of the residents, including another member of the ruling House of Bijād. This was not counted a completed mission, for the raiders moved farther south and killed about the same number in an attack on the apostates of al-Ḥarīq.

The intervention of providence secured for the Unitarians a victory they had not been able to win with their own arms when death carried off Ḥasan b. Rāshid al-Bijādī, the Amir of al-Yamāmah and next to Zaid Ibn Zāmil the outstanding opponent of al-Dir'īyah in al-Kharj.[32]

Either at the close of 1195 or in the beginning of 1196/December 1781 to December 1782[33] the old Imam raided in person down to al-Ḥauṭah in Wadi al-Far', where his men killed about fifteen of the townspeople who ventured forth and then cut down all the palms in the grove of al-Ruḥail,[34] one of the largest groves in the oasis. On the way back the Unitarians felled palms belonging to the settlements of al-Furai' and Nutaiqah in the oasis of al-Dilam and still others in the oasis of Na'jān. At al-Yamāmah the Imam's men pulled down some of the defense towers.[35]

[31] Ibn Ghannām, II, 124, places 'Abd Allāh's expedition against al-Yamāmah and al-Ḥarīq after the operations against the fort of al-Bid'; Ibn Bishr, I, 74 places the expedition before the operations.

[32] Ibn Bishr, I, 74. Ibn Ghannām fails to record the decease of al-Bijādī.

[33] Ibn Ghannām, II, 125, gives the later date; Ibn Bishr, I, 74, the earlier.

[34] The name probably means The Little Camel Saddle (diminutive of *raḥl*).

[35] Ibn Ghannām, II, 125; Ibn Bishr, I, 74. Ibn Bishr alone mentions the attacks on al-Dilam and al-Yamāmah during the homeward journey.

Su'ūd's great victory over the Ẓafīr at Mubā'iḍ, 1195/1781

The Imam of the Unitarians, hearing that his old Bedouin enemies the Ẓafīr had gathered near Sudair,[36] sent his son Su'ūd to chastise them for their iniquities. Su'ūd with his mixed force of townsmen and Bedouins came up to the enemy at the watering-place of Mubā'iḍ in Majzal[37] but found them so numerous that he failed to break them at the first onslaught. Withdrawing to Tumair on the edge of Majzal, Su'ūd issued a summons to the levies of Sudair to join him without delay, both horse and foot. With these reinforcements Su'ūd returned to Mubā'iḍ, where the enemy Bedouins were awaiting him confident in the belief that they were more than a match for all the Unitarians. They had underestimated the weight of Su'ūd's veterans, who carried everything before them in the fight. More than a hundred of the Ẓafīr and their friends were killed,[38] and the Unitarians took as booty about seventeen thousand sheep and goats and five thousand camels, as well as fifteen horses and quantities of weapons and household goods and other possessions of the nomads. One fifth of the booty went to the commander Su'ūd; the rest was divided among the Unitarians, two shares to the mounted man and one to the foot soldier.

Rebellion in al-Qaṣīm: the lord of al-Aḥsā' at Buraidah and al-Rauḍah, 1196/1782

At a time when the Unitarians thought that their worst difficulties were in the south, a rebellion of major proportions broke out in

[36] According to Ibn Bishr, I, 75, there were seven branches (*aslāf*) of the Ẓafīr and other unidentified Bedouins in the gathering. Among the chiefs of the Ẓafīr were Muḥsin Ibn Ḥallāf of Āl Sa'īd and Dahhām Abā Dhirā' of the Ṣumdah. Ibn Ghannām, II, 124, says that Bedouins of 'Anazah were among those present.

Sections of 'Anazah, particularly the 'Amārāt headed by Judhai' or Judai' Ibn Hadhdhāl of Āl Ḥablān (see above, p. 155, n. 29), had just been severely mauled by Muṭair in a battle in which Judhai' fell – Ibn Bishr, I, 74–5. Judhai' was an ally of Sa'dūn b. 'Urai'ir of Banī Khālid.

[37] See above, p. 168, n. 4.

[38] Among the chiefs who fell were Dahhām Abā Dhirā' and Thawwāb Ibn Ḥallāf.

al-Qaṣīm in 1196/mid-December 1781 to early December 1782.[39] The Unitarians were strong enough to maintain themselves in only three towns in the district, Buraidah, al-Rass and al-Tanūmah;[40] in all the others the agents of disaffection gained the upper hand. These men met in secret conclave to lay their plans, which called for concerted risings to slaughter the Unitarian representatives in all the towns of the province. To insure the success of the undertaking, the plotters informed Sa'dūn b. 'Urai'ir of al-Aḥsā' of their plans and asked for his co-operation, which he willingly pledged. Sa'dūn mustered his Bedouins of Banī Khālid and enlisted as allies contingents from 'Anazah and Shammar and the Ẓafīr;[41] then he marched with this host for al-Qaṣīm. The advance of Sa'dūn was the signal for the plotters to put their plans into execution. The people of al-Khabrā' to the southwest of 'Unaizah[42] cut down their Imam, Manṣūr Abā al-Khail, as he led the congregational prayer on a Friday; Thunayyān Abā al-Khail[43] was also killed. The inhabitants of Jannāḥ hard by 'Unaizah seized a blind Unitarian and crucified him, driving the nails through the calves of his legs.[44] The people of Shamās in the neighborhood of Buraidah slew their Unitarian Amir 'Alī b. Jaushān, and

[39] Not in the spring of 1783, as stated by Philby, *Arabia*, p. 35.

[40] Ibn Ghannām, II, 125; Ibn Bishr, I, 75. Philby, *Arabia*, p. 35, names only the first two, probably because the copyist of Ibn Ghannām has omitted the "t"of al-Tanūmah, making the name difficult to decipher.

[41] Apparently he made no attempt to secure aid from Muṭair, who had recently been fighting against him and his allies of 'Anazah.

[42] Al-Khabrā' lies a very short distance below al-Hilālīyah and al-Bukairīyah – see above, p. 130, n. 58. It is Doughty's Khubbera (or Khobra), a "clay-built town … without palms or greenness. The tilled lands are not in sight; they lie, five miles long, in the bottom of the Wady er-Rummah [al-Rimah]" – Doughty, *Travels in Arabia Deserta*, II, 407. A *khabrā'* is "a naked clay bottom in the desert, where shallow water is ponded after heavy rain" – Doughty, II, 238.

[43] The brother or relative of Manṣūr.

[44] *'Aṣabat rijlih* – Ibn Ghannam, II, 127.

When Doughty was at 'Unaizah in the late 1870s he was told that Jannāḥ, which had been founded centuries before by Banī Khālid, had been abandoned for ninety-five years. "Jannaḥ in the beginning of the Wahāby Power, held with *Thuèyney el-Múntefik* [see below, pp. 195–6]… but Aneyza was allied with the Wahāby. The Khalidies of Jannaḥ were overcome in the troubles ensuing, and they forsook the place: many of them went to live in the north, the rest withdrew to Aneyza." – *Travels in Arabia Deserta*, II, 354–5. It may be that the people of Jannāḥ began to abandon the town after the collapse of the rebellion of 1196/1782, which was just about ninety-five years before Doughty's visit.

so it went in all the towns. The plotters in 'Unaizah lacked the courage to strike directly at their Unitarian instructors, 'Abd Allāh al-Qāḍī and Nāṣir al-Shiblī,[45] but they sent the two to Sa'dūn with a message indicating that they would be glad to have them put out of the way; Sa'dūn executed them in cold blood. In Buraidah, from early days a chief center of Unitarianism in the north, there were also plotters, but the able governor, Ḥujailān b. Aḥmad Ibn 'Ulayyān, nipped the plot in the bud by killing the ringleaders, Sulaimān al-Ḥujailānī, a member of his own family, and Ibn Ḥuṣayyin.

Sa'dūn hurried forward as consternation overtook the Unitarians upon the swift and merciless carrying out of the plot. The anti-Unitarians felt success within their grasp if they could beat down the resistance of Buraidah, but the subjection of Buraidah with Ḥujailān in command was not an easy matter, as Sa'dūn discovered when his first assaults on the walls were repulsed with heavy losses. The lord of al-Aḥsā' then sat down before Buraidah for a protracted siege, which was in itself virtually an admission of defeat, since his army composed mainly of Bedouins was not the instrument for that type of warfare. Sa'dūn tried prodding the laggards to make his attacks more formidable, but still the Unitarians held their ground. At a conference between Sa'dūn and the local leaders of the rebellion it was decided that the only way to take the town was to smash the walls with artillery. Having few or no cannon at hand on this occasion,[46] Sa'dūn tried to cast new ones on the spot. The people of al-Qaṣīm brought in bits of brass and copper[47] from all over the province for this purpose, but every effort to produce a barrel from the mold proved fruitless.

The siege wore on week after week. The besiegers built a fort to strengthen their position, but the Unitarians came out at night and tore it down; only one man of the garrison escaped to take the news to his fellows. Sa'd b. 'Abd Allāh, the Amir of al-Rass who had remained loyal to the Unitarians, assisted his beleaguered coreligionists by taking about four hundred sheep and goats[48] that Sa'dūn's

[45] Ibn Ghannām, II, 127. Ibn Bishr, I, 75, gives the name of the latter as al-Shubailī.

[46] The cannon Sa'dūn left at al-Yamāmah the year before (see above, p. 174) may have been all he had.

[47] *Anwā' al-ṣufr* – Ibn Ghannām, II, 129.

[48] *Ghanam* that were called *dughaimawāt*/"black ones" – Ibn Ghannām, II, 129.

Bedouins had in pasture. The men of Buraidah made a sally and seized a hair tent[49] that had been set up on a height by 'Abd Allāh b. Rashīd[50] to serve as a store for weapons and ammunition.

After four or five months had gone by,[51] the attackers set to work to build a contrivance similar to the reinforced box that had been used at al-Bid' in al-Kharj,[52] made of wood in such a way that leaden bullets could not pierce it. They pushed this contrivance to the watchtower of the town,[53] which was held by a detachment of ten men. There the men pushing the box tried to persuade the defenders that they were coming as friends and believers in Islam; though they met with a measure of success at first, their trickery was discovered before long and they were all driven off.

Before abandoning the siege Sa'dūn threw all his troops into one last assault on the walls and towers, pricking on with the sword any who held back, but he still could not dislodge the Unitarians. Ḥujailān, the steadfast governor, chose this moment to celebrate his nuptials. When Sa'dūn heard the drums and learned that they were beating for Ḥujailān's wedding feast, he knew there was no hope for him to prevail over such an adversary, and he brought the siege to an end.[54]

When Sa'dūn had departed, Ḥujailān shouldered the task of visiting punishment on the rebels throughout al-Qaṣīm and reordering the affairs of the province.[55] In the settlement of Shamās he killed all

[49] *Bait min al-sha'r* – Ibn Ghannām, II, 129.

[50] Ibn Ghannām, II, 129. There is no indication as to whether this 'Abd Allāh b. Rashīd belonged to the famous House of Rashīd of Shammar or not. The House of Rashīd, who as lords of Ḥā'il ruled much of the interior of Arabia in the latter half of the 19th century, did not rise to prominence until the first half of that century – Musil, *Northern Neğd*, p. 237.

[51] Ibn Ghannām, II, 129, says the siege lasted about five months; Ibn Bishr, I, 76, four months. The incident here described took place almost at the end of the siege.

[52] For the reinforced box, see above, p. 173. Ibn Ghannām, II, 129, calls the contrivance built at Buraidah a *mintarīs* or *muntarīs*, an inexplicable form derived from *turs*/"shield" (compare *mitras*/"bulwark, rampart, entrenchment"). Ibn Ghannām then says that the Arabs named the contrivance *'ajal*/"a car or cart, something that rolls" (compare *'ajalah* in the sense of "wheel"), a word that he himself had used for the device on which the reinforced box of al-Kharj was mounted.

[53] *Marqab al-balad* – Ibn Ghannam, II, 129.

[54] Ibn Bishr, I, 76, is the only source that gives the story of the wedding and the drums.

[55] The chroniclers offer no explanation as to why the Imam and the Unitarians at al-Dir'īyah

the rebels he could find; many of the inhabitants of the settlement had fled with Sa'dūn's forces. The other rebellious towns were brought to book and required to accept Unitarianism again; Ḥujailān levied fines on them for their misconduct. Town after town, with the sole exception of 'Unaizah, sent delegations to swear allegiance.[56]

In addition to regulating the affairs of al-Qaṣīm, Ḥujailān sent out a party of men to follow the tracks of Sa'dūn and his army. In the land known as al-Mustawā the men of Buraidah encountered a detachment of the enemy and wiped it out completely. Among the booty taken the Unitarians found considerable property that was identified as belonging to people from the holy city of Medina. When this was reported to the Imam 'Abd al-'Azīz, he ordered that every bit of it should be restored, since it was all *waqf* property, which in the eyes of the Unitarians was inviolate.[57]

In the meantime Sa'dūn had moved with his host to the neighborhood of al-Zilfī, where he paused for a while. There he was joined by a large number of the apostates of al-Kharj. Proceeding to the watering-place of Mubā'iḍ,[58] he paused again. Despite his failure to take Buraidah, the size of his force was so impressive that anti-Unitarians and the discontented from many quarters flocked in to his standard: exiles from Ḥarmah and al-Zilfī and other towns that had felt the weight of Unitarian vengeance, and Zaid Ibn Zāmil from al-Kharj. Sa'dūn took counsel with his allies as to which town in Sudair they should strike at first. Among those who joined him at Mubā'iḍ were members of the House of Māḍī, the rulers of al-Rauḍah,[59] and in agreement with them it was decided that a part of the army should advance on al-Rauḍah.[60] After the Feast of the Sacrifice had come and gone,[61] the members of the House of

remained entirely inactive during the long siege of their people at Buraidah. They also gave Ḥujailān a free hand in the reorganization of al-Qaṣīm, probably because they themselves were occupied by the developments in Sudair – see below, pp. 179–81.

[56] Ibn Ghannām, II, 130–1.

[57] Ibn Ghannām, I, 131. A *waqf* or *ḥabs* is property that has been established as a pious endowment.

[58] See above, pp. 168, n. 4; 175.

[59] See above, p. 164, n. 34.

[60] Ibn Bishr, I, 76, is the only source to give the details of Sa'dūn's progress from Buraidah to al-Rauḍah.

[61] The Feast of the Sacrifice in 1196 fell about the middle of November 1781.

Māḍī,[62] the exiles of the House of Mudlij of Ḥarmah and others from Sudair and al-Zilfī, and Zaid Ibn Zāmil with the men of al-Dilam and al-Kharj marched on al-Rauḍah, where they found the Unitarians of the town entrenched in the citadel.[63] A siege of some days compelled the Unitarians to surrender on terms,[64] whereupon Sa'dūn came down from Mubā'iḍ and joined his allies, helping to install the House of Māḍī in firm control of the town. Next the anti-Unitarians struck at the town of al-Dākhilah, where Muḥammad b. Ghushayyān[65] was stationed with a company of Unitarian cavalry. Ibn Ghushayyān stopped the enemy and prevented them from enlarging their foothold in Sudair beyond al-Rauḍah; the other towns in the province proved loyal to Unitarianism and refused to join the rebellion. Ḥasan b. Mishārī with Unitarian forces at Jalājil[66] also lent a hand in containing the invaders and upstarts.

Now at last the Imam 'Abd al-'Azīz at al-Dir'īyah, who had watched the year's developments without sending forth a single expedition, began to take action. He ordered his son Su'ūd to Thādiq in al-Maḥmal to build his formations from the contingents supplied by the Unitarian districts. Before Su'ūd could leave Thādiq for Sudair, Sa'dūn had made up his mind to bring his adventure in Najd to an end and had departed, abandoning the members of the House of Māḍī to their fate in al-Rauḍah. Ibn Ghushayyān, Ḥasan b. Mishārī, and the Unitarians from all over Sudair swarmed down upon al-Rauḍah to take vengeance. In the fighting the rebel 'Aun b. Māni', the head of the House of Māḍī, fell, being succeeded by his brother

[62] The men of the House of Māḍī who allied themselves with Sa'dūn were 'Aun b. Māni' and his brothers, and Turkī b. Fauzān b. Māḍī and his brother Manṣūr – Ibn Bishr, I, 76.
[63] Ibn Ghannām, II, 131, who indicates that Sa'dūn was present when the citadel was taken, states that the people of al-Rauḍah had of their own accord risen against the Unitarians, who took refuge in the citadel. Ibn Bishr, I, 76, says that the citadel in the center of the town was occupied by a garrison appointed by the Imam and made up of men from al-'Āriḍ and other places; with them were Sulaimān b. Mūsā b. Qāsim and 'Alī b. Aḥmad, the Qadi of al-'Aṭṭār.
[64] Ibn Ghannām, II, 131, says that the besiegers won the citadel by cutting off or threatening to cut off its water supply.
[65] Ex-commandant of the fort of al-Bid' in al-Kharj – see above, p. 173.
[66] See above, p. 169.
[67] Ibn Ghannām, II, 132; Ibn Bishr, I, 77.
[68] Ibn Bishr, I, 77. This must have been after Ibn Ghushayyān left al-Dākhilah.

'Uqail, and the rebels lost much ground, though they managed to hold the citadel and its towers, where they were supported by a small detachment left behind by Sa'dūn. Su'ūd arrived with the main body of the Unitarians to take a hand in the siege by having his men fell palms in al-Ḥuwaiṭah, al-Rufai'ah and other groves. Seeing that all hope was gone, the rebels made peace with Su'ūd, who subjected them to a heavy fine and appropriated all the property in the town, which he allowed the repentant rebels to repurchase for cash from the Unitarian treasury.[67] Su'ūd assigned exile as the lot of the members of the House of Māḍī and appointed 'Abd Allāh b. 'Umar as the new Amir.

The town of al-Dākhilah having served as a refuge for anti-Unitarians during this war,[68] Manṣūr b. Aḥmad b. Ibrāhīm, the Amir of al-Far'ah, sent twenty men there.

13

Najd Finally Submits

First Unitarian raid into Jabal Shammar, 1197/1783

In 1197/early December 1782 to late November 1783, Su'ūd set out from al-Dir'īyah with the intention of chastising al-Kharj, whose inhabitants had sided with Sa'dūn of al-Aḥsā' and the rebels of Sudair the year before. At al-Ḥā'ir on the road to al-Kharj Su'ūd learned that the Bedouins of Āl Murrah, who had inflicted severe defeats on the Unitarians on two occasions,[1] were present in al-Kharj in force; this intelligence caused Su'ūd to switch from the raid southward to a raid into the far north, where the Ṣahabah, a section of Muṭair, were reported to be wandering in Jabal Shammar. No Unitarian expedition had yet penetrated into Jabal Shammar, the region that lies beyond al-Qaṣīm, to the northwest of the twin cities of 'Unaizah and Buraidah, with its center at Ḥā'il between the mountains of Aja' and Salmā.[2] In pursuit of the Bedouins of Muṭair the Unitarians now went all the way to al-Mustajiddah, on the pilgrim road south of Ḥā'il, not far from the southwestern extremity of Jabal Salmā. Attacking the Bedouins in the morning and putting them to rout, Su'ūd and his men killed many of them, including two of their chieftains, Khalaf Āl Fughum[3] and Dakhīl Allāh b. Jāsir Āl Fughum,[4] and took much booty in livestock, including ten horses.

[1] See above, pp. 127, 160.

[2] Aja' and Salmā are famous in Arab history and legend as Jabalā Ṭayy'/the Two Mountains of Ṭayy', the tribe that inhabited this area in the time of the Prophet.

[3] The House of Fughum are still the chiefs of the Ṣahabah – Sulaimān Ibn Saḥmān, *Tatimmat ta'rīkh Najd*, p. 132. Khalaf means "substitute, compensation, a good son"; Fughum or Fughm means "mouth, chin".

[4] Ibn Ghannām, II, 132–3; Ibn Bishr, I, 77.

Death of Zaid Ibn Zāmil of al-Kharj, 1197/1783

Zaid b. Mishārī Ibn Zāmil of al-Dilam in al-Kharj, who had taken the place of Dahhām b. Dawwās as the stoutest foe of Unitarianism in the south, rode out with several hundred men[5] to raid the Bedouins of Subai', of all the nomads perhaps the most constant in following the principles of the Shaikh. In the neighborhood of al-Riyāḍ Zaid came upon his quarry and deprived them of their camels. At that moment Sulaimān b. 'Ufaiṣān, the Unitarian Amir of al-Kharj who had been driven out when the apostates seized the region,[6] happened to be not far away with about thirty mounts on a mission for the Imam, looking for highway robbers. When Sulaimān heard what Zaid had done to Subai', he set out after him, discouraged not a whit by the disparity in numbers, and in the land of al-Ḥanīyah, west of Ṭuwaiq, he made him give battle. In the fray a shot from Sulaimān's side hit Zaid and nearly pitched him off his camel, but the sleeve of his cloak caught in a piece of the saddle[7] and held his dead body swaying there as his mount raced away at top speed. The death of Zaid struck terror into the hearts of his followers, and Sulaimān rescued the camels belonging to Subai'. Zaid's son Barrāk succeeded his father.

Relations with the Sharif Surūr of Mecca: resumption of the pilgrimage by the Unitarians, 1197/1783

In Dhū al-Qa'dah 1186/January to February 1773 the House of Musā'id b. Sa'īd rose against their uncle, the Sharif Aḥmad b. Sa'īd,[8] and drove him into exile,[9] his nephew Surūr b. Musā'id becoming Sharif of Mecca in his stead.[10] Thus was inaugurated a period of well over fifty years during which the sons and grandsons of Musā'id held

[5] Ibn Ghannām, II, 133, says more than three hundred; Ibn Bishr, I, 77, about two hundred.
[6] See above, p. 159, n. 13.
[7] *Ghazāl al-kūr* – Ibn Bishr, I, 78.
[8] They were all members of the branch of Dhawī Zaid of the House of Abū Numayy, since Sa'īd was the grandson of Zaid. For Musā'id, see above, p. 140.
[9] Aḥmad b. Sa'īd died in exile at Jiddah in 1196/1782 – Ibn Bishr, I, 77.
[10] Snouck Hurgronje, *Mekka*, I, 136 and Table III; Ibn Bishr, I, 59.

the Sharifate[11] without intrusion by scions of the rival branches of the House of Abū Numayy; Surūr himself ruled for the first fifteen years of this period. Surūr established himself as a ruler of such influence and eminence that the prince of Morocco in the far west of Islam sent to him in 1779, at the time of the pilgrimage, costly presents and his daughter to become the Sharif's bride.[12]

It had become the policy of the Unitarians of Najd, upon the accession of a new Sharif in Mecca, to endeavor to secure from him permission for their people to make the pilgrimage. When the request for such permission was made of Surūr, he, being interested chiefly in greater profits from the pilgrim traffic, offered to grant the desired permission if the Unitarians would pay the higher taxes that the Persians were accustomed to pay. Eager as the Unitarians were to make the pilgrimage, which like all good Moslems they considered one of the pillars of their religion, they could not submit to this indignity, and they scornfully refused Surūr's offer.[13]

In 1197/1783, ten years after Surūr's accession, the Imam 'Abd al-'Azīz reopened negotiations on the subject by sending a gift of horses and camels to Surūr. Out of appreciation for this gift and the rendering of honor that it signified the Sharif agreed to permit the Unitarians to come, and about three hundred of them went that year to make the circuit of the House of God in Mecca and to stand on 'Arafāt.[14]

[11] According to Snouck Hurgronje, Table III, their respective rules were as follows:

Surūr b. Musā'id	1186–1202/1773–88
Ghālib b. Musā'id	1202–28/1788–1813
'Abd al-Mu'īn b. Musā'id	1202 and 1218/1788 and 1803
Yaḥyā b. Surūr	1228–42/1813–27
'Abd al-Muṭṭalib b. Ghālib	1243/1827

Muḥammad b. 'Abd al-Mu'īn b. 'Aun of Dhawī 'Aun, a branch of the 'Abādilah, ousted 'Abd al-Muṭṭalib as Sharif in 1243/1827, after which the Sharifate was held by Dhawī 'Aun, with two brief interruptions, until the abolition of the office about a century later.

[12] Snouck Hurgronje, *Mekka*, I, 137. The lady was accompanied by two of her brothers.

[13] Snouck Hurgronje, *Mekka*, I, 139. The Unitarian chroniclers have nothing at all on these negotiations.

[14] Ibn Ghannām, II, 134. The pilgrimage season in 1197 reached its climax in early November 1783, not in the early summer of 1785, as stated by Philby, *Arabia*, p. 38. Philby points out that the number of people who made the pilgrimage was low because of the hard times that began in 1197 – see below, p. 185. There is no evidence in the sources to support Philby's explanation, p. 39, that Unitarian attacks on the pilgrim caravans from Iraq and Persia had reduced the number of pilgrims, which led the merchants of Mecca and Medina to demand of Surūr that he allow the Unitarians to come.

Drought and hard times: government measures to alleviate the suffering, 1197–1200/1783–6

Central Arabia suffered one of its periodic droughts beginning in 1197/December 1782 to November 1783 and enduring until 1200/November 1785 to October 1786, a span of three years or so without even the scant rainfall that the area usually has.[15] Food became scarce and prices soared very high. Famine wrought suffering among the people far and wide; conditions grew even worse during the second year as the slender stocks of food dwindled away. Many of the beasts upon which the people subsisted died, and many of the people themselves, men, women, and children. Men going to pray would suddenly stagger and then collapse. Towards the end of 1199 and in early 1200/fall and winter 1784–5, a disease attacked the camels of the country and carried off large numbers of them. The disease was so quick and deadly that mounts were falling down and dying under their riders.[16]

The Imam 'Abd al-'Azīz was greatly disturbed by the plight of his subjects. He issued orders to every Unitarian town to prepare a census of the poor and the weak, giving special attention to widows and orphans, and to make sure that as the civic larders held any food it went to those registered on the lists. In this way the Imam and his followers carried out the injunctions of their God and His Prophet to protect and care for the ones in need.

In 1200/early November 1785 to late October 1786 the break came at last. Rains fell, vegetation sprang up, food became more abundant, and the prices of wheat and other staples returned to more reasonable levels. The Unitarian state had weathered another crisis and in so doing had further cemented the solidarity of its members.[17]

[15] Philby, *Arabia*, pp. 37–8, is wrong in saying that the famine began in the summer of 1784, and lasted about two years. Both Ibn Ghannām, II, 133, and Ibn Bishr, I, 78, place the beginning in 1197/1783; Ibn Ghannām says the trouble continued for years, and Ibn Bishr, I, 80 dates the end of the drought 1200/1786.

[16] The year 1199 was called Jizām or Jazām – Ibn Bishr, I, 79. If the name referred to the famine, it was probably derived from *jazama* in the sense "to cut off, to eat one meal a day"; if it referred to the camel disease, it may have come from *jazama* in the sense "(of camels) to be watered."

[17] Ibn Bishr, I, 78, says that this period of hard times was known as Dālūb, but on p. 80 he

Continuation of the war with al-Kharj, 1198/1783–4

Barrāk b. Zaid Ibn Zāmil of al-Dilam intended to play his father's part in waging war against the Unitarians. Supported by the people of al-Yamāmah, he came up in 1198/late November 1783 to mid-November 1784[18] to attack the oasis of Manfūḥah not far below the capital al-Dir'īyah. The people of the oasis came out to meet him and killed about fifteen of his men, some of them known apostates. When news reached the capital of this act of aggression, Su'ūd mounted his men and rode south to deal with Barrāk, but he failed to overtake him.

When Su'ūd was returning from his raid into al-Aḥsā' later in the year,[19] he decided to pass by al-Yamāmah. There he found many of the townspeople enjoying an outing among the flowers of the *rauḍah*s outside the town. The pitiless Unitarian horsemen rushed in among the unprepared picnickers and cut down eighty of them.[20]

Unitarian raid against al-'Uyūn in al-Aḥsā', 1198/1784

More than a score of years had gone by since 'Abd al-'Azīz, then a captain in the prime of his life, had led the Unitarian raiders over the sands of the Dahnā' into the eastern land of al-Aḥsā' for the first time.[21] Now that the faith was more firmly installed in Najd, it was time to begin to look to the east again. Moreover, the drought of Daulāb still had its grip on the heart of the Peninsula, and the sheep of al-Aḥsā' were fatter than those of the decimated flocks of Najd. Su'ūd called out his raiders to speed with him straight across the dunes to al-'Uyūn at the northern end of the central series of oases, a settlement on the site where centuries before the capital of al-Aḥsā'

gives the name as Daulāb, which is probably the correct form. *Daulāb*, a word of Persian origin, may be applied to any rotary machine; the name was no doubt given to this period because of the recurrence of the drought year after year.

[18] Ibn Ghannām, II, 134; Ibn Bishr, I, 78. Not at the beginning of 1786, as stated by Philby, *Arabia*, p. 40.

[19] See below, p. 187.

[20] Ibn Ghannām, II, 134; Ibn Bishr, I, 78.

[21] See above, pp. 102–3.

had stood.[22] Taking al-'Uyūn by surprise, Su'ūd and his men rounded up much of the town's livestock, after which they broke into the houses and plundered them of food and furnishings. Ibn Muhannā and a number of the townspeople fortified themselves in the castle and held it against the Unitarians, who did not tarry for a siege. Su'ūd carried his booty back to Najd in a hurry, pausing only to slaughter the picnickers at al-Yamāmah.[23]

Unitarian raid against 'Unaizah, 1198/1784

When Ḥujailān b. Aḥmad of Buraidah subjected al-Qaṣīm to Unitarian rule after the rebellion of 1196/1782, the one place that refused to submit was the city of 'Unaizah, resentful of the leading role assumed by its rival Buraidah in the Unitarian drama. Ḥujailān unaided lacked the strength to bend 'Unaizah to his will, so the central government was constrained to take a hand in the matter. Su'ūd led his dreaded raiders northwards against 'Unaizah and launched an attack with his cavalry on the outskirts. The men of 'Unaizah defended themselves valiantly, and neither party could overpower the other. They stopped fighting to discuss terms of peace, but no agreement was reached. Su'ūd departed, leaving the settlement of his business at 'Unaizah for another day.[24]

Subjection of al-Kharj: submission of the south to Unitarianism, 1199/1784–5

The year 1199/mid-November 1784 to early November 1785, a year of great triumphs for Unitarianism in the south, began modestly enough with a minor raid conducted by Su'ūd against camels belonging to al-Ḥarīq that were being tended by Bedouins of Subai'.[25] Su'ūd

[22] The House of al-'Uyūn ruled over the central oases, al-Qaṭīf, Bahrain, and their dependencies from the 10th to the 13th centuries AD.

[23] See above, p. 186. The raid against al-'Uyūn took place in 1198/1784, not in 1786, as stated in Philby, *Arabia*, p. 40.

[24] Ibn Ghannām, II, 135; Ibn Bishr, I, 78.

[25] These Bedouins were elements of Subai' who had not yet accepted Unitarianism or who wore their religion so lightly that it was no impediment to their trafficking with the enemy.

got what he was after from the Bedouins.

Next Su'ūd headed south looking for Bedouins of the southern marches,[26] and he found them in the land of al-Ruwaiḍah.[27] Their chief took refuge in the castle of al-Ruwaiḍah, where the Unitarians killed him, after which they turned on his followers in the open. The Unitarian horse were about to make short work of the Bedouins when a large force of cavalry belonging to the Bedouins of the Suhūl appeared on the scene. These Suhūl were loyal Unitarians, but they failed to recognize Su'ūd and his men and they rode through them, putting them to flight and spoiling their action against the southern Bedouins. The Suhūl were repentant when they later learned the mistake they had made.

The Unitarian cause profited when the cousins of Barrāk b. Zaid Ibn Zāmil[28] of al-Dilam rose against him and killed him. The cousins hoped to make themselves rulers in succession to Barrāk, but the people of the town refused to have them and drove them out, for they were notorious for their corruption and evil ways. They made their way to al-Dir'īyah and tried to ally themselves with the Unitarians, but again they were rejected; in the end they fled to al-Aḥsā'.

Starting out for al-Kharj again,[29] Su'ūd learned while on the way that a heavily laden caravan belonging to the people of al-Kharj and Wadi al-Far' was coming up from al-Aḥsā'. At the watering-place of al-Thulaimā'[30] Su'ūd prepared an ambush, for he knew that the

It is a common practice in Arabia for townspeople to hire Bedouins to watch over their herds and flocks in the open spaces.

[26] Ibn Ghannām, II, 135, refers to them simply as *firqān al-Yaman*, using *firqān* as a plural of *farīq*/"a branch or section".They may have been elements of the 'Ajmān – see above, p. 106, n. 1.

[27] *Ruwaiḍah* is the diminutive of *rauḍah*.

[28] Ibn Ghannām, II, 136, and Ibn Bishr, I, 79, name as responsible for the murder of Barrāk his cousin Zāmil or Zuwaimil, who may have been aided by his brothers, and a certain 'Abd Allāh b. Muḥammad b. Rāshid al-Abraṣ (the Leprous), who may also have been a cousin.

[29] Ibn Ghannām, II, 136, places this raid after the murder of Barrāk Ibn Zāmil; Ibn Bishr, I, 79, places it before the murder.

[30] Al-Thulaimā' is probably derived from *thalm* or *thulmah*/"a notch, nick, indentation, or breach". Al-Hamdānī, *Ṣifat jazīrat al-'arab*, p. 139, names al-Thalmā' as a water in the Bayāḍ; this is obviously the same place with the name now being used in the diminutive form.

caravaneers would be badly in need of water after the crossing of the Dahnā'. When the van of the caravan arrived and made for the water, the Unitarians came out of their ambush and killed them to the last man. The main body[31] of the caravan couched its camels and made ready to defend itself. The Unitarians were not to be denied: out of the three hundred men or so accompanying the caravan they killed seventy or ninety[32] and compelled the rest to surrender, which meant the loss of all their camels and the variety of goods that the camels bore, including a large supply of cloth.

The Unitarian cause gained another important accession when Rubayyi' b. Zaid and Badan b. Zaid, the chiefs of the Makhārīm, a section of the Dawāsir domiciled in Wadi al-Dawāsir, appeared in al-Dir'īyah with a number of notables of their people to request the Shaikh and 'Abd al-'Azīz to accept them as followers of the true religion. From this time on the Makhārīm and their chiefs were counted among the leading exponents of Unitarianism in the great southern valley. Since many of the settlers in al-Kharj were of Dausirī extraction,[33] this development made an impression on them, and the spread of Unitarianism to the regions south of their own country, taking them as it were in the rear, weakened their will to resist. Moreover, the murder of Barrāk Ibn Zāmil had created a confused situation in al-Dilam, so that the time was opportune for the Unitarians to strike a final and decisive blow at apostasy in al-Kharj.

As the year 1199 was about to close, in the last part of the month of Dhū al-Ḥijjah/late October and early November 1785, Su'ūd and the Unitarian troops entered the oasis of al-Dilam for the last reckoning with the apostates. When the attackers occupied the palm groves and the outer defenses, the defenders had resort to the citadel. Instead of settling down for a long siege, Su'ūd constructed a fort among the palms to contain the enemy and made preparations to depart. The men of al-Dilam left the citadel and flung themselves upon the Unitarians in a desperate sally, but it was in vain, for they were beaten off with the loss of over twenty of their ranks, one of

[31] *Al-ẓahīrah* or *al-ẓuhairah* in Ibn Ghannām, II, 136; *al-ḥadrah* in Ibn Bishr, I, 79.

[32] Ibn Ghannām, II, 136, gives the lower figure; Ibn Bishr, I, 79, the higher. Among the slain were Zāmil b. Zaid (of al-Dilam?) and Ibn Zaid al-Hazzānī (of al-Ḥarīq?).

[33] Especially in al-Dilam, al-Salamīyah and al-Yamāmah.

the dead being Turkī b. Zaid Ibn Zāmil, who had succeeded his brother Barrāk as Amir of al-Dilam. Despite this setback, the besieged in the citadel were considering another sally when a member of the House of Zāmil, their ruling family, who was present in Su'ūd's company, came and prevailed upon them to accept the customary terms of surrender. All the weapons, animals, food and other property in the town were sequestered by the Unitarian treasury and then sold back to the townspeople at fixed prices. All the palm gardens became possessions of the Unitarian state. The leaders of apostasy were sentenced to exile, and Sulaimān b. 'Ufaiṣān was reappointed Amir.[34]

The occupation of al-Dilam marked the end of resistance throughout al-Kharj and Wadi al-Far'. Before Su'ūd returned home he received delegations from al-Yamāmah and al-Salamīyah, from al-Ḥauṭah and al-Ḥarīq, and from all the other towns of the region. Each delegation pledged obedience in the future; for their opposition in the past Su'ūd levied fines upon them, which they had to pay in cash.

After Su'ūd reached al-Dir'īyah, representatives came there from al-Aflāj, the intermediate district between al-Kharj and Wadi al-Far' to the north and Wadi al-Dawāsir to the south, to interview the Shaikh and the Imam 'Abd al-'Azīz and enlist themselves and their people as adherents of Unitarianism.

The capture of al-Dilam and the submission of the surrounding areas made the outgoing year of the 12th century of the Hegira a year of moment in the history of the spread of Unitarianism. For the first time since the beginning of the campaigns of the House of Su'ūd, the Unitarians were entirely free of the annoyance or threat of enemies lodged close to the heart of their domains. Save for the extremities, Jabal Shammar in the north[35] and Wadi al-Dawāsir in the south, Najd acknowledged the reign of the faith. The conquest of

[34] Ibn Ghannām, II, 138; Ibn Bishr, I, 79. For the first appointment of Sulaimān as Amir of al-Kharj, see above, p. 158.

[35] Although Jabal Shammar is sometimes reckoned as lying outside the confines of Najd, the prevalent opinion among the Arabs is that the Jabal does form a part of the great central province.

[36] See below, p. 203.

[37] See below, p. 207.

Najd could for all practical purposes be considered complete, for Jabal Shammar was to be overrun with little difficulty within the next two years,[36] while the submission of the Makhārīm of the Dawāsir had given the Unitarians a *point d'appui* from which they completed the subjection of the southern valley only three years later.[37] Beginning with the year 1200 of the Hegira/1785–6, the prime concern of the Unitarian strategists and captains was to be foes and unbelievers from beyond the limits of Najd. Invasions of Najd by outsiders were still to come, but all were to result in failure until the advance of the Egyptian forces some thirty years later. Moreover, the invasions were to be few in number, for fighting abroad in the lands of others was the common calling of the missionary soldiers of Najd. In particular, al-Aḥsā' to the east and the Holy Land of the Hijaz to the west invited the progress of Unitarian arms, and there they were soon to go.

PART IV

The Last Years of the Shaikh and the Beginnings of the Expansion of Unitarianism Beyond Najd

1200–1206 AH/AD 1786–1792

14

Campaigns East, North and South

Revolt against the lord of al-Aḥsā', 1200/1786

Ever since the Shaikh had begun preaching Unitarianism in al-'Uyainah, his movement had been opposed by the power of Āl Ḥumaid, the chiefs of Banī Khālid and lords of al-Aḥsā'. On two occasions the members of the House of Ḥumaid had fallen to fighting among themselves, but on each occasion a strong man had arisen and quickly put an end to the fighting, first 'Urai'ir b. Dujain in 1166/1752–3[1] and then 'Urai'ir's son Sa'dūn in 1189/1775–6.[2] For a decade after his accession Sa'dūn had sacrificed no chances to make trouble for the Unitarians in Najd. The Unitarians, however, kept gaining strength, while the foundations of Sa'dūn's rule were gradually weakening. In the year 1200/November 1785 to October 1786[3] the men of the ruling family of al-Aḥsā' went to war against each other once more; this time they brought closer their final overthrow by inviting an outsider to take part in the strife.

The leader of the party who desired the expulsion of Sa'dūn b. 'Urai'ir was 'Abd al-Muḥsin b. Sirdāḥ of Āl 'Ubaid Allāh, another section of Banī Khālid. Instead of trying to appropriate the office of ruler for himself, 'Abd al-Muḥsin put forward as candidate his nephew Duwaiḥis,[4] a brother of Sa'dūn. Not feeling strong enough to unseat Sa'dūn without aid from abroad, 'Abd al-Muḥsin referred to Thuwainī b. 'Abd Allāh Āl Shabīb, the paramount Shaikh of the

[1] See above, p. 90 [and Table, p. 254].
[2] See above, p. 152 [and Table, p. 254].
[3] Not at the beginning of 1787, as incorrectly stated by Philby, *Arabia*, p. 41.
[4] Duwaiḥis was the son of 'Urai'ir b. Dujain and 'Abd al-Muḥsin's sister – Ibn Bishr, I, 85. Duwaiḥis is the diminutive of Dāḥis/Whitlow.

great Bedouin confederation of the Muntafiq in lower Iraq,[5] who supplied him with men and money. The chiefs of two sections of Banī Khālid, the Mahāshīr[6] and Āl Subaiḥ, threw in their lot with ʻAbd al-Muḥsin.

In the spring[7] of 1200/1786 Saʻdūn met his enemies, both his kinsmen and their alien supporters at Ḍajʻah[8] in the lands of Banī Khālid. The battle went against Saʻdūn,[9] who had to flee with his intimates on horseback. His brother Duwaiḥis succeeded him as chief of Banī Khālid and lord of al-Aḥsā', but the real power was in the hands of ʻAbd al-Muḥsin b. Sirdāḥ.

Saʻdūn b. ʻUraiʻir of al-Aḥsā' at al-Dirʻīyah, 1200/1786

When Saʻdūn fled from the field of Ḍajʻah, leaving his newer enemies in control of his homeland, he rode towards al-Dirʻīyah, the capital of his older enemies the Unitarians, sending on ahead to the Imam ʻAbd al-ʻAzīz a request for safe conduct. The Imam, who had made an agreement with Thuwainī of the Muntafiq stipulating peace and friendship,[10] forbade Saʻdūn entry into the town until the Unitarians had had an opportunity to consult with Thuwainī.

[5] Thuwainī had become head of the Muntafiq for the first time in 1175/1761–2 upon the death of his father ʻAbd Allāh b. Muḥammad – al-Nabhānī, *al-Tuḥfah al-nabhānīyah: al-Muntafiq*, p. 56, where the Christian date corresponding to 1175 is wrongly given as 1760. He became a famous figure in his area before his death in 1212/1797 while on an expedition against the Unitarians of Najd. The English writers of his time called him Twiney or Twyney – Longrigg, *Four Centuries of Modern Iraq*, p. 213, n. 1; 214, n. 2.

Although Longrigg lists Thuwainī under the family of Saʻdūn in his index, p. 374, he was not of this family, as Longrigg himself shows in the genealogy on p. 349. Saʻdūn b. Muḥammad, Thuwainī's uncle, was the ancestor of almost all the heads of the confederation in the 19th and 20th centuries.

[6] Compare the role the Mahāshīr played in driving out Sulaimān b. Muḥammad Āl Ḥumaid in 1166/1752–3 – above, p. 102.

[7] Al-Nabhānī, *al-Muntafiq*, p. 57.

[8] Al-Nabhānī, *al-Muntafiq*, p. 57, says that the name of the place is Ḍajʻah, but that it is commonly called Jaḍʻah. An inversion of consonants of this sort is not unusual in Arabic. Ibn Ghannām, II, 139, and Ibn Bishr, I, 80, both give the name as Jaḍʻah.

[9] Al-Nabhānī, *al-Muntafiq*, p. 57, says that Saʻdūn was betrayed on the field by some of his own men. Thuwainī carried home much booty as a result of the victory.

[10] *Muhādanah wa-muṣāḥabah* – Ibn Ghannām, II, 139. The sources do not state when this agreement had been made.

Sa'dūn, however, was not to be denied; he made his way in and took the Imam by surprise as he came out of the gate of his palace to attend the Friday congregational prayer. The Imam placed Sa'dūn in the palace and hurried out again to avoid being absent in the mosque. The divine service over, the Imam took counsel with the Shaikh Muḥammad b. 'Abd al-Wahhāb, who despite his years[11] still had the last word in all matters of vital importance affecting the state. To the perplexed 'Abd al-'Azīz the Shaikh cited the words of God in the Koran: "It may be that God will create love between you and those of them who have been inimical towards you, for God is powerful and God is forgiving and merciful."[12] These words and others in similar vein spoken by the Shaikh made the decision easy for the Imam; he granted Sa'dūn the refuge he sought.[13]

Being afraid that Thuwainī might consider the harboring of Sa'dūn a violation of the agreement, the Imam sent a letter to him at al-Ṭaff assuring him that he intended no violation and offering to be the guarantor for anything Thuwainī might desire from the refugees. Thuwainī, however, had gnashed his teeth and flown into a rage at hearing the news, and the Imam's letter failed to soothe him. He began making preparations for war against the Unitarians, calling in his allies from all their districts, but it was not until the following year that he took the road for Najd with his army.[14]

Unitarian raid against Qaḥṭān in the south, 1200/1786

The victorious march of Unitarianism through Najd was strikingly emphasized in 1200/1786 when Su'ūd drove south for a raid against

[11] The Shaikh was in his early eighties.

[12] Ibn Ghannām, II, 140.

[13] Ibn Bishr, I, 80, has nothing on the Imam's hesitancy to receive Sa'dūn or on the Imam's conference with the Shaikh; he says simply that the Imam greeted Sa'dūn with honor and bestowed upon him a rich gift.

Philby, *Arabia*, p. 42, says that "the verdict of history must be that this apparently insignificant incident was the first definite step of the house of Sa'ud on the path that led to Empire". This hardly seems to be in keeping with the facts, for the Unitarians were already well along on the path that led to Empire, and even if the Imam had rejected Sa'dūn's plea it is likely that the conquest of al-Aḥsā' would have been quickly achieved and that other events would have followed much the same course that they did follow.

[14] Ibn Ghannām, I, 140.

Qaḥṭān, the dominant tribe in the desert sector between southern Najd and 'Asīr, a tribe once rich in horses[15] and still rich in camels. In Su'ūd's train went Bedouins of the Ẓafīr and Banī Khālid,[16] nomad groups who had until this time fiercely opposed the spread of Unitarianism and had never appeared in its ranks. When the men of Qaḥṭān heard that the Unitarians were coming, they rejoiced; they were valiant men in a fight, and they thought that southerners could worst any invader. The Unitarian onslaught, however, gave Qaḥṭān a taste of defeat and turned their rejoicing into sorrow, for many of them were slain in the battle. The Unitarians carried off their belongings and herded away their fine camels.

Second Unitarian raid into Jabal Shammar, 1200/1786

The raid to al-Mustajiddah, the first Unitarian venture into Jabal Shammar,[17] was followed in 1200/1786 by a raid into a different part of the district. Ḥujailān b. Aḥmad Ibn 'Ulayyān, the Unitarian governor at Buraidah, learned that a great caravan had left al-Baṣrah and Sūq al-Shuyūkh in Iraq bound across the northern waste of the Peninsula with cloth for Jabal Shammar. Ḥujailān stationed himself at Baq'ā' in the Jabal with soldiers from al-Qaṣīm and Bedouin auxilaries from 'Anazah, and when the caravan arrived he put to rout the townsmen and Bedouins who made it up, after which he took possession of their bundles of goods. Like the raid of Su'ūd against Qaḥṭān in the same year, the purpose of this raid was the acquiring of booty for the state treasury rather than the subduing of enemies of the faith, but the blows in every direction were telling and the name of the Unitarians was becoming a fearful one abroad.[18]

[15] See above, p. 128, n. 52.

[16] Ibn Ghannām, I, 140. Among the representatives of Banī Khālid with Su'ūd there may have been some of the refugees who had come from al-Aḥsā' with Sa'dūn.

[17] See above, p. 182.

[18] On Ḥujailān's raid see Ibn Ghannām, II, 141, and Ibn Bishr, I, 80. Philby, *Arabia*, p. 43, has in an unaccountable manner substituted a campaign by Thuwainī of the Muntafiq for the coming of the caravan.

Invasion of Najd by Thuwainī of the Muntafiq, 1201/1786–7

In Muḥarram 1201/late October to late November 1786[19] Thuwainī b. ʿAbd Allāh Āl Shabīb of the Muntafiq had completed his preparations for the expedition into Najd to take revenge on the Unitarians for giving shelter to Saʿdūn b. ʿUraiʿir. In addition to his own Bedouins he had assembled contingents from the tribes of Shammar and Ṭayy' and the town of al-Zubair.[20] For the guns of his soldiers and the cannon he carried along he was said to have had seven hundred packloads of ammunition.[21] Just after entering the province of al-Qaṣīm, Thuwainī and his army camped before the Unitarian town of al-Tanūmah,[22] the inhabitants of which refused to open their gates or grant passage. For some days Thuwainī pounded the place with his cannon and engaged in maneuvers with his cavalry, but the Unitarian defenders held out. At length, Thuwainī found a certain ʿUthmān b. Aḥmad, a comrade of the defenders, who consented to betray his fellows. Using ʿUthmān as an intermediary, Thuwainī induced the defenders to agree to terms and to allow some of his men to come into their citadel. Thuwainī's men who got inside seized the citadel and turned on the defenders, slaying all who were unable to flee,[23] after which the rest of the army poured into the town and plundered it.[24] From al-Tanūmah Thuwainī

[19] Ibn Bishr, I, 81. Al-Nabhānī, *al-Muntafiq*, p. 61, says that the expedition took place early in 1201; Ibn Ghannām, II, 142, places it in 1201 after the trouble at al-Yamāmah (see below, p. 202, n. 38) without stating what part of the year it was in. Philby, *Arabia*, p. 43, incorrectly states that the expedition was carried out in the winter season of 1787–8. Although Longrigg, *Four Centuries of Modern Iraq*, has much information on Thuwainī's career, he does not mention this expedition.

[20] Ibn Bishr, I, 81; al-Nabhānī, p. 61. Musil, *Northern Neǧd*, p. 260, speaks of Turkish troops under the leadership of Thuwainī; they were Turkish only in the sense that Thuwainī owed allegiance to the Ottoman Pasha in Baghdad. There is no indication in the sources that the Ottoman government had anything to do with the going out of the expedition.

[21] Ibn Bishr, I, 81.

[22] The copyist of Ibn Ghannām has again omitted the "t" from this name (compare above, p. 176, n. 40) – Ibn Ghannām, II, 143. This time Philby, *Arabia*, p. 43, mistakes the "n" for a "t" and reads the name as Tuma.

[23] It is said that 170 men were killed – Ibn Bishr, I, 81.

[24] Ibn Ghannām, II, 143–4, who does not bear out the statement by Philby, *Arabia*, p. 43,

marched on to Buraidah, the key possession of the Unitarians in al-Qaṣīm, and blockaded the city.[25] While the siege of Buraidah was in progress, Bedouin politicians from Iraq[26] arrived in Thuwainī's tent and persuaded him that he ought to give up frittering away his strength far from home in Najd and return to take advantage of the troubles then besetting the Ottoman Pasha of Baghdad.[27] Thuwainī broke off the siege of Buraidah abruptly and took his army off towards Iraq.[28]

When the Imam 'Abd al-'Azīz in al-Dir'īyah had learned of Thuwainī's advance into Najd, he had issued the summons for the Unitarian troops to turn out in full force and had placed them under the command of his son Su'ūd to go to the rescue of Buraidah. Su'ūd, who arrived in the north soon after Thuwainī's departure, hastened after the retiring invaders. Although he failed to catch the main body of Thuwainī's army, he did come upon elements of Shammar under Ibn Jady; the Unitarians killed many of these Bedouins and took as booty everything they had.[29]

that Thuwainī pretended "to sue for peace and to be desirous of entering the Wahhabi fold". Ibn Bishr, I, 81, says that Thuwainī took the town by force.

[25] The sources do not reveal whether Ḥujailān b. Aḥmad Ibn 'Ulayyān was at home or away on his expedition into Jabal Shammar, for which see below, p. 203.

[26] Sulaimān Ibn Shāwī, head of the tribe of the 'Ubaid and one of the greatest Bedouin chiefs in Iraq, who was in revolt against the Ottoman government, encouraged Thuwainī to seize the city of al-Baṣrah and to attempt to make himself Governor of the whole of Iraq in place of the Ottoman Pasha of Baghdad. According to al-Nabhānī, p. 61, n. 1, Ibn Shāwī came to Thuwainī while he was in Najd, apparently during the siege of Buraidah, and won his acceptance of these plans.

Moreover, either Ibn Shāwī or other Bedouins informed Thuwainī at about the same time that his position in his own tribe the Muntafiq might become insecure if he did not return home without delay. Throughout the latter part of Thuwainī's career his nephew Ḥumūd b. Thāmir b. Sa'dūn was a powerful rival for the headship of the Muntafiq and did succeed in supplanting him in office on several occasions.

[27] On these troubles and the situation in Iraq in general, see Longrigg, *Four Centuries of Modern Iraq,* pp. 203–4.

[28] Ibn Ghannām, whose whole account of this campaign is poetic rather than straightforward, says that a great pain overtook Thuwainī and fright induced him to return home defeated. Ibn Bishr, I, 81, and al-Nabhānī, p. 61, who attribute his return to the internal situation in Iraq, seem to be closer to the mark.

[29] Ibn Ghannām, II, 144–5, is the only source for Su'ūd's pursuit of Thuwainī and attack on the elements of Shammar. Philby, *Arabia*, pp. 43–4, who reads Ibn Ghannām carelessly at this point and does not check him with other accounts, places Thuwainī's capture of al-Baṣrah and defeat by Sulaimān Pasha of Baghdad (for which see below, pp. 201–2) between

While Thuwainī was retreating in the direction of Iraq with Su'ūd and the Unitarians on his trail, Duwaiḥis b. 'Urai'ir and 'Abd al-Muḥsin b. Sirdāḥ appeared in Najd with the levies of Banī Khālid and the townsmen of al-Aḥsā', expecting to join Thuwainī in assaults on the centers of Unitarianism.[30] Before leaving al-Aḥsā' they had been convinced that Thuwainī would be staying in Najd for a long time, trustworthy informants having told them that Thuwainī had compelled all the men of al-Zubair in his army to bring along their women and children as well as goods for buying and selling.[31] Upon finding that Thuwainī and his settlers had already gone, the allies from al-Aḥsā' wheeled about and headed straight for home, even though it meant crossing the dunes of the Dahnā' in summer[32] without an adequate supply of water. Many of the people died of thirst in the Dahnā' and in the stony desert of the Ṣummān to the east.

Thuwainī, upon arriving in Iraq in the summer of 1787, lost no time in making himself master of the city of al-Baṣrah[33] and in trying to undermine the position of Sulaimān Pasha, the Ottoman governor of Baghdad. The Bedouin chief, however, had overplayed his hand; the government at Istanbul stood firm behind its Pasha, who marched south to chastise Thuwainī. In Muḥarram 1202/October 1787 Sulaimān Pasha with his Janissaries and Kurds and Arabs of 'Uqail and the tribe of Ka'b[34] smashed the army brought out by Thuwainī[35] in the neighborhood of Sūq al-Shuyūkh. The

the lifting of the siege of Buraidah and Su'ūd's attack on the Bedouins of Shammar. When one counts as an expedition led by Thuwainī Philby's description of the Iraqian caravan that was plundered by Ḥujailān (see above, p. 198, n. 18), he discovers that Philby has on record three separate expeditions by Thuwainī into Najd at this time when actually there was only one.

[30] Thuwainī had no doubt called upon Duwaiḥis and 'Abd al-Muḥsin to support him in return for the aid he had given them in overthrowing Sa'dūn – see above, pp. 195–6.

[31] Ibn Ghannām, II, 145.

[32] The summer of 1787: Sha'bān 1201 began in mid-May, Ramaḍān in mid-June, and Shawwāl in mid-July.

[33] Thuwainī held al-Baṣrah for about three months until the beginning of Muḥarram 1202/mid-October 1787 – al-Nabhānī, pp. 63–4. Therefore, his occupation of the city must have taken place in July 1787. On the occupation see al-Nabhānī, *loc. cit.*, and Longrigg, *Four Centuries of Modern Iraq*, pp. 204–5.

[34] Ḥumūd b. Thāmir b. Sa'dūn, Thuwainī's nephew and rival, was also present on Sulaimān Pasha's side.

[35] Ibn Bishr, I, 82–3; al-Nabhānī, pp. 63–4; Longrigg, p. 205.

crestfallen Bedouin sought safety in the region of al-Kuwait;[36] after a while he moved on to join his friends of Banī Khālid in the Ṣummān. It may have been at this time that he made his journey to al-Dir'īyah and asked to be accepted as a believer in Unitarianism, a conversion that did not hold good, since he soon broke with the Unitarians and rejoined the ranks of their enemies.[37]

Apostasy in al-Yamāmah, 1201/1786–7

Early in 1201/October 1786 to October 1787[38] Su'ūd was at Malham in al-Maḥmal assembling the Unitarian forces when the chiefs of the Rūsah of al-Yamāmah came and informed him that the House of Bijād, the old rulers of their oasis, were planning to violate the compact with the Unitarians. Su'ūd led his troops down from Malham to al-Yamāmah; his appearance was sufficient to cow the would-be rebels, who even sent their women to him in order to placate him. The Shaikh and the Imam instructed Su'ūd to deliver the members of the House of Bijād to the capital, but on the way the guilty ones darted off to the right and escaped to al-Aḥsā'. As a consequence, the Imam ordered that their homes and their settlement, al-Bannah, in the oasis of al-Yamāmah, should be destroyed. Su'ūd appointed 'Abd Allāh Āl Ruwais[39] Amir of al-Yamāmah and built a fort to strengthen the Unitarian position there. Muḥammad b. Ghushayyān, the former commandant of the

[36] Ibn Ghannām, II, 144, says that he went to al-Kuwait; Ibn Bishr, I, 83, and al-Nabhānī, p. 64, say that he went to al-Jahrā', a village and gathering-place for Bedouins twenty miles west of al-Kuwait. Brydges, II, 176, states that Thuwainī took refuge with "the Shaik of Grain [al-Kuwait]," who, "notwithstanding he was offered large bribes on the one hand, and threatened with the whole power of the Paçhalik of Bagdad, on the other, refused to give up his guest."

[37] It is not clear when Thuwainī's journey to al-Dir'īyah was made. Ibn Ghannām, II, 144, mentions it following his account of Thuwainī's defeat by Sulaimān Pasha in 1202/1786, but he gives no date and it may have taken place some time later. Longrigg, p. 206, n. 1, places the journey to al-Dir'īyah after Thuwainī's return to power as head of the Muntafiq and the expulsion of him from Iraq for the second time in the middle of 1203/early 1789 – see below, p. 211, n. 72.

[38] Ibn Ghannām, I, 141–2, describes this affair under the year 1201 before dealing with Thuwainī's expedition to Najd, which perhaps should have been placed first, since it started out in the opening days of the year.

[39] One of the Rūsah.

nearby fort of al-Bid‘,[40] was made Amir of the garrison in the new stronghold.[41]

Expedition of Ḥujailān of Buraidah: submission of the whole of Jabal Shammar, 1201/1786–7

Acting under instructions from the Imam ‘Abd al-‘Azīz,[42] Ḥujailān b. Aḥmad Ibn ‘Ulayyān of Buraidah in 1201/1786–7[43] entered Jabal Shammar with an impressive array made up of townsmen from al-Qaṣīm and Bedouins from various tribes. Although it was not the first time the Unitarians had gone into the Jabal,[44] it was the first time they went there with the intention of imposing their faith by military means. Ḥujailān confronted the inhabitants of the Jabal with the alternatives: accept Unitarianism or we shall make war on you, and after we subdue you, you shall pay fines. Many accepted the teachings of the Shaikh of their own free will and desire, others to escape the alternative of fighting and fines, and others only after they had been beaten in battle.[45] Before Ḥujailān marched back to Buraidah he had subjected the whole district of Jabal Shammar to Unitarianism.[46] From that year to the present day the faith of Najd has had large numbers of devoted adherents in the Jabal.

[40] See above, p. 173.

[41] Both ‘Abd Allāh Āl Ruwais and Ibn Ghushayyān were probably subject to the authority of Sulaimān b. ‘Ufaiṣān, who was Amir of the whole district of al-Kharj.

[42] Ibn Bishr, I, 82.

[43] The time of the year is not given. Ḥujailān may have been absent on this expedition when Thuwainī laid siege to Buraidah – see above, p. 200, n. 25.

[44] Philby, *Arabia*, p. 44, says that "now for the first time [Jabal Shammar] comes within the purview of Wahhabi history". For the first two Unitarian expeditions into Jabal Shammar, see above, pp. 182, 198. Philby also errs in placing this expedition in 1788.

[45] Ibn Ghannām, I, 146.

[46] Ibn Bishr, I, 82, also mentions a raid carried out by Ḥujailān against the Bedouins of Shammar after the departure of Thuwainī. About a hundred of the Bedouins were killed and many camels and much other booty taken. This may have been a part of the operation carried out by Su‘ūd against the Bedouins of Shammar during his pursuit of Thuwainī – see above, p. 200.

[47] Qarmalah was the name of Hādī's mother – Ibn Ghannām, II, 146. It is not uncommon for a Bedouin to use his mother's name.

Submission of Hādī Ibn Qarmalah of Qaḥṭān, 1201/1786–7

Hādī b. Ghānim, more commonly known as Ibn Qarmalah,[47] a minor figure from the great tribe of Qaḥṭān in the southwest, arrived in al-Dir'īyah during the year 1201/1786–7 to express to the Imam his desire to enlist in the Unitarian cause. Hādī may have been inspired by the impressive victory of the Unitarians over his fellow tribesmen the year before,[48] or he may have been moved by a conviction that the Bedouins needed the Word of God to redeem them from their idolatry and superstitions. He pledged himself in the presence of the Imam to carry on the struggle against the Mushrikūn and the enemies of the faith. The adherence of an ally in the *dīrah* of Qaḥṭān was a noteworthy gain for the Unitarians, since that area was to be of strategic importance in the impending conflict between Najd and the Sharifs of the Hijaz. Ibn Qarmalah by embracing Unitarianism took the first step on the road towards making himself with the aid of his new allies commander of all Qaḥṭān.

Progress of Unitarianism in Wadi al-Dawāsir, 1202/1787–8

The chiefs of the Makhārīm of the Dawāsir, Rubayyi' b. Zaid and Badan b. Zaid, after returning to their valley in the south as the leading representatives of Unitarianism there,[49] concerned themselves with the propagating of their new faith among their neighbors. Realizing that they might encounter opposition, they began by constructing a fort in which they could shut themselves up in case of war. Next they embarked on their campaign against idolatry and *shirk* by burning down a sacred tree that existed in the valley. The opposition they had anticipated now crystalized, and the sons of Zaid found themselves besieged in their new fort. The anti-Unitarians, being unable to take the place by storm, slaughtered a donkey and cast it into the well outside the fort on which the sons

[48] See above, pp. 197–8.
[49] See above, p. 189.

of Zaid depended for their water supply, and in a short time the well was stinking. The sons of Zaid, however, succeeded in finding another spring, after which they bought off their enemies by the gift of a mare.

The sons of Zaid sent a message to the Imam 'Abd al-'Azīz informing him of the resistance to Unitarianism that had developed in the valley. The Imam directed that weapons, money and provisions should be dispatched to the Makhārīm and appointed Mubārak b. 'Abd al-Hādī in command of reinforcements for the cause in the south. No sooner had Mubārak arrived at the fort of the sons of Zaid than the Khaṭāṭibah, another element of the Dawāsir,[50] went to work to build a fort overlooking the new post of the Unitarians. Rubayyi' and his allies were able to thwart the builders at their task, only to have the whole valley rise in a surge of anti-Unitarianism. Those who had gathered together against the sons of Zaid built two boxes of wood,[51] each large enough to hold thirty men.[52] The boxes were pushed towards the Unitarian fort on rollers, but both came to a halt before reaching the walls, one having been smashed and the other uncovered.[53] Nine of the occupants were killed by the gunfire of the defenders. Undiscouraged by this failure, the besiegers kept up the pressure until they had broken down part of the walls, whereupon the Makhārīm agreed to evacuate on terms, which called for no more than the surrender of the weapons they had taken from the attackers during the period of the siege. Having left the fort, the Unitarians

[50] The Khaṭāṭibah are a subsection of the Rijbān or Rajbān of the Dawāsir.

[51] Although Ibn Ghannām, II, 148, uses the plural throughout most of his account, indicating that there were more than two boxes, at the end he shifts to the dual, so that it may be assumed that only two were built or at least only two were used.

[52] The men inside the boxes were protected by coats of mail and equipped with instruments for tearing down the mudbrick walls of the fort. Philby, *Arabia*, p. 46, interprets Ibn Ghannām's *mafātīḥ* as referring to duplicate keys for the locks on the gate of the fort; while *mafātīḥ* ordinarily does mean keys, it may be used for any sort of instrument employed for the purpose of opening something, and the context in Ibn Ghannām suggests that the reference is to crowbars or similar instruments to be employed in opening the fort by tearing down the walls.

[53] Compare the boxes used before this at al-Bid' in al-Kharj and at Buraidah – above, pp. 173, 178. Ibn Ghannām, II, 148, here calls the contrivances *zaḥḥāfāt*/"creepers"; he says that the rollers on which the boxes were mounted were called by the people of Wadi al-Dawāsir *'ajal*.

of the valley joined Mubārak b. 'Abd al-Hādī, who had apparently remained at a safe distance in the days of the siege, and soon thereafter traveled to al-Dir'īyah to see the Imam, who received them with honor and gave them gifts of food and other things.

Returning from al-Dir'īyah to their home district, the Makhārīm resumed their enterprise by building a fort opposite the village of Tamrah,[54] which they used as a base for raids directed against the towns and forts held by the anti-Unitarians in the valley. As the months went by Rubayyi' and Mubārak achieved such success that three elements of the Dawāsir – the Ḥanābijah, the 'Umūr, and the Walāmīn – joined them in professing Unitarianism. Rubayyi' b. Zaid himself left his fort and mingled with the Ḥanābijah, instructing them in the principles of the religion preached by the Shaikh.[55]

Third attack on the Unitarians by the lord of Najrān, 1202/1788

When the anti-Unitarians of Wadi al-Dawāsir saw the Unitarians making headway with their raids and propaganda, they turned to the lord of Najrān for aid. Jamāhir, the chief of the Rijbān, and Ḥuwail, the chief of the Wadā'īn,[56] journeyed to Najrān to make their appeal in person. They pointed out to the lord that if the Unitarians brought Wadi al-Dawāsir under their control no barrier would remain between them and the land of Najrān itself. The lord answered their plea by coming up to Wadi al-Dawāsir with his turnout of fighting-men, but it was no longer the redoubtable force it had once been. Even though supported by the Rijbān and the Wadā'īn, the lord of Najrān lacked the strength to overcome the Ḥanābijah, fired as they were by zeal after the preaching tour of Rubayyi' b. Zaid. The lord of Najrān had no stomach for crossing swords with the greater armies of the Unitarians; he retraced his steps, leaving Wadi al-Dawāsir vulnerable to conquest by the faith from the north.[57]

[54] "In the gap of the Tuwaiq ridge which commanded the main route between the Wadi settlements and Sulaiyil [in the eastern part of the valley]" – Philby, *Arabia*, p. 46.

[55] All the details given here are taken from Ibn Ghannām, II, 146–50.

[56] Ḥuwail had supported the second invasion of Najd by the lord of Najrān in 1189/1775–6 – see above, pp. 150, n. 6; 154, n. 26.

Submission of the whole of Wadi al-Dawāsir, 1202/1788

The slipping away of the lord of Najrān was the signal for the Rijbān to enroll themselves among the Unitarians by means of a compact with Rubayyi' b. Zaid of the Makhārīm. Their example was followed immediately by the Wadā'īn and by the towns and villages scattered throughout the valley. The conversion of some of the newcomers was, however, no more than nominal, and their lack of enthusiasm for the true tenets of Unitarianism soon became apparent. To combat this situation Rubayyi' and a group of the leading men of the Dawāsir went up to al-Dir'īyah to ask the Shaikh and the Imam to assign a Unitarian instructor to the region; they were again received with honor and 'Abd Allāh b. Fāḍil was nominated to return with them in the capacity of instructor.

About six months later the Rijbān and the Wadā'īn made an outright break with Unitarianism. The Imam ordered Sulaimān b. 'Ufaiṣān, the Amir of al-Kharj, down to Wadi al-Dawāsir to cope with the disloyal elements. Sulaimān soon taught them the futility of their conduct and had them begging to be reaccepted as Unitarians. Singling out the leaders, Sulaimān compelled them to go with him to al-Dir'īyah, where their readmission into the Unitarian state was approved by the Imam on condition that they should at once pay a fine of two thousand riyals and one thousand muskets.[58] Thus was one more important district attached to the rapidly growing Unitarian state.

Unitarian expeditions against 'Unaizah and 'Anazah, 1202/1787–8

During the year 1202/October 1787 to October 1788 Su'ūd led his Unitarian forces into the city of 'Unaizah in al-Qaṣīm. Reports had

[57] Ibn Ghannām, II, 150–1, is the only source that deals with the expedition of the lord of Najrān.

[58] Ibn Ghannām, II, 151–2, is again the main source for events in Wadi al-Dawāsir. Ibn Bishr, I, 83, says simply that during 1202/1788 all the people of the valley swore allegiance to the religion of God and His Prophet and sent delegations to the Shaikh and the Imam after a number of maneuvers and battles.

reached him that there was a party favoring apostasy in the city,[59] and he had come to investigate. A close study of affairs in ʻUnaizah convinced Suʻūd that the place would be better off without the members of the ruling House of Rashīd; these he sentenced to exile and appointed Ibn Yaḥyā as the new Amir.[60]

Later in the year[61] Suʻūd moved northwards again to upper Najd beyond al-Qaṣīm, where he conducted a successful raid against the Bedouins of the tribe of ʻAnazah who were encamped at the hills of Qinā and Qunayy.[62]

Unitarian raids against Qaṭar and al-ʻUqair, 1202/1787–8

Although the Unitarians had carried out hit-and-run raids into al-Aḥsā' before 1202/October 1787 to October 1788, they had not yet reached the coast of the Persian Gulf. This year saw their armed men ride as far as salt water for the first time in raids inaugurating a series of campaigns that soon brought about the subjection of the whole region of al-Aḥsā'.

The Amir of al-Kharj, Sulaimān b. ʻUfaiṣān, who was rapidly coming to the forefront as one of the ablest and most reliable of the Unitarian captains, drove all the way across al-Aḥsā' for an attack on the peninsula of Qaṭar, which juts out into the Gulf about halfway down the western coast.[63] Taking the members of Āl Abū Rumaiḥ by surprise, Sulaimān defeated them, killing about fifty of their men and seizing all the camels, sheep and goats, weapons and other

[59] Ibn Ghannām, II, 152–3. This would indicate that ʻUnaizah had previously submitted at some unspecified time after having been the last to hold out following the suppression of the revolt in al-Qaṣīm – see above, pp. 178–9.

[60] Ibn Ghannām, II, 153, identifies him as ʻAlī Ibn Yaḥyā; Ibn Bishr, I, 83, as ʻAbd Allāh Ibn Yaḥyā.

[61] Apparently after the formal designation of Suʻūd as heir apparent, for which see below, pp. 209–10.

[62] Ibn Ghannām, II, 155; Ibn Bishr, I, 83. [*Cf.* Ch. 8 p. 127, n. 47 on Qinā and Qinā. Ed.]

[63] The series of raids into the east had actually been begun before this by Suʻūd, who in this year had started across the Dahnā' for an attack on Banī Khālid. While on the way he received news that his quarry had moved off to the north; he then turned about and went home – Ibn Ghannām, II, 153.

possessions they had with them. Returning towards Najd, Sulaimān struck in the early morning at the settlement of al-Jishshah in the central oases; the townspeople sprang up to defend their dwellings and prevented the Unitarians from adding to their collection of booty.[64]

Before the year was out Sulaimān was off to the east again, under orders from the Imam to swoop down on al-'Uqair, the port of entry for the central oases.[65] On the way towards the Gulf,[66] when he and his men arrived at Ḥaraḍ, a watering-place south of the central oases, they met a party of about fifty of the exiles of al-Yamāmah under 'Uwais b. Ghufayyān[67] who were starting out on a raid against the Unitarians in Najd. In the fight at Ḥaraḍ Sulaimān's company killed most if not all[68] of the enemy, including their captain, and took their mounts and weapons. Continuing on to the main objective, Sulaimān reached al-'Uqair one morning and made a rich haul of merchandise in the caravanserai. The soldiers stationed at the port fled to their citadel, while the Unitarians set fire to the palm-branch huts in the settlement.

Designation of Su'ūd as heir apparent, 1202/1788

The Unitarian state was now so firmly established in Najd and its future was so bright that the aged Shaikh Muḥammad b. 'Abd al-Wahhāb decided to designate Su'ūd formally as the one who ultimately would succeed his father the Imam 'Abd al-'Azīz. Su'ūd on many a field of battle had shown that he was deserving, and the Imam himself was at one with the Shaikh in making the selection. Instructions went out the length and breadth of the Unitarian dominions that recognition should be accorded Su'ūd's new position and allegiance sworn to him in the traditional manner.[69] The

[64] Ibn Ghannām, II, 153; Ibn Bishr, I, 83.

[65] Philby, *Arabia*, p. 47, mistakenly describes the attack on Qaṭar and the attack on al-'Uqair as having taken place during a single raid by Sulaimān to the east.

[66] Not on the return march, as incorrectly stated by Philby, *Arabia*, p. 47.

[67] Ibn Ghannām, II, 155. Ibn Bishr, I, 83, who calls him 'Īsā instead of 'Uwais, says that he was a slave who was famous as a poet and a knight.

[68] Ibn Ghannām, II, 155, says that all of them were killed; Ibn Bishr, I, 83, most of them.

[69] Ibn Ghannām, II, 154, says that the Unitarians were instructed by the Shaikh to swear allegiance to Su'ūd as the Amir after his father; Ibn Bishr, I, 83, that the Shaikh instructed them to swear allegiance to Su'ūd, who was to be the heir apparent (*walī al-'ahd* – see above, p. 116, n. 7.)

prescriptions of the religious law applying to a ceremony of this nature were scrupulously observed.

Su'ūd's raid against Banī Khālid in al-Aḥsā', 1203/1788–9

On the first campaign of 1203/October 1788 to September 1789 the newly designated heir apparent made for the nomad encampments of Banī Khālid in their *dīrah* in al-Aḥsā'. After searching around Su'ūd discovered the whereabouts of the people of Duwaiḥis b. 'Urai'ir and 'Abd al-Muḥsin b. Sirdāḥ, the two who ruled the region at this time. Su'ūd was accompanied by an unusually powerful force and the men of Banī Khālid were split up into little groups over the countryside, but the Unitarian leader held back from a full-scale offensive, contenting himself with letting his cavalry skirmish with the enemy. Su'ūd suspected treachery within his own ranks,[70] and so he withdrew without a battle.

On the way home Su'ūd passed by the villages of Banī Khālid in al-Ṭaff and plundered them of the food and other provisions they contained. He also caught and killed a few of 'Abd al-Muḥsin's scouts, but he accomplished nothing else on this raid.[71] The retreat of Su'ūd on this occasion when he vastly outnumbered the enemy increased the confidence of Banī Khālid in themselves, but they were soon to learn that not every Unitarian raid would have such an outcome.

Su'ūd's victory over Thuwainī in al-Āḥsā', 1203/1788–9

Not long after the return from the disappointing operations against Banī Khālid, messengers left al-Dir'īyah to notify the levies of townsmen and tribesmen that they should meet Su'ūd at Khufaisat al-Dijānī for another expedition to the east. As soon as all the levies

[70] Ibn Ghannām, II, 156; Ibn Bishr, I, 84–5. Ibn Bishr says that Su'ūd's suspicions were directed towards some Bedouins of Banī Khālid who were with him.

[71] Ibn Bishr, I, 85, says that the raid was named Waiqah or Wīqah.

had arrived Su'ūd sent a message to his father the Imam asking for his recommendation as to the objective of the coming campaign. The Imam suggested that his son should try to overtake Thuwainī b. 'Abd Allāh of the Muntafiq, then roaming in the *dīrah* of Banī Khālid, who had not yet been chastised by the Unitarians for his attack on them in al-Qaṣīm. As Su'ūd advanced his scouts reported to him that Thuwainī and his party were in camp at Ḥamḍ.[72] There the Unitarian cavalry launched a charge against the enemy, but the Muntafiq held their ground and repulsed them. Su'ūd ordered his horsemen to dismount and to remember how disgraceful flight would be. Bethinking themselves of the sweet alternatives before them, rich booty in life or an abode in Paradise after death, the Unitarians returned to the fight with such spirit that the Muntafiq had to give way at last. The wealth of the camp, including a famous tent[73] that must have belonged to Thuwainī himself, fell into the hands of the victors.[74]

After the victory Su'ūd's raiders all expected that they would go to Qaryah to get water. Su'ūd himself desired to go there, but a voice that he took to be the voice of his Lord turned him away. The men fretted and Ṣāliḥ Abū al-'Alā', the guide of the party, came to Su'ūd as their spokesman. Ṣāliḥ tried cajolery until he learned that Su'ūd intended to water at al-Wafrā', whereupon the guide exclaimed: You

[72] Ibn Ghannām, II, 156–7. Ibn Bishr, I, 84, says that Su'ūd overtook Thuwainī in the Ṣummān in the *dīrah* of Banī Khālid. Ibn Ghannām, though he states that Su'ūd was seeking Thuwainī, does not refer to Thuwainī's participation in the battle.

It is not clear whether this affair took place before or after the expulsion of Thuwainī from Iraq for the second time. Early in 1203/late 1788 the Ottoman Mutasallim of al-Baṣrah had induced Sulaimān Pasha of Baghdad to reappoint Thuwainī head of the Muntafiq – al-Nabhānī, pp. 64–5; Longrigg, p. 205. Sulaimān Pasha was aware, however, that the Mutasallim and Thuwainī were plotting against him, and in Jumādā II, 1203/February 1789 the forces of the Pasha defeated the plotters and drove them out of the country – al-Nabhānī, pp. 65–6; Longrigg, p. 206.

[73] *Ṣīwān mashhūr* – Ibn Ghannām, II, 157.

[74] After describing Su'ūd's victory over Thuwainī in the Ṣummān and the capture of his camp in I, 84, Ibn Bishr in I, 85, speaks of a second raid by Su'ūd against the Muntafiq at al-Rauḍatain between al-Miṭla' and Safwān in which the Unitarians took tents and other equipment from the camp of the enemy. Since this second raid is described before the visit of the Unitarians to al-Wafrā' (see below), Ibn Bishr must be mistaken in dividing the operation up into two separate raids. Ibn Bishr's whole record for the year 1203/1788–9 is somewhat confused.

will get to your own home in better shape than you will reach al-Wafrā' in. But Su'ūd would not be dissuaded; they went to al-Wafrā' and from there they headed for Ḥafar al-Bāṭin. As they drew near the Ḥafar they were informed that men were laying in wait for them there. A fall of rain provided them with the water they needed at the moment, and they advanced to the Ḥafar to find Ibn Maghjal with nearly ninety men of the Saḥbān of Banī Khālid there. The Unitarians in their fury cut down every man of the Bedouins.

Su'ūd's operations against the central oases of al-Aḥsā', 1203/1788–9

For the third straight time during 1203/October 1788 to September 1789 Su'ūd penetrated into al-Aḥsā', where he alighted at night outside the large settlement of al-Mubarraz in the central oases. In the morning the townspeople ascended to the roofs of their houses and kept the raiders at a distance. Next the defenders made a sortie in such strength that Su'ūd deemed it best to draw off. Passing by the nearby town of al-Hufūf, Su'ūd did not pause, for he could count on a reception there similar to the one he had had at al-Mubarraz. Leaving the oases, the Unitarians fell upon the village of al-Fuḍūl in the eastern part of al-Aḥsā'. In all the wars in Najd there had been few examples of killing without quarter, but now that the Unitarians were beyond the limits of their homeland they reckoned the men about them a more sinful lot. When the Unitarians fought their way into al-Fuḍūl, they blocked off all avenues of escape, so that the men of the village had no refuge other than their own homes, where the raiders hunted them down and slaughtered them. It was said that three hundred were slain in one building, and that was not the total for the village. Stories such as this repeated throughout the lands surrounding Najd undermined the will of the people to resist when the warriors of the One God came riding down upon them. On the day of the holocaust at al-Fuḍūl efforts had been made to bring out the troops of al-Aḥsā' and the men of al-Mubarraz against Su'ūd, but to a man they refused to move.[75]

[75] Ibn Ghannām, II, 159. Ibn Bishr, I, 85, describes this campaign with fewer details.

Battle of Ghuraimīl in al-Aḥsā', 1204/1789–90

Su'ūd had devoted all of his campaigning in 1203/1788–9 to al-Aḥsā'. He knew that the power of Banī Khālid there was crumbling and that the whole district was ripe for annexation to the Unitarian state. In 1204/September 1789 to September 1790 he aimed another and heavier blow at Banī Khālid. With the flower of the Unitarian troops, supported by the Bedouins of the Ẓafīr and the Bedouins of al-'Āriḍ and accompanied by Zaid b. 'Urai'ir and other exiles from al-Aḥsā',[76] Su'ūd sought out the ruling chiefs of Banī Khālid, Duwaiḥis b. 'Urai'ir and his uncle 'Abd al-Muḥsin b. Sirdāḥ, in their home country. The decisive battle took place at the hill of Ghuraimīl.[77] Upon learning of the approach of the Unitarians 'Abd al-Muḥsin sent his brother Thawwāb into the central oases to bring out the soldiers of the settlements, but he found them as reluctant to face the Unitarians as they had been on the day of the pillage of al-Fuḍūl. Even without the hoped-for reinforcements the men of Banī Khālid numbered some thousands, but they were not enough. The fight was a long one[78] that ended with the utter defeat of the

[76] Zaid was the fifth of the sons of 'Urai'ir to play a part in the events of the time. He had probably accompanied his brother Sa'dūn in the flight to Najd after the successful revolt engineered by 'Abd al-Muḥsin b. Sirdāḥ – see above, p. 196.

[77] Ghuraimīl is a solitary hill with a watering-place below it a short distance south of Abqaiq (properly Buqaiq), an important oil field in the zone of operations of the Arabian American Oil Company.

[78] Ibn Ghannām, I, 160, says that the fight lasted from the beginning of the day until the evening, with an interruption during which the Unitarians prayed the late-afternoon prayer (*al-'aṣr*). Ibn Bishr, I, 85, gives the duration of the fight as three days.

[79] Ibn Ghannām, I, 161, says that 'Abd al-Muḥsin and the members of 'Urai'ir's family who were with him fled to al-Zubārah on the coast of Qaṭar. Ibn Bishr, I, 85, says that 'Abd al-Muḥsin took refuge with the Muntafiq. Not long after this 'Abd al-Muḥsin was killed and his son Barrāk, setting aside the family of 'Urai'ir, took over the leadership of the opposition to the Unitarians – Ibn Ghannām, II, 178; Ibn Bishr, I, 98.

[80] *Ghazā Rubayyi' al-musammā Qa'id bi-jamā'ah min qaumih fa-shammara li-'azmih al-sa'id wa-sarā bi-man ma'ah* – Ibn Ghammām, II, 161. The meaning of the passage as it stands is obscure, and Philby, *Arabia*, p. 50, has been misled into thinking that it refers to an otherwise unmentioned person named "Rubai'a al Qaid". However, Ibn Ghannām, II, 195, speaks of a raid conducted five years later by Qa'id b. Rubayyi', who is obviously the man referred to here, the word *ibn* before Rubayyi' having been omitted by the copyist.

[81] This affair was known as *al-Waq'ah al-Lailīyah*/the Night Battle – Ibn Ghannām, II, 162.

[82] Ibn Ghannām, I, 162. Ibn Bishr has nothing on these events in the southern valley.

rulers of al-Aḥsā', who fled away beyond the limits of their realm.[79] This victory in reality marked the termination of the many years of independent reign of Banī Khālid in al-Aḥsā'.

Although the chiefs had not stayed, the majority of the Bedouins of Banī Khālid preferred to adopt Unitarianism and cleave to their homes. This may have been the principal reason why Su'ūd chose to name the exile Zaid b. 'Urai'ir as Amir in succession to his brother. However, when Su'ūd desired to take Zaid with him into the central oases to impose Unitarianism on the residents, Zaid held back. Su'ūd started off without Zaid, but he had not gone far before he changed his mind and turned back to Najd. The Unitarians had opened the road into al-Aḥsā', but it was to be a little while yet before they trod it all the way.

Apostasy in Wadi al-Dawāsir, 1204/1789–90

During 1204/September 1789 to September 1790 Qa'id b. Rubayyī',[80] son of the champion of Unitarianism in Wadi al-Dawāsir, commanded the Unitarians of the south in a raid against Bedouins of the tribe of Banī Hājir who had shown opposition to the faith. When the test came many men in the attacking force melted away from their captain, their loyalty to the beliefs they were called upon to fight for being only superficial, and there remained steadfast with Qa'id and his camelry only Hādī Ibn Qarmalah of Qaḥṭān and a certain Aḥmad Ibn Najjān as the battle wore on past the end of the day and into the night.[81] About twenty of the Unitarians were killed and the same number captured by Banī Hājir.

The failure of the Unitarians in their attempt to subdue Banī Hājir and the inconstancy shown by their supporters gave heart to the chiefs of the Dawāsir who found irksome the Unitarian control to which they had been subjected. Jamāhir, chief of the Rijbān, and Ḥuwail, chief of the Wadā'īn, together with the men of their sections, broke the compact they had recently made and departed from the Unitarian fold.[82]

15

War with the Hijaz
1204–5/1789–91

Unitarian mission to Mecca, 1204/1789–90

After a reign of fifteen years, the Sharif Surūr b. Musā'id died in Rabī' II 1202/January to February 1788, and in the same month his brother Ghālib embarked on a reign that was to be over ten years longer than Surūr's,[1] during which the long and bitter war between Najd and the Hijaz raged until at last the men from the interior marched into the Holy Cities. Although Ghālib b. Musā'id at the time of his accession must have been aware of the existence of Unitarianism in Najd, he may not have had a clear idea of the Shaikh Muḥammad b. 'Abd al-Wahhāb's teachings. In order to learn more about these teachings, Ghālib wrote to the Imam 'Abd al-'Azīz in 1204/September 1789 to September 1790 and expressed a desire to have a learned religious man come and enlighten him. As it had once before,[2] the choice of the Shaikh and the Imam for this mission fell on 'Abd al-'Azīz b. 'Abd Allāh Āl Ḥaṣīn al-Nāṣirī. The Shaikh 'Abd al-'Azīz carried with him the following letter:

> From Muḥammad b. 'Abd al-Wahhāb to the noble 'Ulamā' in the Holy City, may God grant aid through them to the lord of men [the Prophet], upon whom be the best of blessings and peace, and to the followers of the noble Imams [the founders of the four schools of Islamic law].
>
> Peace be upon you and the mercy of God and His blessings. We

[1] Snouck Hurgronje, *Mekka*, I, Table III. Another brother, 'Abd al-Mu'īn, held the office of Sharif for a few days in Rabī' II between the death of Surūr and the accession of Ghālib. Snouck gives no details in his text and the pertinent passages in Aḥmad b. Zainī Daḥlān, *Khulāṣat al-kalām*, are not at hand at the moment of writing.

[2] See above, p. 144.

have undergone the troubles that you and others have heard about as a result of the tearing down of structures over the graves of the righteous in our land. Along with this we forbade them to pray to the righteous and ordered them to direct their prayers to God alone. When we brought up this matter and tore down the buildings over the graves, some of those who pretend to learning played upon the superstitions of the common people for reasons that are obvious to the likes of you, such as indulgence of their passions. They spread rumors about us to the east and the west to the effect that we revile the righteous and are not on the path of the 'Ulamā' and other things that a man of sense would blush to mention.

I shall inform you of our beliefs, since men like you will pay no heed to lies about people who reveal where they stand to all and sundry. We, praise be to God, are followers, not innovators, in the school of the Imam Aḥmad Ibn Ḥanbal. You, may God strengthen you, know that persons in authority in many regions, if these matters [the Shaikh apparently refers to worship of God alone and the destruction of tombs] are raised, will play upon the superstitions of the common people, who, like their fathers before them, follow the opposite course.

You, may God have mercy on you, know that in the reign of the Sharif Aḥmad b. Sa'īd there came to you the Shaikh 'Abd al-'Azīz b. 'Abd Allāh [Āl Ḥaṣīn], and you learned what our beliefs are after they brought out the Hanbalite books which we regard as authoritative, like *al-Tuḥfah* and *al-Nihāyah* in the eyes of the Shafiites.[3] When the Sharif Ghālib, may God strengthen and aid him, made his request of us, we complied and he [the Shaikh 'Abd al-'Azīz] is coming to you. If the question concerns *ijmā'* [the establishing of religious truths by the consensus of opinion in the Moslem

[3] *Al-Tuḥfah* by al-Ramlī and *al-Nihāyah* by Ibn Ḥajar are well known commentaries on *Minhāj al-ṭālibīn* by al-Nawāwī [d. 7th century of the Hegira/late 13th century AD], the standard Shafiite work of jurisprudence – Laoust, *Essai*, p. 33, n. 4, and p. 524.

The Sharifs of Mecca, like the majority of the inhabitants of Lower Egypt, Syria and western Arabia, were Shafiites, and the Imam or leader of the Shafiites in prayer usually if not always took precedence over the Imams of the other schools in the Sacred Mosque at Mecca, where he had the honor of standing at the particularly holy spot of Maqām Ibrāhīm – Rif'at Pasha, *Mir'āt al-Ḥaramain*, I, 251; Snouck Hurgronje, *Mekka*, I, 89; Laoust, *Essai*, p. 33. It should be mentioned, however, that the Ottomans, who claimed sovereignty over the Holy Cities, were Hanafites, not Shafiites.

The Shaikh Muḥammad b. 'Abd al-Wahhāb had studied under the Shaikh 'Abd Allāh b. Muhammad b. 'Abd al-Laṭīf, a Shafiite scholar in al-Aḥsā' – see above, pp. 35–6.

community], there is no need of discussion, and if it is a question of *ijtihād* [the establishment of religious truths by the interpretations of individual scholars], you know that there is naught to be condemned in questions of *ijtihād*. Whoever proceeds according to his own school in the region of his authority is not to be condemned.[4]

I bear witness to God and His Angels, and I testify to you that I believe in the religion of God and His Prophet and that I am a follower of the men of learning. Peace be upon you and the mercy of God and His blessings.[5]

According to the Unitarian chronicler,[6] the Sharif Ghālib received the envoy from Najd with honor and had a number of meetings with

[4] *Fa-in kānat al-mas'alah ijmā'an fa-lā kalām wa-in kānat mas'alat ijtihād fa-ma'lūmukum annah lā inkār fī masā'il al-ijtihād fa-man 'amala bi-madhhabih fī maḥall wilāyatih lā yunkar 'alaih* – Ibn Ghannām, II, 163.

The Unitarians of Najd limit the exercise of *ijmā'* to the consensus of opinion among scholars in the time of the Prophet and those who came immediately after him, provided that that consensus agrees with the Koran and the traditions and practice of the Prophet – R. W. van Diffelen, *De leer der Wahhabieten*, p. 73. The Unitarians reserve for themselves the right to interpret the views of the early authorities in their own fashion, though they deny that they were sponsoring a revival of *ijtihād*, the practice of which by latterday scholars is not favored by Sunnites in general, though it is prevalent among the Shiites. For detailed discussions of this involved theological question, see the *risālah* by Aḥmad b. Nāṣir Ibn Mu'ammar in *Majmū'at al-rasā'il al-Najdīyah*, II, sec. 3, pp. 2–24, and van Diffelen, *op. cit.*, pp. 73–6.

The attitude of the Unitarians is greatly influenced by that of the Syrian Hanbalite Ibn Taimīyah (d. 728/1328), which is described by Macdonald: "He ... went back to first sources and principles in everything. His self-confidence was extreme, and he smote down with proud words the Rightly Guided Khalifas, Umar and Ali, themselves. His bases were Qur'an, tradition from the Prophet and from the Companions and analogy. Agreement, in the broad sense of the agreement of the Muslim people [i.e. *ijmā'*], he rejected. If he had accepted it he would have been forced to accept innumerable superstitions, beliefs, and practices – especially the whole doctrine of the *wali*s [saints and holy men] and their wonders – for their basis was agreement. The agreement of the Companions he did accept, while convicting them right and left of error as individuals." – D. B. Macdonald, *Development of Muslim Theology, Jurisprudence and Constitutional Theory* (New York, 1903), p. 275. [A proper reading of the writings of Ibn Taimīyah, and of the proponents of the reform movement in Najd, will show that this account by Rentz of the attitude of the *muwaḥḥidūn* to *ijma'*/consensus as presented by R. W. van Diffelen, of their approach to interpreting the early religious texts, and of Ibn Taimīyah's views on *ijma'*/consensus as presented by D. B. Macdonald, is marred by a certain amount of misunderstanding and erroneous deduction. KAPL]

[5] Ibn Ghannām, II, 162–3.

[6] Ibn Ghannām, II, 163.

him, during the course of which the Sharif was given the letter by the Shaikh Muḥammad b. ʻAbd al-Wahhāb to read.[7] After a time, however, the Sharif's attitude changed, and instead of sympathy for the doctrines expounded by the envoy he began to show hostility. The Shaikh ʻAbd al-ʻAzīz then requested an opportunity to debate the principles of Unitarianism with the ʻUlamā' of Mecca, but these worthies refused to present themselves and warned the Sharif that the Unitarians of Najd desired to destroy the beliefs of his fathers and grandfathers and to undermine his control over the practices that prevailed in his own country.[8] The Unitarian mission to Mecca had resulted in failure; the opportunity to reach an understanding with the ruler in the west had slipped away; the settlement of the issue between the two regimes was to depend in the future upon soldiers rather than scholars.[9]

First attack on the Unitarians by the Sharif Ghālib, 1205/1790–1

The situation developed so rapidly that the first clash of arms between the Unitarians of Najd and the forces of the Sharif took place only a year or less after the mission of the Shaikh ʻAbd al-ʻAzīz Āl Ḥaṣīn. Through the agency of Hādī Ibn Qarmalah the Unitarians were acquiring influence among many of the tribesmen of Qaḥṭān, who were a power in the region lying between the domain of the Unitarians and that of the Sharif. Unitarian propaganda was advancing with great speed through the Bedouin tents on the deserts of this intervening region and was reaching the towns and tribes on the

[7] It should be noted that the letter was addressed to the ʻUlamā' of Mecca, not to the Sharif – see the text of the letter above.

[8] *Rafʻ yadik ʻan muʻtādik wa-jawā'iz bilādik* – Ibn Ghannām, II, 163.

[9] Aḥmad b. Zainī Daḥlān, *Khulāṣat al-kalām*, p. 261, the chronicler of Mecca who writes with a strong anti-Unitarian bias, says that the Sharifs Masʻūd, Musāʻid, Aḥmad b. Saʻīd, and Surūr had all refused to allow any of the followers of Ibn ʻAbd al-Wahhāb to make the pilgrimage, and that when Ghālib became Sharif the Unitarians asked permission to come as pilgrims, which Ghālib refused to grant, threatening instead to attack them. If the letter of the Shaikh to the ʻUlamā' of Mecca is genuine, as it appears to be, Ghālib's stand as portrayed by Daḥlān was probably not taken until after the visit of the Unitarian mission.

borders of the Hijaz.[10] The Sharif Ghālib, a shrewd politician who by now was alive to the danger, decided that it would be better to strike first before the tide drew any closer.

In the year 1205/September 1790 to August 1791 the first expedition against the Unitarians set out under the command of Ghālib's brother, the Sharif 'Abd al-'Azīz b. Musā'id.[11] Numbering about six hundred men at the time of departure from Mecca,[12] the force swelled as it made its way eastwards and the Bedouin allies of the Sharif came trooping up. The men of Qaḥṭān who had not yet been won over by Ibn Qarmalah, Bedouins of Muṭair under Ḥusain Āl Dawīsh,[13] and representatives of Shammar were among the nomads who rallied to the standard of the Sharif.[14] As the army penetrated into Najd, town after town capitulated, some after a fight and others without resistance.[15] The size of the Sharifial army and the ease of its progress frightened many in Najd whose Unitarianism was only skin-deep, and cases of apostasy multiplied.

The Sharif 'Abd al-'Azīz continued on his triumphal course for three hundred miles or so until he came to the small Unitarian outpost of Qaṣr Bassām[16] at the southern end of the district of al-Sirr. Here for the first time he met a complete band who were prepared to die for their faith before surrendering. With neither cannonballs nor scaling ladders could the Sharif 'Abd al-'Azīz overcome the resis-

[10] See below, p. 231, n. 18.

[11] Ibn Ghannām, II, 168, calls him simply 'Abd al-'Azīz the Sharif. He is identified as Ghālib's brother by Ibn Bishr, I, 86, and Aḥmad b. Zainī Daḥlān, *Khulāṣat al-kalām*, p. 262.

[12] Daḥlān, p. 262.

[13] Shortly before the Sharif's expedition Su'ūd had carried out a raid against elements of Muṭair under their chief al-Ḥumaidānī in the region known as al-Juraisīyah and had killed over fifty of them – Ibn Ghannām, II, 163–4.

[14] Ibn Bishr, I, 86, says that the army was made up of about ten thousand men, which is no doubt an exaggeration. He also says that the Sharif 'Abd al-'Azīz had with him more than twenty cannon, which may be a more nearly accurate figure than the first.

[15] Daḥlān, p. 262, names among the towns taken along the route of march Ḍarīyah, "the first town of Najd," Muskah, Suwāj, Athlah, Waḍāḥ, and al-Kibrītīyah. The Unitarian chroniclers give no details on the operations prior to the siege of Qaṣr Bassām.

[16] Ibn Ghannām, II, 166, says that the garrison of Qaṣr Bassām numbered about twenty men. Ibn Bishr, I, 86, says that there were about thirty men, who were the residents of the place and a few members of the pariah tribe of Hutaim; Ibn Bishr also emphasizes the weakness of the defenses of the fort. Daḥlān, p. 262, on the other hand, states that the fort was a strong one.

tance of these brave men who barred the way; after some days[17] he raised the siege and moved off.[18] Notifying his brother the Sharif Ghālib in the Hijaz that he needed more men and equipment, the Sharif 'Abd al-'Azīz remained on the flank of the Unitarian state in the district of al-Sirr.[19] During the period of waiting he decided to make another attempt to break into Qaṣr Bassām.[20] Clothed in coats of mail, the attackers came on to ascend the walls, but the defenders beat them down as before.

In the meantime the Imam 'Abd al-'Azīz in the Unitarian capital had been making strenuous efforts in the preparation of countermeasures. The Unitarian contingents called up were informed of the seriousness of the danger in the west; it was also impressed upon them that the Sharif's aggression had provided them with a great opportunity. The heir apparent Su'ūd was entrusted with the command of all the forces and instructed to go out and keep watch on the movements of the enemy. Su'ūd took up a position in the region known as Rumḥain in the neighborhood of Nafūd al-Balādīn, where he awaited the tardy elements of his army. Ḥasan b. Mishārī with a party of Unitarian Bedouins fell upon some of the Bedouins supporting the Sharif and took away their camels. While still in this place Su'ūd had to detach some of his men to rectify matters in Wadi al-Dawāsir, since a grave threat to the maintenance of the Unitarian front had arisen there.

The Sharif Ghālib and Wadi al-Dawāsir, 1205/1790–1

The Sharifs in the Hijaz were well enough informed on Bedouin affairs and on events in the interior to be able to take advantage of

[17] Ibn Bishr, I, 86, says that the siege lasted more than ten days; Daḥlān, p. 262, some days. Neither Ibn Bishr nor Daḥlān mentions the renewal of the siege.

[18] Daḥlān, p. 262, attributes 'Abd al-'Azīz's failure to take Qaṣr Bassām to the length of time he had been away from Mecca – half a year – which made his men, especially the Sharifs among them, so restless that many of them broke away from the army and returned home.

[19] Ibn Ghannām, II, 166, says that 'Abd al-'Azīz stayed in al-Sirr four months.

[20] Philby, *Arabia*, p. 52, says that the attack on Qaṣr Bassām was resumed after 'Abd al-'Azīz had received reinforcements. However, Ibn Ghannām, the source used by Philby, says nothing about the arrival of reinforcements at this time.

chinks in the Unitarian armor. Unitarianism was a recent growth in Wadi al-Dawāsir, and some of the prominent chiefs there had accepted it under duress and had broken with it at the first chance.[21] The Sharif Ghālib delegated one of his lieutenants, the Sharif Shākir, to lead a number of troops to the support of the anti-Unitarians and the backsliders in the south, at the head of whom were the Bedouins of Banī Hājir and two of the chiefs of the Dawāsir, Ḥuwail of the Wadā'īn and Jamāhir of the Rijbān.[22]

The Unitarians sent by Su'ūd from Rumḥain under the command of a certain Nughaimish[23] proved to be more effective than the troops of the Sharif Shākir. Joining forces with Rubayyi' b. Zaid and Mubārak b. 'Abd al-Hādī, Nughaimish plunged into battle without hesitation. The anti-Unitarians and Shākir's men were encamped about the large settlement of al-Lidām[24] in the valley, and there the combined Unitarian forces attacked and defeated them. The Unitarians lost three men and the enemy twenty.

Arrival of the Sharif Ghālib in Najd: failure of his expedition, 1205/1791

While the Sharifial army marked time in the district of al-Sirr, Su'ūd, who was watching it, struck out suddenly at one of its elements, Bedouins of the tribe of Muṭair under their chief Ḥusain Āl Dawīsh. The men of Muṭair gathered and swept down on the approaching

[21] See above, p. 214.

[22] Ibn Ghannam, II, 167. Philby, *Arabia*, p. 52, makes the mistake of thinking that Ḥuwail and Jamāhir were the names of sections of the tribe, though Ibn Ghannām, II, 150, makes it clear that they were the chiefs of the sections here named.

[23] Ibn Ghannām, II, 167, does not identify this captain, who here appears for the first time in the Unitarian campaigns.

[24] Philby, in *Arabia*, p. 52, and elsewhere in his books and on his maps erroneously gives this name as Dam. If the name were Dam preceded by the definite article *al*, it would be written الدام and pronounced by the Bedouins *addām*, for they never fail to assimilate the "l" of the article with a following sun letter such as "d". The fact is, however, that the name is properly written with two distinct "l's", one for the article and the other as the initial letter of the name اللدام (see, for example, Ibn Ghannām, II, 167), and is pronounced by the Bedouins *aldām*, the short vowel "i" being elided and the two "l's" coalescing because of the disappearance of the vowel. *Lidām* means "patchwork".

Unitarians "like the wings of vultures and ravens",[25] but the soldiers of Su'ūd stopped their charge and killed more than twenty of them. The Sharif's Bedouins had to yield some of their camels to the Unitarians.

Late in the month of Sha'bān 1205/end of April 1791[26] the Sharif Ghālib left Mecca for Najd with a large body of troops and a number of cannon.[27] As his brother 'Abd al-'Azīz had been held up at the Unitarian outpost of Qaṣr Bassām, so was Ghālib himself held up at another outpost, al-Sha'rā', not far to the west of al-Dawādimī on the road to Mecca.[28] To make the cannon fire more destructive the Sharif's cannoneers linked their shot together with iron chains and iron bars.[29] The Sharif 'Abd al-'Azīz arrived from al-Sirr to join his brother in prosecuting the siege, but their Bedouin allies, disappointed in the trifling quantities of plunder they had secured during the campaign, grumbled and wavered in their support. It is not clear whether Ghālib succeeded in forcing the garrison to come to terms,[30]

[25] *Ka-annahum ajniḥat al-nusūr wal-ghurbān* – Ibn Ghannām, II, 168. The *nasr* [pl. *nusūr*] is in Arabia a huge vulture, not an eagle.

[26] Daḥlān, p. 262, says that Ghālib left Mecca on 23 Sha'bān. Ibn Ghannām, II, 169, who is probably less reliable in this case, places the departure of Ghālib a week or more later, in Ramaḍān/early May to early June. Ibn Ghannām here refers to Ramaḍān as the month in which "the gates of fire are shut", an allusion to the old prohibition against waging war in this month because of its sacred character.

Ibn Ghannām states that the Sharif 'Abd al-'Azīz had informed his brother Ghālib that he had achieved his aim and had captured towns and had struck terror into the hearts of the people of Najd; at the same time 'Abd al-'Azīz asked Ghālib to come quickly with reinforcements. Philby, *Arabia*, p. 52, goes beyond the text of Ibn Ghannām in saying that 'Abd al-'Azīz wrote to Ghālib that he had conquered Najd and that it only remained for Ghālib to make an appearance to receive the formal submission of tribes and towns.

[27] Ibn Bishr, I, 86–7, says that according to report Ghālib brought with him seven cannon.

[28] Ibn Bishr, I, 87, and Daḥlān, p. 262. The word *sha'rā'*, the feminine of the adjective *ash'ar*/"hairy", when used with reference to the earth means "covered with plants".

This town of al-Sha'rā' should not be confused with a place of the same name much farther to the west in the neighborhood of Qarn al-Manāzil. Al-Sha'rā' near al-Dawādimī is mentioned by Doughty, *Travels in Arabia Deserta*, II, 461, and al-Sha'rā' near Qarn al-Manāzil is described by him in II, 476.

[29] *Ḍulū' al-ḥadīd* – Ibn Bishr, I, 87.

[30] Daḥlān, p. 262, states definitely that the garrison did ask for terms, which were granted by Ghālib. The Unitarian chroniclers are vague on this point: Ibn Ghannām, II, 169, says that Ghālib returned home, failing to carry out his oath not to leave until Najd had been destroyed by his troops; Ibn Bishr, I, 87, says that Ghālib departed from al-Sha'rā' after meeting with failure (*'alā fashl*). Ibn Bishr gives the strength of the garrison as about forty

but it is clear that Ghālib did not go beyond al-Sha'rā'. Giving up the operations in Najd either because of the stubbornness of Unitarian resistance or because of the approach of the pilgrimage season at home,[31] Ghālib, accompanied by his brother 'Abd al-'Azīz and the whole of their array, withdrew to his capital Mecca.

As long as the Sharifial army had stayed at al-Sha'rā', Su'ūd with the main body of the Unitarians had not felt strong enough to risk a battle. As soon as word came that the army was moving westwards, Su'ūd ordered Muḥammad b. Mu'aiqil of Shaqrā'[32] out to harry it on its march. While carrying out these orders Ibn Mu'aiqil encountered a party of Qaḥṭān from whom he captured a large number of camels and fifteen thoroughbred horses.[33]

In this first expedition into Najd the Sharif Ghālib had taken a few insignificant towns in the frontier region between the Hijaz and Najd. By so doing he had gone to war with the Unitarians, an action that he was to live to regret. The Unitarians had not repulsed the army from the Hijaz in the open field, but the courage of the garrisons in the outposts had shown how well the central territory of the Unitarian state was protected against aggression from outside. Moreover, the danger of the loss of newly won Wadi al-Dawāsir in the south had been met and disposed of.

Great Unitarian victory over Bedouin allies of Ghālib, 1205/1791

As the Sharif Ghālib marched back to the Hijaz, large numbers of his Bedouin allies separated themselves from his army and moved off

men and says that they killed more than fifty of the Sharif's men during the siege which lasted a month.

[31] Ibn Ghannām, II, 169, and Ibn Bishr, I, 87, attribute the withdrawal of Ghālib to his failure to make headway against the Unitarian defenders; Daḥlān, p. 262, attributes it to the coming on of the pilgrimage season. According to Daḥlān, Ghālib arrived in Mecca 21 Dhū al-Qa'dah 1205/late July 1791, less then twenty days before the pilgrimage reached its climax.

[32] This is the first appearance of Ibn Mu'aiqil, one of the great Unitarian captains. Philby, *Arabia*, p. 53 and *passim*, incorrectly gives the name as Mu'aiqal. Philby is often weak in the voweling of names having a diminutive form, placing an "a" where there should be an "i".

[33] Ibn Ghannām, II, 170.

towards their own ranges in the north. Su'ūd led his Unitarians in that direction, hoping to meet with the Bedouins of Muṭair and Shammar, who had been conspicuous as auxiliaries in the Sharif's train. At the watering-place of al-'Adwah in Jabal Shammar[34] Su'ūd found elements of Muṭair, men of the Barā'iṣah and 'Ubayyāt,[35] under the command of Samrah, the chief of the 'Ubayyāt and a famous knight, and Mas'ūd, nicknamed Satan's Charger.[36] In the closing days of the year 1205/late August 1791[37] the Unitarians burst into the camp of these Bedouins at al-'Adwah. In the sanguinary battle Satan's Charger and his son fell, as did Samrah of the 'Ubayyāt and another stalwart named Abū Hulaibah, besides many of the lesser ones in the tribe. An ample store of goods lay at hand as the prize of the Unitarians.

The Bedouins who fled from al-'Adwah hastened off to bear the tidings to their kinsfolk and allies and to raise the countryside against the victors. Among the Bedouin nobility who responded was Muslaṭ b. Muṭlaq al-Jarbā',[38] the son of a great man of Shammar;[39] Muslaṭ

[34] Al-'Adwah, in the neighborhood of Jabal Salmā less than fifty miles SE of Ḥā'il, was a place where the Bedouins of Shammar cultivated a few crops (*mazra' li-Shammar*) – Ibn Bishr, I, 87.

[35] The Barā'iṣah are a subsection of the Mawahah of 'Ilwah of Muṭair; the 'Ubayyāt are a subsection of Wāṣil of Muṭair – Fu'ād Ḥamzah, *Qalb jazīrat al-'arab*, pp. 193–4, on the authority of the Amir 'Abd Allāh b. 'Abd al-Raḥmān, brother of King Ibn Saud.

[36] Ḥiṣān Iblīs – Ibn Ghannām, II, 170; Ibn Bishr, I, 87. Since Samrah was chief of the 'Ubayyāt, Mas'ūd was probably chief of the Barā'iṣah, though this is not mentioned by the sources. Ibn Ghannām states that Satan's Charger was head of all the Bedouins who fought on this day.

Max Freiherr von Oppenheim, *Die Beduinen*, I, 134, takes Satan's Charger to have been a chief of Shammar, which is also possible.

[37] Ibn Bishr, I, 87, says the fight took place at the end of al-Aḍḥā, i.e. the month of Dhū al-Ḥijjah.

[38] Ibn Ghannām, II, 172, gives his first name as Muṣlaṭ; Ibn Bishr, I, 87, as Muslaṭ. The first form is the proper one; the second is the one in commoner use among the Bedouins of Arabia – see Count Carlo de Landberg, *Glossaire de la langue des Bédouins Anazeh*, published by K. V. Zettersteen, *Uppsala Universitets Arsskrift*, 1940: 2, p. 31, who vowels the name as either Muṣlaṭ or Muṣliṭ. Oppenheim, *Die Beduinen*, I, 134, gives the name as Meṣlaṭ. It apparently means The One to Whom *Sulṭān*, i.e., Power or Authority, Has Been Given. The Arabians usually pronounce and often write the name Sulṭan with a *ṣād* instead of a *sīn*; Ibn Ghannām prefers the form with *ṣād*. See also J. J. Hess, *Beduinennamen aus Zentralarabien*, in *Sitzungsberichte der Heidelberger Akademie der Wissenschaften: Philosophisch-historische Klasse* (1912) 19, Abhandlung, p. 35, who gives Muṣlaṭ and Ṣulṭan.

vowed that he would trample down the tent of Su'ūd himself with the hooves of his war-mare.[40] The men who were stirring up the Bedouins against the Unitarians told the camelherds and shepherds in the vicinity that if Su'ūd remained at al-'Adwah they could not get water for their animals. Many nomads were persuaded to bring along their wives and children and their worldly goods as they came in for the fight; their leaders believed that they would be better men on the field if they knew that the fate of all they held dear was at stake.

When the assembly of Bedouins was complete, the leaders sent word to Su'ūd: Come out and fight, or we shall come after you. Su'ūd, unperturbed, sat still at al-'Adwah, where he and his men were busy dividing the spoils of their first victory. The Bedouin host moved down upon them there. For the time of attack the Bedouin leaders selected twilight, hoping to take advantage of the familiarity of the country to them and its strangeness to the enemy; they thought that if the Unitarians were beaten they would be easy game as they wandered about aimlessly in the dark, while if the Unitarians won on the field the Bedouins could escape by tracks they knew well. These leaders placed their hope of victory in the tactics they had devised for this battle: they tied large numbers of camels together and drove them into the Unitarian camp, intending thus to shield themselves from the bullets of Su'ūd's men and at the same time to create confusion in the camp.[41] The Unitarians, however, held firm

Muslaṭ b. Muṭlaq was a famous poet whose verses are still repeated; the text of a short poem attributed to him is given by R. Montagne in "Contes poétiques bédouins", *Bulletin d'Etudes Orientales,* V (Damascus 1935), 104.

[39] According to Oppenheim, *Die Beduinen,* I, 134, this is the first reference in history to the family of al-Jarbā', the present rulers of the tribe of Shammar. The great Shaikhs of Shammar in modern times have been descendants of Muslaṭ's uncle Fāris, the younger brother of Muṭlaq.

Muṭlaq Ibn Muḥammad, Muslaṭ's father, was killed by the Unitarian Khuzayyim Ibn Liḥyān, chief of the Bedouins of the Suhūl, during a raid led by Su'ūd into Iraq in 1212/1798 – Ibn Bishr, I, 112.

The name of the family is the feminine form of the adjective *ajrab*/"scabby".

[40] *Wa-kāna qad nadhara an yujashshima farasah ṣīwān Su'ūd* – Ibn Bishr (Mecca), I, 87; *wa-qad nadhara an taṭa'a farasuh khaimat Su'ūd* – Ibn Bishr (Baghdad), p. 52.

[41] *Wa-qad zayyana lahum Iblīs an yaj'alu al-ibil lahum 'an al-raṣāṣ muntaris* – Ibn Ghannām, II, 171 (the page number here is incorrectly given by the copyist as 271). On the word *muntaris,*

until the rows of camels had nearly reached their tents; then they concentrated their fire on the men who were driving the camels forward and put them to flight. While this maneuver was being executed the Bedouin warriors came dashing in. Muslaṭ al-Jarbā' was in the van, determined to carry out the vow he had made to wreck Su'ūd's tent. One of the Unitarians struck him off his horse,[42] and when he fell the others closed and killed him. With the maneuver of the camels thwarted and the champion of Shammar dead, the Bedouins lost their enthusiasm for the battle; they broke and fled away into the night. For two days or more[43] the Unitarians pursued the enemy and augmented the booty victory had bestowed upon them. When the final reckoning was made, this booty was said to include over a hundred thousand sheep and goats and some thousands of camels, not counting the animals that had perished in the wastelands after being deserted by their herders.[44] Returning from the pursuit, the Unitarians again set about making the division of what they had captured. A fifth part was set aside for the treasury of the state; the remainder went to the men who had participated in the expedition, with each horseman receiving a double share.[45]

compare above, p. 178, n. 52. Ibn Bishr, I, 87, speaks of the Bedouins advancing *muqarrinīn al-ibil*, and of *al-ibil muqarranah fi al-ḥibal.*

[42] Ibn Bishr (Mecca), I, 87, says that a man hit him with a *mishwā qurṣ*, apparently an implement used in baking bread. On the use of the word *qurṣ* among the Bedouins of Arabia, see J. J. Hess, *Von den Beduinen des Innern Arabiens* (Zürich and Leipzig 1938), p. 113: "*gyrṣ* pl. *gyrṣan* – das ungesäuerte Brot in Fladen."

Ibn Bishr (Baghdad), p. 52, on the other hand, says that one of the Unitarians hit Muslaṭ with a piece of wood he had in his hand used for stirring the fire. Oppenheim, *Die Beduinen*, I, 134, has used the Baghdad edition.

The story still retold among the Bedouins of Shammar is that Muslaṭ fell among the tents of the kitchen servants in Su'ūd's camp, where he was strangled as he lay on the ground by an old slave who had been left there as unfit for combat duty – R. Montagne in *Bulletin d'Etudes Orientales*, V, 105, n. 6.

[43] Ibn Ghannām, II, 172, says for days and nights; Ibn Bishr (Mecca), I, 87, for about two or three days; Ibn Bishr (Baghdad), p. 52, for two days.

[44] Ibn Ghannām, II, 172, and Ibn Bishr, I, 87, agree on the number of sheep and goats (*ghanam*). Ibn Ghannām gives the number of camels as over six thousand; Ibn Bishr, about eleven thousand or more. Mengin, *Histoire de l'Egypte*, II, 505, who may have used a different MS of Ibn Ghannām, also mentions sixty horses among the booty. Mengin in his description of this battle refers to disheveled women who with martial chants encouraged the Bedouin attackers to conquer or die.

[45] Ibn Bishr, I, 87.

16

The Shaikh's Final Year

Unitarian conquest of al-Qaṭīf in al-Aḥsā', 1206/1792

The oasis of al-Qaṭīf with its large Shiite population[1] on the shores of the Persian Gulf was the place more detested by the Unitarians of Najd than any other in the region of al-Aḥsā'. In the first half of 1206/end of 1791 or beginning of 1792,[2] Su'ūd marched eastwards to stamp out with force the Shiite practices condemned by Unitarianism.[3] First he surrounded the town of Saihāt in its oasis a short distance south of the main groves of al-Qaṭīf. The towns-people attempted to defend the place, but they could not prevent the Unitarians from scaling the walls and breaking in. As they had done at al-Fuḍūl, the Unitarians cut down their victims right and left; it was estimated that they killed about fifteen hundred.[4] After stripping Saihāt of everything of value, the Unitarians repeated the performance at the smaller isolated oasis of 'Anik[5] and at the settlements of al-Qudaiḥ and al-'Awwāmīyah in the depths of the main groves of al-Qaṭīf. By this time most of the residents of al-Qaṭīf who had not fallen had taken refuge in the fortifications at the port.[6] Advancing to

[1] See above, p. 101, n. 95.

[2] Ibn Bishr, I, 88, says that Su'ūd went raiding *fī awwal Jumādā*. Jumādā I 1206 began in the closing days of December 1791; Jumādā II in the closing days of January 1792.

[3] Ibn Ghannām, II, 173, denounces in strong terms the religion of the people of al-Qaṭīf without mentioning Shiism as such.

[4] Ibn Ghannām, II, 173.

[5] Ibn Bishr, I, 88, says that more than four hundred were killed at 'Anik, though it is possible that this figure of his may refer to the number killed at both 'Anik and Saihāt, in which case there would be a great discrepancy between him and Ibn Ghannām (compare the discrepancy between them with regard to the amount paid to buy the Unitarians off from the attack on the port – see below).

[6] Both Ibn Ghannām, II, 173, and Ibn Bishr, I, 88, refer to the port as al-Furḍah. The word

these fortifications, Su'ūd and the men of Najd called upon the people inside to acknowledge Unitarianism, but they refused to do so. For some days the Unitarians laid siege to the Shiite stronghold until an agreement was reached stipulating that they should withdraw upon payment of a number of gold pieces.[7] Before the Unitarians left al-Qaṭīf, though, they smashed a number of objects held sacred by the people and destroyed the Shiite places of worship.[8]

Death of the Shaikh Muḥammad b. 'Abd al-Wahhāb, 1206/1792

The armed forces of Unitarianism were parading through the land in ever-widening circles and the number of converts, both willing and unwilling, was steadily growing, but the strength of the Shaikh Muḥammad b. 'Abd al-Wahhāb, the founder of the movement, was fast slipping away in al-Dir'īyah. The Shaikh was nearly ninety,[9] and when he went to pray two men had to support him until he took his place in the line of the faithful.[10] During the month of Shawwāl 1206/late May to June 1792 he fell sick, and either at the end of this month or the end of the next, Dhū al-Qa'dah/late June to late July,[11] his spirit left his body.

furḍah is used in eastern Arabia with special reference to a pier or jetty. At the present time there is a customs jetty at al-Qaṭīf very near the extensive fortifications occupied by the Turks in the 19th and early 20th centuries, and it is not unlikely that there was a jetty there in the 18th century, since the water of the harbor is unusually shallow (one can wade across to the island of Tārūt that faces al-Qaṭīf and shelters the harbor).

[7] Ibn Ghannām, II, 173, gives the number as three thousand *zarrs*; Ibn Bishr, I, 88, as five hundred *aḥmars*. Ibn Bishr's *aḥmar* is the same as Ibn Ghannām's *zarr*. The higher figure is probably closer to being the correct one.

[8] *Kanā'is al-rafḍ* – Ibn Ghannām, II, 174. The Shiites are popularly known as Rawāfiḍ in Arabia.

[9] According to the Christian calendar. According to the Moslem calendar with its shorter years, the Shaikh was nearly ninety-two at the time of his death – Ibn Ghannām, I, 60; Ibn Bishr, I, 95.

[10] Ibn Bishr, I, 95.

[11] Ibn Ghannām, II, 174, says: "The beginning of the sickness was in Shawwāl, and his death was on Monday at the end of the month"; Ibn Bishr (Mecca), I, 95, says that he died at the end of Dhū al-Qa'dah, while the Baghdad edition simply places his death in Dhū al-Qa'dah. Philby, *Arabia*, p. 54, is incorrect in giving the date as about the middle of April 1792.

The Unitarians in the capital and throughout the realm knew that they had lost their greatest man, but their stern beliefs would allow neither the holding of any elaborate ceremonies[12] nor the raising of any memorial in clay or in stone.

The Unitarian state at the death of the Shaikh

In his long life the Shaikh Muḥammad b. ʿAbd al-Wahhāb had builded well with his own hand and with the aid of his associates. He and they had transformed a small oasis in Wadi Ḥanīfah into the capital of a strong expanding state the likes of which had never before been known in the recesses of the Arabian Peninsula. He more than any other had given the Arabs of his time and place a common purpose and had harnessed and directed their abilities and energy in working to attain a common goal.

The Unitarian state rested on twin foundations: the beliefs of its people and the arms they bore. The Shaikh had proclaimed the faith, and at the same time he had trained others to carry on the work of proclaiming and preaching and teaching. Four of his sons were scholars cast in their father's mold,[13] and there were grandsons too who had learned their lessons at the feet of the Shaikh. Besides his own progeny, the Shaikh had given instruction to many another man of religion, such as Aḥmad b. Nāṣir Ibn Muʿammar and ʿAbd al-Raḥmān b. Nāmī, both of whom were afterwards to go on missions to Mecca as representatives of Unitarianism, and ʿAbd al-Raḥmān b. Khumayyis, the Qadi in al-Dirʿīyah in the reigns of ʿAbd al-ʿAzīz and Suʿūd and the Imam in the palace mosque under Suʿūd.[14] Nor

[12] Ibn Bishr was present in Mecca when the Shaikh Aḥmad b. Nāṣir Ibn Muʿammar, the Qadi of al-Dirʿīyah and a former student of the Shaikh Muḥammad b. ʿAbd al-Wahhāb, died there a few days after the pilgrimage in Dhū al-Ḥijjah 1225/January 1811, and he gives a brief description of the funeral of this scholar. Suʿūd, who had succeeded his father ʿAbd al-ʿAzīz as Imam of the Unitarians, and a large throng offered prayers for the deceased – Ibn Bishr, I, 152. The same was likely done at al-Dirʿīyah when the Shaikh Muḥammad b. ʿAbd al-Wahhāb died, though neither Ibn Ghannām nor Ibn Bishr makes any reference to the funeral.

[13] Ibn Bishr, I, 93, gives a brief notice of the career of each of the four: Ḥusain, ʿAbd Allāh, ʿAlī and Ibrāhīm. Another son, ʿAbd al-ʿAzīz, died the year before his father – Ibn Ghannām, II, 164. There is no indication as to whether ʿAbd al-ʿAzīz was also a religious scholar.

had the Shaikh's classes ever been held for men of religion alone; all who wished to hear the Word of God were welcome, and they came in throngs – officials, fighting men, merchants, men of every calling. By this means and the industrious composition of letters, tracts and books, the Shaikh had led the way in disseminating the principles of Unitarianism among his followers and those they sought to convert. How well he wrought is shown by the tenacity with which the people of Najd have held to those principles down to the present day.

In directing the use of Unitarian arms and in administering the mundane affairs of the state, the Shaikh relied more heavily on his associates than he did in religious matters and missionary labors, though even in the military and governmental spheres he continued to be active – as an advisor at least – until a short time before his death. In choosing the House of Su'ūd as his partners he had chosen wisely, for this virile family produced a succession of rulers endowed with rare ability. When Muḥammad, the Shaikh's first ally in the House of Su'ūd, died, his son 'Abd al-'Azīz took his place and surpassed him in accomplishments. When, eleven years after the Shaikh succumbed to sickness, the Imam 'Abd al-'Azīz fell under an assassin's dagger in the mosque of al-Ṭuraif in al-Dir'īyah,[15] his son Su'ūd, the designated heir apparent, became Imam in his stead and proved himself the greatest of his line before the advent of the 20th century.[16] In the reign of Su'ūd the Unitarian faith and state came

[14] Ibn Bishr, I, 94, gives brief notices on Ibn Mu'ammar, Ibn Nāmī and Ibn Khumayyis.

[15] Ibn Bishr, I, 123, places the assassination in the last ten days of Rajab 1218. According to Wüstenfeld and Mahler's tables, Rajab 1218 ran from 17 October through 15 November 1803 (Gregorian). Mengin, *Histoire de l'Egypte*, II, 529, dates the assassination 18 Rajab 1218/14 October 1803, apparently using the Julian calendar, though there is an error of some days in the correspondence of dates, since the difference between the Gregorian and Julian calendars at this time was only twelve days. Philby, *Arabia*, p. 84, dates the event 4 November 1803; Philby's source is uncertain, Ibn Ghannām's chronicle having come to an end before this time.

[16] Su'ūd ruled as Imam the better part of eleven years, dying at al-Dir'īyah of an affliction in his lower belly. Ibn Bishr, I, 176, dates his death on the eve of Monday 11 Jumādā I, 1229. According to Wüstenfeld and Mahler's tables, this month ran from Thursday 21 April through Friday 20 May 1814, which would make the 11th of the month fall on Sunday, not Monday. Mengin, II, 20, n. 1. dates Su'ūd's death on 8 Jumādā I/17 April; again there is an error of some days in the correspondence of dates – compare above, n. 15. Philby, *Arabia*, p. 96, gives the date 1 May 1814.

to the high point of the course upon which they had been set by the Shaikh and Su'ūd's grandfather; at Su'ūd's death the enemies of Unitarianism sent by Muḥammad 'Alī Pasha of Egypt were in Arabia, and in the following years they whittled away the authority of the Unitarian state until they captured the capital al-Dir'īyah in 1233/1818 and then razed it to the ground, but they could not so easily destroy the faith that had gone out from there.

In 1206/1792 much of the Arabian empire had not yet been conquered by the Unitarians, but their armies of conquest were well advanced. They and their beliefs held the heartland of Najd in a positive grip. In the east the oases, ports, and grazing grounds of al-Aḥsā' lay virtually defenseless, and this province was to be

[17] Brydges, II, 9, says: "... when I arrived at Bassora [al-Baṣrah] in the year 1784, his [Su'ūd's] proceedings and marauding marches caused great anxiety and alarm to the paçha of Baghdad, to his governor at Bassora, as well as to the best informed Turks. For these last were aware that his doctrines, when examined by the simple text of the Koran, were perfectly orthodox, and consonant to the purest and best interpretations of that volume." Brydges mistakenly believed that Su'ūd at that time had already "assumed the character of temporal and spiritual leader".

[18] Daḥlān, *Khulāṣat al-kalām*, pp. 262–3, states that in Rabī' II 1206/late November to late December 1791, i.e. about half a year before the death of the Shaikh, the Sharif Ghālib sent out an army under the command of his brother the Sharif 'Abd al-'Azīz "to fight the tribes that had adopted the religion of 'Abd al-'Azīz b. Muḥammad b. Su'ūd". This expedition went down to Tarabah, Ranyah, and Bīshah, all of which are important positions on the route into the Hijaz from the southeast.

[19] Aḥmad b. Zainī Daḥlān in his chronicle of Mecca, *Khulāṣat al-kalām*, pp. 262–91, describes fifty-six different campaigns in the period between 1205/1791 and 1220/1806, the year in which peace was concluded between the Unitarians and the Sharif Ghālib.

[20] The Shaikh's son 'Abd Allāh, who was present at the entry of the Unitarians into Mecca, gives a brief description of the historic occasion in *al-Hadīyah al-sunnīyah*, pp. 35–6. 'Abd Allāh says that the entry took place at midday on Saturday 8 Muḥarram 1218. According to Wüstenfeld and Mahler's tables, Muḥarram ran from Saturday 23 April through Sunday 22 May. Philby, *Arabia*, p. 83, places the entry in April 1803. Ibn Bishr, I, 122 (2), describes the entry into Mecca under the events of the year 1217, which ended 22 April, but the fixing of the time by Ibn Bishr is so vague that no injustice is done to his narrative when one accepts the exact date given by 'Abd Āllāh. [See also O'Kinealy 1874, cited in Introduction. Ed.]

The Unitarian troops had shaven heads because they entered the Holy City as pilgrims performing the lesser pilgrimage (*al-'umrah*).

[21] The Amir Faiṣal b. 'Abd al-'Azīz, the Minister of Foreign Affairs of Saudi Arabia and head of his country's delegation to the United Nations, is descended from the Shaikh on the distaff side.

incorporated almost immediately into the Unitarian empire as the first important possession beyond the borders of Najd. To the north of al-Aḥsā' the richer land of Iraq had heard of the Unitarian exploits with an alarm[17] that events were to demonstrate was not misplaced, even though the Unitarian onrush into Iraq never went beyond the destruction of shrines and the pillaging of cities to the subjection of the whole territory. In the west Unitarian propaganda out of Najd was spreading over the deserts and winning adherents in the home country of the Sharifs.[18] The Sharif Ghālib had flung down the gage and the long war[19] had began, a war whose clamors were not to be stilled until Unitarianism had become supreme in the Holy Cities and throughout the greater part of Arabia.

The Shaikh Muḥammad b. 'Abd al-Wahhāb did not live to see the shaven-pated warriors of the faith crowding into Mecca on 8 Muḥarram 1218/30 April 1803,[20] but he himself had achieved a greater triumph by implanting the belief in One God in the hearts and minds of his fellowmen. The Imam 'Abd Allāh, the successor of his father Su'ūd in 1228/1814, suffered defeats where his forefathers had won victories, but the utmost disaster in battle was not enough to crush this belief. Over a century and a half after the death of the Shaikh, one of his descendants[21] sits in the assembly of the nations of the world, and the inscription on the green flag of Saudi Arabia floating there proclaims the essential tenets of Unitarianism: "There is no God but God; Muḥammad is the Prophet of God."

PART V

Bibliographical Essay and Bibliography

Bibliographical Essay

So far as can be determined, no documentary sources as such exist for the period of Arabian history dealt with in this study. A certain number of contemporary documents are quoted in full or in part in the Arabic chronicles, but that is all. Although the authenticity of the texts that are quoted cannot be established beyond any doubt, there appears to be no reason for not accepting them as authentic. All such documents, other than those that are exclusively theological in content, have been used in the preparation of this study.

Lacking documents, one must rely on the contemporary and near-contemporary chronicles composed by men who were privy to the affairs of the Unitarian state in the days of the Shaikh and not long thereafter. The two of these that have been preserved[1] constitute the principal sources from which the information in this study has been derived. The older of the two is the work of Ḥusain b. Ghannām (1),[2] a learned religious man of al-Aḥsā'. Ibn Ghannām died as an old man in 1225/1811, less than a score of years after the death of the Shaikh, so that much of his lifetime was spent within the period covered by this study. It is possible, though definite evidence has not been found, that he left his homeland to settle in Najd and be near the founder of the Unitarian movement whom he greatly admired. He was at any rate a well-known figure in his time, particularly as a teacher of the Arabic language. His extensive knowledge of Arabic, however, proved to be other than a blessing when he took up the writing of history, for the chief defect of his work is the obscurity

[1] No indication has been found that there were others that have since been lost.

[2] The figures in parentheses throughout this essay refer to the works listed in the following bibliography.

or vagueness of many passages resulting from the use of rhymed prose and other literary devices. Nevertheless, Ibn Ghannām's work remains extremely valuable, particularly when it can be checked by another source, such as Ibn Bishr, that recounts the same events.

Ibn Bishr's chronicle (2) is not simply a rewriting of Ibn Ghannām's.[3] 'Uthmān b. 'Abd Allāh Ibn Bishr al-Ḥanbalī al-Nāṣirī al-Tamīmī,[4] a native of the town of Shaqrā' in the heart of Najd, died in 1288/1871–2. While Ibn Ghannām was still alive Ibn Bishr as a youth had already become a student of the Unitarian religion, and the year of Ibn Ghannām's death found his successor a pilgrim in Mecca. Ibn Bishr studied under some of the leading teachers of the first half of the 19th century in Najd, and he made a point of seeking out and interrogating people who had first-hand recollections of the early days of Unitarianism. Thus he drew upon a number of sources in addition to Ibn Ghannām in the gathering of material for his chronicle. It may be noted that Ibn Bishr in a number of cases records events in al-Aḥsā' more fully than does Ibn Ghannām, even though Ibn Ghannām came from that area. Ibn Bishr is also a mine of information on the history of Shaqrā' and the neighboring towns in the valleys of Najd, and he is usually superior to his forerunner in the handling of Bedouin affairs. Ibn Bishr has a further advantage in that his style is more factual and straightforward than that of Ibn Ghannām.

Two editions of Ibn Bishr's work have been printed. The Mecca edition is sometimes misleadingly called the second edition, simply because it was printed at a later date. In reality, the Mecca edition was printed from an earlier draft of Ibn Bishr's manuscript,[5] which would tend to make the Baghdad edition the more valuable. Unfortunately, however, the Baghdad edition is only a condensation of the first volume of the whole work. The first volume contains 251 pages in the Mecca edition and 142 in the Baghdad edition, and the pages of the Mecca edition are larger. Abundant material that occurs in the Mecca edition is omitted from the Baghdad edition with the comment by the editors that nothing of interest took place

[3] Philby, *Arabia*, p. x, errs in suggesting that it is.

[4] Ibn Bishr, like the Shaikh, was a townsman descended from the tribe of Tamīm.

[5] For the evidence of this, see above, p. 49, n. 45.

in such-and-such a year. For this reason the Mecca edition is the one that has been used more than the other in this study; when reference is made to Ibn Bishr, the Mecca edition is intended unless the Baghdad edition is specified.

Both Ibn Ghannām and Ibn Bishr follow the usual form for annals. All of the events of a given year are grouped together in one section, after which comes another section listing the events of the next year, and so on. If a certain affair runs on for two or three years or more, the account of it is interrupted and then resumed. Ibn Bishr in his first volume also employs a technique that is not at all common in Arabic countries – to give it a name one may borrow the term "flashback" from modern American literature. After the sections on certain years in the main body of the annals, Ibn Bishr pauses to recount the events of certain years in the more remote past. There is no relationship between the material in the flashbacks and the material in the annals proper beyond the fact that the bulk of all the material is concerned with the history of Najd. For this study the flashbacks have been found useful in giving information on affairs in Najd before the beginning of the Unitarian movement.

The present study is the first in any language to be based on a careful and systematic comparison of Ibn Ghannām and Ibn Bishr. Philby (26) has used Ibn Ghannām, but his account is neither as complete or as accurate as it should be because Ibn Ghannām has not been checked and supplemented by reference to Ibn Bishr. Mengin (30) apparently has also used Ibn Ghannām, but Ibn Bishr's work was still in the process of composition when Mengin's account was published. Hartmann (29) has based his survey mainly on Ibn Bishr. Musil (27) cites both Ibn Ghannām and Ibn Bishr among his sources, but his treatment of the Shaikh's career is short and contains a number of mistakes. Al-Rīḥānī, with his knowledge of Arabic and his experience in Arabia and with both the old chronicles at hand, had an opportunity to write an authoritative work, but, being by nature a poet and a man of letters rather than a historian, he let the opportunity slip.

Among the handful of Westerners who visited Arabia in the 18th and early 19th centuries, the only one before Burckhardt (11) who has much to offer is Niebuhr (3). Having great gifts as an explorer,

Niebuhr left a work that is one of the classics of travel literature, and he was the first to inform the Western world of the movement inaugurated by the Shaikh in Arabia. The information he collected on the movement, however, was based only on hearsay, since he did not reach any of the regions where Unitarianism existed at the time of his journey. Seetzen (7), who was in the Hijaz shortly after the Unitarians occupied the Holy Cities, might have had a wonderful story to tell if he had not been killed before getting out of Arabia. Seetzen's descriptions of his travels in the lands bordering on the Peninsula contain scattered references to the Wahhabis, but the detailed record of his experiences in their own domains has been lost forever.

Raymond (8), Corancez (9), and Rousseau (10) were men whose knowledge of Iraq and Syria far outstripped their knowledge of Arabia. Their accounts are of value for the period in which they wrote, when the Unitarians were threatening to overrun the Fertile Crescent, but they are practically worthless for the earlier period.

Burckhardt (11), an accomplished Swiss traveler who spent some time in the Hijaz after it had been conquered by the forces of Muḥammad ʻAlī of Egypt, learned as much as he could about the Wahhabis by questioning the people he met there. His work is indispensable for the history of the Egyptian occupation, but his attempt to reconstruct the origins and early progress of the Unitarian movement leaves much to be desired.[6] Burckhardt stated without reservations that "nobody, in this country [the Hijaz], thinks of committing to paper the events of his own times",[7] though there were Arab chroniclers at work then both in Mecca and Najd.

Of the later accounts of the Unitarian movement, one of the best is the brief one that appeared in the now defunct Cairo monthly *al-Zahrā'* (25), probably by the hand of the editor, Muḥibb al-Dīn al-Khaṭīb. The work by al-Ālūsī (16), a scholarly member of a famous family of scholars with pro-Unitarian leanings in Iraq, though entitled *The History of Najd*, is rather a hodgepodge of miscellaneous facts about Najd and Unitarianism, often useful in providing

[6] Burckhardt himself admitted that he was able "to give with accuracy very few dates prior to the campaign of Mohammed Aly" – *Notes on the Bedouins and Wahábys*, II, 99.

[7] Burckhardt, *Travels in Arabia*, I, 412.

background information. The book by al-'Āmilī (17) is a lengthy composition, partly historical and partly polemical, with a strong anti-Unitarian bias.

The history of the Wahhabi movement by Philby (26), the greatest explorer of Arabia in the 20th century and in some respects the greatest of all time, is the most detailed account in any Western language and probably the one most frequently referred to by persons seeking reliable information on the subject in English. One who reads the footnotes of the present study may derive a false impression of the opinion the author entertains of Philby's work, since a number of mistakes or slips by Philby are cited there. Philby's story of the 18th century in Arabia is derived almost exclusively from Ibn Ghannām's chronicle. Philby has on the whole reproduced the information given by his Arabic source with fidelity, so that the general outlines of his story may be accepted as valid. The form of the narrative is of course a great improvement over the original, and the Englishman has added much in the way of analysis that is of value. The book is further enriched by Philby's first-hand knowledge of the land of Arabia and its people. Philby's account is much less detailed than the present study, giving only fifty-six pages to the period covered here, but it is felt that it can still be read with profit and pleasure by a student of the Unitarianism of the Shaikh.

★

Since the present study is concerned only in passing with the dogmas of Unitarianism, no attempt has been made to include in the bibliography references to the extensive literature on that subject. Anyone desirous of pursuing the matter further may find guidance in:

R.W. van Diffelen, *De Leer der Wahhabieten* (Leiden: E. J. Brill 1927) 83, 4 pp.

Henri Laoust, *Essai sur les doctrines sociales et politiques de Taḳi-d-Dīn Aḥmad b. Taimīya* (Cairo: Imprimerie de l'Institut Français d'Archéologie Orientale 1939) 755 pp.

Laoust, besides giving an excellent picture of the intellectual and theological climate out of which the Unitarianism of Arabia developed, has a section of over thirty pages on Wahhabism itself.

Bibliography

I. Contemporary and nearly contemporary Unitarian chronicles

(1) Ḥusain b. Ghannām. *Rauḍat al-afkār wal-afhām li-murtād ḥāl al-imām wa-ti'dād ghazawāt dhawī al-Islām* (Bombay: al-Maṭba'ah al-Muṣṭafawīyah, n.d.) 2 vols.

(2) 'Uthmān [b. 'Abd Allāh] Ibn Bishr. *'Unwān al-majd fī ta'rīkh Najd* (Mecca: al-Maṭba'ah al Salafīyah 1349/1930–31) 2 vols.

'Uthmān b. 'Abd Allāh Ibn Bishr. *'Unwān al-majd fī ta'rīkh Najd*, vol. I, ed. Muḥammad b. 'Abd al-'Azīz b. Māni' and Sulaimān al-Dakhīl (Baghdad: Maṭba'at al-Shābandar 1328/1910) 142 pp.

II. Contemporary and nearly contemporary data from Western travelers

(3) Niebuhr, Carsten. *Beschreibung von Arabien, aus eigenen Beobachtungen und im Lande selbst gesammleten Nachrichten* (Copenhagen: Hofbuchdruckerey 1772) xlvii, 431 pp.

(4) Brydges, Sir Harford Jones. *An account of the Transactions of His Majesty's Mission to the Court of Persia, in the Years 1807–11. To which is Appended, a Brief History of the Wahauby* (London: J. Bohn 1834) 2 vols., Vol. II: "A Brief History of the Wahauby", 238 pp.

(5) Valentia, George Viscount [George Annesley, second Earl of Mountnorris]. *Voyages and Travels to India, Ceylon, the Red Sea, Abyssinia, and Egypt, in the years 1802, 1803, 1804, 1805, and 1806* (London 1809) 3 vols.

(6) Badia y Leblich, Domingo ['Alī Bey al-'Abbāsī]. *Voyages d'Ali Bey el Abbasi en Afrique et en Asie pendant les années 1803, 1804, 1805, 1806 et 1807* (Paris: Imprimerie de P. Didot l'aîné 1814) 3 vols.

—. *Viatjes de Ali Bey el Abbassi (Domingo Badia y Leblich) per Africa y Assia durant los anys 1803, 1804, 1805, 1806 y 1807* (Barcelona: Imprenta "La Renaixensa" 1889) 3 vols. in 1.

(7) Seetzen, Ulrich Jasper. *Ulrich Jasper Seetzen's Reisen durch Syrien, Palästina, Phönicien, die Transjordanländer, Arabia Petraea und Unter-Aegypten. Hrsg. und commentirt von Professor Dr. Fr.* [Friedrich Carl Hermann] *Kruse, in Verbindung mit Prof. Dr.* [Hermann F. W.] *Heinrichs, Dr. G. Fr.* [Georg F. H.] *Müller und mehreren andern Gelehrten* (Berlin: G. Reimer 1854–9) 4 vols. in 3.

—. In Freiherr Franz Xaver von Zach, ed., *Monatliche Correspondenz zur Beförderung der Erd- und Himmelskunde*:
"Fortgesetzte Reise-Nachrichten des Dr. U. J. Seetzen", XI (April 1805) 360–367, XII (September 1805) 234–241.
"Aus einem Briefe des Kammer-Assessors Dr. Seetzen an seinen Bruder, Pfarrer in Heppens", XII (October 1805) 341–347.
"Auszug aus einem Schreiben des Russ. Rais. [*sic* – read Kais.] Kammer-Assessors Dr. U. J. Seetzen", XXVI (October 1812) 381–399, XXVII (January and February 1813) 61–79, 160–182, XXVIII (September 1813) 227–253.
"Auszug aus dem Reisejournal des Hádschy Mústaphá Ibn Ibrahim Aga Schabénder, von Haléb nach Mekka mit einer Kjerwane von Pilgrimmen im J. 1182 der Hédschre [1769 A.D.]. Aus dem Arabischen übersetzt [by U. J. Seetzen?]" XII (October 1805) 348–350.

—. In *Annales des Voyages*:
"Mémoire pour servir à la connoissance des tribus arabes en Syrie et dans l'Arabie déserte et pétrée", VIII (1809) 281–324.
"Voyage de M. Seetzen sur la Mer Rouge et dans l'Arabie", XXII (1813) 309–333. Translated from Von Zach's *Monatliche Correspondenz*.

(8) Raymond, Jean. *Mémoire sur l'origine des Wahabys, sur la naissance de leur puissance et sur l'influence dont ils jouissent comme nation. Rapport de J. M. daté de 1806, document inédit extrait des archives du ministère des affaires étrangères de France,* pref. by Edouard Driault (Cairo: Imprimerie de l'Institut Français d' Archéologie Orientale 1925) viii, 40 pp. [Société Royale de Géographie d'Égypte: publications spéciales]

(9) Corancez: L. A. ••• [Louis Alexandre Olivier de Corancez]. *Histoire des Wahabis, depuis leur origine jusqu'à la fin de 1809* (Paris: Imprimerie de Crapelet 1810) viii, 222 pp.

(10) Rousseau: M. ••• [J. B. L. J. Rousseau]. *Description du pachalik de Bagdad, suivie d'une notice historique sur les Wahabis, et de quelques autres pièces relatives à l'histoire et à la littérature de l'Orient* (Paris: Treuttel et Würtz 1809) viii, 261 pp.

—. "Nouveaux renseignemens sur les opérations militaires des Wahabis, depuis l'année 1807 jusqu'au milieu de 1810" *Annales des Voyages*, XIV (1811) 102–112.

—. *Voyage de Bagdad à Alep 1808*, ed. Louis Poinssot (Paris: J. André 1899) xv, 168 pp.

(11) Burckhardt, John Lewis [Johann Ludwig]. *Notes on the Bedouins and Wahábys, Collected during his Travels in the East, by the late John Lewis Burckhardt* (London: Henry Colburn and Richard Bentley 1831) 2 vols. II, 95–357, 363–378: "Materials for a History of the Wahábys."

—. *Travels in Arabia, Comprehending an Account of those Territories in Hedjaz which the Mohammedans Regard as Sacred* (London: Henry Colburn 1829) 2 vols.

—. *Travels in Nubia* (London: John Murray 1819) xcii, 543 pp. [Burckhardt's works were "published by the authority of the Association for Promoting the Discovery of the Interior of Africa".]

(12) Finati, Giovanni. *Narrative of the Life and Adventures of Giovanni Finati, Native of Ferrara; who, under the assumed name of Mahomet, made the campaigns against the Wahabees for the recovery of Mecca and Medina; and since acted as interpreter to European travellers in some of the parts least visited of Asia and Africa. Translated from the Italian, as dictated by himself, and edited by William John Bankes, Esq.* (London: John Murray 1830) 2 vols.

(13) Maurizi: Shaik Mansur [Vincenzo Maurizi]. *History of Seyd Said, Sultan of Muscat; together with an Account of the Countries and People on the Shores of the Persian Gulf, particularly of the Wahabees. Translated from the original Italian MS hitherto not published* (London: John Booth 1819) xxii [unnumbered], 174 pp.

(14) Buckingham, J. S. [James Silk]. *Travels among the Arab Tribes Inhabiting the Countries East of Syria and Palestine, including a Journey from Nazareth to the Mountains beyond the Dead Sea, and from thence through the Plains of the Hauran to Bozra, Damascus, Tripoly, Lebanon, Baalbeck, and by the Valley of the Orontes to Seleucia, Antioch, and Aleppo, with an Appendix, Containing a Refutation of Certain Unfounded Calumnies Industriously Circulated against the Author of this Work, by Mr. Lewis Burckhardt, Mr. William John Bankes, and the Quarterly Review* (London: Longman, Hurst, Rees, Orme, Brown, and Green 1825) xv, 679, viii pp.

(15) Sadlier, Captain G. F. "Account of a Journey from Katif on the Persian Gulf to Yamboo on the Red Sea. With a Route" *Transactions of the Literary Society of Bombay*, III (London 1823) 449–493.

III. Later accounts in Arabic

(16) al-Ālūsī, al-Sayyid Maḥmūd Shukrī. *Ta'rīkh Najd*, ed. Muḥammad Bahjat al-Atharī, together with Sulaimān Ibn Saḥmān, *Tatimmat ta'rīkh Najd*, 2nd ed. (Cairo: al-Maṭba'ah al-Salafīyah 1347/1928–9) 148 pp.

(17) al-'Āmilī, al-Sayyid Muḥsin al-Amīn al-Ḥusainī. *Kashf al-irtiyāb fī atbā' Muḥammad b. 'Abd al-Wahhāb* (Damascus: Maṭba'at Ibn Zaidūn 1346–7/1927–9) 17, 506, 26 pp.

(18) al-Batānūnī, Muḥammad Labīb. *Al-Riḥlah al-ḥijāzīyah*, 2nd ed. revised and enlarged (Cairo 1329/1911) iv, 334 pp.

(19) Fu'ād Ḥamzah. *Qalb jazīrat al-'arab* (Cairo: al-Maṭba'ah al-Salafīyah 1352/1933) viii, 463 pp.

(20) Ḥāfiẓ Wahbah. *Jazīrat al-'arab fī al-qarn al-'ishrīn* (Cairo: Maṭba'at Lajnat al-Ta'līf wal-Tarjamah wal-Nashr 1354/1935) ix, 436 pp.

(21) Kurd 'Alī, Muḥammad. *Al-Qadīm wal-ḥadīth* (Cairo: al-Maṭba'ah al-Raḥmānīyah 1343/1925) 247 pp.

(22) al-Rīḥānī, Amīn [Ameen Rihani]. *Ta'rīkh Najd al-ḥadīth wa-mulḥaqātih* (Beirut: al-Maṭba'ah al-'Ilmīyah 1928) x, 432 pp.

(23) Shaikhū, al-Ab Luwīs [Louis Cheikho, S. J.]. "Ḥaul jazīrat al-'arab", *Al-Mashriq* [*Al-Machriq*], XVIII (1920) 24–35, 107–117, 178–184, 282–287, 332–338, 425–429, 534–538, 621–628.

(24) Wajdī, Muḥammad Farīd. "Al-Wahhābīyah", *Dā'irat Ma'ārif al-Qarn al-Rābi' 'Ashar (al-'Ishrīn)* (Cairo 1353/1925) X, 869–873.

(25) Anonymous [Muḥibb al-Dīn al-Khaṭīb?]. "Al-Wahhābīyah", *al-Zahrā'*, III, No. 2 (Cairo: al-Maṭba'ah al-Salafiyah, Ṣafar 1345/August-September 1926) 81–99.

—. "Shaikh al-Islām Muḥammad b. 'Abd al-Wahhāb 1115–1206 h. [A.H.]" *al-Zahrā'*, III, No. 7 (Rajab 1345/January-February 1927) 417–431.

IV. Detailed accounts in Western languages: Philby and Musil

(26) Philby, H. St.J. B. [Harry St. John Bridger]. *Arabia* (New York: Charles Scribner's Sons 1930) xix, 387 pp. [*The Modern World. A Survey of Historical Forces*, ed. H. A. L. Fisher, no. 14].

(27) Musil, Alois. *Zur Zeitgeschichte von Arabien* (Leipzig: S. Hirzel, Vienna: Manz 1918) 102 pp. [K. k. Oesterreichische Orient und Uebersee-gesellschaft].

—. *Northern Neğd. A Topographical Itinerary* (New York 1928) xiii, 368 pp. [American Geographical Society, *Oriental Explorations and Studies*, ed. J. K. Wright, no. 5. Published under the patronage of the Czech Academy of Sciences and Arts and of Charles R. Crane.]

V. Other detailed accounts in Western languages

(28) Caskel, Werner. *Altes und neues Wahhabitentum* (Leipzig 1929) 10 pp.

(29) Hartmann, Richard. "Die Wahhabiten", *Zeitschrift der Deutschen Morgenländischen Gesellschaft*, LXXVIII [Neue Folge, III], Heft 2 (1924) 176–213.

(30) Mengin, Félix. *Histoire de l'Égypte sous le gouvernement de Mohammed-Aly, ou récit des évenemens politiques et militaires qui ont eu lieu depuis le départ des Français jusqu'en 1823, par M. Félix Mengin; ouvrage enrichi de notes par MM. Langlès et Jomard, et précedé d'une introduction historique, par M. Agoub* (Paris: Arthus Bertrand 1823) 2 vols. II, 449–544: Appendix "Précis de l'histoire des Wahabys".

(31) N. •••, Auguste de. "Notice sur les Arabes et sur les Wahabis", *Annales Encyclopédiques*, V (Paris 1818) 5–30.

(32) Phoenix. "A Brief Outline of the Wahabi Movement", *Journal of the Central Asian Society,* XVII (1930) 401–416.

(33) Margoliouth, D. S. "Wahhābīya", *Encyclopaedia of Islam*, IV, 1086–1090.

(34) Prisse d'Avennes, E. "Les Wahhābi", *Bulletin de la Société de Géographie de l'Est*, XXX (Paris 1909) 41–47.

(35) Rehatsek, E. [Edward]. "The history of the Wahhábys in Arabia and in India", *Journal of the Bombay Branch of the Royal Asiatic Society*, XIV (1880) 274–401.

(36) Rihani, Ameen [Amīn al-Rīḥānī]. *Maker of Modern Arabia* (Boston and New York: Houghton Mifflin Co. 1928) xvii, 370 pp.

VI. Works by later travelers: in Arabic

(37) Fu'ād Ḥamzah. *Al-Bilād al-'arabīyah al-su'ūdīyah* (Mecca: Maṭba'at Umm al-Qurā 1355/1936–7) 8, 273 pp.

(38) Muḥammad Shafīq Muṣṭafā. *Fī qalb Najd wal-Ḥijāz* (Cairo: Maṭba'at al-Manār 1346/1927) 67 pp.

(39) al-Rīḥānī, Amīn [Ameen Rihani]. *Mulūk al-'arab au riḥlah fī al-bilād al-'arabīyah*, 2nd ed. revised (Beirut: al-Maṭba'ah al-'Ilmīyah 1929) 2 vols.

(40) al-Ziriklī, Khair al-Din. *Ma ra'aitu wa-ma sami'tu* (Cairo: al-Maṭba'ah al-'Arabīyah 1342/1923) 190 pp.

VII. Works by later travelers: in Western languages

(41) Rüppell, Eduard. *Reisen in Nubien, Kordofan und dem petraïschen Arabien vorzüglich in geographischstatistischer Hinsicht* (Frankfurt am Main: Friedrich W. Imans 1829) xxvi, 338 pp.

(42) Descoudray. "Voyage à la Mekke, dans les années 1826–1827", *Nouvelles Annales de Géographie* 2e série, XI (1829) 198–216.

(43) Tamisier, Maurice. *Voyage en Arabie. Séjour dans le Hidjaz. Campagne d'Assir* (Paris: L. Desessart 1840) 2 vols.

(44) Wallin, Georg August. "Notes taken during a Journey through Part of Northern Arabia, in 1848", *Journal of the Royal Geographical Society*, XX (1850) 293–344.

—. "Narrative of a Journey from Cairo to Medina and Mecca, by Suez, Arabá, Tawilá, al-Jauf, Jubbé, Háil, and Nejd, in 1845", *Journal of the Royal Geographical Society*, XXIV (1854) 115–207.

(45) Burton, Sir Richard F. *Personal Narrative of a Pilgrimage to Al-Madinah and Meccah*, ed. by his wife, Isabel Burton, with an introduction by Stanley Lane-Poole (London: George Bell and Sons 1898) 2 vols. [The first edition appeared in 1855–6 in 3 vols.]

(46) Didier, Charles. *Séjour chez le grand-chérif de la Mekke* (Paris: Hachette 1857) vii, 310 pp.

(47) Palgrave, William Gifford. *Narrative of a Year's Journey through Central and Eastern Arabia* (1862–63), 3rd ed. (London and Cambridge: Macmillan and Co. 1865–6) 2 vols.

(48) Pelly, Lieut.-Colonel Lewis. "A visit to the Wahabee capital, Central Arabia", *Journal of the Royal Geographical Society*, XXXV (1865) 169–191.

(49) Guarmani, Carlo. *Northern Najd. A Journey from Jerusalem to Anaiza in Qasim*, translated from the Italian by Lady Capel-Cure, with an introduction and notes by Douglas Carruthers (London: The Argonaut Press 1938) xliv, 134 pp.

(50) Doughty, Charles Montagu. *Travels in Arabia Deserta*, Introduction by T. E. Lawrence (New York: Random House, n.d.) 2 vols. in 1 [reprint of 3rd ed. (in facsimile) of 1921].

(51) Blunt, Lady Anne. *A Pilgrimage to Najd* (London: John Murray 1881) 2 vols. II, 251–270: Appendix "Historical Sketch of the Rise and Decline of Wahhabism in Arabia" by Wilfrid Scawen Blunt.

(52) Euting, Julius. *Tagbuch einer Reise in Inner-Arabien* (Leiden: E. J. Brill 1896, 1914) 2 vols. I, ch. VII, 157–172: "Die Wahhabitische Religionsbewegung. Sa'ūdiden, Raschīdiden."

(53) Huber, Charles. *Journal d'un voyage en Arabie (1883–4) avec atlas,* eds. E. Renan, Barbier de Meynard, C. Maunoir (Paris: Imprimerie Nationale 1891) xii, 778 pp. [Publié par la Société Asiatique et la Société de Géographie sous les auspices du Ministère de l'Instruction Publique.]

(54) Snouck Hurgronje, Christiaan. *Mekka. Mit Bilder-Atlas* (The Hague

1888–9) 2 vols. and atlas. [Herausgegeben von "Het Koninklijk Instituut voor de Taal-, Land- en Volkenkunde van Nederlandsch-Indië te 's-Gravenhage"] I, 138–162: "Die Beziehungen der Wahhabiten zu Mekka."

—. *Het Mekkaansche Feest* (Leiden: E. J. Brill 1880) 199 pp.

(55) Nolde, Baron Eduard. *Reise nach Innerarabien, Kurdistan und Armenien. 1892* (Brunswick: Friedrich Vieweg und Sohn 1895) xv, 272 pp.

(56) Zwemer, S. M. [Samuel Marinus]. *Arabia, the Cradle of Islam* [New York, Chicago, &c.: F. H. Revell Co. [1900]) 434 pp.

—. "The Wahabis: their origin, history, tenets, and influence", *Journal of the Transactions of the Victoria Institute or Philosophical Society of Great Britain*, XXXIII (1901) 311–330.

(57) Musil, Alois. *Arabia Petraea* (Vienna: A. Hölder 1907–08) 3 vols. in 4. [Kaiserliche Akademie der Wissenschaften.]

—. *The Northern Heǧaz* (New York 1926) xii, 374 pp. [American Geographical Society. *Oriental Explorations and Studies*, no. 1]

—. *Arabia Deserta* (New York 1927) xvii, 631 pp. [American Geographical Society. *Oriental Explorations and Studies*, no. 2].

(58) Philby, H. St.J. B. *The Heart of Arabia. A Record of Travel and Exploration* (London, &c.: Constable and Co. 1922) 2 vols.

—. *Arabia of the Wahhabis* (London: Constable and Co. 1928) xiv, 422 pp.

(59) Twitchell, K. S. [Karl S.]. *Saudi Arabia, with an Account of the Development of its Natural Resources*, with the collaboration of Edward J. Jurji (Princeton: Princeton University Press 1947) xiii, 192 pp.

VIII. Works giving general information about Arabia.

(60) Avril, Adolphe d'. *L'Arabie contemporaine, avec la description du pèlerinage de la Mecque et une nouvelle carte géographique de Kiepert* (Paris: E. Maillet/Challamel aîné 1868) 313 pp.

(61) Great Britain, Admiralty. *A Handbook of Arabia, Compiled by the Geographical Section of the Naval Intelligence Division, Naval Staff,*

Admiralty (London: His Majesty's Stationery Office [1920] 2 vols. [vol. II never published?]

(62) Great Britain, Foreign Office. *Arabia* (London: His Majesty's Stationery Office 1920) 122 pp. [Handbooks prepared under the direction of the Historical Section of the Foreign Office, ed. G. W. Prothero [Peace Handbooks], no. 61.]

(63) Hogarth, David George. *The Penetration of Arabia. A Record of the Development of Western Knowledge Concerning the Arabian Peninsula* (London: Alston Rivers, Ltd. 1905) xv, 359 pp. [The Story of Exploration, ed. J. Scott Keltie.]

(64) Jomard, E. F. [Edme François]. *Études géographiques et historiques sur l'Arabie, accompagnées d'une carte générale de l'Arabie; suivies de la relation du voyage de Mohammed-Aly dans le Fazoql, avec des observations sur l'état des affaires en Arabie et en Égypte* (Paris: Firmin Didot Frères 1839) xxxvii, 272 pp.

(65) Kiernan, R. H. *The Unveiling of Arabia: The Story of Arabian Travel and Discovery* (London, &c.: George G. Harrap and Co.) 1937, 360 pp.

(66) Lesch, Walter. *Arabien: eine landeskundliche Skizze* (Munich 1931?) 153 pp. [Sonderabdruck aus den *Mitteilungen der Geographischen Gesellschaft in München*, XXIV, Heft 1 (1931).]

(67) Moritz, B. [Bernhard]. *Arabien. Studien zur physikalischen und historischen Geographie des Landes* (Hanover: Orient-Buchhandlung Heinz Lafaire 1923) 133 pp.

(68) Nallino, Carlo Alfonso. *L'Arabia Sa'ūdiana*, ed. Maria Nallino (Rome: Istituto per l'Oriente 1939) xii, 303 pp. [Raccolta di scritti editi e inediti, I.]

(69) Roloff, Max. *Arabien und seine Bedeutung für die Erstarkung des Osmanenreiches* (Leipzig: Verlag von Veit & Co. 1915) 26 pp. [Länder und Volker der Türkei. Schriften des Deutschen Vorderasienkomitees, ed. Hugo Grothe, Heft 5.]

(70) Scheltema, J. F. "Arabs and Turks", *Journal of the American Oriental Society*, XXXVII (1917) 153-161.

(71) Sprenger, A. *Die alte Geographie Arabiens als Grundlage der*

Entwicklungsgeschichte des Semitismus (Commissionsverlag von Huber & Co. 1875) 343 pp.

(72) Zehme, Albrecht. *Arabien und die Araber seit hundert Jahren. Eine geographische und geschichtliche Skizze* (Halle: Verlag der Buchhandlung des Waisenhauses 1875) viii, 407 pp.

IX. The Hijaz

(73) Aḥmad b. Zainī Daḥlān. *Khulāṣat al-kalām fī bayān umarā' al-balad al-ḥarām min zaman al-nabī 'alaih al-ṣalāh wal-salām ilā waqtinā hādhā bil-tamām* (Cairo: al-Maṭba'ah al-Khairīyah 1305/1887–8) 4, 332 pp.

X. The Yemen

(74) al-Wāsi'ī al-Yamānī, 'Abd al-Wāsi' b. Yaḥyā. *Ta'rīkh al-Yaman al-musammā furjat al-humūm wal-ḥazan fī ḥawādith wa-ta'rīkh al-Yaman* (Cairo: al-Maṭba'ah al-Salafīyah 1346/1927–8) 400 pp.

XI. Oman

(75) Salīl Ibn Ruzaiq [?]. *History of the Imāms and Seyyids of 'Omān, by Salīl-ibn-Razīk, from* A.D. *661–1856; tr. from the original Arabic, and ed., with notes, appendices, and an introduction, by George Percy Badger* (London 1871) cxxviii, 435 pp. [Works issued by the Hakluyt Society, XLIV.]

XII. Bahrain

(76) al-Nabhānī, Muḥammad b. Khalīfah. *Al-Tuḥfah al-nabhānīyah fī ta'rīkh al-jazīrah al-'arabīyah: al-Baḥrain*, 2nd printing (Cairo: al-Maṭba'ah al-Maḥmūdīyah 1342/1923–4) 262 pp.

XIII. Kuwait

(77) al-Qinā'ī, Yūsuf b. 'Īsā. *Safaḥāt min ta'rīkh al-Kuwait* (Cairo: Dār Sa'd Miṣr 1365/1946) 105 pp.

XIV. The Persian Gulf

(78) Vadala, R. *Le golfe Persique* (Paris: Rousseau et Cie 1920) 152 pp.

(79) Wilson, Lt.-Col. Sir Arnold T. *The Persian Gulf: An Historical Sketch from the Earliest Times to the Beginning of the Twentieth Century* (Oxford: The Clarendon Press 1928) xvi, 327 pp.

XV. Iraq

(80) al-Nabhānī, Muḥammad b. Khalīfah. *Al-Tuḥfah al-nabhānīyah fī al-jazīrah al-'arabīyah: al-Baṣrah*, 2nd printing (Cairo: al-Maṭba'ah al-Maḥmūdīyah 1342/1923–4) iii, 428 pp.

—. *Ibid.: al-Muntafiq*, 2nd printing (Cairo: al-Maṭba'ah al-Maḥmūdīyah 1344/1925–6) 190 pp.

(81) Longrigg, Stephen Hemsley. *Four Centuries of Modern Iraq* (Oxford: The Clarendon Press 1925) xii, 378 pp.

XVI. Syria

(82) Lammens, Henri *La Syrie, précis historique* (Beirut: Imprimerie Catholique 1921) 2 vols.

XVII. Egypt

(83) al-Jabartī, 'Abd al-Raḥmān b. Ḥasan. *'Ajā'ib al-āthār fī al-tarājim wal-akhbār* (Cairo: 1297/1880) 4 vols.

(84) Gouin, Édouard. *L'Égypte au XIXe siècle. Histoire militaire et politique, anecdotique et pittoresque de Méhémet-Ali, Ibrahim-Pacha, Soliman-Pacha (Colonel Sèves)* (Paris: Paul Boizard 1847) iv, 470 pp.

(85) Mouriez, Paul. *Histoire de Méhémet-Ali, vice-roi d'Égypte* (Paris: L. Chappe 1858) 5 vols. in 4.

XVIII. Ottoman Empire

(86) Wāṣif, Aḥmad. *Maḥāsin al-āthār wa-ḥaqā'iq al-akhbār* (Cairo: Maṭba'at Būlāq 1243[?]–46/1827–8 [?]–1830–31) 2 vols. in 1.

(87) Hammer, Joseph Freiherr von [Hammer-Purgstall]. *Geschichte des osmanischen Reiches, grossentheils aus bisher unbenützen Handschriften und Archiven* (Pest: C. A. Hartleben 1827–35) 10 vols.

(88) Zinkeisen, Johann Wilhelm. *Geschichte des osmanischen Reiches in Europa* (Hamburg and Gotha: F. Perthes 1840–63) 7 vols.

[*Geschichte der europäischen Staaten*, hrsg. von A. H. L. Heeren und F. A. Ukert.]

(89) Jorga, N. [Nicolae Iorga]. *Geschichte des osmanischen Reiches. Nach den Quellen dar gestellt* (Gotha: F. Perthes 1908–13) 5 vols. [*Allgemeine Staatengeschichte*, hrsg. von K. Lamprecht.]

APPENDIX

Genealogical Tables

THE BANĪ KHĀLID SHAIKHS FROM 1080/1669 TO 1210/1799

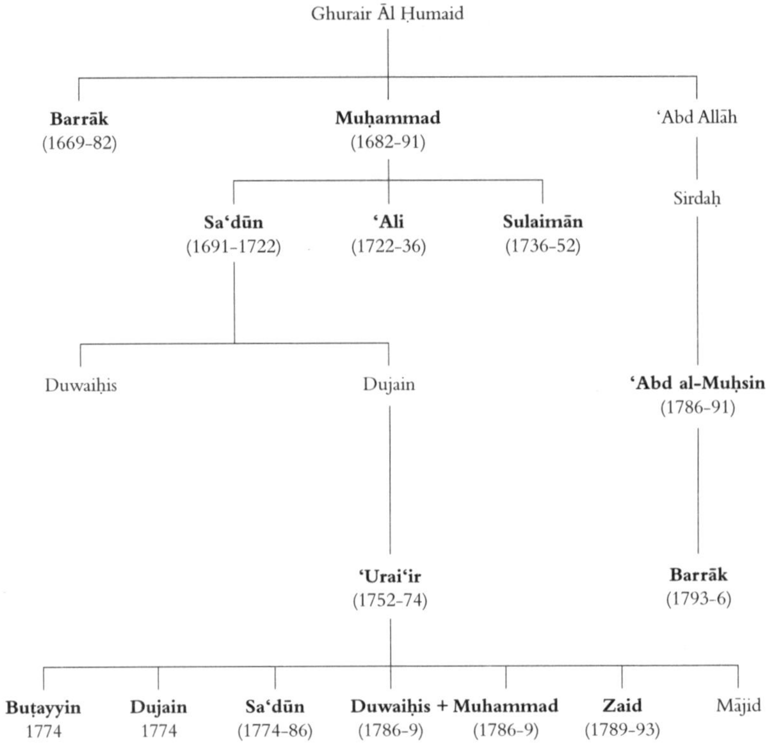

THE RULERS OF THE HOUSE OF SAUD

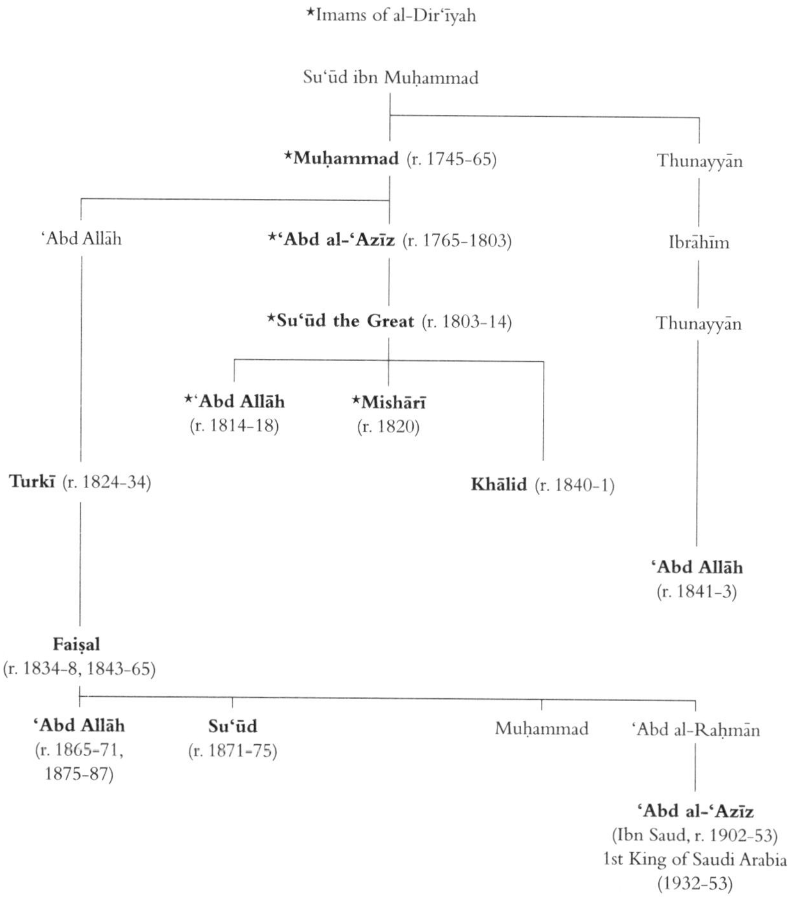
*Imams of al-Dir'īyah
Su'ūd ibn Muḥammad
*Muḥammad (r. 1745-65)
Thunayyān
'Abd Allāh
*'Abd al-'Azīz (r. 1765-1803)
Ibrāhīm
*Su'ūd the Great (r. 1803-14)
Thunayyān
*'Abd Allāh (r. 1814-18)
*Mishārī (r. 1820)
Turkī (r. 1824-34)
Khālid (r. 1840-1)
'Abd Allāh (r. 1841-3)
Faiṣal (r. 1834-8, 1843-65)
'Abd Allāh (r. 1865-71, 1875-87)
Su'ūd (r. 1871-75)
Muḥammad
'Abd al-Raḥmān
'Abd al-'Azīz (Ibn Saud, r. 1902-53) 1st King of Saudi Arabia (1932-53)

INDEX

In alphabetizing, al-, *Āl,* b. *and* Ibn *are ignored.*